RONALD REAGAN

AND HIS QUEST
TO ABOLISH
NUCLEAR
WEAPONS

RONALD REAGAN

AND HIS QUEST TO ABOLISH NUCLEAR WEAPONS

PAUL LETTOW

RANDOM HOUSE | NEW YORK

Published in the United States by Random House, an imprint
of The Random House Publishing Group, a division
of Random House, Inc., New York.

RANDOM HOUSE and colophon are registered trademarks
of Random House, Inc.

Library of Congress Cataloging-in-Publication Data
Lettow, Paul Vorbeck.
Ronald Reagan and his quest to abolish
nuclear weapons / Paul Lettow.
p.   cm.
Based on the author's thesis (Ph.D.)—
University of Oxford, 2003.
Includes bibliographical references (p.) and index.
ISBN 1-4000-6307-8
1. Strategic Defense Initiative.   2. Ballistic missile
defenses—United States.   3. Reagan, Ronald—Views on
ballistic missile defenses.   I. Title.
UG743.L386   2005
358.1'74'097309048—dc22   2004050805

Printed in the United States of America
on acid-free paper

Random House website address: www.atrandom.com

2 4 6 8 9 7 5 3 1

First Edition

BOOK DESIGN BY BARBARA STURMAN

To my parents,

Charles and Sue Lettow

CONTENTS

INTRODUCTION

R ONALD REAGAN, beginning in 1945 and extending throughout his public life, loathed nuclear weapons and the threat of nuclear war. Long before he became president, Reagan desired to intervene in and solve the nuclear dilemma. He sought to abolish all nuclear weapons, and pursued that goal as a personal mission.

Reagan's nuclear abolitionism, which grew out of his deeply rooted personal beliefs and religious views, resulted in some of the most significant—and least understood—aspects of his presidency. As early as the 1960s, Reagan called for the United States to lead an arms race that he believed the Soviet Union could neither keep up with nor afford. He saw such an arms race as part of a larger competition through which the United States could pressure the Soviet system and compel Soviet leaders to change the system from within. In a related sense, he believed that if confronted with a U.S.-led arms race, the Soviets would conclude that they could not compete and would be willing to negotiate reductions in nuclear weapons. Reagan emphasized, time and again, that the aim of his arms buildup was to attain deep cuts in nuclear weapons; most people did not listen to what he was actually saying.

During Reagan's presidency the United States put forward a series of arms control proposals to reduce drastically the number of nuclear weapons. Many commentators claimed that the proposals were so radical that the Reagan administration must have set them forth because it did not want to negotiate with the Soviet Union. In fact, those proposals grew out of Reagan's sincere desire to get rid of nuclear weapons.

Reagan's nuclear abolitionism also led him to create the Strategic Defense Initiative (SDI). In his cherished SDI, Reagan saw more than a defense against ballistic missiles. He intended that SDI would catalyze the total elimination of nuclear weapons. An effective missile defense, he believed, would make not just ballistic missiles but all nuclear arms negotiable. The United States and the Soviet Union, and then the other nuclear powers, would negotiate reductions in—and ultimately the elimination of—their nuclear arsenals. The United States would then "internationalize" the defense system by sharing it with other countries, including the USSR, and the shared defense would ensure the safety of a nuclear-free world. Despite protestations from nearly all his advisers, Reagan held unwaveringly to that vision of SDI, which he espoused publicly on many occasions.

Contrary to the conventional wisdom, Reagan himself, not his advisers or outside influences, was the driving force behind the creation and subsequent shaping of SDI, and his singular views regarding nuclear weapons guided his aims for the initiative. Reagan directed the emergence of SDI in his first term and then carefully controlled the shaping of the initiative during the rest of his presidency, constantly pursuing his goal of the elimination of nuclear weapons.

In a series of highly classified National Security Directives, Reagan established early in his presidency a Cold War policy that derived from his own often highly unusual views. Over time, he came to perceive and use SDI as a strategic tool for furthering his Cold War policy objectives.

This book is based substantially on primary sources and interviews. It draws heavily on previously classified material that has recently been declassified and released by the U.S. government, including National Security Directives, intelligence reports from the Central Intelligence Agency (CIA) and other sources, internal government memoranda, and the official U.S. transcripts of the summits between Reagan and Soviet General Secretary Mikhail Gorbachev. The author conducted nearly thirty interviews with former Reagan administration officials, among them both of Reagan's secretaries of defense, four of his six national security advisers, both of his ambassadors to the Soviet Union, and other senior officials from the State and Defense Departments, the Joint Chiefs of Staff, and the National Security Council (NSC) staff, as well as White House political and policy aides.

The book revises our understanding of Reagan's motives and his modus operandi. Reagan held audacious, unorthodox views regarding nuclear weapons and U.S. policy toward the Soviet Union—ideas that he formulated on his own, before he became president. Reagan's nuclear abolitionism was visionary, even utopian. But he determinedly and skillfully used his presidential power to establish and pursue his ideas as official U.S. policy. The result was that Reagan brought about a string of major, distinctive turns in U.S. foreign and national security policy. By identifying and tracing Reagan's ideas, and his successes and setbacks in seeing them realized, one finds that some of the most puzzling events of his presidency—such as the emergence of SDI in 1983 or the outcome of the Reykjavík meeting between Reagan and Gorbachev in 1986—are in fact explicable.

Reagan's antinuclearism is one of the best kept secrets of his political career, for it fails to conform to conventional wisdom. Reagan's quest to abolish nuclear weapons is only now becoming widely known, sixty years after it began.

This book offers a fresh portrayal of Reagan, drawn largely from newly available evidence. Reagan was much more complex than is generally understood, and his personal influence on his administration was direct and extensive.

RONALD REAGAN

AND HIS QUEST TO ABOLISH NUCLEAR WEAPONS

CHAPTER

I

ORIGINS

I N DECEMBER 1945, Ronald Reagan almost helped lead a mass anti-nuclear rally in Hollywood, California. The rally was entitled "Atomic Power and Foreign Policy," and the notice bills included the subcaption "Atomic Energy—Slave or Master?" It was sponsored by the awkwardly named Hollywood Independent Citizens Committee of Arts, Sciences and Professions (HICCASP).[1] HICCASP had been founded during the Second World War to provide high-profile liberal support for the policies of President Franklin D. Roosevelt, but by late 1945 it lacked a raison d'être and shifted to the left.[2] The thirty-four-year-old Ronald Reagan, recently discharged from U.S. Army service and an established film star, then considered himself to be a liberal Democrat and was an earnest, if "naïve," member of HICCASP.[3]

The basic theme of the December rally in Hollywood was to argue for international control over atomic energy and for the abolition of atomic weapons (on which the United States then had a monopoly).[4] At the time, such ideas were being widely debated. Assistant

Secretary of State Dean Acheson argued within the U.S. government for an international system of controls that would eliminate atomic weapons and regulate the peaceful uses of atomic energy. Secretary of War Henry Stimson advocated international control of atomic power along similar lines. On October 3, 1945, President Harry S Truman told the U.S. Congress that

> The hope of civilization lies in international arrangements looking, if possible, to the renunciation of the use and development of the atomic bomb, and directing and encouraging the use of atomic energy and all future scientific information toward peaceful and humanitarian ends.[5]

The Truman administration set forth a blueprint for the internationalization of atomic energy in its ill-fated "Baruch Plan," unveiled in June 1946. Even Edward Teller, the Hungarian-born American physicist, veteran of the Manhattan Project, and eventual bête noire of the Cold War Left, gave his support to the internationalization of atomic energy, writing an article in early 1946 that endorsed what would become the Baruch Plan.[6]

Ronald Reagan, the actor, was an early and ardent proponent of the abolition of atomic weapons and the internationalization of atomic energy. The United States dropped atomic bombs over Japan on August 6 and 9, 1945, to end World War II. By August 25, 1945, Reagan had signed on as an officer of the Hollywood chapter of the American Veterans Committee (AVC), a liberal political group. Among the causes that the AVC endorsed was the "cession of American nuclear power to the United Nations." The founder of the AVC later recalled that Reagan was particularly drawn to the "idea of expanding the Committee into an international lobby under the aegis of the United Nations, working to contain the A-bomb."[7]

Reagan intended to appear at HICCASP's "Atomic Power and Foreign Policy" rally on December 12, 1945, at the Hollywood Legion Stadium. Scheduled to speak at the rally alongside Reagan were U.S. Congresswoman Helen Gahagan Douglas (D-Calif.), Harvard astronomer Harlow Shapley, and a U.S. Marine Corps colonel. Reagan was supposed to read an antinuclear poem, "Set Your Clock at U-235," authored by the then-famous radio dramatist Norman Corwin.[8] Corwin's poem went so far in the direction of international control of atomic energy that it veered toward one-worldism:

> The secrets of the earth have been peeled, one by one, until the core is bare: The latest recipe is private, in a guarded book, but the stink of death is public on the wind from Nagasaki: The nations have heard of the fission of the atom and have seen the photographs: skies aboil with interlocking fury, mushrooms of uranium smoke ascending to where angels patrol uneasily./ . . . Unless we work at it together, at a single earth,/ . . . [T]here will be others out of the just-born and the not-yet-contracted-for who will die for our invisible daily mistakes.[9]

Corwin's boiling skies and single earth proved too much for Warner Bros., the studio to which Reagan was contracted as a film actor. After the program for the HICCASP rally was advertised in the press on December 6, a Warner Bros. official sent a telegram to Reagan's talent agent stating that Reagan's participation in the rally "as a dramatic performer" would violate his contract with the studio. Chastened, Reagan replied to Warner Bros. through his agent that he would not, in fact, appear. (Reagan did get one, less public, opportunity to declaim "Set Your Clock at U-235," at a dinner for Shapley on December 10.)[10]

The fervor during the immediate post–World War II years for the international control of atomic power and the abolition of nuclear weapons slipped out of mainstream American politics as tensions between the United States and the USSR rose in the mid- to late 1940s. The notion that international cooperation could bring about the abolition of nuclear arms and administer peaceful uses of atomic energy was seen to be unrealistic long before Truman declared in a July 1949 meeting that

> [W]e have made every effort to obtain international control of atomic energy. We have failed to get that control — due to the . . . contrariness of the Soviets. I am of the opinion we'll never obtain international con-

trol. Since we can't obtain international control we must be strongest in atomic weapons.[11]

Throughout his political career, Reagan wistfully cited the Baruch Plan and similar U.S. government efforts to internationalize nuclear energy. He eventually retrieved the notion of internationalizing nuclear energy—in his mind, redeemed it—when he announced, in 1983, that he intended to internationalize any missile defense system that resulted from SDI by sharing it with the Soviet Union and other countries.

Many views that Reagan held in the mid-1940s changed as he evolved from liberal to conservative. Reagan's experiences with Communists and Communist sympathizers in HICCASP and the AVC during 1946 and 1947 would catalyze the development of his fervent anticommunism.[12] He shed the vestiges of his immediate postwar liberalism and by the late 1950s had adopted a political outlook compatible with his later worldview and ideology—what international relations scholar Alexander George has called an individual's "belief system."[13]

Yet it will be shown that Reagan never abandoned his hatred of nuclear weapons and his desire to eliminate them. Reagan's "dream" —as he himself described it—was "a world free of nuclear weapons." "[F]or the eight years I was president," he wrote in his memoirs, "I never let my dream of a nuclear-free world fade from my mind."[14] Reagan pursued that dream as a personal religious mission.

Despite overwhelming primary and interview-based evidence, historians and international relations scholars have thus far neglected to investigate the impact of Reagan's nuclear abolitionism on his presidency. In fact, the impact of that "dream" was direct and significant. For example, Reagan's nuclear abolitionism contributed greatly to his determination to engage in a U.S. arms buildup that he believed the USSR could neither afford economically nor keep up with technologically; he intended that the Soviets would thus be forced to agree to vast reductions in the two countries' stockpiles of nuclear arms. It led to SDI, one of the most important and least understood of Reagan's

Cold War policies. To Reagan, SDI served as a catalyst for—the enabler of—his "world free of nuclear weapons." Reagan's nuclear abolitionism also pervaded his administration's approach to arms control, and his interactions with Soviet leaders.

LIFEGUARD

Ronald Wilson Reagan was born in 1911 in Tampico, a tiny farming town in western Illinois. He was the second and last child of John Edward "Jack" Reagan, an Irish Catholic shoe salesman, raconteur par excellence, and partisan Democrat, and Nelle Wilson Reagan, a seamstress, amateur actress, and devoted member of the Disciples of Christ, a Protestant evangelical denomination.[15] Ronald Reagan's early childhood was an itinerant one. His family moved constantly, first to Chicago and then to a succession of small Illinois towns—Galesburg, Monmouth, and back to Tampico—whenever Jack Reagan's ambition, or chronic alcoholism, made it seem best to do so.[16]

In 1920, the Reagan family finally settled in Dixon, Illinois, a mid-sized town on the Rock River. A slight and myopic young boy, Ronald Reagan was pleasant and made friends, yet he displayed an early tendency toward a peculiar inwardness.[17] He found delight and reward in an inner world of thought and imagination to which others were not often privy.[18] As he later wrote, "I was a little introverted. . . . I've been inclined to hold back a little of myself." He added that "[i]n some ways I think this reluctance to get close to people never left me completely."[19]

Reagan's nonscholastic pursuits focused on the outdoors and on reading. Recalling the later effect of his childhood reading, Reagan stated in 1977 that he had been, and remained, "a sucker for hero worship." "All in all," he noted, "as I look back I realize that my reading left an abiding belief in the triumph of good over evil."[20]

Nelle Reagan's religiousness deeply permeated both her youngest son's upbringing and his later life. Ronald Reagan went to prayer meetings on Wednesday nights, church services on Sunday morning, Sunday school, Sunday-evening youth prayer meetings, and then evening services following that. Ronald's older brother, Neil, a less resolute worshiper, later declared that the boys had "had religion up to our ears."[21] As a politician, Reagan was famously reticent regarding his own religious beliefs. (Interviewer: "You have a deep religious faith?" Reagan: "Yes.") He briefly overcame that reticence during a 1980 interview, however, when he allowed that "[m]y mother left me with a faith that as the years go on I realized was deeper and stronger than I ever thought it would be."[22] In particular, Reagan absorbed a central message from his mother's faith and carried it over into his own: "I was raised to believe that God has a plan for everyone."[23]

As he moved through adolescence, Reagan grew rapidly and developed a genial personality that made him popular with his peers. He became a capable athlete, actor, and student. Midway through his high school years, he took on a summer job as a lifeguard at a local Rock River beach. He returned to take up the job each summer for the ensuing five years.

Reagan's experience as a lifeguard was a formative one. He relished his responsibility of saving lives (and had plenty of opportunity to exercise it; the stretch of Rock River that he oversaw was treacherous).[24] Initially frustrated that few of those he saved thanked him for it, Reagan began to mark a notch in a log for each person he rescued.[25] While reconciling himself to public ingratitude—"I got to recognize that people hate to be saved"—he felt an increasing sense of accomplishment as the notches, eventually seventy-seven in all, spread over the log.[26]

Reagan's lifesaving left an indelible sense of purpose and satisfaction in the young man. According to William Clark, Reagan's friend and national security adviser, and "the only man who ever got within a furlong of intimacy" with Reagan, in Edmund Morris's phrase,[27] Reagan's lifesaving instilled in him the "value of each person's life as well as the power of one man's actions."[28] Lou Cannon, who as a journalist covered President Reagan and has written several biographies of him, has said that Reagan "loved being a lifeguard, a job perfectly suited to his personality. Lifeguards are solitary objects of adoration who intervene in moments of crisis and perform heroic acts without becoming involved in the lives of those they rescue."[29]

Close aides and observers from his political life recall that the theme of lifeguarding underpinned Reagan's aims and instincts as a political leader. Edmund Morris, Reagan's authorized biographer, stated that "Reagan's subsequent career, his political career, was devoted to the general theme of rescue."[30] Michael Deaver, who served under Reagan from 1967 to 1985, noted that Reagan's lifeguarding days "were a parable of his larger life as he saw it." After Alzheimer's disease had rendered even Reagan's family and friends unrecognizable to him, the former president would lead his visitors to a picture, either of himself as lifeguard or of the Rock River, and recall the exact number of people he had pulled from the river waters.[31]

Beginning with his adolescent experience as a lifeguard, Reagan harbored a fundamental impulse to intervene in the course of events in order to rescue others from peril. In time, that impulse would fuse both with his belief that he had a mission to fulfill in life and with his abhorrence of nuclear weapons. From the confluence came Reagan the determined nuclear abolitionist, and Reagan the father of SDI.

As an undergraduate at Eureka College, a small Disciples of Christ–sponsored school in Illinois, Reagan was a campus political leader, athlete, and actor. His academic career as an economics and sociology major, while above average, did not rank as his top priority.[32] His awakening interest in becoming an actor during this period coincided with his seeing, and performing in, antiwar plays.[33] In a production of Edna St. Vincent Millay's *Aria da Capo*, Reagan played one of two shepherd friends who construct a wall to separate themselves, proceed to fight over the distribution of resources on each side of the wall, and finally—in a vivid portrayal of mutual destruction—kill each other in a frenzy of mistrust and fear.[34]

Many years afterward, Reagan recalled that his experience watching a professional production of the World War I antiwar trench drama *Journey's End* convinced him that he wanted to become a professional actor (he later performed the lead role when Eureka students put on the same play).[35] Perhaps inspired by *Journey's End*, Reagan authored two unpublished antiwar short stories in 1931 that center on World War I trench life.[36] Around that time he also flirted with outright pacifism, although he soon retreated from that conviction (he volunteered for the U.S. Army Cavalry Reserves in 1935).[37]

After finishing his undergraduate degree in 1932 and spending one last summer as a lifeguard on the Rock River, Reagan found employment as a radio announcer in Davenport, Iowa. He was promptly transferred to the larger city of Des Moines, where he spent the next five years as a popular sportscaster and regional celebrity. During a 1937 trip to California to cover a baseball team's spring training, Reagan managed to arrange a screen test with Warner Bros. The studio signed him on as a film actor.

In 1940 and 1941, Reagan acted in a number of well-received films that elevated him to the status of Hollywood star.[38] A reservist, he entered active duty in the U.S. Army in 1942 and served for the duration of World War II. Reagan never left the United States during the war (poor eyesight disqualified him from combat duty); he narrated training films for the U.S. Army Air Corps and then served as the adjutant for the base in California that produced the films.

The war intensified Reagan's political interests. Known before the war to read extensively and expound at length on current events, he did so with fervor as the conflict progressed.[39] In keeping with his inherited loyalty to the Democratic Party, Reagan strongly supported President Roosevelt and identified himself as a liberal in terms of domestic politics.[40] Through the end of the war, Reagan's views on foreign affairs remained, in Lou Cannon's later description, "patriotic, idealistic and unformed."[41] As we have seen, however, there was one aspect of world affairs on which Reagan's views had formed instantly and deeply—and, as it turned out, permanently: he loathed nuclear weapons.

THE DEVELOPMENT OF REAGAN'S BELIEF SYSTEM

After the war, Reagan determined that he would use his speaking skills and political activism to help bring about, as he described it, "the regeneration of the world."[42] This determination led him to HICCASP and the AVC.[43] Both groups then had a high national profile because of their celebrity members: early AVC members included Dwight Eisenhower, Bill Mauldin, and Audie Murphy, while Albert Einstein, Frank Sinatra, and Orson Welles supported ICCASP, HICCASP's national organization.[44]

While Communists and Communist sympathizers did not constitute a majority in either HICCASP or the AVC in the immediate aftermath of the war, they began to exercise increasing control over both.[45] Reagan, meanwhile, was "not sharp about communism" (in his later words).[46]

One of the first stirrings of what Reagan would eventually call his "awakening" occurred when he attended the AVC's California state convention in early 1946 and noticed that it was dominated by a well-organized Communist minority.[47] Then, after making several well-received speeches to liberal citizens' groups warning of fascism, Reagan added a section that denounced communism as well. It elicited "dead silence."[48] In July 1946, Reagan attended a HICCASP executive council meeting at which James Roosevelt, the late President Roosevelt's son, introduced a measure that repudiated communism. Roosevelt fell under severe verbal attack. Reagan endorsed Roosevelt's proposal, at which point he found himself "waist-high in epithets." Stung and appalled, Reagan joined a group of moderate liberals within HICCASP, including Roosevelt, who conspired to force through a resolution against communism. They were met with fierce resistance and resigned from HICCASP.[49]

At the same time that Reagan began to engage in "philosophical combat" with Communists in Hollywood, he became involved in a labor dispute that shaped his rapidly developing anticommunism.[50] During the war, Reagan took on a leadership role with the Screen Actors Guild (SAG), the powerful actors' union.[51] Immediately after the war, SAG was confronted with a jurisdictional dispute between rival unions of studio craft workers; a new and left-wing union called the Conference of Studio Unions (CSU) sought to poach workers from the established International Alliance of Theatrical Stage Employees (IATSE). SAG's response to the CSU strike was crucial to the outcome; if the actors refused to cross the picket lines, the motion picture industry would shut down altogether.

Deeply wary of the CSU's radicalism and suspecting that it was a Communist front, Reagan helped lead SAG to cross the picket lines. Eventually the strike—and the CSU—collapsed, but not before it had resulted in months of violence. In the midst of the turmoil, Reagan received a telephone call on the set of a film shoot. The anonymous caller told him that his face would "never be in pictures again." The threat never materialized, but the police issued Reagan a concealed handgun and briefly placed him under protection.[52] Soon after that incident, two agents from the Federal Bureau of Investigation (FBI) visited Reagan's home.[53] They told him that the Communist Party was seeking to assert influence among Hollywood workers and in the content of films. Reagan provided information to the FBI on a handful of occasions over the next two years.[54]

Morris has posited that because of Reagan's personal experiences in 1946 and 1947 in Hollywood, he "became a rock-ribbed anticommunist then and there."[55] In his presidential memoirs, Reagan wrote that the "strike and the efforts to gain control over HICCASP and other organizations had a profound effect on me." "These were eye-opening years for me," he stated, adding that

> Now I knew from firsthand experience how Communists used lies, deceit, violence, or any other tactic that suited them to advance the cause of Soviet expansionism. I knew from the experience of hand-to-hand combat that America faced no more insidious or evil threat than that of Communism.[56]

Reagan's experiences during the mid- to late 1940s convinced him that the Soviet Union sought to expand communism worldwide, and was constantly orchestrating means to achieve the end of world domination; he believed the Communist activities he had encountered were products of that effort.[57] That view formed the early essence of Reagan's anti-Communist approach.[58]

Reagan served as president of SAG in the late 1940s and early 1950s. His leadership of the union gave him self-confidence in his own negotiating abilities, as several of his presidential aides later testified.[59] As SAG president, Reagan made frequent public appearances and speeches, which he came to enjoy.[60] Anticommunism always lay at the heart of his comments, which emphasized Moscow's expansionism; the Soviet Union, he claimed in 1951, "aimed at world conquest."[61]

In 1954, General Electric (GE) offered Reagan a unique job. He was to host a new weekly television show sponsored by the company and was also to serve as a company spokesman and ambassador. In the latter capacity, Reagan was expected to travel for several months of the year, visiting GE plants around the nation and appearing at various events. Reagan accepted. The immediate and sustained popularity of the *General Electric Theater* television show meant that he was broadcast to a large audience of viewers throughout the nation each week until 1962, when he left GE.[62]

Initially, Reagan's traveling appearances on behalf of GE consisted of meeting employees and making anecdotal remarks, usually to do with his Hollywood experiences.[63] After a year or so, however, the company began to arrange speaking engagements for him before civic groups, business associations, and community meetings and gave him free rein to speak on whatever topic he chose. During the first years of his appearances, his talks began to evolve into an exposition of his political views, and by the late 1950s, Reagan had honed what was effectively one speech (although he was constantly revising it), which consisted of spelling out his political approach.[64] He delivered variations of that speech, which he wrote entirely on his own, to countless audiences across the nation over ensuing years.[65] After Reagan left GE in 1962, he continued to travel extensively and give his speech, and it constituted the basis for his entry into politics during the mid-1960s.

The speech was premised upon the notion that the USSR intended to expand communism around the world; as a result of that Soviet expansionism, the United States found itself in a "world struggle."[66] Believing that the Soviets ultimately sought nothing short of the complete destruction of capitalism (and lacing his speech with quotes to that effect from Soviet leaders),[67] Reagan criticized those in the United States who sought to find "accommodation" with the USSR.

In 1961, he stated that "peaceful coexistence on Russia's terms is a satanic, diabolical device of the enemy to blunt our sword while he moves in for the kill."[68] In 1964, he said that "the spectre our well-meaning liberal friends refuse to admit is that their policy of accommodation is appeasement."[69] While Reagan maintained through the mid-1960s that America's overall military strength prevented the Soviets from a direct attack on the United States, he asserted that Moscow sought to achieve its objectives through subversion and the use of proxies, and by lulling the United States into a position of weakness.[70]

Reagan's view of the Cold War also influenced his approach to domestic politics. By advocating an ever-expanding federal government, Reagan asserted, liberals were unwittingly aiding the rise of government at the expense of individual liberty, a process that he feared could lead the United States toward socialism and thus accomplish the Soviets' goals for them.[71]

In setting forth his own recommended approach to foreign and domestic affairs, Reagan rejected the possibility of merely containing Soviet advances abroad or limiting the growth of the federal government at home. Instead he advocated rolling them back. "Containment won't save freedom on the home front any more than it can stop Russian aggression on the world front," he stated. "We must roll back the network of encroaching control."[72] Reagan specifically repudiated any search for accommodation with the Soviet Union based upon the geopolitical status quo, criticizing those who "say to a billion enslaved human beings behind the Iron Curtain—'Give up your hopes of freedom because we've decided to get along with your slave masters.'"[73]

Because scholars have not often returned to Reagan's speeches from this period, they have tended to overlook the extent to which he had formed—and espoused, over and over again—deeply held views regarding America's Cold War policy before he entered even state politics. (They have also missed the fundamental connection that he drew between Soviet objectives abroad and the expansion of the federal government in the domestic arena, expressions of which he later toned down as he sought votes.) As early as the late 1950s, Reagan chafed at the U.S. Cold War policy of containing Soviet expansionism, thinking it insufficient and immoral. As president, Reagan's long-standing inclination to move beyond containment in dealing with the Soviets contributed to his unprecedented decision to establish roll-back as official U.S. Cold War policy. It also led him to ensconce as official U.S. policy the further aim of weakening the Soviet system itself through pressure.

In 1963, Reagan wrote a speech in which he claimed that it is "painfully clear that our foreign policy today is motivated by fear of the bomb." He chastised the Kennedy administration and "the liberal establishment of both parties" for asserting that a policy of "accommodation" was "the only (and you can underline only) method for avoiding a nuclear holocaust." Reagan criticized American foreign policy makers for not exploiting the weaknesses of the Soviet economy, which he saw as fundamentally vulnerable. The average Soviet citizen, Reagan declared, did not even have a pot, much less a chicken to put into it. He said:

> If we relieve the strain on the shaky Russian economy by aiding their enslaved satellites, thus reducing the danger of uprising and revolution, and if we continue granting concessions which reduce our military strength giving Russia time to improve her's [sic] as well as to shore up her limping industrial complex—aren't we perhaps adding to the communist belief that their system will through evolution catch up and pass ours?

Instead of seeking ways to ameliorate the Cold War conflict, Reagan stated, the United States should take the initiative by pressuring the Soviet internal system: "If we truly believe that our way of life is best aren't the Russians more likely to recognize that fact and modify their stand if we let their economy come unhinged so that the contrast is apparent?" Seeking accommodation with the USSR, he claimed,

> is based on wishing not thinking. . . . The other way is based on the belief (supported so far by all evidence) that in an all out race our system is stronger, and eventually the enemy gives up the race as a hopeless cause. Then a noble nation believing in peace extends the hand of

friendship and says there is room in the world for both of us. We can make those rockets into bridge lamps by being so strong the enemy has no choice.[74]

Reagan was probably unique among public figures with any political standing in 1963 in stating that by pursuing a vigorous competition with the USSR—including but not limited to leading a military buildup—the United States could compel the Soviets to reduce nuclear weapons, and furthermore to change the aims and nature of their regime. This was not the policy of the Kennedy administration, or of the Democratic Party on the whole.

Nor were those views shared by Republicans. Some of Reagan's political beliefs were most compatible with those of Barry Goldwater, the Republican senator from Arizona, leader of the conservative wing of the Republican Party, and failed presidential candidate in 1964. Goldwater sought to reorient U.S. foreign policy toward seeking "all out victory" in the Cold War and championed the idea that America should take to the offensive against the USSR by choosing its own terms and places of competition.[75] Goldwater, however, did not see the Soviet system as being economically vulnerable to U.S. pressure but hoped for a Cold War victory in which "the captive peoples [would] revolt against their Communist rulers."[76] In fact, in a 1962 book outlining his foreign policy beliefs, Goldwater warned that extensive domestic and foreign programs could lead to the "economic collapse" of the United States.[77]

Reagan's arguments in 1963 that the Soviet economy represented an important area of vulnerability in the Cold War and that the United States could exploit that vulnerability via an arms race and political and economic competition ran contrary to the prevailing wisdom among American politicians and opinion shapers.[78] Reagan never dropped those ideas. He would repeat and refine them in later years, particularly during his presidential campaigns in 1976 and 1980 and throughout his presidency. Those beliefs helped shape both his administration's formal written Cold War policy and the implementation of that policy during his time in office.[79]

Reagan's idea of engaging in an all-out competition with the USSR, particularly in the military sphere, in order to exacerbate the inherent weaknesses of the Soviet economy was directly linked to his desire to eliminate nuclear weapons. He set forth the notion as an alternative "method for avoiding a nuclear holocaust," as opposed to what he derided as the method of "accommodation." Reagan believed that if the Soviets were confronted with a U.S.-led competition, especially in the form of an arms race, they would conclude that they could neither afford nor keep up with that competition, and would agree to reduce nuclear arms. He also felt that if faced with that competition, the Soviet Union would be forced to "modify [its] stand" in a broader sense. Reagan implied that this would include a realization that the USSR could not win the Cold War, that the Soviets would see aspects of the Western "way of life" as attractive, and that they would begin to change their system. (He did not claim that if subjected to an arms race, the Soviet Union would bankrupt itself and fall apart.) In Reagan's mind, destroying nuclear weapons and winning the Cold War were closely tied together.

Other specific clues to Reagan's later policies and rhetoric can be found in versions of his standard speech from the 1960s. During a speech in March 1964, for example, Reagan called the Soviet Union "the most evil enemy that has ever faced mankind."[80] He repeated the phrase "evil enemy" in connection with the USSR constantly throughout that year and the next.[81] Nineteen years later, Reagan issued a better-known, but strikingly similar, characterization of the USSR.[82]

Cannon accurately wrote of Reagan's speech making during the 1950s and 1960s that "[n]o American politician-in-the-making ever had such training."[83] In those years, Reagan thought and read extensively about foreign and domestic affairs and developed a policy approach to both. He espoused that approach to large audiences (news clippings from the time state that he often spoke to groups comprising thousands) of influential and politically conscious citizens across the United States.[84]

Reagan thus spent considerable time and effort thinking and speaking about U.S. policy toward the Soviet Union before he ran for political office. It is demonstrably incorrect to argue that Reagan did not, or could not, think for himself, or that he was a mere cipher through which his advisers enacted their own agendas. Some of the most important elements of Reagan's Cold War policy appear puzzling to scholars precisely because they were quite often based upon his own—often wildly unconventional—ideas.

In the autumn of 1964, Reagan agreed to deliver a speech on national television supporting Barry Goldwater in his presidential election bid against the incumbent president, Lyndon B. Johnson. Despite remaining a nominal Democrat until 1962, when he switched his party registration to become a Republican, Reagan had last voted for a Democratic presidential candidate in 1948—President Truman—and since the 1950s had been a popular speaker for conservative causes and candidates.[85] Reagan's address for Goldwater, which was broadcast nationwide a week before the 1964 election, was his standard speech.[86] While Reagan's speech did not rescue Goldwater from overwhelming defeat, it proved a tremendous success, both for the Republican Party and for Reagan himself. The speech was widely praised, even in the media; *Time* magazine called it "the one bright spot in a dismal campaign."[87] It also generated support for Reagan to run for political office.

In 1966, Reagan ran as the Republican candidate in the California gubernatorial election. He surprised virtually everyone, particularly his opponent, the incumbent Democratic governor, when he won the race by a million votes.

REAGAN'S INTRODUCTION TO MISSILE DEFENSE

Shortly after taking office in January 1967, Governor Reagan accepted an invitation from the physicist Edward Teller to visit the Lawrence Radiation Laboratory (now the Lawrence Livermore National Laboratory), a U.S. government nuclear research facility in Livermore, California.[88]

Teller was brilliant and controversial. His scientific contributions and incessant lobbying proved crucial to the development of the U.S. hydrogen bomb. Teller had been interested in missile defense as early as 1945, when he extrapolated from the advent of the atomic bomb and the ballistic missile that the former would eventually be delivered by the latter. His interest in missile defense faded in the postwar years, however, until it was revived by a visit in 1961 to the U.S. Air Command Center in Colorado Springs, Colorado. In that cavernous space inside a mountain, he was struck by the commanding general's frustration that while the center could track an incoming missile twenty minutes before impact, "there is nothing more that we can do, other than to issue a warning."[89] Beginning in the mid-1960s, Teller became an enthusiastic proponent of research on missile defense, in which the Lawrence Radiation Laboratory played a leading role.

Documents from the laboratory reveal that Governor Reagan received an extensive briefing on missile defense concepts and technologies during his visit to Livermore on November 22, 1967. A handwritten agenda for the visit shows that Reagan was briefed on the Spartan and Sprint antimissile systems, which then constituted the most advanced U.S. missile defense technologies.[90] Spartan and Sprint were themselves nuclear missiles, albeit defensive "interceptor" missiles. They functioned by launching toward the other side's incoming ballistic missiles and detonating their nuclear warheads close enough to the enemy missiles to destroy them. Spartan was designed to intercept incoming missiles above the atmosphere, while Sprint attacked at shorter altitudes any that passed into the atmosphere.[91]

According to Teller, the briefing on missile defense, which was conducted by several of the laboratory's scientists, lasted about two hours. He was almost certainly correct in asserting that the topic of missile defense was new to Reagan; as yet there are no indications that Reagan had any awareness of missile defense possibilities before the visit.[92] Teller later wrote that "[w]hat we told the governor was not simple, but he listened carefully and asked perhaps a dozen salient questions."[93] In an interview with the author, Teller commented, "My impression was that his questions showed very little knowledge of the subject but real interest in the subject. And furthermore, they were perfect questions, they were good questions . . . coming from a man who had not looked into that situation before."[94]

Teller recalled that at the time, Reagan did not endorse the work on Spartan and Sprint: "He didn't want to come out for or against it." Much later, knowing of Reagan's antinuclearism, Teller surmised that Reagan disliked the idea of employing nuclear warheads for any purpose, even to destroy incoming nuclear missiles. "If possible," Teller recently claimed, Reagan desired "that the [missile defense] system not utilize nuclear weapons."[95] General James Abrahamson, who headed SDI at the Pentagon during much of Reagan's presidency, suggested that Reagan's visit to Livermore "planted the idea in his head that [missile defense] might be possible—not that any one of the technologies they advocated was the right one."[96]

A few days after Reagan's trip to Livermore, a University of California official who had accompanied Reagan during the briefing wrote a note to the laboratory's director, stating that the "Governor obviously was interested" in what he had seen and heard.[97] Indeed he was. During a March 1968 interview with the *Chicago Tribune* in which he thoroughly criticized the Johnson administration's foreign and defense policy, Reagan warned that the Soviets had begun to deploy an antiballistic missile (ABM) system, which was true. Implicitly scolding the Johnson administration for not advancing further on a system of its own, Reagan declared that the United States was "in great danger."[98] In a July 1968 speech, Reagan mentioned approvingly Teller's efforts to emphasize "the need for the 'development of effective defensive systems.'"[99]

Two weeks prior to his visit to Livermore, Reagan had delivered a speech at a California Institute of Technology banquet in which he noted the rapid pace of technological change around the world and then added that "I cannot help commenting that this same society that makes such technological advance has not yet learned how to live with itself so as to preclude the use of [nuclear] energy for society's destruction."[100] In missile defense, Reagan saw a means of using technology to transcend what he viewed as a disjuncture between the destructive potential of nuclear energy and humans' apparent inability to avoid threatening one another with it. He sought to outflank the danger posed by nuclear weapons by drawing upon high technology to produce a defense against missiles. Reagan made this point explicitly when he announced SDI in 1983.

Many of Reagan's advisers in Sacramento, and then in Washington, later noted that Reagan believed that the biblical story of Armageddon foretold a nuclear war. He thought both that a nuclear war that would end civilization was imminent and that it could be avoided. He was convinced that it was his mission to avert a nuclear holocaust. While there is little evidence as to when Reagan first adopted that conviction, both Cannon and Morris state that he mentioned it to evangelical clergymen, to his advisers, and to a few others, in the late 1960s and continuously thereafter. Reagan's belief in a future nuclear war as Armageddon contributed further to his nuclear abolitionism—and to his desire to pursue a missile defense system.[101]

Those who served with him in Sacramento and in Washington recalled that missile defense occupied a prominent place in Reagan's mind during his tenure as governor of California from 1967 to 1975 (he was reelected in 1970). In those years, Reagan spoke often with his closest aides about his abhorrence of nuclear arms and his desire for a defense against missiles. Edwin Meese, chief of staff to Reagan in Sacramento and later one of his Cabinet officials in Washington, recalled in an interview with the author, "Almost as long as I have known him . . . Governor Reagan then, and later President Reagan, was very interested in some sort of a defense against missiles—ballistic missiles—and nuclear warfare. His view on nuclear warfare is that it could not be won and should never be fought. And he was concerned that there was no defensive measure, technical measure, to defend against ballistic missiles. . . . [H]e felt it was important. He discussed this in general terms when he was governor, and a lot with those of us who were close to him as these things came up."[102]

Caspar Weinberger, who served Reagan as finance director in California and then as U.S. secretary of defense from 1981 to 1987, wrote in his memoirs that Governor Reagan felt strongly that the United States should seek a defense against nuclear missiles and discussed that conviction with Weinberger in Sacramento.[103] During an interview with the author, Weinberger commented that Reagan "didn't like nuclear weapons. . . . The idea of doing something about nuclear weapons was something that he had in mind for a long time."[104] He said that Reagan sought "a defensive capability as the very best way of keeping the peace."[105] Weinberger told the author that, in California, "this was not anything that we ever had a forum about, or a conference about, or anything. These were just discussions."[106] ("[T]hese were just . . . conversations," Weinberger noted, "because the state of California didn't do a great deal about that stuff.")[107] Michael Deaver, who served continuously as a political aide to Reagan from 1967 to 1985, concurred that Reagan had frequently spoken with his gubernatorial advisers of his dislike of nuclear missiles and his belief that the United States should seek a missile defense system.[108]

Thus, driven largely by his antinuclearism, Reagan concluded by the mid-1960s that the United States should vigorously pursue a defense against missiles. At the same time, influential segments of the U.S. foreign policy establishment mobilized to foreclose just that possibility. Robert McNamara, the U.S. secretary of defense from 1961 to 1968, strenuously opposed the deployment of any ABM system. McNamara's anti-ABM position had much to do with his belief in the theory of mutual assured destruction (MAD) and a related view of the Cold War arms race known as the "action-reaction phenomenon."

MAD posited that deterrence against nuclear attack was to be maintained through the ability of each side to inflict "an unacceptable degree of damage" upon the other, "even after absorbing a first strike." According to McNamara, no foreseeable ABM system could be effective enough to negate the other side's ability to inflict unacceptable damage, a view that many scientists vocally supported.[109] A defensive system would only lead the side that had not deployed ABMs to increase its offensive capability in order to guarantee the overwhelming of the defense, thus catalyzing a heightened arms race. This stance reflected McNamara's perception of the arms race as a result of actions and reactions on each side that would lead to a dangerous upward spiral that offered no advantage to either side, since neither could alter the basic calculus of MAD.[110]

Although not the intellectual progenitor of MAD or the "action-reaction phenomenon," McNamara was their principal proponent, fully introducing them within the administration and to the public by the mid-1960s. Soon they achieved, in Lawrence Freedman's phrase, "canonical status." "The legitimization of a balance of terror," Freedman wrote, "once a matter of much liberal and radical distaste, had become a liberal cause. The vice of the perpetual nuclear threat was displaced by the virtue of stability."[111]

Reagan disliked MAD. He also disliked the technocratic McNamara, whom he publicly derided as "that efficient disaster."[112] Reagan likened MAD to an Old West standoff, with "two westerners standing in a saloon aiming their guns to each other's head—permanently."[113] Deaver, Meese, and Weinberger all recalled that Reagan mistrusted MAD and talked with his aides in Sacramento about his objections to it.[114] According to Weinberger, the idea that one was safe from nuclear attack only if vulnerable to it "repelled" Reagan.[115] Meese told the author that Reagan felt that MAD was "politically and diplomatically, militarily, and morally flawed."[116] Martin Anderson, one of Reagan's aides during the 1970s and 1980s, wrote that Reagan described MAD as "the most ridiculous thing" he had ever seen.[117] That the United States should indefinitely base its security from nuclear attack on vulnerability to nuclear attack struck Reagan as morally backward; that it should maintain such a mutual balance of terror with the Soviet Union seemed to him "particularly dangerous."[118]

Reagan's solution to the nuclear dilemma was to eliminate the danger that Soviet nuclear missiles posed to the United States by pursuing a missile defense and to reduce the number of all nuclear arms, ultimately to zero. (Asked whether then-Governor Reagan's antinuclearism encompassed a desire to see all nuclear weapons abolished, Deaver replied, "Oh, yeah. I don't think there's any question that, in conversations that I heard, even in those early years, that he would say, 'That's our goal. We want to get rid of them altogether.'")[119]

For his part, McNamara was not entirely successful in precluding a U.S. missile defense effort. After the Soviets deployed a limited ABM system around Moscow in the mid-1960s, the Johnson administration faced pressure from the military and from members of Congress to come up with a missile defense proposal of its own. The Joint Chiefs of Staff (JCS) unanimously favored developing an ABM system, which put McNamara in an awkward situation.[120] The approval of the Joint Chiefs (or in this case, their nonapproval) can be crucial to the outcome of U.S. defense policy and decision making; as shall be seen, the support of the JCS played a significant role in the inception of Reagan's SDI.

McNamara's solution was to announce, in the fall of 1967, that the United States would proceed with an extremely limited ABM system to protect against a potential missile threat from China, which had just recently developed a ballistic missile capability. At the same time, McNamara emphasized that the U.S. system would pose no threat to the retaliatory power of the USSR. He also insisted that the United States and the USSR should pursue arms talks for the purpose of limiting offensive strategic forces and curtailing missile defense systems.

After taking office in 1969, President Richard M. Nixon and his advisers, most notably Henry Kissinger, were not inclined to depart from the basic logic of MAD and the destabilizing impact of missile defense. The Nixon administration committed itself to engaging the Soviets in talks to foreclose ABM systems and to curb the offensive nuclear arms race. In an attempt to gain momentum and leverage toward achieving that result, the administration announced early in its first year that it would deploy an ABM system to protect intercontinental ballistic missile (ICBM) fields.

That decision sparked a tumultuous debate that centered on the appropriations process in Congress. Opponents of ABM deployment— in Congress and, prominently, many scientists and others in the academic community—argued against missile defense largely along the lines established by McNamara and his colleagues in the mid-1960s. While many of those who supported Nixon's decision did so because they favored actually deploying a missile defense, the fundamental rationale for going ahead with the ABM deployment was to provide an incentive for the Soviets to engage in arms control negotiations, and then to use the system as a bargaining chip during the negotiations.[121] Among those who were motivated to support the deployment as a bargaining chip was Paul Nitze, the eminent national security policy maker who had served as a senior official in the Roosevelt, Truman,

Kennedy, and Johnson administrations. Nitze founded a private group to promote the ABM program; one of the young analysts who undertook much of the group's work was Richard Perle.[122]

At the end of the rancorous debate over the ABM system, the Senate approved appropriations for it by a single vote. The Nixon administration promptly parlayed the leverage accrued by the new program into gaining Soviet consent to bilateral strategic arms control negotiations (to which Nitze was a chief U.S. delegate). Those negotiations—the Strategic Arms Limitation Talks, or SALT I—produced a set of agreements in 1972. One was the ABM Treaty, which restricted the missile defense capability of each side to two fixed installations of ground-based interceptor missiles, limited to 100 interceptor missiles per site. (At that time, the only feasible missile defense technologies consisted of ground-based, nuclear-tipped antimissile missiles, such as Spartan and Sprint.) Beyond the allowance for those two limited sites, the treaty forbade the development, testing, and deployment of ABM systems.[123] The other principal element of SALT I was an interim accord on offensive strategic weapons, which set caps on the number of missiles of various kinds, namely ICBMs and submarine-launched ballistic missiles (SLBMs), allowed each side.[124]

The ABM Treaty killed any foreseeable possibility of developing U.S. missile defenses.[125] A 1974 protocol to the treaty reduced the number of permitted ABM ground-based installations to one; the Soviets deployed theirs around Moscow, while the United States constructed a site at an ICBM field in North Dakota in 1976 and then shut it down within the year, citing cost and ineffectiveness.[126] From that time until Reagan's announcement of SDI in 1983, the United States maintained only a low-priority research program into advanced missile defense technologies.

THE MATURING OF REAGAN'S BELIEF SYSTEM AND CLUES TO HIS FUTURE COURSE

In the overall framework of the Cold War, the SALT I arms control measures embodied Nixon's and Kissinger's détente policy. As John

Lewis Gaddis described it in *Strategies of Containment*, détente was intended to generate stability in the U.S.-Soviet relationship by moving away from "the clash of competing interests" and toward the evolution of what Kissinger called "habits of mutual restraint, coexistence, and, ultimately, cooperation."[127]

Initially, Reagan publicly criticized détente less than he might have done had Nixon not been a Republican and a Californian. But criticize it he did. In 1972, while still governor of California, Reagan gave a speech on foreign affairs in which he warned:

> We must ask ourselves if we are willing to risk all that we call the American way on the naïve hope that our potential enemies have mellowed so much that they no longer have any aggressive designs. . . . The President wants to end the Cold War era of conflict and substitute an era of negotiations and peaceful settlements of disputes before they flare into war. I am sure every American shares that goal. But are we also aware that every nation in history which has sought peace and freedom solely through negotiation has been crushed by conquerors bent on conquest and aggression?[128]

Reagan rejected Kissinger's premise that any large-scale convergence of interests between the two nations could arise from policy shifts in the absence of a transformation of the internal nature of the Soviet regime. Weinberger told the author that Reagan believed that the "two systems were not compatible. They weren't just two systems that could live together and work together and everything would be fine."[129] According to Deaver, Reagan believed that "there was no ultimate gain in getting along. We had to eliminate the threat" posed by the USSR.[130]

Reagan thought that the United States should prosecute the Cold War and that it could win it. Communist expansionism, Reagan believed, was rooted inherently in the ideology and nature of the Soviet regime. Only when the Soviets changed their internal system would the USSR's threat to the United States be neutralized. As discussed earlier, Reagan thought that if the United States engaged in and led a strenuous military, political, and economic competition with the USSR, it could exacerbate the weaknesses of the Soviet system, particularly its economy and technological base, and help compel Soviet leaders to undertake fundamental changes. Reagan's policy approach toward the Soviet Union was linked to his nuclear abolitionism, as previously noted. Reagan believed that if confronted with severe strain on its economic and political system, the USSR would negotiate reductions in nuclear weapons. These ideas lay outside the prevailing wisdom during the rise of Reagan's political career, even among his own conservative milieu and advisers. Reagan appears to have developed them on his own, during a long and intense period of thinking and speaking on foreign and domestic policy.

Détente ran counter to Reagan's Cold War approach. Reagan maintained that the Soviets were using détente as a cover to lull the United States into passivity and self-restraint while they themselves prosecuted the Cold War. In particular, he was adamant that U.S. Cold War policies of the late 1960s and 1970s, exemplified by the SALT negotiations, had led to a precipitous decline in the military position of the United States vis-à-vis the USSR, most crucially in the area of nuclear arms. He felt that the increased military power of the USSR relative to that of the United States allowed the Soviets leverage that they could employ to further their global ambitions. In arguing against détente, Reagan claimed that the United States should compete vigorously against the USSR, particularly in the overall military balance, and should do so by taking the initiative, exploiting areas and aspects in which the United States held advantages.

Reagan assailed détente during his bid in 1976 to defeat incumbent President Gerald R. Ford as the Republican presidential nominee. Challenging an incumbent president of his own party was a bold political move; even some of Reagan's own advisers tried to discourage him from doing so.[131] Reagan was undeterred.

During the 1976 Republican primary campaign, Reagan constantly criticized recent American foreign and defense policy. He charged that the United States had "become second to the Soviet Union in military strength in a world where it is perhaps fatal to be second best."[132] Reagan elaborated on the deleterious effects of this apparent decline during an interview:

I think we have to make darn sure that we improve our military position to the point that we're not second best, so that we can truly be dealing for peace through strength. I believe the Soviet Union, in its great
upsurge of military building—its increased truculence—operates from
a standpoint that the reason we're falling behind is that the American
people no longer have the will to make the effort. The Russians feel
they are more virile—that they are the stronger power. . . . And we are
the Carthage of our time, in a way.[133]

Reagan insisted that the United States should undertake a substantial military buildup, not only to prevent the Soviets from gaining
leverage in the overall Cold War rivalry, but also to exploit what he
viewed as U.S. economic and technological advantages over the
USSR. Throughout the 1960s and early 1970s, he had continually argued that the Soviet economy represented a key vulnerability relative
to the United States. In 1967, he stated that the Soviet Union was
"in the grip of modern day feudalism" and that its political system intrinsically prevented a dynamic economy.[134] During one of the syndi-
cated radio commentaries that he wrote and broadcast after leaving
the California governorship in 1975, Reagan asserted that "Communism is neither an ec.[onomic] or a pol.[itical] system—it is a form of
insanity—a temporary aberration which will one day disappear from
the earth because it is contrary to human nature."[135]

Reagan emphasized that the USSR's exorbitant devotion of its
economic resources to its military exacerbated the inherently "shaky"
Soviet economy. In a 1975 radio commentary, he stated, "One thing is
certain, the threat of hunger to the Russian people is due to the Soviet
obsession with mil.[itary] power. Nothing proves the failure of Marx-
ism more than the Soviet Unions inability to produce weapons for its
mil. ambitions and at the same time provide for their peoples everyday
needs." Linking the USSR's economic shortcomings with his views on
the arms competition and the aims of U.S. Cold War policy, Reagan
continued, "The Russians have told us over & over again that their
goal is to impose their incompetent and ridiculous system on the
world. We invest in armaments to hold them off, but what do we envision as the eventual outcome? Either they will see the fallacy of their

way & give up their goal or their system will collapse or—(and we don't let ourselves think of this) we'll have to use our weapons one day."[136]

During the 1976 primary campaign, Reagan reiterated his long-held belief that a U.S.-led military buildup would strain the relatively weak Soviet economy and force the USSR to concede the arms race and agree to reduce the number of nuclear weapons. In an interview with *U.S. News & World Report*, he stated:

> The U.S. should say to the Soviet Union: "Look, détente as a relaxing of tensions is fine. . . . But, in the meantime, we are not ever going to be second best to anyone else militarily. We're going to be strong and do whatever has to be done to remain strong." If the U.S. would do this and the Soviets see this demonstration of will, they might say: "Oh, wait a minute. If we're going to keep up an arms race, this is going to go on forever, and we can't catch them or match them." Then I think you could have legitimate reduction of arms. My belief is that the Soviet Union right now is surging ahead because it sees no intent on the part of our people to do this. The Russians know they can't match us industrially or technologically.[137]

It does not appear that Reagan expressed this conviction during set, scripted speeches in 1976. It is likely that his advisers took pains to exclude it from those speeches; endorsing a massive military buildup to pressure an adversary's internal system is not a reliable vote winner. But Reagan continued to espouse it during interviews.

Reagan's criticism of détente resonated with voters in the 1976 Republican primaries. His attacks on American foreign policy since the 1960s helped drive his candidacy to a strong showing after an initially sluggish start.[138] Heading into the Republican National Convention in Kansas City, Reagan and Ford were locked in a close fight. In the end, the incumbent Ford won the nomination by a thin margin.

Immediately after he was nominated and had delivered his acceptance speech on the last night of the convention in Kansas City, President Ford asked Reagan to join him onstage and offered him the podium.[139] Political tradition dictated that Reagan should have acknowledged Ford as the party's candidate, given encouragement, and perhaps spoken a few lines from his standard speech. Instead, during brief, spontaneous remarks, Reagan described how he had recently been asked to write a letter for a time capsule. In preparing it, Reagan said, he had thought of how

> we live in a world in which the great powers have aimed and poised at each other horrible missiles of destruction, nuclear weapons that can in minutes arrive at each other's country and destroy virtually the civilized world we live in. And suddenly it dawned on me: those who would read this letter a hundred years from now will know whether those missiles were fired. They will know whether we met our challenge. . . . Will they look back and say, "Thank God for those people in 1976 . . . who kept us now a hundred years later free? Who kept our world from nuclear destruction?"[140]

Martin Anderson, a policy adviser to Reagan who was with him at the convention, recalled during an interview with the author that "I think there you got the pure, the real essence of what Reagan felt. . . . [H]is main concern [was] the threat of nuclear weapons, and what we're going to do about it, and how we're going to solve it. I don't think anyone paid that much attention to the substance of that speech. But if you look at what he did from there on out, the various steps he took from time to time, it all sort of fits in." From the beginning of his involvement in politics, Anderson commented, Reagan had been working toward the goal of "do[ing] something about what he used to call 'Armageddon'—the threat of nuclear war."[141]

Deaver, who was also at the convention, stated in an interview that Reagan's preoccupation with eliminating the nuclear threat, and nuclear weapons altogether, underpinned his determination to win the presidency: "Reagan thought that he *had* to run for president. He was the guy that could get the Soviets to the table and end nuclear war." Deaver concurred with Anderson that the 1976 convention speech provided a glimpse of Reagan's fundamental ambition to intervene in and solve the nuclear dilemma, and he linked that ambition with Reagan's religious beliefs: "This was a guy who believed in predestination, who believed that there was a purpose for everybody's life and we had to fulfill it. And that was his purpose. . . . He was running for president because he believed he was *destined* to do away with nuclear weapons. And I don't know how long it will take before [that] becomes clear to people."[142]

Many years after the 1976 convention, Cannon, who covered it as a journalist, and who has no incentive to champion Reagan, wrote that in the brief convention speech, Reagan "addressed the issue that mattered most to him, speaking from his heart and without notes or cue cards. It was a clue of what was to come." Cannon acknowledged that he and other journalists had missed the significance of that clue regarding Reagan's antinuclearism and his preoccupation with radically altering the nuclear status quo. "This clue," Cannon stated,

> did not lead us anywhere . . . because most of us in the journalistic community did not realize then that there was a mystery to solve. . . . Reagan was a familiar figure on the national political stage. There seemed nothing enigmatic about him. He was stereotyped as a likable and decent man who was lacking in intellectual candlepower. Most reporters focused on the maneuvers of Reagan's strategists rather than on Reagan's inner goals. Often, the strategists were also focused on themselves. They respected Reagan's performing skills and paid little attention to his larger purposes. This attitude was compounded when Reagan reached the White House; many of his advisers viewed his dreamy imaginings and original ideas as irrelevant to his presidency.[143]

Cannon's statement stands equally well as an indictment of scholars today as it does of journalists at the time. Few have ventured to look beyond the stereotype of Reagan as a detached figurehead, a cipher for his advisers.

As will be shown, Reagan's "dreamy imaginings and original ideas" were far from irrelevant to his presidency—as many of his advisers did realize then and as more of them came to appreciate after the fact. Reagan abhorred nuclear weapons early, consistently, and deeply. He was convinced that he could intervene in and resolve the nuclear standoff between the United States and the USSR, and that he must; he believed that it was his purpose and duty to do so. Reagan sought to eliminate the threat that Soviet nuclear weapons posed to the United States and ultimately to abolish all nuclear weapons. He held unique views, held them strongly, and was determined to put them into action.

THE 1980 CAMPAIGN

Reagan never stopped running for president after his close primary defeat in 1976. In 1980, his chances were much better than they had been four years earlier. The travails of President Jimmy Carter, a Democrat, presented Reagan with an opportunity.

Early in his presidency, Carter declared that the United States should move past the notion "that Soviet expansion was almost inevitable but that it must be contained" and past an "inordinate fear of communism" that was distorting U.S. interests.[144] Toward the end of his tenure, Carter's policy with respect to the USSR had produced little success and considerable setbacks, and he significantly altered the approach he had initially set out.

Soon after taking office, Carter dispatched his secretary of state, Cyrus Vance, to Moscow to convince the Soviets that arms negotiations should aim to reduce, not merely limit the growth of, the two sides' nuclear arsenals. The Kremlin emphatically rejected Vance's appeal. The Carter administration ended up negotiating what became the SALT II Treaty, completed in 1979. SALT II, which like its predecessor set caps on various types of nuclear arms, allowed the Soviets an advantage in the total number of ICBM warheads and a monopoly on "heavy" ICBMs; it effectively codified the evolution of the arms race during the 1970s.[145] That, in addition to Carter's cancellation or postponement of several major U.S. weapons programs, led to intense criticism of his defense and foreign policies not just by Republicans, but by Democratic Cold War hawks as well, many of whom, such as Nitze and Perle, later joined the Reagan administration.

Criticism of Carter's Cold War approach was particularly acute by private organizations such as the bipartisan Committee on the Present Danger, whose goal was to increase support for a harder-line stance toward the USSR and whose members included Reagan, Nitze, Dean Rusk—the former secretary of state under Presidents Kennedy and Johnson—and Richard Pipes, a Russian and Soviet history professor at Harvard. Groups such as the Committee on the Present Danger advanced the idea that the United States might be entering a "window of vulnerability" in which its nuclear retaliatory capability could be threatened by the growing power of the Soviet ICBM fleet.[146]

During the late 1970s, Soviet-backed groups expanded their influence in a variety of regional conflicts. In December 1979, one month after the seizure of the U.S. Embassy in Tehran, the Soviet Union invaded Afghanistan. Following the Soviet invasion, Carter shifted to the right in foreign policy, withdrawing SALT II from Senate consideration, ordering a series of embargoes against the USSR, and calling for substantial annual increases in defense spending. As the 1980 election neared, Carter lacked popular consensus for his foreign policy, especially as pertained to the Soviet Union. This presented an unusual opportunity for an aspiring president to reframe the debate and establish a Cold War policy that differed substantially from that of the recent past.

During his announcement in November 1979 that he was entering the presidential race, Reagan argued that the United States should move away from what he saw as a passive, defensive Cold War approach: "[T]oo often in recent times we have just drifted along with events, responding as if we thought of ourselves as a nation in decline." He called for a new "long-range diplomatic strategy."[147]

In Reagan's speech to the Republican National Convention in the summer of 1980—this time a victory speech, as he defeated his nearest rival, George H. W. Bush, for the party's nomination—he attacked the Carter administration's defense policy, claiming that "America's defense strength is at its lowest ebb in a generation, while the Soviet Union is vastly outspending us in both strategic and conventional arms." As a result, he continued, "[a]dversaries large and small test our will and seek to confound our resolve, but we are given weakness when we need strength, vacillation when the times demand firmness." Reagan emphasized his own optimism, claiming that President Carter and the Democratic-controlled Congress "say that the United States has had its day in the sun, that our nation has passed its zenith. . . . I utterly reject that view."[148]

During a campaign speech on national security in August 1980, Reagan declared that the national defense was "in shambles." He said that "[a]ll over the world, we can see that in the face of declining American power, the Soviets and their friends are advancing. . . . Soviet leaders talk arrogantly of a so-called 'correlation of forces' that has moved in their favor, opening up opportunities for them to extend their influence." Reagan stated that, with a new approach, the United States could prevail in the Cold War:

> The truth is we would like nothing better than to see the Russian people living in freedom and dignity instead of being trapped in the backwash of history as they are. The greatest fallacy of the Marxist-Leninist philosophy is that it is the "wave of the future." Everything about it is primitive: compulsion in place of free initiative; coercion in place of law; militarism in place of trade; and empire-building in place of self-determination; and luxury for a chosen few at the expense of the many. We have seen nothing like it since the Age of Feudalism.

"I believe it is our pre-ordained destiny," Reagan said, "to show all mankind that they, too, can be free without having to leave their native shore."[149]

Strident assaults on Carter's foreign and defense policies, calls for a new, stronger, and more confident Cold War approach, and evocations of American exceptionalism found wide support amongst a U.S. electorate that had suffered a string of international humiliations and that felt the Soviets might be pushing ahead militarily and geostrategically. Yet Reagan's advisers were acutely aware that one of their candidate's key political weaknesses was the potential to be tarred, as Goldwater had been, as a mad bomber.[150] Reagan's geniality largely defused the issue, however, and Carter's overt attempts to exploit it backfired. At one point, Carter declared that the election would determine "whether we have peace or war," a remark that Reagan dismissed as "beneath decency."[151]

In fact, Reagan was anything but a mad bomber. One of Reagan's aides, Fred Iklé, recalled a meeting between Reagan and his advisers in the late 1970s during which they discussed a president's response upon being warned of an incoming missile attack. According to Iklé, one person present said, "If we see that the Russians are attacking, we just launch our missiles before [theirs] hit." Reagan replied, "That would be the wrong thing to do."[152] Neither Reagan nor any of his advisers ever publicly stated that he expressed doubts that he would retaliate if the United States came under Soviet nuclear attack. Such a statement would have undermined the very basis of nuclear deterrence.[153] Yet some of Reagan's presidential advisers were almost certain that he would not retaliate in the event of an attack, as will be seen in Chapter 4.

Most of Reagan's scripted speeches in 1980 excluded calls for applying U.S. pressure to wear down the Soviet economy. (This is not to say that they varnished his real views; during one speech he asked, "Since when has it been wrong for America to aim to be first in military strength? How is American military superiority 'dangerous'?")[154] However, during unscripted moments—usually in interviews—Reagan expounded frequently and at length on his view that the Soviets would recognize that an untrammeled arms race led by the United States would place intolerable strain on the Soviet economy and that they would therefore agree to cut nuclear arms if confronted with one. "The Soviet Union," Reagan told the *National Journal*,

> I believe, is up to its maximum ability in developing arms. Their people are denied so many consumer products because it is all going into the military. They know that if we turned our full industrial might into an arms race, they cannot keep pace with us. Why haven't we played that card? Why haven't we said to them when we're sitting at the SALT table, "Gentlemen, the only alternative to you being willing to meet us halfway on these things is an arms race"? And maybe we wouldn't have to have the arms race because that's the last thing they want us to do.[155]

In an interview with *The Washington Post*, Reagan stated bluntly that it "would be of great benefit to the United States if we started a buildup."[156] "The very fact that we would start would serve a notice on the Soviet Union," he added.[157] "I think there's every indication and every reason to believe that the Soviet Union cannot increase its production of arms. Right now we're hearing of strikes and labor disputes because people aren't getting enough to eat. They've diverted so much to military [spending] that they can't provide for the consumer needs."[158] During a later interview with the Associated Press, Reagan again emphasized his belief in the value of a U.S. military buildup: a Soviet negotiator, he argued, "will be far more inclined to negotiate in good faith if he knows that the United States is engaged in building up its military. . . . The one card that's been missing in these negotiations has been the possibility of an arms race." Reagan took pains to demonstrate that his unorthodox approach was intended to reduce the nuclear threat: "My goal is to begin arms reductions. My energies will be directed at reducing nuclear weaponry in the world."[159]

Anderson later wrote that on "numerous occasions during the presidential campaigns when [Reagan] was talking privately to his policy advisers he would say, 'The only way the Soviets will stop their drive for military superiority is when they realize that we are willing to go all out in an arms race. . . . If we release the forces of our economy to produce the weapons we need the Soviets will never be able to keep up. And then, and only then, will they become reasonable and willing to seriously consider reductions in nuclear weapons.'"[160] Anderson, an economist, commented during an interview with the author that among all of Reagan's campaign advisers and staff, the candidate "was the only person in the campaign that was saying that, that was thinking that."[161] Reagan's idea that Soviet fears of the economic ramifications of a massive U.S. military buildup would force the USSR to accept reductions in nuclear weapons appears to have been his own.

While Reagan's expressions of that belief, and his intention to act on it as president, did draw some attention in the press during the 1980 campaign (*The New York Times* ran the front-page headline "Reagan Calls Arms Race Essential to Avoid a Surrender or Defeat"),[162] they did not unduly hurt him at the ballot box. Reagan was elected president by a wide margin.

REAGAN AND MISSILE DEFENSE
IN THE 1980 CAMPAIGN

In retrospect, Reagan's long-standing determination to pursue a missile defense was conspicuous by its absence from the 1980 presidential campaign. Missile defense was never far from Reagan's mind after he left the governorship of California in 1975. During one of his radio commentaries in 1977, he claimed that "[a]pparently the Russians have a laser beam capable of blasting our missiles from the sky if we should ever try to use them."[163] It is not clear where Reagan got this information, which was inaccurate; although the Soviets were pursuing a research program into advanced missile defense technologies, including lasers, they were not even close to deploying a system based on such technologies. It is significant that Reagan was taken with using nonnuclear, advanced technology in order to defend against missiles. He had been wary of methods involving nuclear warheads, and the prospect of pursuing missile defense with nonnuclear means recommended itself to him.

In the summer of 1979, Reagan visited the North American Aerospace Defense Command (NORAD), in Colorado Springs, Colorado, the U.S. military's nerve center for tracking a potential nuclear attack. Anderson, who accompanied Reagan on the trip to NORAD, later wrote that Reagan "was keenly interested in finding out how this system worked and what information it could provide." During the visit, Reagan received a briefing on the nature and number of the Soviet Union's nuclear forces. He was shown the main command room, an enormous space — "several stories high," according to Anderson — with a large display screen that represented U.S. airspace. In response to questions posed by Reagan and Anderson, the commanding general informed them that a direct hit by one of the USSR's SS-18 "heavy" ICBMs on the massively protected and sealed NORAD "would blow us away." Responding to the visitors' queries as to what would happen if the Soviets launched an ICBM at an American city, the general replied, "Well, we would pick it up right after it was launched, but by the time the officials of the city could be alerted that a nuclear bomb would hit them, there would be only ten or fifteen minutes left. That's all we can do. We can't stop it."[164]

In an interview, Anderson stated that before the visit both he and Reagan "knew that there was nothing you could do" if the USSR launched a missile attack on the United States. But "there's something about seeing" how NORAD worked, and how events would occur in the event of a nuclear attack, Anderson said, "that drives the point home. It somehow coalesces your thinking on it."[165]

NORAD (then under a different name) was the same facility that Edward Teller had visited in 1961, when he had received his own briefing from the then–commanding general. That 1961 visit had convinced Teller of the need for missile defense. In 1979, Reagan needed no convincing on that count. On the plane ride back to California, Reagan told Anderson, "We have spent all that money and have all that equipment, and there is nothing we can do to prevent a nuclear missile from hitting us."[166] As Anderson recounted to the author, "We were just sitting, talking. He was musing, I believe thinking about if things went well . . . if he got elected, he'd be the guy who had to make the decision. He was thinking in those terms and running through the options. And he didn't like the options. He was really clear that he did *not* like the options."[167] Reagan said to Anderson, "The only options we would have would be to press the button or do nothing. They're both bad. We should have some way of defending against nuclear missiles." The two then discussed the debate over ABMs in the late 1960s and the ABM Treaty. Reagan readily agreed with Anderson that the campaign should look into missile defense, particularly at new technologies.[168]

A few weeks after the trip to NORAD, Anderson produced an internal campaign memorandum on national security, which, he later explained, "drew on what [Reagan] had said on the plane and what I knew about his general attitude and what he said."[169] Reagan's campaign at that stage had no full-time national security adviser, so Anderson, as the head of the overall policy unit, drew it up himself.

Included in that paper was a section on missile defense, which read in part:

> During the early 1970s there was a great debate about whether or not this country should build an anti–ballistic missile system. The ABM lost, and is now prohibited by SALT agreements. But perhaps it is now time to seriously reconsider the concept. . . . Of course, there is the question of feasibility, especially with the development of multiple entry warheads, but there have apparently been striking advances in missile technology during the past decade or so that would make such a system technically possible. If it could be done, it would be a major step toward redressing the military balance of power, and it would be a purely defensive step.[170]

The memorandum touched off considerable debate within the Reagan camp regarding missile defense.[171] All of the major policy advisers to the campaign, including Meese and Iklé (and Richard Allen, who signed on to the campaign after the memo had been written and who would become Reagan's first national security adviser in the White House), supported the idea of pursuing missile defense.[172] So did Reagan, who nevertheless asked tough questions: "Can we do it? Is the technology available? How soon can we do it? How much will it cost?"[173]

In the end, however, "a political call was made" (in Anderson's later words). Reagan's political advisers, led by Deaver, argued that "in the 1980 campaign, it would be politically very difficult for Reagan to run on national security issues and talk about nuclear weapons, et cetera, et cetera, because as soon as you put Reagan and nuclear weapons in the same sentence, people would go up a tree." Reagan's policy advisers saw the wisdom in this—as did the candidate himself. As a result, Anderson stated, "a decision was made to slow that down," and the campaign avoided any public calls for the development of missile defense capabilities.[174]

The success of this political strategy was threatened numerous times by Reagan himself during the 1980 campaign. In several unscripted moments, he came perilously close to revealing publicly his desire to seek a missile defense. During an interview with Cannon in

October 1979, Reagan stated that "we have allowed ourselves to believe in the MAD system . . . [that] neither country will ever want to push the button because of what it will do to their own people in the exchange of nuclear weapons." After claiming that Soviet military improvements were rendering America's deterrent capability tenuous, Reagan continued, "We have to see what now, with the least lead time, will allow us to come back to a position where we cannot, in the next few years, reach a point at which the Soviet Union could deliver an ultimatum and our only response would be pushing the button."

Cannon asked if Reagan had any particular system—meaning offensive system—in mind to redress the situation. "No," replied Reagan, "I think that maybe it's too simple to go back and say, 'Let's go back to the things we postponed.' Maybe the delay now is such that they would not be effective enough in time." He then mentioned "ABM technology." Cannon asked whether Reagan was "basically in favor of some kind of antimissile defense." Reagan hedged: "I think that we should be looking at and researching, perhaps more than we are, some defensive system. Recently I had a briefing at NORAD, and we know that we can, by radar, pick up the Soviet missiles, if they were ever launched, virtually from launch, we can track them and know exactly when and where they are going to hit this country. We can do nothing to prevent them from hitting this country."[175]

In a later interview with journalist Robert Scheer, Reagan again mentioned his visit to NORAD. "NORAD is an amazing place," he said, and then described how it could track the smallest of items orbiting in space. "I think the thing that struck me," he continued, "was the irony that here, with this great technology of ours, we can do all of this yet we cannot stop any of the weapons that are coming at us. I don't think there's been a time in history when there wasn't a defense against some kind of thrust, even back in the old-fashioned days when we had coast artillery that would stop invading ships if they came." Reagan proceeded to criticize Robert McNamara for ensconcing the "Mutual Assured Destruction plan" in national policy and for creating the conditions "that resulted in our doing away with our antiballistic missile system."

He then stated, "I do think that it is time to turn the expertise that we have in [the scientific] field . . . to turn it loose on what do we need in the line of defense against their weaponry [to] defend our population, because we can't be sitting here—this could become the vulnerable point for us in the event of an ultimatum." After Scheer diverted his interviewee by asking about bomb shelters, Reagan returned to his theme of missile defense: "One of the first things I would do would be to turn to those who are knowledgeable in military affairs, knowledgeable in the weaponry that would be coming at us, and so forth, to find out what we could do."[176]

In March 1980, Reagan again briefly discussed his interest in missile defense. During an interview with the *National Journal*, Reagan claimed that the United States "must restore our ability to deter the Soviet Union. I tell you, I think we're talking about the next few years that we must change the situation, not eventually down the road." The interviewer asked what a potential solution might be and in his question specifically mentioned missile defense. Reagan responded affirmatively to missile defense, stating that the United States "certainly" needed "a defensive weapon," but did not elaborate.[177]

So Reagan's long-standing and newly rejuvenated desire to seek a missile defense was kept from the public during the 1980 presidential campaign, if only barely. While Reagan and his advisers did not specifically advocate missile defense, however, the issue did arise in the campaign. The 1980 Republican Party platform contained a section on missile defense. It stated, "We reject the mutual-assured-destruction (MAD) strategy of the Carter administration which limits the President during crises to a Hobson's choice between mass mutual suicide and surrender." The platform endorsed "vigorous research and development of an effective ballistic-missile system, such as is already at hand in the Soviet Union, as well as more modern ABM technologies."[178] One of the principal drafters later stated in an interview that the substance of the platform had been fully coordinated with the Reagan campaign.[179] Reagan was preparing the political ground for a missile defense decision in the future.

CHAPTER

II

1981–1982

I n selecting his administration's top foreign policy and defense officials during the transition period between his election in November 1980 and his inauguration in January 1981, Reagan drew for the
most part on aides who had worked for him in California, or on his
presidential campaign staff, who were familiar with his approach and
instincts concerning the Cold War.

There was a notable exception. Reagan chose General Alexander
Haig to be his secretary of state. Haig was a West Point graduate and
career Army officer who had served as supreme Allied commander in
Europe during the mid-1970s. He also had extensive political experience, having been military assistant to Henry Kissinger and then
deputy national security adviser during President Nixon's first term,
and subsequently Nixon's last White House chief of staff as Nixon
struggled to handle the Watergate scandal. Haig was strong-minded,
quick-tempered, and ambitious. He had gauged the prospects for running for president himself before backing Reagan. Reagan and Haig

met on a handful of occasions during the 1980 campaign, during which Haig impressed Reagan.[1] Over the objections of his political advisers, Reagan picked Haig to head the State Department.[2] Unlike his advisers, Reagan harbored no doubts regarding Haig's loyalty.

Haig, concerned about his lack of familiarity with Reagan, believed he needed someone at the State Department with close connections to Reagan who could serve as an "interpreter" between the secretary and the president.[3] For that reason he asked William Clark to serve as deputy secretary of state.

Clark was a fourth-generation Californian, the grandson of a U.S. marshal and the son of a police chief. A devout Catholic, he had dropped out of Stanford for a time to attend an Augustinian seminary.[4] Before beginning a law career in California, he served as an enlisted man in military counterintelligence in West Germany. Clark worked on Reagan's first gubernatorial campaign in 1966 and became Governor Reagan's first Cabinet secretary. From 1967 to 1969, he served as Reagan's chief of staff in Sacramento. Clark, who spoke slowly, softly, and not very much, and whose real love was ranching, developed a singularly close relationship with Reagan.[5] After Reagan failed to convince Clark to become lieutenant governor, he appointed him to a series of judgeships that concluded with a seat on the California Supreme Court. There Clark had remained, while keeping in constant contact with Reagan, until he took the State Department job in 1981. Clark, then forty-eight, frankly admitted that he did not know much about foreign policy, which he demonstrated during his Senate confirmation hearings.[6] As he told Haig, however, he did know Reagan's "ways."[7]

Haig filled many of the State Department's other top slots with career Foreign Service officers who were conservative enough to satisfy the White House. He also recruited Robert "Bud" McFarlane, a former Marine Corps colonel and veteran of the NSC staff under Nixon and Ford, to serve as counselor. McFarlane, who held a graduate degree in strategic studies, had most recently worked on arms control issues for conservative Republican Senator John Tower and had helped draft the defense and foreign policy portions of the 1980 Republican

Party platform.[8] Haig selected Richard Burt, another young strategic expert, as the department's director of political-military affairs. Burt had worked at the International Institute for Strategic Studies in London and had covered national security affairs for *The New York Times*.

In choosing his secretary of defense, Reagan turned to Weinberger. A native San Franciscan, Weinberger earned his undergraduate and law degrees at Harvard before enlisting as an infantryman in World War II, which he spent in the Pacific theater, including service on the staff of General Douglas MacArthur. Back in California, he entered state politics. He joined Reagan's gubernatorial administration in 1968 as director of finance and formed lasting friendships with Reagan and several of his other aides, including Meese and Clark.[9] Weinberger then moved on to a variety of senior positions in the Nixon and Ford presidential administrations, including director of the Office of Management and Budget and secretary of health, education, and welfare.

While in those posts, Weinberger earned a reputation as a budget cutter. His approach to defense was quite different, however. Weinberger viewed the Soviet Union as a distrustful enemy, and as defense secretary he deployed his formidable skills toward securing the U.S. military buildup that Reagan championed. He was aided by Deputy Secretary Frank Carlucci, an experienced government official who had worked with Weinberger in several departments during the Nixon and Ford years but had few direct ties to Reagan. Fred Iklé, a Swiss-born conservative academic who had previously served as director of the Arms Control and Disarmament Agency (ACDA) under Nixon, became undersecretary of defense for policy. As seen in the previous chapter, Iklé had been involved with Reagan's 1980 campaign; through his participation in several sessions with Reagan during the campaign he became fully aware of Reagan's views.[10] In the summer of 1981, Richard Perle joined the Pentagon as assistant secretary for international security policy. That post, which was under Iklé's purview, had broad responsibility for arms control policy within the Defense Department. Perle, a Democrat, had spent the 1970s as an influential Senate staff member who had criticized both détente and the SALT treaties as disadvantageous to the United States.

Reagan chose his 1980 campaign manager, William Casey, to head the CIA. Casey, a New York lawyer, had served in a series of economic positions, including as undersecretary of state for economic affairs, in the Nixon and Ford administrations. He was also a veteran of the Office of Strategic Services, the forerunner of the CIA. Casey disdained both communism and the USSR. According to one CIA official who worked closely with him, Casey "came to CIA primarily to wage war against the Soviet Union."[11] Meant figuratively, that description encapsulated Casey's preoccupation throughout his tenure at the CIA with identifying and exploiting Soviet vulnerabilities.

Reagan appointed Richard Allen, his principal foreign and defense policy assistant during the 1980 presidential campaign, as White House national security adviser. Allen had worked briefly on Henry Kissinger's NSC staff, to the discomfort of both Allen and Kissinger, since the former argued for a harder line toward Moscow. In 1981, Allen assembled his NSC staff from a variety of fields, including the military, academia, investment banking, and business. Of particular consequence was his selection of Richard Pipes as director of Soviet and Eastern European affairs. After immigrating to the United States from his native Poland in 1940, Pipes served with the U.S. Army Air Force during World War II before embarking on his academic career at Harvard. Pipes had been active during the Cold War policy debates of the 1970s, first as chair of "Team B," an independent panel that reviewed the CIA's intelligence estimates of the USSR, and then as a member of the Committee on the Present Danger.

From the outset, Allen faced a significant bureaucratic handicap as national security adviser. During the 1980 campaign, Reagan publicly criticized the rivalry between the national security adviser and the secretary of state that had characterized both the Nixon and Carter administrations, when the occupants of the two posts struggled for primary control over the determination and implementation of foreign policy. The Carter administration, he claimed, had been "unable to speak with one voice in foreign policy."[12] In an effort to prevent similar internecine tensions, Reagan downgraded the post of national security adviser.[13] Instead of reporting directly to the president, Allen reported through the White House counselor, a new position created to oversee both foreign and domestic policy.

That decision decimated the influence of the national security adviser, whose bureaucratic power derives almost entirely from a close working relationship with and constant access to the president; otherwise, the national security adviser has only a small staff and budget and no real operational capabilities. One result of the decision was that Allen's ability to act as an independent source of policy formulation within the government—a role adopted by successive national security advisers since the Kennedy administration by tradition rather than by statute[14]—was severely limited. Another, unintended consequence was that Allen, who had little standing with the president and thus virtually no leverage over the departments or their secretaries, had difficulty accomplishing the tasks that the NSC had been charged by law to accomplish—namely, to act as a centripetal force for coordinating the various foreign and defense policies of the administration and to serve as the president's arbiter of different options and views.[15]

The holder of the new post of White House counselor, through whom Allen reported to the president, was Edwin Meese, Reagan's principal policy adviser and 1980 campaign chief of staff. Meese, another fourth-generation Californian, had been an assistant district attorney in northern California before he joined Governor Reagan's administration as legal affairs secretary. In 1969, he replaced Clark as Reagan's chief of staff and he remained at Reagan's side throughout the presidential campaigns in 1976 and 1980. Meese constituted one third of Reagan's White House "triumvirate," an unusual arrangement in which three officials—the others were Chief of Staff James Baker and Deputy Chief of Staff Michael Deaver—shared responsibilities related to the president's political agenda.

Of the three, Reagan knew Baker, a close ally of Vice President Bush, the least well. In addition to overseeing the administrative side of the White House, including personnel and what papers did or did not reach Reagan, Baker focused on the mechanics of the political process. Like Clark and Meese, Deaver had been with Reagan since the beginning of his career in elected politics. Deaver concentrated on Reagan's public image, but his influence extended beyond that.

Reagan would make a small number of important changes both to his administration's personnel and to his national security policy-making system over the course of his first two years as president. He did so to assert control over the system, attempting to ensure that it effectively reflected and sought his broad objectives. The above review of personnel acts as a brief background to illuminate their later roles in the 1980s.

PRIORITIES

During the transition, Reagan continued to discuss privately his desire for a defense against missiles. In particular, he conveyed his views on MAD and missile defense to those who would have to play important roles in promoting a missile defense program.

Harrison Schmitt, a Republican senator from New Mexico, happily reported to the press the details of a conversation he had with the president-elect in December 1980. Schmitt, a former astronaut and one of a handful of U.S. senators then interested in high-technology missile defense,[16] said that Reagan had expressed frustration that existing strategic policy held "tens of millions of people hostage to annihilation in order to maintain a deterrent." Reagan told Schmitt that he wanted to develop a missile defense and prodded Schmitt on "the technological possibilities of altering [U.S.] strategic policy toward one of protection rather than mutually assured destruction." Schmitt, soon to be chairman of the Senate Subcommittee on Science, Technology, and Space, replied that he thought such technologies feasible given concerted effort to achieve them.[17]

Reagan reemphasized his desire for a missile defense to Secretary of Defense–designate Weinberger.[18] As described previously, Weinberger knew from discussions he had had from the late 1960s onward with then-Governor Reagan that Reagan "had a very deep revulsion of the whole idea of nuclear weapons"[19] and longed to "acquire a defensive capability" against them.[20] Reagan told Weinberger that "I'd like to set our scientists loose" on missile defense "because I think it could be done and I'd feel a great deal safer."[21]

Weinberger pointed out during an interview with *The New York Times* before Reagan's inauguration that the new administration would consider building an extensive missile defense system. He stated that the administration would be interested in defenses based on "later technology" than those of the early 1970s and that continued U.S. adherence to the ABM Treaty was "not automatic."[22] Twenty years later, Weinberger specifically recalled the interview, commenting that the reporter had "practically dropped his pen, he was so astonished at this idea."[23] While the *Times* story noted that Weinberger had mentioned the potential for using a missile defense capability to protect ICBM sites, it did not say whether he had discussed employing it to shield the American population, which Weinberger knew was Reagan's intention.

In the same interview, Weinberger warned that the Reagan administration would not "rush into" arms negotiations with the Soviets. He stated that it would wait until its promised military buildup was perceived to have taken effect, particularly after the administration had secured increased defense budgets for 1981 and 1982, so that when the United States entered negotiations, it would do so "from a position of greater strength."[24]

The Reagan administration's immediate priority during 1981 was to push its domestic economic plan and its defense buildup through Congress.[25] Anderson, who served as the principal White House domestic policy adviser, recalled that "in terms of timing, the first thing [we] had to do was economics."[26] A review of Reagan's schedule and statements during the first half of 1981 illustrates that the majority of his activity was devoted to rallying public support and congressional votes for his economic plan, particularly his tax cuts and budget reductions, which he signed into law in August 1981.[27]

Reagan's economic plan and defense buildup were inextricably linked. He sought across-the-board increases in defense spending. While the sums for the modernization of strategic nuclear forces (those that could reach targets in the USSR from the United States) and the naval buildup received the most attention and criticism, Reagan also "provided substantial additional funding for all the major categories of the defense budget."[28] Reagan told his advisers that his foremost priority was to increase defense spending, not to balance the budget.[29] (He believed that the budget would eventually come into balance through economic growth, which would generate larger revenues, and domestic spending cuts.) Anderson later recalled that "Reagan's first priority was not to balance the budget, it was to do something about the threat of nuclear war. And by God, he was going to do that."[30]

To Reagan, the defense buildup was necessary to reverse what he viewed as the United States' deteriorating ability to deter the Soviets from attack and to foil the USSR's global ambitions. He explained during a press conference in August 1981 that the Soviets intended to "get to the point of dominance" by continuing their military buildup while restraining the defense efforts of the United States and its allies. From that position, he stated, the Soviets could "issue to the free world an ultimatum of 'surrender or die.'" "[I]f they could achieve such a superiority by conning everyone else into being quiescent, they could then say, 'Look at the difference in our relative strengths. Now, here's what we want.' This is what I mean by an ultimatum, 'Surrender or die.'" Reagan claimed that his administration's determination to carry out its own defense buildup was already causing the Soviets "anguish." "They are squealing like they're sitting on a sharp nail simply because we now are showing the will that we're not going to let them get to the point of dominance."[31]

Reagan also viewed his administration's military buildup as a means of eventually reducing the Soviets' ability to pay for their own nuclear program and to force the USSR to change from within. By embarking on a major defense buildup, he had begun to put into place his aim of confronting the Soviet Union with an arms competition that would threaten its internal system.[32]

FURTHER IMPETUS FOR REAGAN'S DESIRE TO PURSUE MISSILE DEFENSE AND TO INTERVENE PERSONALLY IN U.S.-SOVIET RELATIONS

Reagan's presidency almost ended only two months after it began. On March 30, 1981, after delivering a speech at a Washington hotel, Reagan was shot by a deranged would-be assassin. The bullet that struck the president lodged within an inch of his heart, and he ended up losing more than half of his body's blood. Reagan, then seventy years old, very nearly died.[33]

When he returned to the White House after spending almost two weeks in hospital following the shooting, Reagan wrote in his diary, "Whatever happens now I owe my life to God and will try to serve him every way I can."[34] He expressed the same conviction—"I have decided that whatever time I may have left is left for Him"—to Terence Cardinal Cooke of New York in a private meeting on Good Friday, April 17.[35] Reagan thought he knew why he had been "spared." "Perhaps having come so close to death," Reagan stated, "made me feel I should do whatever I could in the years God had given me to reduce the threat of nuclear war."[36]

These events were a confirmation for Reagan. His desire to seek a missile defense grew in intensity.[37] And his inclination to intervene personally in and change the nature of U.S.-Soviet relations came to the fore.

The day after his Good Friday meeting with Cardinal Cooke, Reagan decided to write a personal letter to Soviet leader Leonid Brezhnev, as "I wanted to let him know that we had a realistic view of what the Soviet Union was all about, but also wanted to send a signal to him that we were interested in reducing the threat of nuclear annihilation."[38] When Reagan told Haig that he intended to write the letter, Haig (according to Reagan) "was reluctant to have *me* actually draft it. If I was going to send a letter, he said the State Department should compose it."[39] Through a series of incidents, Haig had already caused concern among some of his colleagues that he was seeking sole control over the administration's foreign policy.[40] Reagan later commented that Haig's reluctance to let him write the letter "was probably the first indication I had that it wasn't only other members of the cabinet and White House staff whom Al didn't want participating in foreign affairs."[41]

Reagan proceeded to write the letter by hand. It was then forwarded to the State Department, which returned it to the White

House with "heavy editing."[42] Reagan "didn't like what they'd done to it," so he "revised their revisions" and sent it with most of his original wording intact.[43] He did agree, however, to send his personal letter together with a separate, more formal message, which was prepared by the State Department. The two missives, both signed by Reagan, were sent on the same day, April 24.

It is probable that Haig disliked Reagan's letter as originally written in large part because it included statements regarding nuclear weapons that Haig viewed as overly idealistic. Richard Pipes later commented that "Reagan, for all his toughness, was terribly afraid of nuclear war." He spontaneously mentioned the first draft of Reagan's handwritten letter to Brezhnev by way of illustration. According to Pipes, Reagan wrote about "how important it was for us to collaborate, and to prevent, for the sake of our children and grandchildren, nuclear war, et cetera." Pipes said that most of his administration colleagues who saw the draft when it was circulated for comment were "absolutely dismayed" by Reagan's overt antinuclearism. "So we revised it," Pipes said, "and some of the worst sentences were omitted."[44]

Years afterward, Haig told Cannon that "[v]ery early on" in Reagan's presidency, Reagan had shown him the handwritten draft of a letter to Brezhnev. Haig was aghast when he read the letter: "I found myself astonished at [Reagan's] attitude when I measured it against the backdrop of what he was saying publicly, and what was attributed to him as a classic cold warrior." Haig stated that the letter "talked about a world without nuclear weapons, it talked about disarmament." It also emphasized Reagan's desire to engage in one-on-one diplomacy with the Soviet leader: "It reflected a demeanor that if only these two men could sit down as rational human beings, the problems of the world would be behind us." Haig felt that Reagan's message was "naïve" and that the president's unorthodox views on nuclear arms would be "confusing to the Soviet leaders." Haig remarked to Cannon that he had persuaded Reagan not to send that letter.[45]

It is possible that Haig misremembered the deletion of antinuclear portions from Reagan's April 24 letter as a separate episode, or that Pipes confused the changes made to the April 24 letter with another occasion on which the president wrote a letter that was discarded entirely, as Haig recalled.[46]

In any event, the handwritten letter that Reagan sent to Brezhnev on April 24 did not include any explicit antinuclear language. In the letter, Reagan recalled meeting Brezhnev in California in 1973, when Reagan had still been governor. On that occasion, Reagan wrote, he had asked Brezhnev if he was "aware that the hopes and aspirations of millions and millions of people throughout the world were dependent on the decisions that would be reached" in the Soviet leader's meetings with then-President Nixon. At the time, according to Reagan, Brezhnev replied that he was "dedicated . . . to fulfilling those hopes and dreams." Reagan continued by writing that "the peoples of the world . . . have very much in common. They want the dignity of having some control over their individual destiny. They want to work at the trade or craft of their own choosing and to be fairly rewarded." "Government exists for their convenience," Reagan stated, "not the other way around."[47]

Reagan then asked Brezhnev, "Mr. President, should we not be concerned with eliminating the obstacles which prevent our own people—those we represent—from achieving their most cherished goals? And isn't it possible some of those obstacles are born of govt. objectives which have little to do with the real needs and desires of our people?"[48]

The essence of Reagan's letter was that the Soviet leadership was pursuing its ideological ambitions at the expense of its people's welfare and wishes. Reagan's focus lay on the relationship between the nature of the USSR's internal regime and its international behavior. He cited specific Soviet actions abroad only in the context of the USSR's domestic affairs: "Will the average Soviet family be better off or even aware that the Soviet Union has imposed a government of it's [sic] own choice on the people of Afghanistan?"[49] The way to resolve the Cold War, Reagan suggested, would be for the Soviet leadership to turn away from its own ideological aims and toward serving the interests of its citizens—to allow them, in his words, "some control over their individual destiny."

Reagan's handwritten letter differed in both tone and substance from the State Department–drafted letter that accompanied it. In particular, the latter message did not address the nature of the internal Soviet regime.[50]

Possibly confused by receiving two letters sent from Reagan on the same day, the Soviet leadership replied via two letters from Brezhnev to Reagan, sent on May 25 and May 27. Each of them blamed the United States for Cold War tensions generally and for the collapse of détente specifically. They also argued for further arms agreements along the lines of SALT I and II.[51] One of them assailed "war preparations that doom the peoples to a senseless squandering of their material and spiritual wealth."[52] Reagan later described the replies from Brezhnev to his letters as "icy." "So much for my first attempt at personal diplomacy," he added.[53] The episode led Reagan to view with skepticism the prospect of making progress with the Brezhnev regime.

REAGAN, HAIG, AND THE DIRECTION OF THE REAGAN ADMINISTRATION'S SOVIET POLICY

In his public statements, Reagan denounced the USSR with the same vehemence and along the same lines as he had before taking office. During his first press conference, he asserted that "so far détente's been a one-way street that the Soviet Union has used to pursue its own aims." Asked what he saw as the "long-range intentions of the Soviet Union," he responded, "I don't have to think of an answer as to what I think their intentions are; they have repeated it." The Soviets "hold their determination that their goal must be the promotion of world revolution and a one-world Socialist or Communist state, whichever word you want to use," he claimed. He charged that Soviet leaders "have openly and publicly declared that the only morality they recognize is what will further their cause, meaning they reserve unto themselves the right to commit any crime, to lie, to cheat, in order to attain that."[54]

Reagan continually espoused his belief that the Soviet system was unsustainable. He proclaimed that the West "won't contain communism, it will transcend communism. . . . [I]t will dismiss it as some bizarre chapter in human history whose last pages are even now being written."[55] For "communism is an aberration. It's not a normal way of living for human beings, and I think we are seeing the first, beginning cracks, the beginning of the end."[56]

The Soviet system, Reagan said, could not withstand the economic and technological strain of an extensive, U.S.-led military competition. A central objective in seeking a military buildup was to secure reductions in nuclear arms; the Soviet leadership could be forced to turn its attention to its economic shortcomings and thus agree to cuts in nuclear weapons. As was the case during the election campaign, Reagan outlined this view only in general terms during prepared speeches. In a speech in September 1981, Reagan said that "we are going to continue to urge them to sit down with us in a program of realistic arms reduction. But it will be the first time that we have ever sat on our side of the table and let them know that there's a new chip on the table. And that chip is: there will be legitimate arms reduction, verifiable arms reduction, or they will be in an arms race which they can't win."[57]

During unscripted moments, when aides could not restrain his comments, Reagan was more expansive. In a question-and-answer session with reporters in October, Reagan stated, "I think that we can sit down and maybe have some more realistic negotiations because of what we can threaten them with." "There's one thing sure," he continued:

> They cannot vastly increase their military productivity because they've already got their people on a starvation diet as far as consumer products are concerned. But they know our potential capacity industrially, and they can't match it. So, we've got the chip this time, that if we show them the will and determination to go forward with a military buildup in our own defense and the defense of our allies, then they have to weigh, do they want to meet us realistically on a program of disarmament or do they want to face a legitimate arms race in which . . . they can't keep up.[58]

Reagan's approach to the Cold War centered on challenging the Soviet system itself, not just the expansion of the USSR's influence throughout the world. Haig did not share Reagan's enthusiasm for the former objective. His own focus was geopolitical; as Raymond Garthoff accurately summarized, the secretary of state aimed to "wage a vigorous competition focused on containing and countering direct or indirect Soviet expansion beyond the Soviet bloc in Eastern Europe, but not to carry the challenge to Soviet rule in the Soviet Union or the bloc."[59] Haig did not think that a U.S. policy of trying to exploit and exacerbate internal Soviet weaknesses was either viable or wise.[60] While he spoke of "fundamental systemic failures" in the Soviet Union,[61] he did not believe, as Reagan did, that the Soviet system was vulnerable to U.S. pressure, that under U.S. pressure it would reach a point at which it could no longer continue its emphasis on defense and international commitments, or that it could change in any fundamental way.[62] Haig evidently tried to block any formal drawing up of administration policy toward the Soviet Union for fear that Reagan would insist on pursuing a course of pressuring the Soviet system to compel change within it.[63]

TENTATIVE STEPS TOWARD MISSILE DEFENSE

Throughout the first half of 1981, Reagan refrained from publicly discussing his desire for a defense against missiles, although Weinberger continued to signal that the administration was considering an expanded missile defense research program. "If indeed you can develop an effective defense to some of these missiles," Weinberger said, "you could, I think, perhaps strongly encourage deterrence against actually employing them, and that, of course, is the goal of all of these things. The ABM Treaty was entered into because a lot of people had somewhat the opposite theory."[64]

Early in 1981, the Defense Department undertook a review of U.S. deterrence strategy and "the adequacy of the forces now available for carrying out that strategy."[65] In the autumn, the Pentagon completed a proposal for improving strategic forces that was approved by the NSC and ensconced as formal U.S. policy in a secret National Security Decision Directive (NSDD) in October 1981.[66] NSDDs, signed by the president, were "used to promulgate Presidential decisions implementing national policy and objectives in all areas involving national security."[67] They constituted the fundamental, authoritative statements of U.S. national security policy during the Reagan administration. Each presidential administration since the founding of the NSC in 1947 has issued similar documents; Truman's, for example, were titled NSC-xx, such as NSC-68.[68] Coordinated and debated at the highest level, NSDDs were usually highly classified and kept from congressional or public knowledge. Almost all of them have been declassified and released in recent years.[69]

The strategic forces improvements established in NSDD 12, "Strategic Forces Modernization Program," consisted of five elements. One was to increase the survivability of command-and-control systems. And each leg of the strategic nuclear "triad"—bomber aircraft, land-based ICBMs, and submarine-launched ballistic missiles (SLBMs)—was to be upgraded; the United States would construct B-1 bombers and develop advanced "stealth" technology bombers, continue steady construction of Trident submarines, develop a larger and more accurate SLBM, and deploy the new MX ICBM. In order to strengthen the potential survivability of the MX in the face of an attack, the NSDD set forth for study a number of possible basing modes for the missile, one of which was protection by ballistic missile defense.

The fifth element included in the NSDD was "improving strategic defenses." Apart from proposing a missile defense to protect ICBM silos, the NSDD stated that a "vigorous research and development program will be conducted on ballistic missile defense systems."[70]

When he publicly announced his administration's plans for improving strategic forces during a press conference the day after signing NSDD 12, Reagan mentioned only that he had "directed that we end our long neglect of strategic defenses."[71] Although the press did not question him further on the subject, Weinberger was asked to elaborate. The defense secretary stated that "the decision on . . . our ballistic missile defense, is simply to see if we can get something more effective than we have now." He noted that the administration would research an array of possible advanced missile defense technologies, including space-based systems. "[T]here are some brand new things that look quite promising," he said. "And these are the things that we are going to be exploring because obviously if we are able to destroy incoming missiles effectively, I don't think it's destabilizing, I think it would be extremely comforting."[72]

During an interview with *Fortune* magazine in mid-October, Weinberger stated that the administration was seeking "both offensive and defensive strategic strength." He made clear that its ambitions extended to an overall national missile defense: "What we would like to have is something that makes a ballistic-missile attack on the U.S. fully ineffective." *Fortune* reported that the administration was studying the potential for a layered defense that would combine a number of different defensive systems, including space-based ones, and was interested in increasing research on possible future technologies such as directed-energy (e.g., laser) weapons. Senator Schmitt told *Fortune* that President Reagan had been "most receptive" to the notion of using directed-energy weapons in a missile defense system when they discussed it during a conversation.[73]

During its first two years, the Reagan administration thus established in presidentially directed policy papers that the United States would pursue a "vigorous" missile defense research program. Weinberger indicated this publicly. Yet little concerted work was undertaken on missile defense in terms of either strategic analysis and planning or actual research and development until after Reagan announced SDI in March 1983. There was no "bottom-up" impetus from within the national security bureaucracy—the Defense Department, the State Department, and NSC staff—to pursue a missile defense program.[74]

In the fall of 1981, a small group of Reagan's White House policy advisers, motivated by their knowledge of the president's desire for a defense against missiles, informally began looking into the feasibility of pursuing a new missile defense project. Each morning, Meese convened a policy-planning session in the White House with Allen, Anderson, and Edwin Harper, deputy director of the Office of Management and Budget. By the autumn of 1981, according to Anderson, Reagan's economic program "was largely in place," and "other policy ideas began moving up on the priority list."[75] In an interview with the author, Anderson stated that "[w]e discussed missile defense policy and that Reagan was interested in it and wanted to do it." Meese, Allen, and Anderson were all acutely aware that missile defense "was something that Reagan knew about and thought a lot about and wanted to do."

The group included Reagan's White House science adviser, George "Jay" Keyworth, in their discussions on the subject.[76] Anderson recalled that Keyworth was "generally supportive of missile defense," although he "had some concerns."[77] Keyworth, who regarded Edward Teller as his mentor, had joined the Reagan administration from the Los Alamos National Laboratory, where he had been director of the Physics Division. Unlike Teller, however, Keyworth at the time was "a skeptic of strategic defense," in his later words. Yet Keyworth knew that the president was inclined toward missile defense; Reagan had expressed to him on several occasions his discomfort with the "nakedness" of not being able to defend the United States against missile attack.[78] Keyworth kept his skepticism as to the feasibility of missile defense quiet.

In late 1981 and early 1982, the White House policy group stayed in contact with a set of outside missile defense proponents.[79] In mid-1981, Daniel Graham, a retired Army general, former director of the Defense Intelligence Agency, and erstwhile adviser to Reagan's 1980 campaign, had joined with Karl Bendetsen, a conservative Democrat and Truman administration Pentagon official, to form a panel to promote the issue of missile defense within the Reagan administration. They recruited several members of Reagan's "kitchen Cabinet"— wealthy political supporters of the president—and Edward Teller. The panel suffered from disunity of purpose. In addition to advocating unrelated military and economic plans for space, Graham wanted the United States to deploy "off-the-shelf" missile defense technologies, which the other members refused to endorse, and he soon left the panel. Teller favored a missile defense system based on the X-ray laser, which required a nuclear explosion to generate its energy.

Without Graham, the members of the panel concentrated on encouraging a missile defense effort that would lie outside the normal channels of departmental or agency oversight.[80] During the autumn of 1981, various members of the panel discussed their idea, as well as more general issues regarding the cost and technological possibilities of missile defense, with Meese, Allen, Anderson, and Keyworth.[81] Bendetsen and two other panel members met briefly with Reagan in January 1982 to present their case.[82] As Anderson later wrote, Reagan "did not have to be convinced that building a missile defense was the right thing to do. His only concern was whether or not it was possible or affordable." Reagan focused his questions on the "technical feasibility" of an extensive missile defense system.[83]

Keyworth later stated that the efforts of the outside panel had had little impact on Reagan's later announcement of SDI. He described the January 1982 meeting as "token" within the context of Reagan's long-standing desire—and determination—to seek a missile defense.[84]

REAGAN'S ANTINUCLEARISM AT WORK

In November 1981, the Reagan administration faced an important arms control decision. During the late 1970s, the USSR began to deploy a three-warhead, intermediate-range ballistic missile, the SS-20, which could strike targets in Western Europe but not the United States. Several Western European leaders, most prominently West German Chancellor Helmut Schmidt, called for deployment of American intermediate-range missiles in Europe as a guarantee against any weakening of the extended deterrence provided to Western European nations by the U.S. nuclear arsenal. In 1979, President Carter and Western European leaders agreed on a two-track policy: the United States would deploy new intermediate-range ballistic missiles in West Germany and intermediate-range ground-launched cruise missiles (GLCMs) in several Western European countries, while also entering into negotiations with the Soviets to limit intermediate-range nuclear weapons in Europe.

In late 1981, the Reagan administration worked to prepare a negotiating position before heading into the intermediate-range nuclear

forces (INF) talks with the Soviets. During intra-administration deliberations, Weinberger and Perle set forward the "zero-zero" proposal: if
the USSR would dismantle its SS-20 and similar missiles, the United
States would cancel the deployment of its intermediate-range ballistic
and cruise missiles to Western Europe. Haig and his principal arms
control adviser, Richard Burt, objected to zero-zero, arguing that the
Soviets would never accept it.[85] Reagan seized on the plan, however,
and announced it publicly during a speech on November 18, twelve
days before the start of the INF negotiations in Geneva.[86]

Weinberger later recalled that the zero-zero proposal suited Reagan's fundamental antinuclearism. "It was consistent with what I knew
the President's feeling was of basically very great unhappiness with nuclear weapons," Weinberger said. "Very few people seem to recognize
that he was basically against nuclear weapons."[87] Iklé concurred that
zero-zero was "a solution that moved in the direction that Ronald Reagan wanted to move in the nuclear field . . . that is, essentially to get
rid of nuclear weapons."[88] That is in fact how Reagan saw the zero-zero
proposal: in his memoirs, he stated that he "viewed [it] as the first step
toward the elimination of all nuclear weapons from the earth."[89]

In an interview with the author, Burt, too, noted that Reagan "had
an aversion to nuclear weapons" and that MAD "bothered" the president. He commented that Reagan conveyed this during "offhand remarks at things like NSC meetings." The president "was attracted to
bold arms control initiatives" as a result of his antinuclearism, Burt
stated.[90]

Those within the administration who did not know Reagan well,
such as Burt, were bemused by his unorthodox views regarding nuclear
weapons. Frank Carlucci later recalled that Reagan said to his advisers that nuclear weapons were "horrible" and "inherently evil."[91] It became apparent to Carlucci and other senior administration officials
that Reagan "had always been very much against nuclear weapons,
even before he got into office." Carlucci added that "some of us didn't
realize that" until they interacted with Reagan.[92]

Reagan apparently asked his advisers on two separate occasions
during 1981 and 1982 for plans to abolish nuclear weapons. At that

time, none of his advisers thought the abolition of nuclear weapons was feasible or desirable, and they did not provide any such plans.[93]

Weinberger later said that Reagan's abhorrence of nuclear weapons was "reinforced" by briefings and exercises related to his responsibilities and possible responses in the event of nuclear war.[94] The president "had an aversion to this kind of thing," remarked Weinberger.[95] Reagan "shrank from" "the instant response that he would have to make, and the short time for it—a launch has taken place, and you have eighteen minutes, and this sort of thing."[96] "What do you do?" Weinberger asked hypothetically. "You don't do very much. There's not an awful lot you can do." Weinberger stated that the exercises drove home to Reagan the inability of the United States to defend itself against missiles.[97]

In an interview with the author, Carlucci recalled a meeting with Reagan on the subject of strategic weapons in which the president said, "Wouldn't it be wonderful if we could design a system that would protect everybody from wars?" "I thought it was a little utopian," commented Carlucci, "but it was something that was clearly on his mind at the time. Later on, when SDI came out, I thought of that conversation."[98]

ESTABLISHING A COLD WAR POLICY FRAMEWORK

In its first year, the Reagan administration accomplished little by way of Cold War policy planning. As previously noted, this was in part because of the administration's focus on its economic plans and defense buildup, which Reagan and his advisers saw as prerequisites for a successful approach to the USSR.

Bureaucratic disarray was also a factor. Robert Kimmitt, then a senior member on the NSC staff, later noted that national security policy making in the first year of the Reagan administration was "more disorganized than might have appeared."[99] The departments and agencies responsible for foreign and defense policy operated with a low degree of coordination, due both to Allen's inability to take a lead role in developing central guidance and to conflict between Haig and his colleagues, including the president. Allen later stated that "everything seemed paralyzed."[100] John Poindexter, then military assistant to the national security adviser, remarked that "we got very little done in the national security and foreign policy areas during that first year. We didn't issue a single decision document during the first year because there was constant fighting over wording."[101] Poindexter was not exactly correct; the administration did produce a number of NSDDs during 1981, including NSDD 12, but none of them addressed broad policy themes.

Toward the end of the year, Reagan and his senior White House staff concluded that the national security policy-making system was not functioning properly.[102] In an effort to assert personal control over his administration's policy making, Reagan made a key personnel change and rearranged the bureaucratic process. He replaced Allen with William Clark in early January 1982 and simultaneously restored the position of national security adviser to one that reported directly to the president.[103]

Clark's relationship with Reagan was singularly close, both personally and philosophically. Robert McFarlane, who left the State Department with Clark to become his deputy, noted that the new national security adviser "was closer to the president than anyone" in the administration.[104] Anderson told the author that Reagan and Clark "shared the same values, they were very, very close, they got along terrifically."[105] Poindexter recalled that Clark "understood the president and what the president believed."[106] Clark later stated that whenever Reagan "came into the room, as governor or president, he didn't need to say anything, I could tell what he wanted."[107]

Poindexter later said that "one of the reasons the system worked with Bill [Clark] and didn't without him was primarily because of the close personal relationship between Bill and the president."[108] The nature of Clark's relationship with Reagan, and his constant access to him, meant that Clark wielded considerable influence and authority within the government.

"[A]t the president's direction," Clark immediately pushed for the administration to set out formally its national security policy, and particularly its Cold War policy, in NSDDs.[109] According to Meese, Clark felt it was "important to have these things down on paper and to have a documentary record of it so that it was clear what the policy was." "The purpose," continued Meese, "was to develop a coherent and comprehensive strategy for dealing with the Soviet Union, as well as with other aspects of national security policy."[110] Clark, who was "totally devoted to Ronald Reagan,"[111] intended that the directives establishing fundamental policy should reflect Reagan's approach—that they should, as Clark later put it, "reduc[e] to careful writing" the president's own views.[112] As Anderson noted, "What you saw happen after Bill Clark came in was very close to pure Reagan": the administration established Reagan's own approach as the basis for an unprecedented and assertive Cold War policy.[113]

McFarlane later stated that Reagan "was quite clear in saying that he wanted this process to be premised upon some fairly different assumptions about how we should approach the Soviet Union" from those that had guided past American policy. As discussed earlier, Reagan emphasized that he did not believe the Soviet political and economic system could or would survive indefinitely. McFarlane commented that Reagan rejected the notion that "the best we could hope for was to limit the pace of their expansion": he sought rather to challenge directly, and weaken, the Soviet system. "As an optimist, and a person of great conviction in the power of the American idea, the American economy, to compete and win in any competition," McFarlane added, "Reagan believed that we should compete very aggressively with the Soviet Union."[114]

On February 5, 1982, Reagan signed a National Security Study Directive that instructed his administration to develop an overarching strategic framework for U.S. national security policy. The administration was to undertake this task by a two-step process. The first step was to produce an extended study paper that identified "[f]undamental U.S. national security objectives" and established a definitive strategic rationale and agenda to guide all aspects of national security policy. The second step was to incorporate formally the findings of the study in an NSDD.

The two-page NSSD signed in February stated that the process culminating in the extended study paper and NSDD was to be conducted by an interagency group. That group, chaired by the NSC staff and including assistant secretary–level participants from the State Department, Defense Department, CIA, and Joint Chiefs of Staff, was to present the study paper to the NSC by mid-April. The NSSD ascribed the utmost sensitivity to the project.[115]

As directed, the interagency group submitted the study paper to the NSC in April 1982. The substance of that top secret, eighty-seven-page study, titled "U.S. National Security Strategy," was neither leaked nor otherwise made available to the press or public. The NSC declassified and released the report in 1996.

The study was divided into three parts. The first consisted of a general overview of the international environment and a statement of the objectives of U.S. national security strategy. The second directed that these objectives were to be implemented through an "interlocking" set of diplomatic, information, politicoeconomic, and military strategies. The third part outlined in detail the Reagan administration's military strategy in pursuit of its overarching policy objectives.

In setting forth the objectives of the Reagan administration's national security policy, the paper went beyond what any previous administration had established as the aims of its Cold War approach.[116] One of the principal "global objectives" proposed by the document was "to contain and reverse the expansion of Soviet control and military presence throughout the world."[117] Containing the spread of Soviet influence had served as the foundation of U.S. policy toward the USSR since the late 1940s, although specific strategies for achieving that goal had differed considerably among the various administrations.[118] Yet the notion of rollback—of actually reversing Soviet influence where it had already been established—had never before been an element of U.S. Cold War policy. The Eisenhower administration had considered rollback as an element of U.S. strategy with respect to Eastern Europe but ultimately rejected it on the grounds that the USSR's interest in maintaining control over the region made a rollback approach unfeasible "except by Soviet acquiescence or war."[119]

The "U.S. National Security Strategy" study took a step beyond rollback. The document declared that another U.S. policy objective was "[t]o foster, if possible in concert with our allies, restraint in Soviet military spending, discourage Soviet adventurism, and weaken the Soviet alliance system by forcing the USSR to bear the brunt of its economic shortcomings, and to encourage long-term liberalizing and nationalist tendencies within the Soviet Union and allied countries."[120] Clark later stated that this objective was based directly upon Reagan's view that the Soviet system was vulnerable and that U.S. pressure could help compel systemic change within the USSR, and called it a "sea change" in American Cold War policy.[121]

By establishing containment, rollback, and pressure on the internal Soviet system as the principal aims of American Cold War policy, the paper directed the Reagan administration both to expand the scope of the U.S.-Soviet competition and to take to the offensive in it.[122]

The second part of the study, which was only a few paragraphs long, directed that "the various instruments of U.S. national power," namely diplomatic, economic, political, military, and intelligence and covert operations capabilites, were to be linked in a "mutually supportive" fashion in order to pursue the objectives established in the first part.[123]

The final and largest section of the study was devoted to setting out a military strategy to achieve the administration's objectives. A central assumption of that portion of the study was that the growth of the Soviet strategic arsenal during the 1970s had led to "a shift in the U.S.-U.S.S.R. nuclear balance from clear U.S. superiority to a state of rough parity with the prospect of U.S. inferiority." Of particular concern was that the Soviets "prefer possession of superior capabilities and have been working to improve their chances of prevailing in a conflict with the US." The paper stated that a primary aim of the USSR's leadership in attempting to achieve nuclear superiority over the United States was to call into question the credibility of the deterrent value of American nuclear forces, and thereby to generate leverage with which to pursue the global expansion of Soviet influence: "A tenet in [Soviet] strategic thinking appears to be that the better prepared the USSR is to fight in various contingencies, the more likely it is that potential enemies will be deterred from attacking the USSR and its allies and will be hesitant to counter Soviet political and military actions."[124]

The study claimed that the Soviets "may increasingly expect that the burden of avoiding confrontation should shift to the US—reflecting the change in the 'correlation of forces' since the 1962 Cuban missile crisis." It noted that the Reagan administration's plans to modernize U.S. strategic forces as directed by NSDD 12 were adequate to foreclose the Soviet bid for nuclear supremacy but warned that "without these investments, the risks of nuclear blackmail that unduly restrict our political latitude . . . would dangerously increase."[125]

In making their assessment of the opportunities and threats faced by the United States in the Cold War, the authors of the military strategy component of the paper devoted considerable attention to the ramifications on the Soviet economy of the USSR's military buildup. The study stated that the Soviets "face severe economic problems" and "a bleak economic outlook" and that "[l]iving standards in the USSR will probably stagnate owing to the growing defense burden and inefficient investment practices. As Soviet citizens perceive a decline in the quality of life, productivity growth will also decline. . . . These problems will force Moscow to make difficult choices among priorities." "[I]t will become increasingly difficult for the Soviets to sustain their military buildup as their economic growth slows," the paper claimed.[126]

The United States, therefore, should seek to exacerbate the Soviet leadership's concern regarding the economic consequences of its defense spending. The study flagged the issue of whether the Soviets could maintain their massive defense expenditures in the face of a deteriorating economy as one to which the United States should devote intelligence attention and resources. As "key intelligence issues of continuing concern for further collection and analysis," the document identified several questions: "Is it likely that the Soviet Union would significantly reduce defense spending in response to domestic economic problems? How severe will these problems be? Will there be any radical change in the policy objectives of the current and post-Brezhnev leaders?"[127]

The study argued that American "political and social heritage" militated against "supporting large forces in peacetime" and that it "impels us rather to seek security in our national genius for technological innovation and industrial efficiency." It emphasized U.S. superiority over the USSR in developing and applying advanced technologies. It claimed that among the shortcomings of the Soviet economy were "continuing difficulties in introducing new technology." Furthermore, it asserted, the Soviet leadership's anxiety over the ramifications of this technology gap served as an important factor in the Kremlin's perceptions of and approach to the Cold War, especially with respect to bilateral relations:

> Parallel to Moscow's military effort, the Soviets will try to pursue an arms control dialogue. . . . The strategic arms control process in particular remains important as a means of constraining military competition with the US. A major Soviet motivation in this dialogue has been to reduce the possibility of a US technological breakthrough that might jeopardize Moscow's strategic nuclear status.[128]

The paper went on to say that, to impede a "US technological breakthrough," the Soviets were dedicated to maintaining the ABM Treaty. They were "concerned that the US could eventually deploy effective ABM systems," the study claimed.

The report reiterated NSDD 12's guidance that the United States should develop missile defense capabilities in language identical to that in the earlier document: "a vigorous research and development program will be conducted on a ballistic missile defense system." Near the end of "U.S. National Security Strategy," the authors of the study addressed missile defense at some length. That portion of the study included the statement that

> The United States should pursue the development of effective BMD [ballistic missile defense] technology, evaluate its role in our overall strategic posture, and preserve the options to modify or withdraw from international agreements that would limit the deployment of a BMD system. . . . Strategic defenses need not be impenetrable to enhance our nuclear strategy. They can still enhance deterrence by increasing

both our civil survivability as well as the certainty that sufficient offensive strategic firepower will remain after an attack. This would reduce Soviet perceptions of advantages to be gained by initiating a nuclear attack.[129]

A principal theme of the study was that perceived advantages in the military sphere of the Cold War translated into expanded influence and freedom of action in the overall U.S.-Soviet competition, and thus that America should seek and exploit opportunities to bolster its standing in the military balance. The development of a missile defense system, the paper stated, could check the apparent Soviet bid for nuclear superiority and provide military advantage for the United States, and thereby alter the "correlation of forces." The authors of the study indicated that U.S. pursuit of a missile defense was particularly well suited to generating leverage over the Soviet Union in that it would exploit the high-technology gap between the two nations. A U.S. missile defense system would represent exactly the kind of "technological breakthrough that might jeopardize Moscow's strategic nuclear status"—and that the Soviets therefore sought to restrain, according to the study.

After its completion in April 1982, the study went before the NSC for debate. Clark, in an interview with the author, stated that the idea of attempting to pressure the Soviet system "didn't have a lot of support" among top State Department officials, particularly Haig.[130] But that idea had originated with the president, who favored it, as did most of his senior officials, including Clark, Weinberger, Casey, and Meese.[131] By this time, Haig's position within the administration had become tenuous, and his reservations were overridden.[132]

In May 1982, Reagan approved the study in full and formally adopted it as the foundation of American foreign and defense policy in a top secret NSDD. That document—NSDD 32, "U.S. National Security Strategy"—stated in the presidential first person that "I have carefully reviewed the NSSD 1-82 study in its component parts, considered the final recommendations of the National Security Council, and direct that the study serve as guidance for U.S. National Security Strategy. Our national strategy," it continued, "requires development and integration of a set of strategies, including diplomatic, informational, economic/political, and military components. NSSD 1-82 begins that process. Part I of the study provides basic U.S. national objectives, both global and regional, and shall serve as the starting point for all components of our national security strategy." The eight-page NSDD 32 listed the "global objectives" outlined in the study and then summarized the rest of the study in general terms. The text of the study accompanied NSDD 32 as an attachment.[133]

Shortly after Reagan approved the study paper and NSDD 32, Clark delivered a speech at Georgetown University in which he discussed the documents in broad terms.[134] He stated that Reagan's motivation in launching the study was to "review the results of [the] first year with decisions often being made at the departmental level, to see where we were, to make sure our various policies were consistent, and to set the course for the future" by a "well-thought through and integrated strategy for preserving our national security."

Clark underscored that the "conversion of [Reagan's] philosophy to policy has been one of the President's major efforts since January." He remarked that Reagan played "an extraordinarily active role" in the policy development process, reviewing and commenting on draft segments and sometimes sending them back "to the drawing board." Clark added that while the NSC staff had led the interagency effort of preparing the documents, the senior leadership of the Pentagon, State Department, CIA, and Joint Chiefs of Staff had been thoroughly involved, and the Treasury and Commerce Departments had been included as well. He noted that Weinberger's internal Pentagon reviews had provided a foundation for the defense portion of the study.

In his comments on the substance of the study and the decision directive, Clark avoided specific mention of the administration's aim of pressuring the Soviet system so as to encourage change and did not announce any of the "global objectives" listed in the documents. Borrowing elements of Reagan's rhetoric, however, Clark said that "collectivism and the subordination of the individual to the state" were a "bizarre and evil episode of history whose last pages are even now being written. We have something better to offer—namely freedom." "[W]e cannot sit back and hope that somehow it all will happen,"

Clark continued. "We find we must be prepared to respond vigorously to opportunities as they arise and to create opportunities where they have not existed before." Later in the speech, he quoted directly from the study when he stated that the United States must force its "principal adversary, the Soviet Union, to bear the brunt of its economic shortcomings." Clark concluded his speech with a general summary of the administration's Cold War approach: "It is our fondest hope that with an active yet prudent national security policy, we might one day convince the leadership of the Soviet Union to turn their attention inward, to seek the legitimacy that only comes from the consent of the governed, and thus to address the hopes and the dreams of their own people."[135]

The April 1982 study paper and NSDD 32 are essential to an understanding of the rest of the Reagan presidency. They codified a single, unifying conceptual framework for the Reagan administration's national security policy, which in practice centered on Cold War policy. The documents introduced and formalized the notion that the United States should seek not simply to contain the spread of Soviet influence but to reverse it as well, and to pressure the internal Soviet system so as to encourage change. They were intended to reorient U.S. Cold War policy away from a defensive, reactive approach toward one that went on the offensive.[136] The documents also catalyzed a period of intense policy planning across a range of issues that lasted until the spring of 1983. Between February 1982 and March 1983, the administration issued seventy-five NSDDs—twice the number, on average, that it generated annually throughout the rest of Reagan's tenure.[137] As shall be seen, one of those NSDDs set out U.S. policy toward the USSR, drawing heavily on the "global objectives" of the "U.S. National Security Strategy" study and NSDD 32.

ARMS CONTROL, REAGAN'S VIEWS ON THE USSR, AND THE EXERTION OF PRESIDENTIAL CONTROL OVER SOVIET POLICY

In May 1982, Reagan gave a speech at Eureka College, his alma mater, in which he announced his administration's proposals for strategic

arms reductions. He insisted that the name of the U.S.-Soviet negotiations on strategic arms should be changed from SALT (Strategic Arms
Limitation Talks) to START (Strategic Arms Reduction Talks) to emphasize his determination to cut the two sides' nuclear arsenals rather
than cap their growth. Reagan set out a two-phase START proposal: In
the first phase, both sides would reduce their ballistic missile warheads
by a third, allowing half of the remaining warheads to be carried on
ICBMs, while simultaneously cutting the total number of missiles. In
the second phase, they would limit the throw weight—a measure of
total destructive power—of their missiles to equal levels.[138] The proposals aimed to cut the number and size of Soviet land-based missiles
and warheads while maintaining the American advantage in SLBMs
and bombers.

Two days before his Eureka College speech, Reagan sent a letter
to Brezhnev that suggested that the two sides commence negotiations
on START and outlined the U.S. proposal. By that time, the two leaders had already exchanged a series of messages, most of them harsh. In
one letter to Reagan, Brezhnev wrote that "American officials, yes,
even you personally, are defaming our social and state system, our internal order. We resolutely repudiate this." He added that the Reagan
administration "has already done enough to disrupt or at the very least
undermine everything positive which was achieved at the cost of great
effort by previous American administrations in the relations between
our countries. Today, unfortunately, little remains of the reciprocal
positive political gains which were achieved earlier."[139]

Despite these tensions, in the wake of Reagan's Eureka College
speech the United States and USSR agreed to begin START negotiations, which opened in Geneva in late June. The Soviets sharply criticized Reagan's specific proposals for START. Brezhnev conveyed
those criticisms in a letter to Reagan. Reagan's notes in the margin of
the letter provide insight into his perception of Brezhnev and the Soviet leadership. By the side of vitriolic statements by Brezhnev, Reagan
made notes such as "History does not confirm" and "He has to be kid-
ding." When the Soviet leader referred to "the existing balance of
forces" between the USSR and United States, Reagan wrote, "He
means imbalance." Another note read, "[The Soviet people] haven't

been told the truth for years."[140] Reagan's marginal notes indicated that he did not see the Brezhnev regime as one with which he could interact and deal constructively, either on arms control or on much else.[141]

By the spring of 1982, Reagan's relationship with Haig—and the relationship of other senior officials in the administration with the secretary of state—had frayed badly. The president and his staff viewed Haig as power-hungry and felt "uneasiness" as to whether "his philosophies were consistent with" Reagan's.[142] Reagan resolved to force Haig out. He stated in his memoirs that Haig "didn't want anyone else, me included, to influence foreign policy," and that he disagreed with the secretary of state on certain issues.[143] In a later interview, Anderson described Reagan as "warmly ruthless." "If you were in his way," Anderson said, "you were gone."[144]

The president replaced Haig with George Shultz. Shultz, who had spent time in both academia and business, had occupied a series of Cabinet-level economic posts in the Nixon administration, including labor secretary and Treasury secretary. He was an experienced negotiator, and it was clear that he would bring those skills and experiences to his new post. Although Shultz did not know Reagan well, he seemed to share the president's foreign policy approach and professed to follow Reagan's lead.[145]

Throughout 1982, Reagan constantly claimed that the Soviet system was politically and economically weak and vulnerable, and that it could be forced to change. Those ideas served as the leitmotif of virtually all of his public statements regarding the USSR. During a speech in January, for example, he said that "[t]he Soviet Union should realize that its resources might be better spent on meeting the needs of its people, rather than producing instruments of destruction . . . the bankruptcy of communism has been laid bare for all to see—a system that is efficient in producing machines of war but cannot feed its people."[146] In an interview in March, he asserted, "I think the economic signs are there now of what has happened to the Soviet Union from this big [military] buildup. They are in deep trouble . . . they economically are very vulnerable right at the moment."[147] At a press conference later that month, Reagan stated that the Soviets were in a "more desperate situation" economically than he had assumed when

he took office. "Their great military buildup," he continued, "has —
and at the expense of consumer products, up to and including food for
their people — has now left them on a very narrow edge."[148]

During a speech in May, Reagan said that "the Soviet dictatorship
has forged the largest armed force in the world . . . by preempting the
human needs of its people, and, in the end, this course will undermine
the foundations of the Soviet system." He emphasized that his administration's policy was to force the Soviet Union to "make the difficult
choices brought on by its military budgets and economic shortcomings." Adding that "[w]e are now approaching an extremely important
phase in East-West relations as the current Soviet leadership is succeeded by a new generation," he noted that "a Soviet leadership devoted to improving its people's lives, rather than expanding its armed
conquests, will find a sympathetic partner in the West."[149] He reiterated the last point during an interview in May: "It seems to me that
now, with the Soviets having the economic problems I mentioned,
that this is an opportunity for us to suggest to them that there might be
a better path than they've been taking. And if so, we'd like to explore
that path."[150]

In June 1982, Reagan delivered an address to the British Parliament that summarized his views regarding the Soviet Union.[151] In the
speech, Reagan stated,

> I believe we live now at a turning point. In an ironic sense Karl Marx
> was right. We are witnessing today a great revolutionary crisis, a crisis
> where the demands of the economic order are conflicting directly with
> those of the political order. But the crisis is happening not in the free,
> non-Marxist West, but in the home of Marxism-Leninism, the Soviet
> Union. It is the Soviet Union that runs against the tide of history by
> denying human freedom and human dignity to its citizens. It also is in
> deep economic difficulty.

"The dimensions of this failure," he went on,

> are astounding. . . . Overcentralized, with little or no incentives, year
> after year the Soviet system pours its best resources into the making
> of instruments of destruction. The constant shrinkage of economic

growth combined with the growth of military production is putting a heavy strain on the Soviet people. What we see here is a political structure that no longer corresponds to its economic base, a society where productive forces are hampered by political ones.

The West should wage a "campaign for democracy," he said, with the intention of encouraging democratic changes in Communist countries—including in the USSR itself. In pursuing those changes, he argued, the United States sought "a process, a direction, a basic code of decency, not . . . an instant transformation." He continued that while "we must be cautious about forcing the pace of change, we must not hesitate to declare our objectives and to take concrete actions toward them."

Faced with the systemic "crisis" that he outlined, the Soviet leadership could turn away from "greater repression and foreign adventure," Reagan stated, and begin "to allow its people a voice in their own destiny. Even if the latter process is not realized soon, I believe the renewed strength of the democratic movement, complemented by a global campaign for freedom, will strengthen the prospects for arms control and a world at peace."[152]

While Reagan publicly emphasized his belief that the Soviet system was fundamentally vulnerable and could be pressured to reform, he also highlighted his related view that the same vulnerabilities could impel the Soviet Union to agree to deep reductions in nuclear weapons. He stated in January that "since [the Soviets] have strained their economy to the limit, they are not really able to adequately provide their people with consumer goods and food, because everything is devoted to the military buildup." "So," Reagan continued, "strained to the limit as they are and suddenly faced with the prospect of trying to have to match the great industrial capacity of the United States now turning to a military buildup, we can get legitimate reductions in arms."[153] In March, Reagan claimed that it was his "dream" that "one of the reasons why we're trying to redress our defensive structure is so we can sit down at a bargaining table with the Soviet Union for once in which they'll have a legitimate reason for wanting to engage in arms reduction with us." "So far we've had nothing to offer them. They are so far ahead," he argued. "But if they find out that we mean it, then maybe we can reduce those threatening weapons, particularly those nuclear weapons that are aimed back and forth at each other. And that's my dream."[154]

In publicly expressing his intention to reduce nuclear weapons, Reagan frequently steered off in directions that caused consternation among his advisers. While Reagan condemned calls by antinuclear groups and protesters for unilateral freezes or reductions of U.S. nuclear arms, he expressed solidarity with their basic antinuclearism: "I know that there are a great many people who are pointing to the unimaginable horror of nuclear war. I welcome that concern . . . to those who protest against nuclear war, I can only say, 'I'm with you.'"[155] A few days later he added, "I have to be heart and soul in sympathy with the people that are talking about the horrors of nuclear war and the fact that we should do everything we could to prevent such a war from happening."[156]

On several occasions, Reagan publicly expressed regret that the Soviets had not accepted the Baruch Plan of 1946, which would have abolished nuclear weapons and internationalized nuclear energy.[157] He also publicly proclaimed his aim of abolishing nuclear weapons, declaring that getting rid of nuclear arms forever was "the ultimate goal."[158] "It just doesn't make sense for the world to be sitting here," he said, "with these weapons aimed at each other."[159]

Establishing U.S. Policy Toward the USSR

In late August 1982, Reagan signed an NSSD directing his administration to formulate a specific policy toward the USSR in a new NSDD. The NSDD was to build upon the policy objectives outlined in the "U.S. National Security Strategy" study and NSDD 32. The purpose, Meese later said, was to establish "a comprehensive approach to the Soviet Union that encompassed economic, political, and military strategies."[160]

The NSSD stated that the policy review that would lead to the NSDD "will proceed on the premise that Soviet international behavior is determined not only by the external environment but also by political, economic, social and ideological features of the Soviet system itself." The NSDD mandated that the review should address the likelihood of changes in the Soviet system; the sources of strains and tensions within that system, as well as the bases for continuity; whether there existed in the Soviet ruling elite elements that favored change (in a liberal or conservative direction) rather than the status quo, and "what actions by foreign powers assist each of these competing groups." It directed that in setting out U.S. policy toward the USSR, the NSDD should emphasize how the "United States, its Allies and other mobilizable forces" could "influence the evolution of Soviet policies and the Soviet regime in directions favorable to our interests." The NSSD dictated that the administration should focus on how to shape the environment in which the Soviet leadership made decisions. The NSSD stated that the NSDD was to be prepared by an interagency group chaired by the State Department and including assistant secretary–level officials from the Pentagon, CIA, and Joint Chiefs, the Treasury, Commerce, and Agriculture Departments, and the NSC staff.[161]

Richard Pipes had drafted the NSSD. He noted in a memo to Clark that in providing guidance for the preparation of the NSDD, he had tried to follow "what I sense to be the President's belief" that Soviet behavior "is the consequence of the [Soviet] system" and that U.S. policy should "aim at modifying the system . . . (e.g., compelling the USSR to alter its economic structure)." That "seems to me to express the quintessence of the President's approach," he added.[162]

While the State Department chaired the interagency group that produced the NSDD, Clark played a significant role in overseeing the process. Pipes drafted most of the NSDD. Pipes fully shared the president's beliefs that the internal system of the USSR was vulnerable, that it could change, and that U.S. pressure could play a part in compelling the Soviet leadership to engage in systemic change. In drafting the NSDD he was guided by those beliefs.[163] It is of significance that he later noted that "the direction of the policy was set by the President and not by his staff."[164]

Poindexter also stated later that the NSDD "was primarily an articulation of the way the president thought about the problem. . . . The basic ideas behind the policy were his," although they were distilled and extended by Pipes and others. "With President Reagan, containment wasn't enough," Poindexter said. He "really wanted to work to change their system." Reagan "didn't say the Russian people were evil, he said their form of government [was]. And he really wanted to change that."[165]

The Soviet policy review group submitted the draft decision directive to the NSC in early December 1982. The nine-page decision directive—which became NSDD 75, "U.S. Relations with the USSR"—grew out of and drew heavily on the objectives and approach prescribed by the "U.S. National Security Strategy" study and NSDD 32.[166] It stated that U.S. policy toward the Soviet Union "will consist of three elements: external resistance to Soviet imperialism; internal pressure on the USSR to weaken the source of Soviet imperialism; and negotiations to eliminate, on the basis of strict reciprocity, outstanding disagreements." It then elaborated on each of these elements. The first was to "contain and over time reverse Soviet expansionism by competing effectively on a sustained basis with the Soviet Union in all international arenas—particularly in the overall military balance and in geographical regions of priority concern to the United States." This element, the document stated, "will remain the primary focus of U.S. policy toward the USSR."

In describing the second element—pressuring the Soviet internal system—the NSDD directed that the United States was

> to promote, within the narrow limits available to us, the process of change in the Soviet Union toward a more pluralistic political and economic system in which the power of the privileged ruling elite is gradually reduced. The U.S. recognizes that Soviet aggressiveness has deep roots in the internal system, and that relations with the USSR should therefore take into account whether or not they help to strengthen this system and its capacity to engage in aggression.

Third, the NSDD stated that the United States would "engage the Soviet Union in negotiations to attempt to reach agreements which protect and enhance U.S. interests and which are consistent with the principle of strict reciprocity and mutual interest."[167]

The directive asserted that "this may be a particularly opportune time for external forces to affect the policies of Brezhnev's successors." It emphasized that the United States should seek to manipulate Soviet leaders' perceptions of the factors that guided and constrained their decision making: "Implementation of U.S. policy must focus on shaping the environment in which Soviet decisions are made both in a wide variety of functional and geopolitical arenas and in the U.S.-Soviet bilateral relationship."

The NSDD outlined the means by which the United States was to alter to its benefit Soviet leaders' decision-making environment, namely military strategy, economic policy, political action, geopolitical strategy, and bilateral relations. The document set out objectives in each of these categories (for example, pursuing "a major ideological/ political offensive which, together with other efforts, will be designed to bring about evolutionary change of the Soviet system," and "loose[ning] Moscow's hold" on Eastern Europe), and though it did set out some specific actions to be taken, it avoided cataloguing them. It noted that the "interrelated tasks of containing and reversing Soviet expansion and promoting evolutionary change within the Soviet Union itself cannot be accomplished quickly." The policy it outlined "is one for the long haul."[168]

Pipes thought that the administration did not have in mind "busting the Soviet Union" but rather "creating difficulties for [the Soviets], and pushing them" in the direction of internal reform. It intended that, under U.S. pressure, "their economic condition" would become "so aggravate[d] that they would undertake reforms." He added that he "didn't expect these reforms to bring down the Soviet Union" but "thought they would lead to very far-reaching changes in the Soviet system and in Soviet policy."[169]

During the drafting of the NSDD, the State Department sought to mitigate the prominence of the objective of encouraging change within the USSR. It succeeded to some extent—hence the inclusion of the phrase "within the narrow limits available to us" in the description of that aim.[170] Once finalized, however, the document met with few objections from the NSC, and Reagan approved it on January 17, 1983.

The Reagan administration self-consciously believed itself to be embarking on a new U.S. policy toward the Soviet Union. A cover memo from Clark to Reagan that forwarded the NSDD to the president in advance of the NSC meeting at which it was considered emphasized the objective of pressuring the Soviet system. That objective, the memo claimed, "represents a new objective of U.S. policy, or at least one that has never before been formally spelled out." "It has always been the objective of U.S. policy toward the Soviet Union," the memo continued,

> to combine containment with negotiations, but the attached document is the first in which the United States Government adds a third objective to its relations with the Soviet Union, namely encouraging antitotalitarian changes within the USSR and refraining from assisting the Soviet regime to consolidate further its hold on the country. The basic premise behind this new approach is that it makes little sense to seek to stop Soviet imperialism externally while helping to strengthen the regime internally. This objective is to be attained by a combination of economic and ideological instrumentalities.[171]

Introducing the NSDD during the NSC meeting at which it was considered, Clark stated that "one of the innovative aspects of this paper is that we strive to contain the Soviet Union not only externally, by blunting its imperialist drive, but also seek to redirect its energies internally by using economic, political, and ideological pressures in this direction."[172]

During Reagan's first two years in office, his administration thus established, in formal directives, a comprehensive and coherent Cold War policy for the United States. The policy aimed not simply to contain the spread of communism globally but to roll it back, and to weaken the Soviet system itself in order to encourage change within it.

That policy reflected Reagan's own views and inclinations as expressed over many years in public statements and in discussions with his aides. The administration saw its Cold War approach as a departure from the past. It sought to win the Cold War, not to mitigate it, and intended to do so by exploiting what it saw as fundamental weaknesses in the Soviet system. While the administration set out the general means by which it would pursue its policy—a vigorous military competition, efforts to destabilize the Soviet economy, covert action, and public diplomacy, for example—it did so more as a means of providing options rather than dictating specific measures. It thus provided itself with strategic flexibility in carrying out its policy objectives.

A large-scale, high-technology missile defense program was included as one long-term possibility for achieving military advantage over the Soviet Union and thus providing overall Cold War leverage. Yet there was little impetus within the administration to create such a program—except from Reagan himself.

CHAPTER

III

THE ANNOUNCEMENT
OF SDI

O N SEPTEMBER 14, 1982, Edward Teller met with Reagan, Clark, Meese, and Keyworth.[1] This was the first meeting between Teller and Reagan since the latter had taken office. Teller, a member of several panels that advised the administration, had expressed regret during an appearance on a television show in the summer of 1982 that he had not been able to convey his views directly to the president.[2] When Reagan, who admired Teller, heard this, he asked Keyworth to arrange a meeting.[3]

During the session, Reagan asked Teller if a missile defense system could work, to which the physicist replied that "present indications are good."[4] Throughout the meeting, Teller focused his remarks to the president on promoting one specific technological possibility for missile defense, the X-ray laser, which was being researched at the Livermore Laboratory.[5] Teller felt that the X-ray laser, which would rely on a nuclear detonation to generate directed energy, could be deployed in space to destroy ballistic missiles.[6]

By all accounts, the meeting did not go well. In an interview with the author, Teller said, "[T]here were lots of interruptions. I don't think I came very clearly through. . . . I don't think I had a chance to put a good case before Reagan."[7] According to Keyworth, he, Clark, and Meese cut the meeting short after Teller made a direct request for increased funds to Livermore for further work on the X-ray laser.[8] Clark and Meese favored a major missile defense effort, yet neither they nor Keyworth viewed Teller's push for the X-ray laser as prudent or appropriate.[9] Keyworth, who at that time was skeptical of the technical prospects for missile defense, was unimpressed with the X-ray laser, although he may not have voiced those concerns in front of his mentor Teller.[10] However, others present expressed doubts about the idea.[11] At the end of the meeting, Reagan conveyed to Teller in general terms his desire to pursue a defense against missiles; but, as had been the case during Reagan's visit to Livermore in 1967, he offered no comments on the particular technology that Teller was championing.[12]

The meeting in September 1982 was the last time Teller saw the president before Reagan delivered his speech announcing SDI in March 1983. Teller later stated that he thought he had not been "particularly influential" regarding Reagan's thinking on missile defense and the announcement of the initiative.[13] After SDI was under way and Reagan had issued instructions to his advisers that a missile defense should be nonnuclear, Teller deduced that Reagan had been disinclined to favor the X-ray laser (and the Spartan and Sprint systems from the late 1960s) because they depended on nuclear detonations to destroy missiles.[14]

Teller was correct in that reasoning, and his statement that he was not "particularly influential" in the inception of SDI was true in a larger, more general sense. "SDI," Reagan wrote in his memoirs, "wasn't conceived by scientists."[15] SDI was not conceived by Teller or by any other scientist, or by any of the president's advisers. Nor did it result from members of Congress, defense contractors, or anyone else pressuring or persuading the president or officials in his administration. Evidence thus far available indicates that SDI—the U.S. government's effort to research and develop an extensive defense against ballistic missiles—originated with Reagan himself.[16]

Reagan had a unique vision for a defense against missiles and a powerful inner motivation to seek the realization of that vision. He saw in missile defense both a means of precluding Armageddon by protecting people from a potential nuclear holocaust and a catalyst for the abolition of all nuclear weapons.

SDI, as Keyworth later put it, was a "top-down" initiative.[17] Reagan prepared and announced SDI through extraordinary use of presidential power. He waited until a moment that seemed to him opportune and then seized it. He carefully manipulated the bureaucratic system, acquiring support for the general idea of a missile defense effort from elements of the bureaucracy whose backing and technological assessment he thought he needed to proceed, particularly the NSC staff and the Joint Chiefs of Staff. Those elements lent their support both because of Reagan's own views and determination and because, in a difficult strategic environment, they saw missile defense research as potentially useful, although their rationales varied. Reagan excluded from the process other elements of the bureaucracy whose support he did not think he needed and whom he thought might try to impede his goal. He ensured that he would be able to announce the initiative at the time and on the terms of his choosing by having the announcement prepared by a very small group under his supervision and with his own extensive involvement. Reagan maneuvered so that SDI, as it was announced, corresponded to his own priorities and instincts.

THE MX DILEMMA

At the time the Reagan administration concluded its long-term Cold War policy-planning effort in late 1982, it was dealt a political setback in its attempt to improve U.S. strategic nuclear forces. The administration struggled unsuccessfully to attain congressional approval for deployment of the MX missile, the new ten-warhead ICBM that was intended to redress the growing disparity between the ICBM capabilities of the USSR and the United States. The USSR had first achieved an advantage over the United States in the number and power of its ICBM warheads in the late 1960s.[18] It had vastly increased that advantage over the course of the ensuing decade.[19] By 1980, the numerical imbalance in ICBM warheads stood at roughly five to two in favor of the Soviets, and it continued to grow during Reagan's first years in office.[20] The United States had more strategic bombers than the USSR and held both a quantitative and qualitative advantage in SLBMs. Yet ICBMs, because of the accuracy of their warheads, were considered counterforce weapons, meaning they could potentially destroy the other side's ICBMs in their silos, and were for that reason the most plausible first-strike nuclear arms.[21]

The USSR's superiority in ICBM missiles and warheads, and its ongoing efforts to compound that superiority, fueled concern within the United States during the 1970s that the overall nuclear competition was becoming increasingly destabilized, and that the Soviets could soon—if not already—be perceived to have the upper hand.[22] To counteract the Soviet advantage in ICBM warheads and to help dispel perceptions of a dangerously deteriorating U.S. nuclear position, President Ford, and then President Carter, supported the development and deployment of the MX.[23] President Reagan included deployment of the MX as part of his package for the extensive upgrading of U.S. strategic nuclear capabilities (as described in Chapter 2).

Devising a survivable basing mode for the MX that would be politically acceptable to Congress proved difficult. President Carter, after reviewing numerous options, had planned to deploy two hundred MX missiles in what was called a "multiple protective shelter" basing mode, whereby each missile would travel back and forth in a network of shelters so as to obscure its exact location. Carter's proposal met with fierce political resistance, especially in the southwestern United States, where the two hundred missiles and their 4,600 shelters were to be located.[24] Reagan rejected Carter's plan. Throughout 1981 and 1982, Weinberger's Pentagon and a panel of outside experts appointed by the Reagan administration deliberated over a variety of basing modes for the MX. Weinberger finally settled on a basing mode known as "dense pack": the missiles were to be placed in close formation, so that incoming enemy warheads would commit fratricide and destroy one another without destroying the bulk of the MXs.

Reagan approved Weinberger's dense pack, which he publicly announced on November 22, 1982. He linked deployment of the MX to his broader objective of building up the U.S. military, and especially strategic forces, to encourage the USSR to agree to deep reductions in nuclear arms. A "secure force," he argued, "increases the prospects of reaching significant arms reductions with the Soviets, and that's what we really want." That point, he continued, "goes to the heart of our policies. Unless we demonstrate the will to rebuild our strength, the Soviets have little incentive to negotiate."[25]

Congress received the Reagan administration's dense-pack proposal with considerable skepticism, as it relied on an untested, somewhat dubious theory. Adverse political circumstances also worked against the administration. A mass movement to freeze the production of nuclear weapons unilaterally was then reaching a peak in the United States, and various groups of religious leaders, including the National Conference of Catholic Bishops, were denouncing the arms race. Many members of Congress, almost all of them Democrats, professed sympathy with the nuclear freeze and related causes and saw in the MX an opportunity to defeat Reagan on a politically sensitive matter. After contentious hearings, the Democratic-controlled House of Representatives voted on December 7 to reject dense pack and to deny funds for production of the MX until a suitable basing mode was identified.[26] The following day, General John Vessey, chairman of the Joint Chiefs of Staff, announced that the Chiefs were also split over the dense-pack basing mode, with three of five opposed.[27] Vessey's acknowledgment that the uniformed military leadership did not endorse a major military proposal by the administration strained the administration's credibility on the issue and provided ammunition for critics of dense pack (and of the MX altogether). Reagan was forced to create a panel of experts outside government to study MX basing modes and issue its own recommendations. The group was known as the Scowcroft Commission, after its chairman, the former (and future) national security adviser.

The MX fiasco stymied the administration's efforts to build up the number and power of American ICBM warheads, thus casting doubt upon an important element of its plans to modernize U.S. offensive strategic forces. It is unlikely that the MX dilemma contributed to Reagan's desire to seek a missile defense, given his already strong predilection to do so. Yet it caused certain officials—notably the Joint Chiefs of Staff and members of the NSC staff—to become disillusioned with the existing nature and parameters of the arms competition between the United States and the USSR. When, in late December 1982, Reagan asked the Joint Chiefs and his White House staff if the United States should explore moving toward missile defense, they returned with a largely positive response, thinking that it might present a new, advantageous direction in the strategic competition. They became followers when other options appeared to have been exhausted.

REAGAN SEIZES THE OPPORTUNITY
FOR STRATEGIC DEFENSE

On December 22, 1982, Reagan met with the Joint Chiefs in the White House. Bush, Weinberger, Carlucci, Baker, Meese, Clark, and McFarlane also attended the meeting.[28] During a previous session with the JCS in September 1982, Reagan had requested to meet with them as a group on a periodic basis "to exchange views," and the December meeting was the first of those occasions.[29] Following a White House recommendation, the Chiefs set the agenda for the meeting, which centered on an overview by the chairman of national strategy requirements and an assessment of current and future military posture, and included progress reports from each of the service chiefs on carrying out "the President's strategic guidance."[30]

It is likely that during the December 22 meeting with the Joint Chiefs, President Reagan instigated the bureaucratic process that led to SDI.[31] According to Anderson, Reagan asked the Chiefs, "What if we began to move away from our total reliance on offense to deter a nuclear attack and moved toward a relatively greater reliance on defense?"[32] This, Anderson noted, was "the way [Reagan] often gave orders. He was very unusual in that respect."[33] Reagan then "continued to press the issue" of missile defense. Following the meeting, one of the Chiefs called Clark to confirm that they had just received "instructions to take a hard look at missile defense," to which Clark responded affirmatively.[34] (As Clark later remembered it, one of the Chiefs called and asked, "Is he serious?")[35]

Anderson had left the White House by then and did not attend the meeting on December 22. The source for his account was Clark.[36] In a letter to the author, Clark wrote that he was "certain" that Anderson's account of the December meeting was "substantially correct." "The President's 'What if?' question was rhetorical but very serious when he posed it" during the "otherwise routine meeting," Clark noted. Reagan was "intent to move away" from MAD.[37]

Weinberger and Meese later concurred that Reagan directly asked the Joint Chiefs to look into missile defense. "He wanted their reaction," Weinberger explained.[38] Meese recalled that Reagan "commissioned the Joint Chiefs of Staff to do a study of our strategic weapons programs and the overall defense strategy related to them. And he asked them to include in that a discussion and analysis of ballistic missile defense. . . . [H]e deliberately asked them to include that in their overall study of our strategic posture." Meese noted that as a result of Reagan's instructions to the Joint Chiefs, missile defense became part of "a specific report that they brought in in February [1983]."[39]

These recollections are consistent with the available documentary record. A few days after the December 22 meeting, Clark wrote to the president's schedulers with a proposal for a follow-up session between Reagan and the Joint Chiefs in early February 1983. The purpose of the February meeting would be for the Joint Chiefs to provide advice "on pending strategic force modernization issues" to Reagan. "I discussed this matter with Ed Meese and General Vessey at the conclusion of the December 22 meeting with the JCS," Clark wrote. He emphasized that the president and Joint Chiefs needed "to address the tough strategic force issues confronting the Administration."[40] Reagan's aides scheduled the follow-up meeting for February 11, 1983.[41]

Reagan's own retrospective version of his meetings with the Joint Chiefs of Staff is generally compatible with the information from

Clark, Weinberger, Meese, and the documentary record. After he left office in 1989, Reagan told Anderson that "I called a meeting of the chiefs of staff in the Cabinet Room, and I said, look, every weapon that's ever been created in the world has resulted in a defense, a defensive weapon—the sword and later the shield. Isn't it—with our technology—possible that we could produce a system that could hit those missiles as they came out of their silos, using space, whatever? They kind of huddled for a minute," Reagan continued, "then they came back and they said could you give us a couple of days on that? I said yes. And in a couple of days they came back. And they said yes, we think it is worthwhile. . . . So I said, all right, we start. Go to it. So we started that plan."[42] It seems plausible that what Reagan remembered seven years after the fact as "a couple of days" was actually the interval between December 22, 1982, and February 11, 1983.

Regardless of how Reagan phrased his directions to the Joint Chiefs during the December meeting, his specific guidance to them to look into missile defense, and his patent desire to pursue a defense, stimulated both the Joint Chiefs and the NSC staff to investigate the issue. Under Clark's auspices, McFarlane and Poindexter led the effort by the NSC staff. According to Poindexter, Clark knew that missile defense was "what [Reagan] wanted to do instinctively."[43]

In an interview with the author, McFarlane stated that "the president's mandate was clear: 'I want to explore strategic defense.'" Like everyone else involved in the inception of SDI, McFarlane was aware that Reagan's conviction to seek a missile defense was long held and deeply rooted. Reagan "came to office with a considerable disdain for assured destruction," McFarlane said, "and wanted to explore how to move away from threatening mutual destruction toward defending Americans." The president, he said, "felt strongly about it."[44]

McFarlane remarked that the notion of the United States embarking on an all-out, high-technology missile defense project was also consistent with the overall Cold War policy that the Reagan administration had recently established in NSDDs. "We had a policy, written down, that said, 'I am the president and I want to challenge the Soviet Union politically, economically, and militarily.' That does tend to have an effect on the Cabinet and on subordinates, as it should. The president was elected, and he says he wants to do this." "The development of programs from that leitmotif," McFarlane continued, "included programs on arms control and human rights and regional disagreements from Afghanistan to Nicaragua and bilateral issues. All of these . . . contained—well, 'aggressive' has a legal connotation to it I don't intend, but an enthusiastic, energetic, competitive content. Not a placid, passive content, but competitive. For example, the economic policies were specifically designed to weaken the Soviet economy and to do so in any way we could think of within legal and moral bounds. . . . We established a policy framework that directed us to explore ways to compete more energetically."

It was in the context of competing with the Soviets in arenas and by means that played to U.S. strengths that McFarlane believed a missile defense program "could play a useful role."[45] In McFarlane's view, the U.S. nuclear deterrent force at that time "was badly out of balance with the Soviet force."[46] The United States faced "an intractable military problem—a worsening counterforce imbalance which we appeared unable to check."[47] McFarlane believed that the entire U.S. ICBM fleet could be vulnerable to a Soviet first strike, and thus the "traditional concept of deterrence was becoming less stable."[48]

McFarlane later said of his thoughts at the time, "You've got an imbalance [in ICBM warheads], six thousand to two thousand, and you can either get them to reduce, which they're not doing, or get us to increase, which we've failed to do, or somehow you cope with the four-thousand-warhead difference, and find a way to deal with that imbalance militarily." "For two years," he added, "we had tried to carry forward assured destruction by modernizing the triad and had failed, certainly in the land-based leg, to field a system that could restore the balance of first-strike systems, hard-target capability." "We had explored just about every deployment option we could using offense," McFarlane continued. "We faced a military problem and had no offensive way to deal with it."[49]

The MX fiasco convinced McFarlane that the nature of the strategic nuclear competition at that time strongly favored the Soviets: "The

United States had been reduced to competing on terms according to which the Soviet Union enjoyed a comparative advantage—that is, in building and deploying ICBMs." He believed that, due to the existing parameters and dynamics of the arms competition, the United States found itself in the position of perpetually trying to catch up with the Soviet Union in ICBM warheads, and that it would perpetually fail to do so. He later wrote that "we could not fashion a political consensus behind a deployment plan [for a new ICBM], so divisive were the effects of partisanship, environmentalist opposition, legitimate military misgivings and antinuclear sentiment."[50] By contrast, the Soviets, uninhibited by legislative control and public opinion, "could always build more than we could."

In Reagan's cherished idea of a missile defense, McFarlane saw "a better way to compete" with the Soviets, "a way in which they would have to spend a lot of money to keep up with us" and in which the United States could "leverage our comparative advantage."[51] That comparative advantage, McFarlane figured, was "excellence in high technology."[52] "Everything I'd read about the Russians," McFarlane told the author in an interview, indicated that "their respect for our technology was very high."

There would be a "psychological dimension" to the United States' engaging in high-priority research into missile defense, McFarlane noted: "The Russians had such a high regard for American technology that you leverage their perceptions dramatically by an investment in high technology. . . . [Y]ou create expectations of discovery, that the Russians expected that surely an investment in high tech was going to have big payoffs on our side." McFarlane "believed that they would conclude that our investment . . . would lead to discoveries that were bound to be enhancing to the American position in the world." He added that a large-scale U.S. missile defense project would exacerbate Soviet fears that, "relatively speaking, the Soviet Union was backward compared to the United States. And that has a very important psychological impact on Russians, so much so [that] their—it's not paranoia, it's defensiveness—would lead them to want to stop the program. And that we could get a price for that; the price would be [for them to] reduce their offensive systems."[53]

This last point was a particularly important one. From the very beginning, McFarlane viewed a missile defense program as a potent source of leverage, particularly with respect to arms control. (He later added that he did not think that it "would bring down the Soviet Union."[54] "All I thought would happen is that they would want us to stop the investment.")[55] McFarlane believed and intended that a missile defense project could serve as an actual bargaining chip in arms negotiations.[56] It could be traded away in exchange for deep cuts in Soviet offensive forces, especially ICBMs. In 1984 and 1985, after he had succeeded Clark as national security adviser, McFarlane attempted to steer the Reagan administration toward an arms control deal that would bring about deep cuts in the Soviet ICBM force in exchange for limitations on SDI. During December 1982 and the first months of 1983, however, McFarlane kept his thoughts regarding the future negotiability of a U.S. missile defense program to himself.[57] He knew that a bargaining chip was not at all what Reagan intended for a missile defense effort.[58]

The administration's defeat in Congress over the MX led Poindexter, like McFarlane, to question the way in which the United States was competing with the Soviets in strategic nuclear weapons. "I became concerned that we simply were not going to be able to gain the public or/and congressional support to continue with new land-based missiles," Poindexter told the author in an interview. "We just could not overcome the public apathy and fear of . . . basing nuclear weapons on the U.S. soil." An admiral in the U.S. Navy, Poindexter later confessed that he was biased from a strategic point of view against ICBMs because their fixed locations rendered them vulnerable. Yet he feared that as time went on, it would become increasingly difficult within the United States to modernize even sea- and air-based systems.

Poindexter concluded "that we ought to think about strategic defense." While he did not necessarily want to build a missile defense system at the time, he thought that "we ought to at least investigate the possibility of doing more research in this area."[59] In his view, pursuing missile defense was strategically sound, it could garner broad and sustained support among the U.S. population, and it might provide "a disincentive to the Soviets to produce offensive systems and an incentive for them to initiate a nuclear pact."[60] Poindexter did not, however, see a missile defense program as a bargaining chip: "From my view, and what I believed was the president's view, it all had to do with really developing a strategic defense capability in the end."

Poindexter was himself a scientist who held a Ph.D. in nuclear physics. Although it seemed to him that the applicable technology was "coming along," he sought to establish whether there existed any basis for optimism that a high-technology missile defense was possible. "What we needed to do was . . . look hard at whether we thought the technology was feasible."[61] Overseen by Clark and McFarlane, Poindexter pulled together a group of specialists from within the White House, including NSC staff members Richard Boverie and Robert Linhard (both of whom were strategic experts and Air Force officers) and Office of Management and Budget official Alton Keel, who was the head of OMB's National Security Division, a former chief of research and development for the Air Force, and an aerospace engineer.[62] The purpose of the group, Poindexter later recalled, was to investigate "whether at some point in the future, if we put some money into the R and D [research and development] budget for this purpose, would it be worthwhile? Were we talking about an impossibility, or were we talking about something that might be feasible?"

Over the course of several sessions in the White House Situation Room, the group "considered the state of the technology, [e.g.,] information processing, sensors, and so forth." It concluded that missile defense "wasn't out of the realm of possibility, and that certainly research in this area was justified." Poindexter's group "provided a technical base upon which you could argue that research could be very profitable and productive." Poindexter reported this to Clark and McFarlane.[63]

In the meantime, McFarlane had been conducting his own investigation, although less formally, into the technological feasibility of missile defense. He conferred with a number of scientists he knew and trusted who had experience in missile defense and related fields. "Happily," McFarlane later stated, and "somewhat to my surprise," those scientists told him that progress in propellants, guidance, the speed of computers, and other areas meant that it "was worth asking the question [of missile defense] again" and that extensive research "might really turn up something that within our lifetimes could make a difference." McFarlane determined that "the state of the art in missile defense had advanced sufficiently to warrant a new effort."[64]

Reagan had been clever in addressing his directions for a study of missile defense (while at the same time clearly conveying his hope to move toward a defense) to the Joint Chiefs of Staff. The support of the Joint Chiefs was a virtual necessity for any major U.S. military project, particularly one that would have as high a profile and as big a budget—not to mention the political and strategic ramifications—as Reagan intended for missile defense.[65] Securing the backing of the JCS for a missile defense program was all the more important in the wake of the recent humiliation brought upon the administration by the Chiefs' public dissent from the dense-pack proposal. McFarlane and Poindexter were acutely aware of all of this. McFarlane said of his thoughts at the time, "It doesn't matter if it's a good idea, if your military establishment is against it, forget it."[66] At the same time as they undertook their studies of missile defense, McFarlane and Poindexter made inquiries as to what support the concept had among the Joint Chiefs. They discovered that Admiral James Watkins, chief of naval operations, was particularly receptive to the idea of a high-priority missile defense research program.[67]

Reagan had promoted Watkins to be the top uniformed officer in the U.S. Navy. Watkins assumed the post in late June 1982, in the midst of deliberations over the MX basing mode. He later said of the strategic force problems then confronting the administration, "I got into it. And I didn't know anything about it. I wasn't a strategic missile person at all. I came from the attack submarine route, and obviously I had experience with nuclear weapons aboard certain ships and that sort of thing, but nothing like this. So I was fresh at it."[68]

During the summer and fall of 1982, the Joint Chiefs met together some forty times to discuss MX basing and related strategic force issues, and Watkins held many more sessions with his own Navy staff and consultants. "I listened to all the arguments on MX basing, every single argument," Watkins told the author, "and finally I said, 'You know, I'm fed up with it. We can't get there from here doing this.'" Watkins believed that under the then-prevailing terms of the U.S.-Soviet nuclear competition, the United States was entering a "strategic cul-de-sac" (he also referred to it as a "strategic valley of death"), a "situation where only the Soviets can win."[69] Given the real and perceived strategic importance of ICBMs and the ever-widening gap between the Soviet and U.S. ICBM arsenals, Watkins believed that the United States was "losing out to the Russians." Regarding the United States' attempts to catch up with the USSR in the number and power of ICBM warheads, he thought, "It was a race we couldn't win, so what are we in it for? Why don't we get in our own race, we'll play by our rules—which is high tech, new systems, defense, doing things they probably could not do as fast as we could."[70] Watkins told his staff:

> Look, the . . . genius of this country is to take a new technological concept (which the Soviets may well have in mind as we do) and build it—field it—which they can't do. So why don't we use our applied technological genius to achieve our deterrent instead of sticking with an offensive land-based rocket exchange which they will win every time? They have bigger rockets . . . and they have no political obstacles in basing their missiles. We shouldn't continue to play in a game like that.[71]

Watkins thought that by pursuing missile defense, the United States could move away from the ICBM quandary and reorient the Cold War strategic competition in a direction that would play to American strengths. In an interview with the author, he said, "We could see us migrating out of offense to defense, and they couldn't. We knew that they could not catch us [in defensive technology]. As capable as they are, they probably couldn't field the systems. They could do it intellectually. They're bright people . . . [but] it's not in their bag to be able to field systems, the way we can here, of that sophistication." (Like McFarlane, Watkins pointed out that he did not intend that the United States would "bring the Russians to their knees" by leading a defensive arms race.) While Watkins thought that a U.S. missile defense program might also help bring about increased willingness on the part of the Soviets to engage in nuclear arms reductions, he never imagined that it might be used as a bargaining chip to be traded away.

Watkins viewed missile defense as a means of enhancing deterrence over the long term.[72] He believed that relying exclusively on the strategy of MAD to deter nuclear attack might not be sustainable in the United States, because he felt that "the American people thought mutual assured destruction morally distasteful—and it was a political loser."[73] Watkins himself considered MAD morally distasteful. He held that the U.S. military had a responsibility to seek protection for the United States against nuclear attack, rather than simply threatening to retaliate against the Soviet Union. He also knew that the president was morally opposed to MAD. Reagan's views helped to validate and encourage Watkins's own moral qualms regarding MAD: "Reagan believed strongly that MAD—mutual assured destruction—was immoral. Well, I happened to agree with him."[74]

In an interview with the author, Watkins stated that he was convinced that if the United States could actually create a missile defense "and take away the political leverage of nuclear weaponry, we've done a great thing for mankind." Watkins was not a nuclear abolitionist. What he was referring to, and what he hoped, was that a functional missile defense would drive down the political leverage that nuclear missiles bestowed upon their owners, particularly the Soviet Union.[75]

After McFarlane and Poindexter learned of Watkins's interest, they arranged a lunch with him in early January 1983 in order to "get specific" about their ideas concerning missile defense. During that lunch, held at the house of the chief of naval operations, Watkins "summarized his view both scientifically and morally that this was the right thing to do," recalled McFarlane, "and, importantly, that he thought the Chiefs would not oppose it—that is, the launching of an R and D program in strategic defense."[76] Watkins commented that he was inclined to propose such a program and asked how it might be received in the White House. "It will be very well received," McFarlane replied.[77]

Soon after the lunch with Watkins, McFarlane briefed Reagan

during a regular morning meeting between the president and his senior White House aides, including Bush, Clark, Meese, Baker, and Deaver, that missile defense appeared feasible and that the administration should move ahead with a research program. According to McFarlane, "The president was palpably excited and leaned forward in his chair and said, 'That's what I've been looking for, that's what we've got to do,' or words to that effect." McFarlane then suggested to Reagan as the next step that his meeting with the Joint Chiefs on February 11 would provide an opportunity to "draw them out on what they think about it."[78]

REAGAN GAINS THE SUPPORT OF THE JOINT CHIEFS OF STAFF

Watkins was confident, based on information he was gathering, that technological advances justified a new missile defense research effort. During his lunch with McFarlane and Poindexter, he had specifically mentioned improvements in computation speed and directed energy systems and expressed enthusiasm about the potential of various space-based technologies.[79]

On January 20, acting on the advice of Keyworth, Watkins met with Teller, who was an acquaintance, to hear the physicist's views on BMD technologies. Watkins was not impressed with Teller's favored X-ray laser, which would have depended upon a nuclear explosion in space: "I said, 'Forget it, Edward, it isn't going to sell politically.'"[80] Watkins did not wish to focus on one specific technology—particularly not that one—but rather wanted a research program that would investigate a wide range of possibilities. In that regard, he was encouraged by his meeting with Teller, for after questioning Teller about a variety of recent advances and potential technologies, Watkins came away impressed with the overall prospects for missile defense, especially for space- and sea-based systems, in the long term.[81] Teller's optimism "more or less confirmed what Watkins had been hearing in JCS briefings on strategic technologies and in discussions with his own R&D advisers."[82]

In late January, Watkins and his aides developed a presentation to take to the other Chiefs in preparation for their February 11 meeting with Reagan. It centered on a plan to initiate a high-priority ballistic missile defense research and development program.[83] Watkins later stated that "my proposal was to shift to defense as an adjunct to [offensive] strategic modernization, which we had to do. Because this defense was long term, way off in the distance, twenty years."[84] He intended that in time the United States would be able to devise defensive capabilities that would enable it to adopt "a long-term strategy based on strategic defense—a position both militarily and morally sound."[85]

Before making his presentation to the Joint Chiefs, Watkins briefed the Chief of Naval Operations' Executive Panel, an advisory group, on its content. Watkins later recalled, "[T]hey said, 'What you're going to do is you're going to raise the expectations of the president that we can do this in a few years.' And I said, 'We [the Joint Chiefs] will make a very strong point that we can't. This is a twenty-year, accelerated R and D program with a lot of unknowns. But we ought to start . . . our laboratories, and some of the best thinkers, can move us in this direction.'"[86]

Before he went to the Joint Chiefs, Watkins also did what he called "homework" on Reagan's dislike of MAD and his desire to pursue missile defense. In addition to reading through Reagan's statements, he spoke with Weinberger, McFarlane, and Keyworth. He found that the president "had been on this kick for some time, that was not something really new." This gave Watkins the feeling that he could "carry the day," particularly with his fellow Chiefs.[87]

On February 5, Watkins delivered his presentation to the rest of the Joint Chiefs. His plan to work toward a missile defense, particularly coming as it did during the ongoing setbacks and wrangling related to the ICBM problem, struck his colleagues as creative and appropriate.[88] General Charles Gabriel, the chief of staff of the Air Force, "whose technical analysis was highly respected by his colleagues," supported the notion of expanded missile defense research.[89] The chairman of the Joint Chiefs, General John Vessey of the Army, endorsed it next.[90] Vessey, like Watkins, had both "moral and military qualms" about MAD.[91] "Relying totally on the idea that you would destroy the other side is not moral, and it's not very logical. It leaves you with two unacceptable alternatives," he later said.[92] The commandant of the Marine Corps and the chief of staff of the Army also approved the idea.[93] Having unanimously agreed to recommend accelerated missile defense research and development to the president, the Joint Chiefs decided that General Vessey would include the proposal in their over-all review of U.S. strategic posture during the February 11 meeting with Reagan.[94]

In addition to the president and the Joint Chiefs, McFarlane and Weinberger attended the February 11 meeting. Meese probably also attended, but not Clark, who was away.[95] It appears that everyone at the meeting, as well as Clark, knew in advance that the Joint Chiefs would recommend missile defense research and development.[96] The White House participants were aware of the proposal before the meeting as a result of communications between Watkins (and possibly others on the JCS and its staff) and the NSC staff. Reagan had been fully briefed ahead of the session by Clark and McFarlane.[97]

In the February 11 meeting, Vessey put forward the Joint Chiefs' missile defense recommendation at the end of a "comprehensive brief-ing on all aspects of the strategic dilemma" during which he reviewed U.S. strategic forces modernization and the difficulty of competing with the Soviets in ICBM warheads. Vessey asserted that a missile de-fense would "move the battle from our shores and skies. Thus, we are kept from the dangerous extremes of (a) threatening a preemptive strike, or (b) passively absorbing a Soviet first strike—we have found the middle ground." He further commented that missile defense would be "more moral and therefore far more palatable to the Ameri-can people" than relying solely on the threat of offensive retaliation.[98] According to Meese, Vessey was "very strong on both the moral imper-atives as well as the military imperatives of a strategic defense in-itiative."[99] Borrowing words from Watkins's presentation to the Joint Chiefs on February 5, Vessey asked rhetorically, "Wouldn't it be better to protect the American people rather than avenge them?"[100] "Ex-actly," Reagan replied.[101]

As for the feasibility of developing a missile defense system, Weinberger recalled that the Joint Chiefs had reported that "we were not able to do it then, but that it was possible that it could be done."[102] The Chiefs did not have in mind the specific form a missile defense might eventually take, and they did not offer one.[103] "There was no program definition. It was the idea that defense might enter the equation more than in the past. It was the idea that new technologies were more promising than they had been in the past."[104] Watkins told the author that Vessey's presentation underscored the Chiefs' view that missile defense was "not a replacement for [offensive] strategic weaponry." Vessey may have been trying, quixotically, to head off any conflation of missile defense and the elimination of nuclear weapons in Reagan's mind.

Following convention, each of the Chiefs had a chance to speak after Vessey's presentation. Watkins reiterated that over the long term, the technological prospects for a missile defense seemed strong. He vigorously supported moving ahead with high-priority research. Reagan "liked" his comments, "because that was his feeling, too."[105] McFarlane then intervened to summarize and emphasize the Joint Chiefs' message: "Mr. President, what Jim is saying is that we may be able to move in our lifetimes from reliance on offense toward defense."[106] "Of course," Reagan responded. "I understand. That's what I want to do." With that, Reagan asked each of the other Chiefs in turn whether they agreed with the recommendation set out by Vessey and Watkins.[107] McFarlane later explained that Reagan wanted to assure himself of the "complete corporate support" of the Joint Chiefs and, cannily, to "get [them] on record here so that they can't later weasel out."[108] One by one, the Chiefs endorsed the proposal.[109] Reagan concluded the discussion by stating, "Well, I would like very much to pursue this."[110]

Later that evening, Reagan wrote in his diary, "So far the only policy worldwide on nuclear weapons is to have a deterrent. What if we were to tell the world that we want to protect our people not avenge them; that we are going to embark on a program of research to come up with a defensive weapon that could make nuclear weapons obsolete?"[111] In both its substance and language, the president's diary entry was essentially a short first draft of his speech announcing SDI. Reagan had obviously taken note of and embraced Vessey's (originally Watkins's) line about protecting rather than avenging Americans, which he later used in his SDI speech. The speech also included the phrase from his diary about a missile defense system making nuclear weapons "obsolete." His choice of words was revealing. Reagan, unlike anyone else involved in the inception of SDI, intended that a missile defense could and would help bring about the total elimination of nuclear weapons, and he spoke with his closest national security aides about that prospect.[112] His advisers worried about the link in Reagan's mind between missile defense and the abolition of nuclear arms.[113]

On February 12, the day after the Joint Chiefs reported back to the president, the Reagans had an informal, private dinner at the White House with Secretary of State George Shultz and his wife. Shultz had recently suggested in a memo to Reagan that the United States should begin "an intensive dialogue with Moscow." He wanted to identify and attain agreements with the Soviets where possible, while pursuing a broad agenda that included human rights and regional conflicts. Shultz wanted U.S.-Soviet meetings up to the level of foreign minister and said that a summit could be useful "if substance warranted."[114] Reagan's comments that night indicated to Shultz that the president, self-confident in both his views and his negotiating prowess, was interested in involving himself directly in talks with Soviet leaders.[115]

Shultz also heard Reagan hold forth on missile defense:

> He talked about his abhorrence of Mutual Assured Destruction (MAD) as the centerpiece of the strategic doctrine of deterrence. The idea of relying on the ability to wipe each other out as the way to prevent war had no appeal to Ronald Reagan. How much better it would be, safer, more humane, the president felt, if we could defend ourselves against nuclear weapons. Maybe there was a way, and if so, we should try to find it. He hoped for the day when there would be no nuclear weapons.[116]

Shultz later wrote that this was his "first intimation" of what was to become SDI, although he "didn't realize it at the time." Neither Shultz nor anyone else at the State Department had been involved in the discussions between the White House and the Joint Chiefs concerning missile defense; those who were involved, including Reagan, feared that State would attempt to derail the idea.[117] In their conversation over dinner, Reagan did not reveal to Shultz the recent series of studies and meetings on the subject, nor did he convey that any action was being considered. Shultz wrote in his memoirs, "As I listened to President Reagan that evening, I understood the importance of what he was saying, but I had absolutely no idea that the views he was expressing had any near-term, operational significance."[118] Reagan was signaling his strong views on missile defense to Shultz and trying to bring him around slowly to the idea—or at least to mitigate his opposition if it came later.

REAGAN DIRECTS PREPARATIONS FOR
THE ANNOUNCEMENT OF SDI

After the February 11 meeting, the Joint Chiefs tasked internal studies to survey potential defense technologies without "a sense of urgency," according to McFarlane, despite warnings from Clark that this was "no paper exercise."[119] Weinberger asked his staff to look into ways to dedicate more research to advanced missile defense technologies.[120]

Reagan was scheduled to deliver a televised speech on March 23 in support of his defense budget. About a week before the speech, he told Clark and McFarlane that in it he would announce a missile defense initiative.

Clark fully supported Reagan. McFarlane balked. He suggested that Reagan first invite support from Speaker of the House Thomas P. "Tip" O'Neill—a Democrat and determined foe of the president—and other congressional leaders, and thereby make missile defense a bipartisan project. (McFarlane later acknowledged that this was a "naive" approach.) He also thought that the allies needed to be forewarned and that Reagan should wait until after the Scowcroft Commission had issued its report on the MX before proceeding with any missile defense effort.[121]

Reagan rejected this. He told McFarlane that he feared that members of Congress would "go public and grandstand with criticism." In his memoirs, McFarlane wrote that the president had "worried about the same sort of thing from within the administration" and instructed that the announcement be prepared by only a small group within the NSC staff. Reagan enjoined McFarlane, "I want you to keep this tightly under wraps. Do the work in your own staff and write the speech and let's get ready to give it."[122]

Reagan was adamant. It was obvious to McFarlane that the president was going to announce his initiative, and he was going to announce it on March 23. Reagan was giving orders. This was relatively uncharacteristic of Reagan and a mark of the extreme—perhaps supreme—importance he attached to his vision of missile defense.[123]

McFarlane, despite genuine concern, followed Reagan's guidance.[124] Later, McFarlane reflected that, given the president's aspirations for missile defense and the massive shift they would bring about, he had been wise to move quickly and secretively: "To take the government in a basic new direction, a China-opening kind of [direction], is going to be resisted." "Through leaks and subversion by people who either oppose it or see it as 'not invented here,'" McFarlane stated, dissenters within the administration would inevitably "ridicule something as breathtaking as the China opening or this."[125]

McFarlane, under the supervision of Clark and aided by Boverie, Linhard, and Raymond Pollock (a defense specialist on the NSC staff), drafted what became the SDI announcement. Reagan intended to annex the announcement to his March 23 speech at the last moment, thereby circumventing the interagency vetting that normally preceded major presidential speeches. (The main body of the March 23 speech was written by the president's speechwriters and reviewed by the relevant departments as usual.)[126]

Poindexter helped McFarlane conceptualize the insert and then edited it. In an interview with the author, Poindexter said (referring to Clark and McFarlane and himself), "We knew that this was completely consistent with what [the president] wanted to do. We thought that from a technology point of view, it was not an impossible situation. There was no rosy view that the technology was just around the corner, but it was very clear to us that it made sense to begin such a program."[127]

Poindexter never shared McFarlane's initial reluctance to move forward in the rushed and closed manner upon which Reagan insisted. In Poindexter's view, that approach was necessary to avoid the "inevitable battering [the initiative] would have gotten from the bureaucracy, because it was a revolutionary idea."[128] "We were convinced there would be a lot of opposition [from within the administration]," he told the author, "and one sure way of killing something is to let it just sort of die a slow death trying to get it out."[129]

From the outset, Meese, Baker, and Deaver, Reagan's closest policy and political assistants in the White House, were informed of and involved with the forthcoming announcement. "They were good," McFarlane later noted; "they knew about it, and to their credit, they didn't leak it." According to McFarlane, Deaver especially "understood the value of surprise, and while he didn't want something stupid to be announced, he knew that this was very likely to evoke a popular grassroots response; it might not from the allies or the Congress, but grassroots reaction we all thought would be positive toward being protected. And that's the way it went."[130]

Meese was particularly enthusiastic about the announcement, having consistently supported the idea of Reagan launching a missile defense effort since at least the presidential campaign (when Deaver, among others, had quashed the idea on political grounds). Meese later recalled that the process of developing the SDI announcement was dictated entirely by Reagan: "He held it very close because he wanted to be the first one to announce it to the world, as he did on the twenty-third of March. And he felt that if there had been any premature disclosure, all the naysayers would have tried to shoot it down before he had a chance to explain it and to start the whole ball rolling from him personally. . . . He got the first shot at making the national announcement."[131]

Technically, McFarlane was mistaken in his belief that Meese had not leaked the White House's preparation of the announcement. Both Meese and Clark were long-standing friends of Weinberger. All three had worked together for then-Governor Reagan in California, and in Washington they almost always sided together, creating an instinctive alliance. From the beginning, Meese and Clark quietly kept Weinberger apprised of the work being done in the White House on missile defense. In his memoirs, Weinberger wrote that Meese and Clark had had to make "Byzantine efforts" to inform him of "the clandestine activities in the White House."[132]

Just a few days before the speech, the NSC staff members working on the insert decided that they ought to bring Keyworth, the president's science adviser, into their small group.[133] On March 19, McFarlane asked Keyworth to come to his office. There Keyworth found McFarlane and Poindexter. McFarlane asked Keyworth what he would think if the president wanted to announce a major national commitment to researching and developing a missile defense. Keyworth, who knew nothing of the speech insert, was "dumbfounded" by McFarlane's question.

As noted previously, Keyworth had been skeptical regarding the technical feasibility of a large-scale advanced missile defense; at the least, he thought there was "a long, long way to go" before it became a possibility. However, Keyworth had recently received the final report of an advisory panel of scientists that he had charged with the task of investigating whether any technologies, offensive or defensive, could present the president with any new strategic options in the near term.[134] The report concluded that among potential missile defense technologies, only one held real promise: a ground-based system that would project directed energy beams into space, where they could then be manipulated and aimed by mirrors. Keyworth thought the concept merited increased research and mentioned this to McFarlane, adding, "If ever there was an exciting time to take a look, now is it." At that point in their conversation, Keyworth did not realize "quite how big a thing we were talking about."

McFarlane handed Keyworth a "very rough one-page draft" of the insert. (Keyworth later surmised that McFarlane had "prepared this draft based on a conversation he had had with the president.") McFarlane then told him that Reagan "would not proceed with this project" unless he, Keyworth, concurred. Keyworth did not know whether this was true, but he "walked out of the room with a heavy sense of responsibility."

When he read the draft insert in his own office, Keyworth was astounded—both deeply worried and intrigued. He was unsure of the technological possibilities and concerned about the reaction among his fellow scientists, as well as about how the allies and the Soviets would respond.[135] At the same time, he felt enormous pressure to be a "team player" and support the president by endorsing the initiative.[136]

Keyworth was strongly influenced by what he knew to be Reagan's intense desire to pursue missile defense. Keyworth respected and deferred to both Reagan's authority and his judgment. In his estimation, the president possessed a "remarkable ability to assimilate information and keep a picture of what it really means in the policy context, a marvelous ability to work the whole while everybody else was working the parts." Keyworth felt that Reagan had "deeply . . . thought this thing through." He reasoned that his own responsibility was to answer the question that had been asked of him: "If you really don't think this is possible, tell me and I won't do it." In answer to that question, Keyworth determined that "I couldn't say that [missile defense was impossible] because I didn't feel it; it wasn't true."

He could not banish his nagging doubts, however. Although he had been told by McFarlane and Poindexter not to discuss the draft with anyone else, Keyworth secretly consulted his chief assistant for national security and space, Victor Reis, on the evening of the nineteenth, and the chair of the White House Science Council, Solomon Buchsbaum, on the twentieth.[137] Both opposed the announcement. (Reis eventually left the White House because of his disagreement with SDI.)

The negative reactions of Reis and Buchsbaum made Keyworth "very nervous." He went to see McFarlane. "I had cold feet and said to Bud, 'Are you sure we are doing something responsible?'"[138] Keyworth told McFarlane, "This is too big, too much of a change, too dramatic."[139] "Bud talked to me for a half an hour or so," Keyworth recalled, "and I walked out having gotten that out of my system." Whatever McFarlane told Keyworth during their meeting evidently eased the latter's uncertainties.[140] Keyworth later stated that after that meeting, "I never had any compunction about strategic defense."

Keyworth then was fully on board what he described as "a very fast moving train." He worked closely with McFarlane to redraft and edit the announcement. He was also assigned what he knew to be the impossible task of trying to establish a consensus in favor of the initiative within the scientific community once the speech had been delivered.[141] For the rest of his tenure at the White House, Keyworth was a prominent defender of SDI.[142]

Years later, looking back at Keyworth's conversion, Victor Reis concluded—accurately, in light of the available evidence—that "Keyworth decided to endorse the program because he felt that the president's political instincts were superior to his own scientific uncertainties, and his job was to ensure that the science was up to the task."[143] Keyworth himself said, "The fact is, I learned much more from the president than he learned from me in preparing that speech."[144]

The Joint Chiefs received a copy of the draft insert, probably the same version that Keyworth first saw, on Sunday the twentieth. General Vessey called Admiral Watkins to meet him at Andrews Air Force Base, whence Vessey was to leave for a trip to Portugal. They hurriedly reviewed the text on board Vessey's plane prior to its departure.[145] Both thought the announcement was premature. "We weren't ready to announce it yet—the necessary policy groundwork had not been laid," Watkins later stated. "We were not expecting the speech. It was unfortunate he gave the speech."[146] Vessey recalled, "We were surprised that it went that fast. It was clear that more study had to be done. But it wasn't in the cards to stop the speech. The White House was full speed ahead."[147]

Vessey and Watkins realized that they would be unable to stop or postpone the announcement; Reagan's determination to proceed was inexorable. Instead, they focused on attempting to moderate language in the draft that they thought would generate unrealistic expectations as to how quickly a defense could be fielded and how effective it might be. "We tried tinkering with the words so that they were acceptable,"

Watkins told the author. The two quickly sent back their comments to the White House, and their suggestions were taken into account. Watkins later noted, "We did all we could." In the end, he added, the speech came out "okay."[148]

During the two days before he was scheduled to deliver the speech, Reagan edited and redrafted the insert extensively. At about the same time, the White House began to notify the top officials of the State and Defense Departments of the imminent announcement.[149] "And then," Poindexter later said, "all hell broke loose." Poindexter told the author that "the initial reaction from everybody, with the possible exception of Cap [Weinberger] . . . was very negative." "When I say negative," Poindexter continued, "it was partly negative with regard to the timing, without consulting with the allies first, and partly, I think, because of a belief that it didn't make any sense."[150]

The civilian leaders of the Pentagon who opposed the announcement, namely Perle and Iklé, belonged to the first camp and not necessarily to the second. Weinberger and Perle were in Lisbon for a NATO Nuclear Planning Group meeting when they received a copy of the insert. Perle was "taken aback" by the text.[151] "That's no way to surface a new policy," he told Weinberger.[152] Perle felt that the administration needed to discuss the initiative with the allies and the Congress before publicly introducing it. He told the author that he immediately "counseled against going public" with the announcement before the allies had been consulted.[153] Poindexter later claimed that Perle "burned up the telephone lines creating friction all over the United States calling everybody he could think of" in an effort to "kill" the announcement.[154] In Washington, Iklé also lobbied strenuously against the insert.[155]

In his criticism of the announcement, Perle did not set forth objections to missile defense per se. He told the author that he had always been "a big advocate of having missile defense" and mentioned his earlier work on behalf of the group organized by Paul Nitze to support the limited ABM system that President Nixon had proposed in 1969 (see Chapter 1). Perle had no love for the ABM Treaty, and he felt that it was just "a matter of time" before the United States began to move toward missile defense. He added that while he was upset at how SDI was announced, he was "happy" and "eager" to support it after Reagan's speech.[156]

Perle later stated that Reagan and those who worked with him to prepare the insert were wise to have overridden his own efforts at the time to stop the speech. "[T]hey made the right decision in going forward," he commented. Looking back, he thought that advance discussions with the allies and the Congress would have generated controversy that might have foreclosed a major missile defense program.[157]

Weinberger generally favored the announcement. Yet he was "particularly concerned at the timing." He told the author, "I was in Europe at a NATO meeting. And I thought that if we had a nice meeting and we adjourned with the usual unanimity and had a reasonably responsible press conference, as we always did, and the next day they read in the paper that the whole strategic approach was going to be upset and I had not told them anything about it, it would be very unfortunate."[158]

Weinberger was aware of, and possibly condoned, Perle's (and Iklé's) intense opposition to the announcement.[159] Other than securing agreement from the White House to brief his NATO counterparts just before the speech, however, Weinberger himself stayed fairly quiet and conveyed that he supported the insert.[160]

The criticisms from the State Department were far more expansive than those from the Pentagon. Shultz and his senior aides opposed not just the way the missile defense initiative was introduced; evidence suggests that they believed that the initiative was an ill-thought-out idea.[161]

Shultz was concerned that a missile defense program could destabilize America's relations with its allies and the Soviet Union. He worried about whether the USSR might perceive the initiative as threatening—although he later claimed to have realized at the time that the Soviets would fear dramatic technological breakthroughs as a result of a U.S. missile defense program and that that fear, and the leverage it would generate for the United States, might prove "the greatest benefit" of the initiative.[162] Shultz argued that the administration had not sufficiently thought through the ramifications for the ABM Treaty. And the initiative might stoke fears among the United States' allies that the administration intended to retreat from the doctrine of extended deterrence, which lay at the heart of NATO strategy, and adopt a "Fortress America" posture.[163] Shultz and his principal aides also doubted that an extensive missile defense was feasible. In short, Reagan's ambitions for missile defense were overlofty, unwarranted, and irresponsible.[164]

Undersecretary of State for Political Affairs Lawrence Eagleburger and Assistant Secretary for European Affairs Richard Burt were furious over Reagan's vision of missile defense as a catalyst for the elimination of nuclear arms (about which more at the end of this chapter).[165] At one point, Shultz said to Burt, "The president has this idea of a world without nuclear weapons." Burt replied, "He can't have a world without nuclear weapons. Doesn't he understand the realities?"[166]

Shultz and his assistants urged that the president neither state nor even imply that the United States would alter its established strategic doctrine in the foreseeable future. While he did not object to research and development into missile defense technologies, Shultz had "great reservations, not about the R and D effort, but about advancing this as something of such tremendous importance and scope." "I can see the moral ground you want to stake out," he told Reagan, "but I don't want to see you put something forward so powerfully, only to find technical flaws or major doctrinal weaknesses." Shultz tried to tamp down the scale and consequences of Reagan's initiative; he tried to make it mundane. In response, he "found great resistance [on the part of the president] to any change in the words for the speech."[167]

In the end, Shultz did win some modifications to the text, namely the addition of assurances that the United States would conduct its missile defense effort under the terms of the ABM Treaty, that it had no aggressive intentions for missile defense (i.e., it did not intend to deploy a defense in order to launch a first strike and then protect itself from a resultant Soviet retaliation), and that it would maintain its existing commitments and responsibilities to its allies.[168] Otherwise, Shultz failed in his attempts to render the initiative insignificant.

According to Poindexter, McFarlane wavered as a result of the critical reaction from within the administration, telling Clark that "he didn't think the president ought to give the speech [because] there was too much opposition to it." Poindexter disagreed with McFarlane: "I said that I think the president ought to go ahead and give the speech. I think the president believes in this, he wants to do it, and I think it makes good sense. . . . [L]et's get it out on the table." Clark—who knew better than anyone that Reagan would not back down—overruled McFarlane's hesitance.[169]

Reagan was neither deterred nor particularly affected by the criticism from within the administration. Keyworth later stated that "there was nothing that was going to change the president's mind."[170] Reagan was equally unfazed by the likelihood that his announcement would generate opposition both at home and abroad. On the day of the speech, Clark warned Reagan that he could expect criticism. "It doesn't bother me," Reagan responded.[171]

Weinberger later commented that Reagan "never regarded the conventional wisdom as very wise. He was always very anxious to—or willing to—test it and to go against it. It's one of the reasons that so many people underestimated him and thought that he simply didn't understand things. . . . He knew what the conventional wisdom was. He knew what MAD theory was, and all the rest, and it did not appeal to him. It did not bother him that to have defenses would violate that conventional wisdom."[172]

THE ANNOUNCEMENT SPEECH AND IMMEDIATE AFTERMATH

Most of Reagan's speech on March 23, 1983, was devoted to a wide-ranging defense of his proposed military budget, including a survey of the Soviet threat. Near the end of the speech he turned to a discussion of deterrence. Deterrence based on the threat of offensive retaliation "has worked," he declared. "We and our allies have succeeded in preventing nuclear war for more than three decades." "In recent months, however," he went on, "my advisers, including in particular the Joint

Chiefs of Staff, have underscored the necessity to break out of a future that relies solely on offensive retaliation for our security. Over the course of these discussions, I have become more and more deeply convinced that the human spirit must be capable of rising above dealing with other nations and human beings by threatening their existence." Reagan then affirmed his determination to negotiate reductions in offensive arms, although he stated that even with dramatic cuts, "it will still be necessary to rely on the specter of retaliation, on mutual threat. And that is a sad commentary on the human condition." He continued:

Wouldn't it be better to save lives than to avenge them? Are we not capable of demonstrating our peaceful intentions by applying all our abilities and our ingenuity to achieve a truly lasting stability?

I think we are. Indeed, we must. After careful consultation with my advisers including the Joint Chiefs of Staff, I believe there is a way. Let me share with you a vision of the future which offers hope. It is that we embark on a program to counter the awesome Soviet missile threat with measures that are defensive. Let us turn to the very strengths in technology that spawned our great industrial base, and that have given us the quality of life that we enjoy today.

What if free people could live secure in the knowledge that their security did not rest upon the threat of instant U.S. retaliation to deter a Soviet attack, that we could intercept and destroy strategic ballistic missiles before they reached our own soil or that of our allies?[173]

I know this is a formidable technical task, one that may not be accomplished before the end of the century. Yet, current technology has attained a level of sophistication where it is reasonable for us to begin this effort.[174] It will take many years, probably decades of effort on many fronts. There will be failures and setbacks, just as there will be successes and breakthroughs. And as we proceed, we must remain constant in preserving the nuclear deterrent and maintaining a solid capability for flexible response.

But isn't it worth every investment necessary to free the world from the threat of nuclear war? We know it is.

There followed Reagan's assurances that the United States would honor its commitments to the allies and that it did not seek to threaten the USSR. Then he concluded:

I call upon the scientific community in our country, those who gave us nuclear weapons, to turn their great talents now to the cause of mankind and world peace, to give us the means of rendering these nuclear weapons impotent and obsolete. [Reagan himself wrote this sentence.[175] Many of his aides objected to it because they knew it reflected his view of missile defense as a catalyst for the abolition of all nuclear weapons.[176] He refused to omit or alter it.]

Tonight, consistent with our obligations of the ABM Treaty and recognizing the need for closer consultation with our allies, I'm taking an important first step. I am directing a comprehensive and intensive effort to define a long-term research and development program to begin to achieve our ultimate goal of eliminating the threat posed by strategic nuclear missiles. This could pave the way for arms control measures to eliminate the weapons themselves. We seek neither military superiority nor political advantage. Our only purpose—one all people share—is to search for ways to reduce the danger of nuclear war.

My fellow Americans, tonight we're launching an effort which holds the promise of changing the course of human history. There will be risks, and results take time. But I believe we can do it.[177]

After he finished the speech, Reagan joined a group of scientists and former and current policy makers—including Edward Teller and Henry Kissinger—whom the NSC staff and Keyworth had invited to the White House. They told him, as he recorded approvingly in his diary that night, that the speech "would be a source of debate for some time to come."[178] In his diary, Reagan also noted that he had "made no optimistic forecasts—said it might take 20 years or more but we had to do it." He ended his entry that night with a concise summary of his emotions at having announced his initiative: "I felt good."[179]

Reagan's speech achieved the surprise he had intended. It came as a complete shock to almost everyone outside the administration—and to quite a few within it—and ignited debate and controversy.

Many scientists and strategic specialists (Robert McNamara was prominent among the latter) instantly denounced Reagan's initiative. They argued in the first place that a defense against ballistic missiles was not and would not be technically feasible. Some claimed that a defense would have to be 100 percent effective in order to be worthwhile—and that such a perfect, hermetic shield could never be realized. They posited that pursuing a defense would destabilize the arms competition between the United States and the USSR, intensifying the arms race not just in defensive systems but in offensive systems as well (so that the Soviets could be sure of overwhelming the U.S. defenses) and dramatically escalating each side's efforts to develop space war–fighting capabilities (so as to knock out the other's satellites and any future space-based missile defense assets).[180] In general, editorial comment in the U.S. national media opposed Reagan's idea, echoing the criticisms espoused by scientists and strategic experts.[181]

Initial U.S. public opinion, as measured in calls, telegrams, and letters to the White House, approved of Reagan's initiative; according to Deaver, the speech generated "the most favorable response" of any since Reagan's election. (Public support for SDI generally remained substantial during Reagan's presidency.)[182] As Weinberger later commented, most of the public was surprised to learn that the United States had no existing defense against missiles.[183]

In Congress, liberal Democrats and some Republicans derided Reagan's initiative as dangerous fantasy. It was largely due to their attacks along those lines that Reagan's initiative became widely known as "Star Wars," a name that intrinsically and devastatingly equated the project to science fiction.[184] The Star Wars moniker is probably one of history's most successful instances of semantic subversion. (After the Star Wars label had already stuck, the administration called the initiative the Strategic Defense Initiative, a title devised by Poindexter.)[185] Reagan himself particularly disliked the name Star Wars, believing that it allowed opponents to parody the initiative as a futuristic, unrealistic space program. In fact, the president had expressed no preference for what kind of defense technologies the initiative might explore; he wanted the United States to look into a wide range of potential systems, which could be based on land, at sea, or in the air or space (or in any combination thereof), to destroy incoming ballistic missiles. In a letter to a supporter, Reagan wrote, "Frankly I have no idea what the nature of such a defense might be. I simply asked our scientists to explore the possibility of developing such a defense."[186]

A few on Capitol Hill delighted in Reagan's announcement.

Mostly conservative Republicans, they were opposed to MAD and the ABM Treaty on both moral and strategic grounds and had desired increased funding for high-technology missile defense research even before the speech.[187] On March 24, Senator Barry Goldwater, whose presidential campaign Reagan had supported nearly twenty years earlier, sent him a one-sentence letter: "That was the best statement I have ever heard from any President."[188]

While some in Congress lambasted SDI and others championed it, more expressed a varying mix of curiosity, ambivalence, and guarded approval.[189] There was an element of political expediency in that muted reaction. Most Republicans sought to maintain solidarity with the White House, and many representatives and senators from both parties saw little advantage in opposing the initiative and thereby, as McFarlane later put it, casting themselves "in the role of champion of nuclear weapons."[190]

America's allies were "startled and shocked" by Reagan's speech.[191] The immediate reaction from most allied capitals was restrained, although many, particularly in Western Europe, viewed the initiative with wariness and confusion.[192] Some expressed unease over a possible delinking of the U.S. nuclear deterrent from Europe, and nearly all agreed "that you had to have something like the ABM Treaty" to restrain the United States and the USSR.[193]

The Soviet response to the initiative was sharply negative and actually began before Reagan delivered his speech. On the afternoon of March 23, Shultz, with White House authorization, showed a text of the speech to Soviet Ambassador to the United States Anatoly Dobrynin. Clearly perturbed, Dobrynin told Shultz that the United States "will be opening a new phase in the arms race."[194] The day after the speech, the official Soviet news agency, TASS, stated that Reagan's "directive clearly indicates his intentions to perpetuate the arms race and to carry it over into the next century." It claimed that the United States was embarking on "new policies . . . aimed at achieving superiority in nuclear armaments over the Soviet Union and destroying the approximate balance of power existing in the world."[195]

On March 26, Yuri Andropov, who had succeeded Leonid Brezhnev as Soviet leader in November 1982 (but who was racked by kidney disease), furiously condemned Reagan's initiative. He set forth a list of charges against SDI: it would lead to the abrogation of the ABM Treaty and undermine past arms control efforts between the two superpowers; it represented a bid by the United States to achieve "military superiority" over the USSR; taken together with the Reagan administration's buildup of offensive strategic forces, the program was intended to render the Soviets "unable to deal a retaliatory strike" and thus to "disarm the Soviet Union in the face of the U.S. nuclear threat."[196] Andropov was particularly vehement in reiterating the argument that Dobrynin had made to Shultz before the speech. SDI, he said, would "open the floodgates to a runaway race of all types of strategic arms, both offensive and defensive. Such is the real purport," he continued, "the seamy side, so to say, of Washington's 'defensive conception.'"[197]

Andropov's litany of objections to SDI laid out the basic arguments that Soviet leaders would employ in their attacks on the initiative over the ensuing few years. The Soviet concern that SDI would result in a new, expansive arms race in both defensive and offensive high-technology systems remained at the center of those attacks. The evolution and urgency of that central Soviet argument proved to be an important element in the unfolding of later events. How the Reagan administration noted and interpreted the argument over the course of the 1980s helped shape its perceptions of, and approach toward, overall U.S. Cold War policy.

That process started immediately. Shultz saw an intriguing and potentially powerful source of leverage for the United States in the Soviets' concern that the initiative would unleash a new, expensive, advanced-technology-oriented phase of the arms race. "Perhaps," he noted, the Soviets were "apprehensive that the president was really on to something. . . . General Secretary Andropov's reaction had been immediate. The Soviets were genuinely alarmed by the prospect of American science 'turned on' and venturing into the realm of space defenses."[198]

In the days and weeks after Reagan's speech, a small number of administration officials, namely Weinberger and Keyworth, publicly elaborated on exactly what Reagan had, and had not, proposed. They stated that the president's initiative was to research and develop a defense against ballistic missiles. (While ballistic missiles were considered the most threatening and destabilizing strategic nuclear weapons, as discussed previously, they were not the only strategic nuclear weapons; a missile defense system would not protect against nuclear armaments delivered by bomber or by the slow, low-flying cruise missile.)

Reagan, his aides asserted, had made the quest for a ballistic missile defense into "a national priority."[199] They emphasized, however, that the realization of a missile defense was "far out on the horizon."[200] In a speech in early April, Weinberger noted, "We have entered into this effort with the full knowledge that we are embarked on a long-term effort that may take many years and may depend ultimately on technologies we have not yet developed."[201] Weinberger added that in time the United States should be able to come to some agreement with the Soviets on deployment of a missile defense, which the ABM Treaty banned.[202]

The officials tried to refute the argument that a missile defense needed to be absolutely leakproof to be effective. They argued that while the United States would pursue perfection as a goal, a defense would be worthwhile if it created enough uncertainty in the mind of the attacker as to whether and how many missiles would get through that he would doubt the ultimate success of the strike. Keyworth claimed that a defense "would not have to be perfect to convince a potential adversary that his attack would fail."[203]

Weinberger stated that the administration did not expect to come up with one "magic bullet" technology or system. It would research an array of potential space-, sea-, air-, and land-based systems with the intention of eventually developing a layered defense comprising several different elements.[204] Ideally, that layered defense would enable the United States to attack ICBMs in each of their three flight phases: boost, midcourse, and terminal. Weinberger stipulated that the administration was seeking to avoid, if at all possible, the use of nuclear weapons in a defense.[205] Weinberger thus followed the wishes and instincts of the president in setting out the parameters of SDI. As Cannon later wrote, Reagan "had no fixed view . . . of the form or shape that the new missile defense system should take. He knew only that he wanted a non-nuclear system." Aside from that one caveat, Reagan felt that the specific design and nature of the defense were "a matter for the scientists to decide."[206]

During an interview in early April, Keyworth acknowledged that "we face great uncertainties developing a workable defensive system," but added, "When we look at it very carefully, we see that we can reasonably make such an attempt." Keyworth and other officials indicated that research would focus on advanced technological concepts such as directed energy and kinetic kill (i.e., hitting an incoming missile with a projectile). Keyworth also noted that in areas that would be integral to any missile defense system—computing, for example, and communications—the United States had made "enormous technological advance in recent years."[207] He commented pointedly that "in most of these areas," the United States had "a substantial edge" over the Soviets.[208]

REAGAN'S AIMS FOR SDI

During a question-and-answer session with reporters on March 25, Reagan was asked why he had put forward his initiative when he did. He replied, "I've been having this idea, and it's been kicking around in my mind for some time here." He stated, "I brought this up one day in a meeting [at] which the Chiefs of Staff were present and others, and we talked about it and discussed it and then discussed it some more." He added that since it was not known how long it would take to achieve a defense, or indeed if it could be achieved, he had come to the conclusion that "the quicker we start, the better." He said, "It is inconceivable to me that we can go on thinking down the future, not only for ourselves and our lifetime but for other generations, that the great nations of the world will sit here, like people facing themselves across a table, each with a cocked gun, and no one knowing whether someone might tighten their finger on the trigger."[209]

Much later, Reagan's aides and his most perceptive observers noted that, with one major exception, Reagan almost never demanded or took sole credit for anything.[210] The exception was SDI.[211] Reagan's possessiveness with respect to SDI illustrated not just the importance that he attached to it but also the importance he attached to his particular purpose for it. In two press conferences soon after he had announced the initiative, he went some way toward explaining that purpose. On March 25, Reagan stated, "I'm quite sure that whatever time it would take and whatever President would be in the White House when, maybe 20 years down the road, somebody does come up with an answer [for missile defense], I think that that would then bring to the fore the problem of, all right, why not now dispose of all these weapons since we've proven that they can be rendered obsolete?"[212] Four days later, at another question-and-answer session with reporters, Reagan declared, "In my opinion, if a defensive weapon could be found and developed that would reduce the utility of these [missiles] or maybe even make them obsolete, then whenever that time came, a President of the United States would be able to say, 'Now, we have both the deterrent, the missiles—as we've had in the past—but now this other thing that has altered this.' And he could follow any one of a number of courses," Reagan continued. "He could offer to give that same defensive weapon to them to prove that there was no longer any need for keeping these missiles. Or with that defense, he could then say to them, 'I am willing to do away with all my missiles. You do away with yours.'"[213]

Those passages, which have been ignored in existing works on Reagan and SDI, are crucial to an understanding of his hopes and aims for SDI. From the very beginning, Reagan had in mind that SDI would catalyze the elimination of all nuclear weapons, and that sharing a missile defense with the adversaries of the United States would play a role in that process. Despite his use of the word "or" in the quotation above, his later statements and actions, as well as testimony by his colleagues, show that he saw the sharing of a missile defense and the abolition of nuclear weapons as complementary. Also, although in the press conference he referred only to abolishing "missiles," he intended that *all* nuclear weapons, not just ballistic missiles, would be abolished. He emphasized that point in hand-drafted letters he sent to supporters of the March 23 speech. In one such letter, Reagan wrote, "Hopefully a defense could result in real negotiations leading to the total elimination of nuclear weapons."[214] In another, he wrote, "My thinking is that if such a defense can be found we could then move to get agreement on eliminating nuclear weapons completely."[215]

Reagan did not imagine that a missile defense in and of itself would do away with all nuclear weapons. A ballistic missile defense would not protect against other forms of strategic nuclear delivery systems—bombers or cruise missiles—and nuclear weapons could also be delivered by theater and tactical means, artillery shells being an example of the latter. (It should be noted, however, that the United States held a significant advantage over the USSR in bombers and cruise missiles. An effective American ballistic missile defense would put Soviet strategic nuclear forces, as then constituted, at a severe disadvantage vis-à-vis U.S. capabilities.)

Reagan believed that if a ballistic missile defense could be made practicable—that is, could cast in strong doubt the success of a ballistic missile attack—it would spur negotiations in which both sides would agree to destroy their entire nuclear arsenals and to share the missile defense as a form of insurance. Those who knew Reagan well were aware that he had held that vision all along and that it had strongly influenced his desire to undertake SDI. Reagan sought to abolish all nuclear weapons. In his view, missile defense would be the catalyst for the realization of that goal.

As Weinberger later commented, Reagan was "against nuclear weapons. He never liked them at all. And that's why the strategic defense. And that we should strive for the elimination of those."[216] Asked by the author if, in Reagan's mind, SDI would have enabled the abolition of all nuclear weapons, Weinberger replied, "Yes, that's what he would have liked to have done." "I think he felt that a strong, effective defense would do a great deal toward eliminating" all nuclear weapons, Weinberger noted, adding, "Bear in mind from the beginning he said that when we got [a defense] we would share it with the Russians."[217]

When the author asked Poindexter the same question—in Reagan's mind, would SDI have enabled the abolition of nuclear weapons?—he responded, "I think [Reagan] clearly viewed it that way." Poindexter said that "the president's goal with SDI was first and foremost to provide a defense, not only to the United States but to all civilization. He was very sincere in his offer to the Soviets to share the technology with them. . . . The president's fundamental logic behind that was that this was a way of doing away with nuclear weapons."[218] In interviews, Deaver and Iklé concurred that Reagan saw missile defense as a way of bringing about the abolition of all nuclear weapons. Deaver added that Reagan's "initial reaction" after meeting with the Joint Chiefs to discuss missile defense prior to the announcement was, "'If this thing works, we can give it to the Soviets, too'—that was his exact instinct—'and then that will eliminate it all.'"[219]

Reagan never gave up his vision of SDI as catalyst for a nuclear weapons–free world and his conviction that the United States should share a defense with the Soviets. Not a single individual within his administration subscribed fully to that concept. Yet Reagan tried to see both of those beliefs formally enacted, most spectacularly at Reykjavík in 1986.

Reagan had instigated and controlled the announcement of SDI to adhere to his own aims. In doing so, he had excluded much of the bureaucracy from the policy-making process, and at first the initiative did not have particularly broad or deep support within the administration. As will be seen in the next chapter, however, most administration officials soon arrived at the conclusion that SDI served a useful purpose in terms of generating leverage over the Soviets regarding arms control, though they disagreed over how to exploit it within that context. Furthermore, Reagan and most of his aides came to believe by 1985 and 1986 that the Soviet leadership perceived the initiative to be a source of economic and technological pressure on the Soviet system.

That raises an important question: Did Reagan foresee and intend from the beginning that SDI would apply pressure on the Soviet economy and technological base? Currently available data provide no answer. It does seem possible that that was the case. Reagan had long believed and expressed his views that the Soviet system was weak and vulnerable, and that U.S. pressure, particularly in the military competition, could encourage fundamental change within it. Those views were very much on his mind during press conferences on January 20, February 22, and March 25, 1983, all around the time he announced SDI, but that is only circumstantial evidence. Reagan himself, in a rare opinion article he authored after he had left the White House, argued that he had intended for SDI to generate economic and technological pressure on the Soviets; he stated that he had known, when he had announced SDI, that

> the Soviets were spending such a large percentage of their national wealth on armaments that they were bankrupting their economy. We also knew that, if we showed the political resolve to develop SDI, the Soviets would have to face the awful truth: They did not have the resources to continue building a huge offensive arsenal and a defensive one simultaneously.[220]

Reagan thus claimed, *ex post*, to have intended this. Whether he actually intended it *ex ante* is as yet unclear.

CHAPTER

IV

1983–1984

R EAGAN'S ANNOUNCEMENT of SDI on March 23, 1983, came two
weeks after he delivered a speech to a conference of evangelicals
in which he called the USSR an "evil empire" and "the focus of evil in
the modern world."[1] In public comments during early 1983, the president stated that better U.S. relations with the USSR would arise from
changes in Soviet behavior, not from "just our own good intentions."[2]
While he did not discuss directly the policy objectives established in
NSDD 32 and NSDD 75, he declared that his administration had
moved the United States from a defensive approach to the Cold War
toward taking the initiative. "For too long," Reagan said during a
speech in February, "our foreign policy had been a pattern of reaction
to crisis, reaction to the political agendas of others, reaction to the offensive actions of those hostile to freedom and democracy. We were
forever competing on territory picked by our adversaries, with the issues and timing all chosen by them." "We can't simply be anti-this and
anti-that," he declared. He stated that his administration had "forged

the beginnings of a fundamentally new direction in American foreign policy—a policy based on the unashamed, unapologetic explaining of our own priceless free institutions and proof that they work and describing the social and economic progress they foster."[3] During a press conference, Reagan said that "we are going to continue not only in the area of disarmament but in every other way we can to convince those who seem to be expansionists today that there is a better course if they're willing to come forth and join the family of nations that want to go forward together in peace and freedom."[4]

Reagan continuously asserted that the Soviets believed they could neither afford nor keep up technologically with the military buildup that was then under way in the United States. The Soviets, he claimed, could be compelled to agree to arms reduction agreements. He said that on arms control, "now we're in a position to get somewhere and I'm determined that we shall."[5] During a press conference, he stated:

> We believe that the Soviet Union has some problems of their own that need to be resolved. And in these negotiations that are going on, we think that it would be in their interest as well as ours [to reduce nuclear weapons]. That's why we are so hopeful and so optimistic that something can be gained here, that they cannot go on down the road they're going in a perpetual arms race. And this is one of the things in connection with our own arms race. It gives us a leverage that has brought them to the table in the first place.[6]

In another press conference, he noted that "it was only when they saw that we were determined to rebuild our defenses—and they know that they cannot over a long period of time match us in that; they are no match for our industrial might—this is why they came to the table and are willing to negotiate with us. They're being stubborn," he added, "but they're there and they're talking."[7]

Reagan continued to express his antinuclearism in public. He again referred approvingly to the Baruch Plan and, days after announcing SDI, declared that it was his goal to try and "persuade [the Soviets] to join us in reducing and, hopefully, eliminating nuclear missiles entirely."[8]

In January 1983, almost exactly six months after taking office as secretary of state, Shultz sent Reagan a memorandum proposing that the administration should seek to engage Soviet leaders in talks up to the level of foreign minister and should work toward a summit "if substance warranted." The memo stated that such talks should encompass regional issues, human rights, economic relations, and bilateral relations (such as consulates and consular exchanges). An invigorated dialogue, Shultz argued, could solve outstanding problems where a solution was feasible, and even if it could not, it would "keep the diplomatic initiative in our hands."[9]

Shultz's effort to initiate expanded talks with the Soviets was greeted with skepticism by Clark.[10] Despite "considerable pulling and hauling" between Shultz and the NSC staff, Shultz won Reagan's authorization to open a regular but limited dialogue with the Soviet ambassador to the United States, Anatoly Dobrynin. Shultz and Dobrynin conducted a series of talks throughout the following months.[11]

Thereafter, Shultz continued to lobby Reagan for expanded formal contacts between the United States and the USSR. During Shultz's private dinner with Reagan in February that was mentioned in the previous chapter, the president indicated that he favored moving cautiously in that direction. Shultz relied on that encouragement to bring Dobrynin to the White House for a secret meeting with Reagan. The president used the occasion to lay out his views to the Soviet ambassador and pressed for Soviet action on a number of particular human rights cases.[12]

During the first weeks of March 1983, Shultz sent two more memoranda to Reagan. The secretary of state emphasized that the United States should both compete vigorously with the Soviets and pursue step-by-step diplomatic negotiations. In the memos and in subsequent meetings with Reagan and with Clark, Shultz advocated that such negotiations should focus on the four broad areas of arms control, human rights, regional issues, and bilateral issues.[13] Clark remained skeptical. Reagan encouraged the secretary of state to move ahead. Nevertheless, Shultz felt that not only Clark but Reagan himself was concerned that Shultz might "run off and initiate actions that would change the atmosphere when they perceived no change was warranted."[14]

In the spring of 1983, Jack Matlock, a foreign service officer who was serving as ambassador to Yugoslavia, joined the NSC staff to fill the position of Soviet affairs director, which had been left vacant by the departure of Pipes. (Pipes had returned to Harvard at the end of his planned two years at the White House.) McFarlane and Poindexter, acting on explicit instructions from Reagan and Clark, told Matlock that Reagan had decided that the U.S. military buildup was proceeding apace and that it was time to begin exploring ways to negotiate with the Soviets. They said that one of Matlock's principal responsibilities was to devise a framework for doing so.[15] Reagan himself soon made that clear to Matlock and the rest of his advisers. Reagan, Matlock later wrote, was convinced that the Soviet system "could change if subjected to sufficient pressure and his personal negotiating skill."[16]

Matlock later said that Clark, who was "very loyal to the president," supported Reagan's decision to start looking for ways to engage with the Soviets. Yet Clark was "very suspicious of the Soviet Union at that time," Matlock added, "and darn well should have been. Until Gorbachev, we had a leadership that lied and cheated and they were almost impossible to deal with. . . . They simply weren't willing to negotiate." Matlock believed, as did Clark, that Shultz "wasn't going to be able to negotiate" successfully with the Soviet leadership at that time: "No matter how much Shultz talked to that group, he wasn't going to get anything." Yet Matlock also believed that it was important to lay out for the future the U.S. agenda for U.S.-Soviet relations, and to begin talking with the Soviets.[17]

Meanwhile, tensions between Shultz and Clark on bureaucratic and strategic issues grew during the late spring and early summer of 1983. Shultz felt that he had been the victim of an end run with respect to the announcement of SDI. In this he was correct, but hardly alone: it was Reagan who had dictated that the development of the initiative was to be entirely a White House effort. Shultz and Clark continued to differ over the pace and extent of talks with the Soviets.[18]

Clark also had a separate but related set of problems brewing with some of the key White House political aides, particularly Deaver. Deaver and others, to some extent including the First Lady, Nancy Reagan, perceived the national security adviser's closeness to Reagan as an obstacle to the introduction of what they saw as more moderate views.[19]

In retrospect, it is apparent that the apogee of Clark's power was during late 1982, when his NSC staff coordinated and largely composed the series of long-term policy documents that established the administration's Cold War policy. Yet by the summer of 1983, Clark was still a formidable, if not the preeminent, player in administration national security policy making.

In mid-June 1983, Shultz presented a long and comprehensive exposition of the Reagan administration's Cold War policy before the Senate Foreign Relations Committee. This formal testimony has occasionally been noted, but rarely analyzed, in the relevant historiography.[20] It provides important insight into the nature and methods of American Cold War policy during the 1980s and into the principles guiding Shultz himself. It also stands as a warning against misinterpreting Shultz's "pragmatism" relative to many of his colleagues within the administration as any sympathy toward a détente approach. He adhered fully to the objectives of NSDD 32 and NSDD 75 and would work to realize them.

Shultz intended his June presentation to be a major public statement that would explain and defend the administration's policy toward the Soviet Union. He took particular care in preparing the text. In doing so, he enlisted the assistance of Matlock. Shultz also reviewed the statement "line by line" with Reagan, who in turn made suggestions and officially "signed off" on the testimony, as Shultz duly reported to the Senate committee.[21] During his testimony, the secretary of state called attention to the fact that he was "speaking not only for myself, but for the president in this statement."[22]

Shultz set out two principal objectives of U.S. Cold War policy, to be pursued simultaneously. The first was to force the Soviet Union to moderate and reverse the external manifestations of its drive for power. The second was to pressure it into reforming the fundamental nature of its internal system:

> Not all the many external and internal factors affecting Soviet behavior can be influenced by us. But we take it as part of our obligation to

peace to encourage the gradual evolution of the Soviet system toward political and economic pluralism and above all to counter Soviet expansionism through sustained and effective political, economic, and military competition.

In laying out this policy, Shultz explained that while "we have, of course, drawn in part on past strategies . . . we have not hesitated to jettison assumptions about United States–Soviet relations that have been refuted by experience or overtaken by events." To illustrate this point, he turned to a criticism of both containment and détente.

Following a policy of strict containment would have two flaws, Shultz said. The first was that "Soviet ambitions and capabilities have long since reached beyond the geographical bounds that this doctrine took for granted." The second was that containment ceded the initiative to the Soviets, forcing the United States to maintain a defensive, reactive stance. He argued that the Reagan administration's policy was instead to take the initiative, to "advance our own objectives, where possible foreclosing and where necessary actively countering Soviet challenges wherever they threaten our interests."

Shultz's critique of détente amounted to a wholesale denunciation. He stated that while détente aimed to induce Soviet restraint through "the anticipated benefits of expanding economic relations and arms control agreements," it had failed on both counts. According to Shultz, U.S.-Soviet economic ties during the 1970s "may have eased some of the domestic Soviet economic constraints that might have at least marginally inhibited Moscow's behavior," while SALT I and SALT II "did not curb the Soviet strategic arms buildup."

Shultz drew attention to the fact that the Reagan administration would actively pursue negotiations with the USSR, asserting that "we now seek to engage Soviet leaders in a constructive dialogue." Yet unlike détente, he stated, the administration's policy did not rest on "a delicate web of interdependence," or on "trust," but rather aimed to demonstrate to Moscow that restraint "was its most attractive, or only, option." The secretary declared that "we attach the highest importance to articulating the requirements for an improved relationship and to exploring every serious avenue for progress. Our parallel pursuit of strength and negotiation prepares us both to resist continued Soviet aggrandizement and to recognize and respond to positive Soviet moves."[23] To Shultz, negotiation and dialogue with the Soviets could serve both to secure concrete benefits for the United States, such as reductions in nuclear arms, and to further the administration's objective of encouraging change within the USSR as established in NSDDs 32 and 75.

In his testimony, Shultz highlighted the importance of perceptions in shaping the environment in which the superpowers made decisions. He particularly focused on perceptions of the military balance, making special note of the fact that "decisions on major strategic weapons systems can have profound political as well as military consequences."[24]

Shultz emphasized that the Soviet economy, particularly with respect to its vast military spending, represented a key vulnerability of the USSR vis-à-vis the United States. He underscored "the continuing Soviet quest for military superiority even in the face of mounting economic difficulties," stating that the USSR's massive, ongoing military buildup came "not only at the expense of the consumer" but "at the expense of industrial development on which the long-term development of the economy depends."[25] At the end of his presentation, Shultz identified pressuring the Soviet leadership to confront economic shortcomings and alter its priorities as a principal strategy of the Reagan administration's objective of encouraging systemic reform within the USSR. He stated:

> Brezhnev's successors will have to weigh the increased costs and risks of relentless competition against the benefits of a less tense international environment in which they could more adequately address the rising expectations of their own citizens. . . . For our part, we seek to encourage change through a firm but flexible U.S. strategy.[26]

Shultz's testimony constituted the most coherent and authoritative public declaration of the Reagan administration's Cold War policy. Its importance in this regard has been entirely overlooked by historians. To a considerable extent, Shultz's presentation amounted to a public exposition of the Reagan administration's objectives and strategic approach from NSDD 32 and NSDD 75. It also placed the administration's Cold War policy in the larger context of past U.S. policy and provided a more subtle treatment of particular topics, such as Soviet economic weakness and the strategic role of negotiations, than was included in the policy documents.

Between mid-1982 and mid-1983, the Reagan administration formulated and coalesced around a Cold War policy that departed from past practice. In terms of the practical implementation of that policy, however, the matter of when to negotiate with the Soviet Union, and to what degree, proved to be an issue on which various administration officials held different views. That circumstance became increasingly important as SDI moved to the forefront of U.S.-Soviet relations.

Shultz's presentation clearly indicated that the Reagan administration as a whole was beginning to focus on the economic weaknesses of the USSR. Throughout 1983, mounting evidence underscored the significance of those weaknesses. In April 1983, the CIA, together with other intelligence agencies within the government, produced a top secret report entitled "Dimensions of Civil Unrest in the Soviet Union." The paper stated that most instances of civil disturbances in the USSR were meant to send a "clear" message to the Soviet leadership regarding economic difficulties—that "the quality of life here is poor; food, especially good food is often scarce; pay is low; and working conditions are disagreeable." The paper noted that "consumer frustrations are rooted in the budgetary priorities of the regime and the inherent sluggishness of the Soviet economy and bureaucracy" and that the situation would probably worsen in the near future: "Intelligence studies show that the earlier growth in per capita consumption in the USSR has declined in recent years and that real growth in consumer welfare will be jeopardized in coming years as the Soviet economic slowdown continues."

The document concluded that continued Soviet economic decline and public dissatisfaction could create "significant future Soviet political problems" and that "the real significance of popular unrest is its potential to disrupt political stability in the USSR." It depicted Soviet leaders as being particularly "sensitive to this danger" and quoted several Soviet insiders as being worried that things could "get out of hand."[27]

The paper constituted one of the first in a series of similar intelligence documents issued during the mid- and late 1980s that focused on the internal situation in the USSR and the Soviet leadership's assessment of its options and priorities.[28] Such papers, which were distributed widely among senior U.S. officials with responsibility for foreign policy and defense matters, garnered attention within the administration.[29]

In the wake of Reagan's announcement of SDI, there followed an initial period during which many Reagan administration officials were both bemused by and wary of the president's initiative. Throughout most of 1983, many officials avoided public comment on the initiative altogether. There was little serious consideration of the program within the administration. Yet Soviet criticism of SDI remained sharp and constant. Prompted by the heated, ongoing Soviet denunciations of SDI, the CIA issued an interagency report in September 1983 entitled "Possible Soviet Responses to the US Strategic Defense Initiative." The Soviet attacks on SDI that were noted in the paper for the most part reiterated the initial charges made by Andropov, outlined at the end of the previous chapter. Yet one theme gradually came to predominate the Soviets' expressed concerns regarding SDI: that it represented a bid by the United States to engage in a broad "militarization of space," to move into an all-out arms race in space.

The CIA paper stated that the Soviets would attempt to prevent the development of U.S. ballistic missile defense systems through a concerted effort involving "propaganda, diplomatic, and negotiating tactics." It predicted that Moscow would continue to generate pressure on the Reagan administration to abandon SDI by targeting specific groups, such as the arms control community and the peace movement, both within the United States and among its NATO allies. The paper's authors posited that the Soviets might offer concessions in arms control negotiations in exchange for limitations on SDI but considered it unlikely either that such concessions would be what the United States "is looking for," or that such concessions would be intended primarily to generate economic "relief" within the USSR.

The document made clear that any Soviet attempt to match SDI with a corresponding program emphasizing advanced technology would pose serious problems for the USSR. The report pointed out that the Soviets had long been engaged in significant research into BMD but that undertaking the kind of large-scale high-technology effort that SDI represented would generate both economic and technological difficulties for the Soviets. Discussing the technological aspect, it stated that "the Soviets are not confident that, over the long haul, they could match US technology if the United States makes a high-level sustained effort, and they would be reluctant to be drawn into a technological 'race' with the United States." On the economic side, the paper judged economic concerns "to be of great importance in conditioning the Soviet response to SDI." Diverting "scarce assets" to a massive high-technology program "would place substantial additional pressures on the Soviet economy and confront the Soviet leadership with difficult policy choices." For these reasons, the document stated, the Soviets would place primary emphasis on propaganda and diplomacy to curb SDI; a military response in the form of a matching high-technology program was a recourse that Moscow would strenuously seek to avoid.[30]

By the autumn of 1983, a set of developments within the Reagan administration was unfolding that would later come to play an important role in shaping how the administration perceived and employed SDI within its overall Cold War policy. One was that the various bureaucratic elements of the administration had coalesced around the objectives and basic strategies of the presidentially approved, comprehensive policy toward the Soviet Union laid out in NSDD 32 and NSDD 75, and in Shultz's public Senate testimony. Second, the notion of expanding negotiations with the USSR was slowly advancing. Third, the administration was growing increasingly aware of the structural weakness of the Soviet economy and the strategic benefits this afforded. And fourth, attention within the administration was very gradually turning toward SDI. The extraordinary nature of the Soviet attacks on SDI prompted reconsideration of the program as something other than a mere vagary of the president.

REAGAN'S NUCLEAR ABOLITIONISM
AND HIS ADVISERS

Throughout 1983, Reagan conveyed his antinuclearism to his advisers frequently and with great fervor. Poindexter later recalled that Reagan "opposed nuclear weapons, period." The president "saw nuclear weapons as very evil and MAD as an evil policy." Poindexter noted that Reagan spoke often of the link he saw between Armageddon and nuclear war.[31]

Kenneth Adelman, who became the director of the U.S. Arms Control and Disarmament Agency (ACDA) in the spring of 1983 after serving for two years as deputy U.S. representative to the United Nations, was shocked by Reagan's antinuclearism. "The more I sat at NSC meetings with him," he told the author in an interview, "the more I was surprised that for an anti-Communist hawk, how antinuclear he was. He would make comments that seemed to me to come from the far left rather than from the far right. He *hated* nuclear weapons."

Adelman stated that "many times [Reagan] would pop out with 'Let's abolish all nuclear weapons.'" Adelman said that Reagan's advisers would ignore or try to push aside the president's nuclear abolitionism. Reagan's conviction that all nuclear weapons should be eliminated was, in their view, "out of the box, it was ridiculous. . . . We wouldn't think to ourselves, 'Oh, the boss thinks that, let's go start to implement it.' That just wasn't the way it was done."

On a few occasions, Adelman noted, he or someone else would try to dissuade Reagan from his nuclear abolitionism. Reagan would listen to the arguments, say "Thank you very much," and carry on repeating it.

To those advisers who had not perceived it from the beginning, it became clear that Reagan intended SDI to catalyze the abolition of nuclear weapons, as described at the end of the previous chapter. Asked by the author if that was Reagan's intention, Adelman responded, "Oh, yeah. Oh, absolutely, absolutely."[32] Matlock told the author that "everybody knew that that's what Reagan wanted, that was his great goal, to get rid of nuclear weapons, that was the whole thing behind SDI to begin with."[33]

Matlock also told the author that he suspected that Reagan would not retaliate in the event of a nuclear attack: "I think deep down he doubted that, even if the United States was struck, that he could bring himself to strike another country with [nuclear weapons]. He could never hint, but I sort of sensed [that]." Matlock believed that Reagan's unwillingness to retaliate against a nuclear attack contributed further to his desire for a missile defense. Matlock paraphrased Reagan's thoughts as: "How can you tell me, the president of the United States, that the only way I can defend my people is by threatening other people and maybe civilization itself? That is unacceptable."

According to Matlock, Reagan considered nuclear weapons "totally irrational, totally inhumane, good for nothing but killing, possibly destructive of life on earth and civilization," and sought to abolish them.[34] Reagan tried to operationalize those views by including them in a letter to Andropov in July. In a handwritten draft, he wrote:

> If we can agree on mutual, verifiable reductions in the number of nuclear weapons we both hold could this not be a first step toward the elimination of all such weapons? Can we as leaders of our two nations allow the people we represent + their children to look toward a future in which they must live under the threat of these destructive weapons? What a blessing [the elimination of nuclear weapons] would be for the people we both represent. You + I have the ability to bring this about through our negotiations in the arms reduction talks.[35]

This was too much for Reagan's aides, including even Clark. Yet Clark, after reviewing the draft letter, decided it was best not to try to dissuade Reagan from his nuclear abolitionism. He knew that would have little effect. Instead, he wrote a memo to Reagan stating that "if we were to make one suggestion" about the letter, "it would be to counter the risk of so emphasizing the importance we attach to arms reductions as to lead the Soviets to up the ante."[36] Reagan evidently thought that this made sense, and he agreed to delete the portion of the draft letter quoted above from the final version he sent to Andropov.[37]

It was of considerable significance to later events that one of Reagan's senior advisers did not object to the idea of abolishing nuclear weapons. Several of his former colleagues told the author in interviews that Secretary of State Shultz—who had had no specialty or previous experience in strategic issues—had "sympathy" for the notion.[38] He not only sympathized with Reagan's desire for a nuclear-free world but asked, as Reagan had in previous years, for studies on the subject. Like Reagan, Shultz received little response from the bureaucracy.[39]

SETTING OUT THE U.S. AGENDA

During the autumn and winter of 1983, the Reagan administration confronted a series of events, some foreseen, some unexpected, which cumulatively constituted a tense period in the Cold War. In early September, a Soviet fighter jet shot down a civilian Korean Air Lines plane carrying a number of Americans, including a congressman. The Soviets' handling of the matter generated widespread outrage and brought about severe exchanges between the two nations, although Shultz argued successfully within the Reagan administration against breaking off ongoing negotiations with the Soviets on the grounds that such "linkage" would prove disruptive and contrary to U.S. interests.

The Cold War issue that most occupied the attention of the Reagan administration during this period, however, was the deployment of U.S. intermediate-range nuclear missiles in a number of NATO countries in Western Europe, namely the United Kingdom, West Germany, Italy, Belgium, and the Netherlands, as had been agreed upon during the late 1970s (see Chapter 1).[40] The matter developed into a tense standoff as the deadline for U.S. deployment of the INF missiles to Europe drew closer. The Soviets, hoping to drive a wedge between the U.S. and its NATO allies, generated enormous political pressure to try to encourage rejection of the deployments by the European nations. In each of the nations due to receive the U.S. missiles, significant popular movements opposed the fielding of the weapons. The episode grew to constitute a serious test of the cohesion of the NATO alliance. In the end, the Western European nations pledged to accept the missiles as planned, and the deployments proceeded on schedule. In response to the deployments, Soviet negotiators walked out of the INF negotiations in Geneva, claiming they would not return while the American missiles were in place. The Soviets subsequently walked out of the START talks as well.

The Soviet decision to boycott both forums of the nuclear arms talks backfired. Moscow had already raised the political stakes of the U.S. missile deployments to Europe and had failed to accomplish its objectives; its subsequent boycott of the arms negotiations damaged its credibility. The Soviet boycott also ceded the diplomatic initiative to the United States. When faced with criticism of its negotiating positions as being inflexible or one-sided, the Reagan administration could (and did) respond by pointing out that the USSR was not even at the bargaining table.

In the midst of the heightened Cold War tensions during the autumn of 1983, a key personnel change took place within the Reagan administration. Clark, weary of bureaucratic and personal opposition, moved to the Department of the Interior. Reagan elevated McFarlane, Clark's deputy, to the position of national security adviser. The move carried considerable ramifications for the course of SDI. As seen in the previous chapter, McFarlane had played a central role in the inception of SDI. He did so largely because he thought that SDI could be used as a means of acquiring leverage over the USSR in arms control negotiations and that it could serve as an actual bargaining chip in those negotiations. McFarlane's rationale was that the Soviets feared the technological and economic ramifications of an all-out competition with the United States in advanced BMD systems (and space weapons generally) and that, if faced with a serious, well-funded American effort, they would agree to significant cuts in their ICBM fleet in exchange for limitations on SDI.[41]

As national security adviser, McFarlane began to consider how best to fulfill the potential he saw in SDI as both bargaining leverage and a bargaining chip. Employing SDI as leverage with which to accrue concrete gains for the United States accorded with McFarlane's larger view of how the Reagan administration should prosecute the Cold War. He was one of the more literal adherents to Reagan's concept of building up overall American strength, and thus leverage, vis-à-vis the USSR and then negotiating agreements that would secure long-term benefits to U.S. interests—such as a reduction in the Soviets' intercontinental missiles. As a result of both personal inclination and the nature of his position as national security adviser, McFarlane devoted much thought and effort to the cultivation, and trajectory, of the various elements that constituted U.S. leverage—including congressional and public support for increasing the defense budget, the overall military balance between the two superpowers, Reagan's political standing, and the cohesion of the Western alliance. McFarlane concerned himself with ensuring that the Reagan administration set about serious negotiations with the Soviets while at the peak of its overall leverage.[42] During a conversation with Reagan soon after taking over from Clark in the autumn of 1983, McFarlane stated that

> the massive increases in the U.S. defense budget were not likely to last, that the earlier Soviet perception of U.S. weakness was being reversed and that it was time to consider a framework for translating the improved U.S. position into permanent gains through negotiations with Moscow.[43]

McFarlane's interest in gradually expanding a dialogue with the Soviets, if only to lock in advantages for the United States within the long-term competition of the Cold War, proved beneficial to Shultz's cause. The replacement of Clark by McFarlane resulted in an important alteration of bureaucratic dynamics. McFarlane later estimated that on substantive matters he had sided with Shultz over Weinberger about 60 percent of the time, but in fact his tenure signaled a distinct shift in bureaucratic influence toward Shultz.[44] Rather than competing with Shultz, as Clark sometimes had, McFarlane more or less provided the secretary of state free access to the president and generally supported his policy maneuvers.

In December 1983, Shultz again argued to the president that expanding diplomatic initiatives with the Soviets presented a valuable opportunity for the United States. Both McFarlane and Shultz reported to Reagan that efforts to build up strength had begun to bear fruit (although McFarlane judged that peak leverage would be reached after about two more years of increased defense spending); that it would be helpful to lower Cold War tensions after the considerable mutual antagonism of 1983; and that the administration would demonstrate readiness to talk seriously "even if the Soviets are not."[45] The fact that 1984 was a presidential election year provided another subtext for enhanced diplomatic efforts.

On January 16, 1984, Reagan delivered a major address on U.S.-Soviet relations. That speech set out the U.S. agenda for expanded dialogue and negotiations with the Soviets. The speech was drafted largely by Matlock, who intended it to establish a framework for working toward improved relations with the USSR.[46] In it, Reagan set out three broad areas for dialogue, based upon those that Shultz had suggested: arms control, regional disputes, and bilateral relations, including human rights (the latter eventually became a separate and fourth category of the administration's "four-part agenda"). Reagan stated that the United States "must and will engage the Soviets in a dialogue as serious and constructive as possible, a dialogue that will serve to promote peace in the troubled regions of the world, reduce the levels of arms, and build a constructive working relationship."[47]

The agenda for dialogue grew out of the objectives of NSDDs 32 and 75. Matlock thought, and Reagan and Shultz concurred, that if the administration handled a dialogue on those agenda topics skillfully—while continuing to apply pressure on the USSR in various forms, such as the military buildup—the administration could impress upon the Soviets that reducing their defense burden and international commitments and turning toward greater political and economic openness domestically was in their own interest, a way of addressing the straining internal Soviet system, particularly economically. Matlock did not believe, however, that the present Soviet leadership would even engage on the topics (aside from arms control), much less adopt them as its own, and that it would take a change in leadership to a new, more flexible Soviet leader before the Reagan administration could find an interlocutor who might. He believed that it was important to set out the agenda for the future, however, and begin to talk with the Soviets. All of the senior Reagan administration officials, including Weinberger and Casey, concurred with the approach of broadening the U.S.-Soviet agenda.[48]

Thus, against a backdrop of increased interest within the Reagan administration in the economic weakness of the Soviet system, the administration, led by the president, Shultz, and Matlock, laid the foundation for broader engagement with the Soviets. That engagement was to encompass topics related not just to the USSR's external behavior but to its internal nature as well. A central aim was to use a broader dialogue to convey to the Soviets that greater systemic openness and change were their best available option.

In his January 16 speech, Reagan also declared his desire for the abolition of all nuclear weapons. He stated that "my dream is to see the day when nuclear weapons will be banished from the face of the Earth."[49] In his State of the Union Address later that month, Reagan said that the "only value in our two nations possessing nuclear weapons is to make sure they will never be used. But then would it not be better to do away with them entirely?"[50] To the chagrin of most of his advisers, he spoke frequently of his desire to eliminate all nuclear weapons during his presidential reelection campaign in 1984. One former NSC official later noted that Reagan's stated hope of abolishing nuclear weapons generated some of the loudest applause during campaign appearances.[51]

SDI MOVES TO THE FOREFRONT OF U.S.-SOVIET RELATIONS

Only in the spring of 1984 did SDI take operational form. Immediately after Reagan's March 1983 speech, the administration established a set of panels, comprising both government officials and outside experts, to work on the technological and strategic aspects of missile defense. Those panels, made up largely but not exclusively of those presumed or known to support the concept, submitted encouraging reports late in 1983.[52] In the spring of 1984, Weinberger decided to manage the initiative through a specially created, free-standing organization within the Department of Defense that would be responsible directly and solely to him.[53] The creation of that organization, the Strategic Defense Initiative Organization (SDIO), isolated the initiative in one compartmentalized structure, free from interservice rivalries and what Weinberger later called intradepartmental "sniping" over budget requests and allocations. He sought to demonstrate that SDI had "the highest priority."[54]

Weinberger later said that while he "didn't know a lot about" the technical side and appreciated that it "was a very difficult task," he believed that the United States had the money and the technical expertise to come up with an advanced missile defense after a serious, long-term effort.[55]

Weinberger's decision to create the SDIO meant that virtually all of the many questions about the cost and technical feasibility of the initiative came to be trained squarely on himself and the members of the SDIO (which was led first by James Abrahamson, an Air Force general and former NASA official). Weinberger told the author that he "recognized that that would happen" when he made the decision.[56] He became a lightning rod for criticism of the president's initiative, as he had foreseen.

In his memoirs, Reagan wrote that Weinberger had been "the chief evangelist" of SDI, "after me."[57] Colin Powell, then Weinberger's military assistant, later stated that Weinberger's "attachment and loyalty to the President were total and visceral." He described Weinberger as "more Catholic than the Pope on the subject of SDI."[58]

As the SDIO took form and the administration set about gaining budget appropriations for the project for fiscal year 1985, officials worked throughout early 1984 to present a case for congressional funding and public support. A fact sheet produced by the Pentagon stated that the aim of the initiative was to "develop sound technical options that could allow future Presidents to decide whether to develop an effective defense against ballistic missiles." It continued:

> [W]e want to emphasize that the strategic defense initiative is not a weapons system development and deployment program, but rather a broad-based centrally-managed research effort to identify and develop the key technologies necessary for an effective strategic defense.

The fact sheet added that it was

> highly unlikely that our research efforts would lead to a single system that could intercept and defend flawlessly against all missiles. . . . There probably is no such "magic bullet." What we anticipate is a defense network, a series of systems not necessarily based on the same technology or physical principles, which taken together will provide an effective defense against ballistic missiles.

The initiative would seek to provide a layered defense, one that would counter ballistic missiles in all stages of their flight, for the protection of the United States and allied countries.[59] In a series of speeches on SDI in 1984, Weinberger emphasized that a defense against ballistic missiles was feasible but was a long-term project.[60]

Throughout early 1984, the Soviets' attacks on SDI intensified. The Soviets focused in particular on the theme that the initiative represented a U.S. attempt to unleash an open-ended arms race in space. Adelman oversaw an ACDA study that concluded that 70 percent of Soviet propaganda around the world was focused on SDI. "This was stunning," Adelman said. He concluded, and conveyed at meetings and hearings, that the Soviets "fear it" and "think there's a lot to it," although privately he was not sure that the Soviets had much to fear in terms of the United States' ability to produce what the initiative aimed to do.[61]

Soviet Ambassador to the United States Anatoly Dobrynin told a senior State Department official that the "space issue" could become "the most dangerously destabilizing factor in our relationship."[62] SDI began to dominate meetings between officials of the two nations. By the summer of 1984, Shultz, like McFarlane, began seriously to think through the potential opportunities that SDI offered the United States in the context of generating Soviet movement on arms control.

Others within the administration also paid increasing attention to the Soviets' reaction to SDI. Weinberger later told the author that the Soviets "were touchy and they were so certain that we could get this, and that they had not been able to."[63] Perle viewed Moscow's protests as a sign that the United States "was doing the right thing": "their caterwauling deepened my conviction that it was the right program." Weinberger and Perle, the latter stated, "were not prepared to give it up at all," but wanted to develop and then deploy a missile defense. They felt that the United States should "work on [SDI] steadily, build it up," and firmly opposed any attempts to limit it.[64]

The extraordinary nature of the Soviet reaction to SDI pushed the initiative to the top of issues of concern between the United States and the Soviet Union. It also led Reagan administration officials to consider how the United States might use SDI to its advantage in the context of its overall approach to the USSR. Reagan administration officials came to see the initiative as a source of leverage over the Soviet Union with respect to arms control, a means of pressuring the Soviets to engage in serious arms talks. Yet officials differed over how SDI should be exploited for arms control purposes. Some, primarily in the State Department and NSC staff, sought to position SDI as a bargaining chip in negotiations. Others, led by Weinberger and Perle, intended to keep SDI out of the negotiating realm entirely. In the meantime, Reagan held to his vision of SDI as both the catalyst and the guarantor of a nuclear-free world.

While SDI moved to the forefront of U.S.-Soviet relations, U.S. officials grew increasingly interested in the relationship between the evidently bleak economic conditions within the USSR and the long-term prospects for the Soviet leadership's resistance to change of any kind. In January 1984, McFarlane sent Matlock a memo relating his view that while he was pessimistic that the current, aged generation of Soviet leaders would move away from their "deeply Stalinistic values," there was at least the potential of "an alternative future among the successor generation."[65] A month after McFarlane wrote the memo, Yuri Andropov, who had replaced the infirm and effectively senile Leonid Brezhnev in 1982, died of kidney failure; in his place the Politburo selected Konstantin Chernenko, who had advanced emphysema. The Reagan administration, in particular Reagan himself, felt frustrated dealing with this procession of the ideologically hidebound and physically decrepit, of whom none seemed willing or able to introduce the flexibility into Soviet policy that the United States hoped to encourage. Yet signs continued to point toward internal decay within the USSR. Matlock sent a memo to McFarlane in April that outlined a crisis in Soviet health patterns and care. In the memo he addressed Soviet difficulties more generally: "Many of us feel that the Soviet regime is facing mounting problems at home, and that this provides some incentive for them to moderate an aggressive foreign policy."[66]

U.S. officials now began to receive signals from Moscow that the Soviets intended to engage in talks aimed at "preventing the militarization of outer space" ("the militarization of outer space" being Soviet terminology for SDI), and on June 29 the Soviets made a formal offer to that effect.[67] Instead of flatly rejecting the proposal, however, and thus handing Moscow a diplomatic victory, McFarlane convened the Senior Arms Control Policy Group (SACPG). That forum comprised representatives from State, Defense, the NSC staff, ACDA, and the Joint Chiefs of Staff. The members of SACPG, prompted by McFarlane, agreed to respond to the Soviet move by offering to hold arms negotiations with the USSR on START, INF, and "other matters of interest to both sides."[68] Reagan approved the idea, and the United States announced the counteroffer immediately.[69] At the same time, the president authorized McFarlane to have SACPG prepare for comprehensive arms negotiations with the USSR, regardless of whether the Soviets ultimately agreed to engage in talks.[70]

The Soviets, caught flat-footed by the American response to expand the proposed talks to include the resumption of START and INF negotiations, declined to meet along the terms set out by the United States, and a series of acrimonious exchanges ensued. In the meantime, the Reagan administration undertook its overall review of arms-negotiating positions and prospects. However, the process, particularly within SACPG, quickly got bogged down over how much flexibility to allow in the U.S. stances with respect to START and INF and especially over how to deal with SDI. Perle and Weinberger resisted any backing away from the administration's established negotiating positions and insisted that SDI be excluded from discussion with the Soviets.[71] The State Department, together with McFarlane and his NSC staff, thought such an approach to be unconstructive and unrealistic.[72]

A harbinger of things to come materialized in the form of a memo from Paul Nitze to McFarlane. Nitze, then chief U.S. representative to the INF talks, had been asked by the NSC staff to send his thoughts on the overall arms control situation to McFarlane as part of the general review. In doing so, Nitze wrote that the Soviets' maneuverings were aimed at curtailing SDI and that the United States "should translate this initiative into Soviet movement on the issues of greatest interest to us—the stabilizing reduction of strategic . . . and intermediate-range offensive nuclear forces." He added that "the United States should examine the relationship between offensive and defensive systems and the linkage we might draw between them."[73] The statement was as close as one could get to advocating a trade-off between restrictions on SDI and deep cuts in offensive missiles without using those exact terms, which Nitze knew would be unacceptable to Reagan.

Nitze was then in his late seventies. He had played major roles in the Roosevelt, Truman, Kennedy, Johnson, and Nixon administrations. As described in Chapter 1, Nitze had led the drive to fund an ABM system in the late 1960s in order to trade it away in the SALT process; as a U.S. negotiator in the early 1970s, he had been central to the process of actually trading it away, having taken part in shaping both the ABM and SALT I agreements. Nitze viewed with skepticism the feasibility of a missile defense system of the sort favored by Reagan. He later said, "I doubted the practicality of the program. It seemed to me that those working on the SDI program had underestimated the technical difficulties involved in working out a program that would produce any useful results. It might be very expensive and get nowhere."[74] What Nitze did see as feasible, and desirable, was a deal that placed limitations on SDI in exchange for reductions in Soviet ICBMs and INF weapons; the prospect of such an outcome, he later said, made his "juices start to flow."[75]

By the autumn of 1984, both McFarlane and Shultz were seeking a way to bypass or overcome the Pentagon's opposition to taking a new aproach to U.S. arms control negotiating positions. In September, McFarlane lobbied Reagan to make personnel changes within the Pentagon and to appoint a single, White House–based coordinator on arms control matters.[76] Reagan refused to do the former but agreed to the latter.

In meetings in October, Shultz and McFarlane took steps that had lasting consequences for the ensuing role of SDI in U.S. policy.[77] The first concerned the issue of an arms control "czar" for the administration. Shultz refused to cede the arms control portfolio to the White House and insisted that any overall adviser with broad responsibility for arms control report first to him and then to the president; McFarlane acceded to this.[78] Shultz and McFarlane agreed that Nitze should occupy the post. Reagan approved, and Nitze was installed as "ambassador-at-large and special adviser to the President and the Secretary of State for arms control." With that decision, Shultz and McFarlane changed the bureaucratic balance of power in terms of SDI and arms control. Shultz's intention had been to make an end run around the interagency decision-making process; he later wrote that he had aimed to manipulate the system so that "interagency committees would meet, and NSC members would fight for their views, but ultimately the decision would be made through the Nitze-Shultz-Reagan lineup."[79] Inevitably, the result did not fully achieve Shultz's plan—which would have been unacceptable to McFarlane, Weinberger, and Perle—but the effect was still significant. Nitze thus became an influential new arms control policy maker in the Reagan administration.

The second successful move by Shultz and McFarlane in October was to acquire Reagan's permission to pursue the opening of "umbrella talks" with the USSR, comprising START, INF, and space issues generally, specifically including SDI. The NSDD that formally endorsed that approach stated that the administration should indicate to the Soviets that it was "prepared to discuss the nature and purpose of the US Strategic Defense Initiative and Soviet ballistic missile defense programs, and the relationship between the limitation of offensive and defensive capabilities."[80] Shultz and McFarlane were able to convince the president to approve this approach by arguing that the Soviets would not likely engage in negotiations that did not encompass SDI. They were both aware, at the same time, that Reagan was adamantly against using SDI as a bargaining chip. That placed them in the awkward position of seeking an end result that the president opposed.[81]

On the day of his landslide reelection in November 1984, Reagan described arms control as one of the key areas on which his administration would focus in its second term. He stated that the Soviets would engage in serious negotiations because they could no longer afford or keep up with the U.S. military buildup:

> I think they know there are difficulties in matching us industrially in such a buildup. And therefore I'm hoping that they will see the common sense value in us achieving a mutual deterrence at a lower level—by reducing the weapons instead of keeping on building them.

Reagan added that SDI "could be the greatest inducement to arms reduction."[82]

Meanwhile, Shultz worked on a proposal to restart arms control negotiations with the Soviets along the lines of the "umbrella talks" concept. His efforts were overtaken by events when the USSR, in mid-November, offered to engage in formal negotiations "on the whole range of nuclear and space weapons."[83] The specific organization and topics for the negotiations were to be worked out during a meeting between Shultz and Soviet Foreign Minister Andrei Gromyko. Reagan accepted the proposal, which amounted to the Soviets returning to the arms talks on exactly the terms hoped for by the United States. The Shultz-Gromyko meeting was scheduled for early January 1985, in Geneva.

By December 1984, Reagan believed—although he did not state

publicly—that the Soviets feared the ramifications of competing with SDI. In a letter to an old friend and frequent correspondent, Reagan wrote, "Just between us I have a suspicion the willingness of those other fellows to talk is born of their respect for our technology; they would like to head off our research on a defense against nuclear missiles."[84] Reagan—always extraordinarily attuned to Soviet economic and technological vulnerabilities—thought that SDI had come to play an important part in the strategy that he had devised more than twenty years before, of engaging in a military buildup against which the Soviets could not compete so as to compel them to accept nuclear arms reductions.

Reagan was well aware that in negotiations the Soviets would seek to stop SDI altogether. But he would not agree to a deal that would curtail SDI in exchange for reductions in nuclear weapons. He never wavered from his original vision for SDI, that an effective missile defense would spur negotiations that would eliminate all nuclear weapons and that the defense would then protect a nuclear-free world. As he wrote to his friend, "I happen to believe an effective defense weapon could bring closer the day when we could all do away with the nuclear threat."[85]

Throughout late November and December 1984, preparations for the Shultz-Gromyko meeting preoccupied the administration. McFarlane presided over at least twelve sessions of SACPG, while Nitze and Shultz set about crafting an appropriate strategy.[86] At the heart of the deliberations within the administration lay the issue of SDI. The period witnessed considerable debate over the purpose and negotiability of the initiative.

Shultz, Nitze, McFarlane, and various State Department officials tried to finesse an approach that would allow SDI to be a part of the negotiations as an actual bargaining chip but that would still be acceptable to Reagan himself. Weinberger and Perle argued that SDI should not even be discussed within a negotiating context. Perle told the author in an interview that he believed at the time that "some people didn't like [missile defense] at all" and saw it as "a bargaining chip to be cashed in right away." He thought there was "very little sympathy for what Ronald Reagan was doing [with SDI] in the Department of State." He added, however, that no one in the administration stated overtly that SDI should be used as a bargaining chip, since that "ran so counter to the president's view." Instead, Shultz, Nitze, et al., tried to allow as much leeway as they could for that possibility.[87]

Each side was fixing its position within the established Cold War policy of the administration—Shultz by arguing that the administration should accrue concrete benefits derived from forcing the USSR to restrain at least the manifestations of its behavior, Weinberger and Perle by stressing that the United States should seize the initiative, push the military competition in directions favorable to it, and seek strategic advantage over the USSR.

From the start of the work in late November, it became clear that Weinberger and Perle were fighting a rearguard action in seeking to preclude SDI from the negotiating talks. This was made evident by the final product of the arduous preparations, the written instructions providing guidance to Shultz for his meeting with Gromyko. The instructions, in the form of a sixteen-page directive—NSDD 153—allowed Shultz to agree to an umbrella negotiating structure under which START, INF, and defensive systems would be treated separately. SDI, then, would be a subject of negotiations between the United States and the USSR. Yet U.S. negotiators were to "protect the promise" of the initiative, a vague but implicit precaution against killing the program outright in a potential deal.[88] The instructions left Shultz—and the negotiators at the arms talks that would follow from the Shultz-Gorbachev meeting—considerable room for maneuver, declaring that

> the overriding importance of SDI to the United States is that it offers the possibility of radically altering . . . dangerous trends . . . by moving to a better, more stable basis of deterrence, and by providing new and compelling incentives to the Soviet Union for seriously negotiating reductions in existing nuclear arsenals.[89]

The NSDD stated that the USSR's "desire to block our Strategic Defense Initiative as soon as possible" was an "important factor influ-

encing Soviet behavior, especially in returning to nuclear arms reduction negotiations." It explained that Moscow "fully recognizes" that
SDI,

> and most especially, that portion of the program which holds out the
> promise of destroying missiles in the boost, post-boost, and mid-course
> portions of their flight—offers the prospect of permitting the U.S. tech-
> nologically to flank years of Soviet defensive investment and to shift
> the "state-of-the-art" in defenses into areas of comparative U.S. advan-
> tage. . . . While the Soviet Union may also be concerned about other
> potential "space weapons" programs, in large part, its focus on space
> reflects an attempt to confine future U.S. defense activity within more
> traditional areas which are consistent with the long-term pattern of
> Soviet investment and where the Soviet Union now holds a compara-
> tive advantage.

The NSDD added that the Soviets were "correct in recognizing the
potential of advanced missile defense concepts . . . to change existing,
and increasingly destabilizing, aspects of the [overall] strategic competition." If the promise of SDI could be achieved, the document continued, "the Soviet advantage accumulated over the past twenty years
at great cost will be largely neutralized." The Soviet Union, the NSDD
stated, "may wish to . . . offer the prospects of a better U.S.-Soviet relationship in return for constraints on specific U.S. programs."[90]

The NSDD also authorized an overarching "strategic concept" of
the U.S. aims for arms negotiations that was intended for public use.
Nitze, its author, meant to frame the concept in terms that were acceptable to Reagan while providing room to negotiate an offense-
defense deal once the arms negotiations were under way. The strategic
concept stated that the United States sought a "radical reduction" in
offensive nuclear weapons while "looking forward to a more stable
world, with greatly reduced levels of nuclear arms and an enhanced
ability to deter war based upon the increasing contribution of nonnuclear defenses against offensive nuclear arms." It declared that such
a process "could lead to the eventual elimination of all nuclear arms,
both offensive and defensive. A world free of nuclear arms is an ultimate objective to which we, the Soviet Union, and all other nations

can agree." NSDD 153 represented one of the first occasions on which the Reagan administration established the abolition of nuclear weapons as a U.S. objective—however distant—in a formal policy paper. It stated that "[f]or the long run . . . both sides seem to be agreed that with respect to nuclear weapons as a whole, the objective should be their total elimination. This should be worldwide and agreed to by all nations."[91]

Reagan himself had to approve the NSDD. He was presented with it during a meeting with Shultz, Weinberger, and McFarlane on December 31, 1984. Weinberger vigorously opposed the document, focusing on how it potentially left SDI open as a bargaining chip. McFarlane told the author in an interview that Weinberger "feared . . . the likelihood that Shultz and I would go off the reservation and would be too flexible, and his points were simply to stress to the president that we must not get ourselves on a slippery slope in which we start off by an openness to talk about space-based systems that will inevitably restrict our latitude. He was fearful, knowing George's inclinations and my own, that we would." According to McFarlane, Weinberger wanted "to put into the [NSDD] proscriptions that 'You will not allow SDI to be put at risk by including reductions in it or alterations to it in the terms of renewed talks.'"[92]

In the end, Reagan sided with Shultz and McFarlane, saying, "Cap, we don't know where it will all come out, but we are going to engage [with the Soviets]. So George, go over there and get it started without giving up anything."[93]

Shultz, McFarlane, and Nitze may have felt that they had gained some control over how SDI would play out in U.S.-Soviet relations, particularly with respect to its potential use not just as bargaining leverage but also as a bargaining chip in arms negotiations. In fact, Reagan controlled the process. The president was happy to allow SDI to serve as pressure on the Soviets to return to the arms negotiations and to discuss seriously deep cuts in offensive arsenals. Yet he had no intention of allowing it to be traded away in a deal. He held firmly to his own purpose for and vision of SDI. Reagan followed the advice of various advisers when that advice seemed to him to further his goals, and did not when it did not.

CHAPTER

V

1985

FOR HIS MEETINGS with Soviet Foreign Minister Gromyko, held on January 7 in Geneva for the purpose of establishing a framework for resumed U.S.-Soviet arms negotiations, Shultz took with him a large delegation, which included Perle. Thus, the group, though outwardly unified, was hardly of one mind on the issue of the U.S. position heading into the talks.[1]

Once the Shultz-Gromyko talks got under way in Geneva, Gromyko focused almost exclusively on SDI. He argued for an outright ban on the development, testing, and deployment of "space strike weapons" and stated that the USSR viewed SDI as "part of a general offensive plan" to create a first-strike capability for the United States.[2] Gromyko displayed a bitter defensiveness concerning the Reagan administration's perceptions of Soviet economic and technological vulnerability. He asserted that the United States believed that "it would be able to create such a [missile defense] system and the Soviet Union would not, so the U.S. would be ahead. . . . The U.S. wants to gain advantage over the Soviet Union, and the defensive system if developed would be used to bring pressure on the Soviet Union." Gromyko also claimed that any effort to portray the USSR's return to arms negotiations as a sign of Soviet weakness would be a "cheap ploy," as the new talks were different from the old: "Space has now appeared as a problem."[3]

Shultz, mindful of Reagan's devotion to the matter, pointed to "the ultimate objective of the total elimination of nuclear arms" and stated that the United States would be prepared to discuss how a missile defense system, if it "proved feasible, could contribute to the goal of eventually eliminating all nuclear weapons."[4] Gromyko replied that the goal of abolishing nuclear arms "is good," and that the Soviets were "in sympathy with it and are impressed by it."[5] He did not pursue the matter, however, and did not seek further information on how the United States envisaged SDI contributing to the aim of eliminating nuclear weapons.

Shultz and Gromyko agreed on a basic framework on how to proceed with future arms negotiations. Each side would send to the arms negotiations one delegation divided into three teams: one each for the START and INF talks and one for space and defense issues. Shultz and Gromyko clashed, however, over whether an agreement could be reached in one area without corresponding deals being made in the other two. Gromyko argued that "implementation of agreements on separate issues would be postponed until an aggregate solution is found and negotiated"; a "comprehensive solution" was "indispensable."[6] Shultz found himself in a difficult position on this point. He could not tie progress in START and INF to limitations on SDI because Reagan would not accept that, but, together with McFarlane and Nitze, he intended to keep open the possibility that such a deal could be made during the course of negotiations.

The outcome of the disagreement was that both sides took recourse to ambiguous language. The relevant portion of the agreement issued by Shultz and Gromyko at the conclusion of the meetings in Geneva read:

> The sides agreed that the subject of the negotiations will be a complex of questions concerning space and nuclear arms, both strategic and intermediate range, with all the questions considered and resolved in

their interrelationship. The objective of the negotiations will be to work out effective agreements aimed at preventing an arms race in space and terminating it on earth, at limiting and reducing nuclear arms and strengthening strategic stability.[7]

While establishing a framework for resumed arms control negotiations with which both nations felt content, that language also produced tension in the U.S.-Soviet relationship. The Soviets maintained that agreements on offensive forces, particularly with respect to START, must be accompanied by a deal that limited SDI. The United States held a different view. As Shultz stated in his press conference immediately following the meetings, "I would say from the U.S. standpoint, if we find an area of importance in which we think it is in the interests of both sides to make an agreement, we will be in favor of making that agreement. But it takes two to make an agreement."[8]

McFARLANE AND SDI

Simultaneously with preparing for the resumption of arms negotiations, the Reagan administration embarked on what McFarlane, in a memo to the president, described as "a process of education and persuasion" with regard to SDI, including speeches and media appearances by senior administration officials.[9] McFarlane's enthusiasm for that "education and persuasion" effort regarding SDI was characteristic of the national security adviser. As illustrated previously, McFarlane intended SDI to be a means of influencing Soviet behavior, particularly in terms of arms control. He called the administration's approach to SDI within the context of U.S.-Soviet relations an "exquisite challenge"—"to exploit a stratagem which had no likelihood of being realized in any near term."

As a "piece of leverage," however, McFarlane saw SDI as being "very perishable." He perceived that perishability to lie in the administration's ability to maintain congressional appropriations for the program. That, in turn, rested upon the support of the U.S. public and upon the weight of criticism from allies and the effectiveness of Soviet propaganda. McFarlane later stated that he was "scared to death that I wouldn't be able to keep the Congress on board" in terms of funding SDI. He summarized his views as follows: "You're maintaining this fine balance. You're betting that the Russians, from the start-up in March of '83, will become ever more worried about [SDI]. But on the American side, you've got a curve that will intersect there, and it's coming down. And that is, whatever support it starts with in the beginning—and the popular support was substantial—as criticisms mount of it, it becomes more at risk. And you just don't want to reach a point on that declining curve where you lose the votes in the Congress."[10]

As a result of his views, McFarlane spent a considerable amount of time organizing measures to increase support for SDI among the United States' allies, with whom he and other officials personally consulted during frequent trips, and among the U.S. public, embodied by the early-1985 media "blitz." Yet his attention was trained particularly on maintaining the "votes in Congress." The son of a New Deal–era Democratic congressman, and himself a former staffer for Republican Senator John Tower, McFarlane was able to cultivate support for SDI among Republicans and key Democrats on Capitol Hill. Nonetheless, he was certain that Congress's will to fund the program was of a finite duration and that that limit was fast approaching.

McFarlane estimated that the two curves—congressional, public, and allied support for SDI on the one hand and leverage accrued by SDI over Soviet behavior on the other—would intersect during 1985 and that SDI "would become a somewhat wasting asset after that." Looking back, McFarlane said that it "turns out I was wrong . . . we did end up sustaining votes for it" beyond 1985; "but that was the way I felt about it." At the time, McFarlane thought that by 1985, the United States should "get on with it" and seek to lock in concrete gains from the USSR on the basis of its fear of SDI: "I was thinking in terms of how do you get the president to a point in negotiations with maximum strength that could give us a basis for reducing Soviet offensive systems."[11] He sought to position the administration to secure a deal limiting SDI in exchange for cuts in Soviet offensive missiles.

SDI and Arms Control

In his second inaugural address, on January 21, 1985, Reagan declared, "We seek the total elimination one day of nuclear weapons from the face of the earth."[12] Thereafter, Reagan continued to elaborate publicly on the ideas that he had begun to express immediately after his speech announcing SDI: that a missile defense would spur an agreement to abolish nuclear weapons and that the technology would be shared. He presented this case incessantly during unscripted, spontaneous back-and-forth sessions. During an interview with reporters in February 1985, for example, Reagan stated that

> My own view would be that if . . . we can produce such a [missile defense], then before deployment I'd be willing to sit down and, in a sense, internationalize. In other words, to negotiate, then, before there would be any deployment or anything, to make sure that they understood that we weren't trying to create the ability of a first strike ourselves, that our goal was still the elimination of nuclear weapons; and that I would see that defensive weapon as another step in attaining that goal; that if we could say that this virtually makes those weapons, if not obsolete, certainly most ineffective—the nuclear weapons—then we've got a real reason for saying, "Now, let's do away with all of them, because we've come up with this defensive weapon."[13]

The president was convinced, as he said at another press interview that month, that "to go forward with this research on a strategic [defensive] weapon is hand in hand with that goal, that ultimate goal" of eliminating nuclear arms. In explaining this notion, he drew from his initial speech announcing SDI, in which he had called for a system to render ballistic missiles "impotent and obsolete":

> If you could have that kind of a defense in which they would have to say: "Well, wait a minute. How many missiles would we have to build to get enough through on a first attack that we wouldn't be threatened with, then, the retaliation?" And then they will see the value that this

is what I mean by making nuclear weapons obsolete—they'll see that this defensive [system] could be a contributing factor to eliminating such weapons.[14]

In March, Reagan said that

once our adversaries fully understand the goal of our research program, it will add new incentives to both sides in Geneva to actually reduce the number of nuclear weapons threatening mankind. By making missiles less effective, we make these weapons more negotiable. If we're successful, the arms spiral will be a downward spiral, hopefully, to the elimination of them.[15]

Although the president put forth these ideas constantly during unscripted talks, they appeared altogether less frequently in his formal speeches. The set speeches were written either by his White House staff or by a department and were thoroughly vetted.

In the meantime, Nitze and McFarlane discussed how to elaborate publicly on SDI.[16] Nitze pushed to establish a set of criteria that would have to be met before deploying any such system: first, that it must be satisfactorily effective; second, that it must be survivable—that is, would not invite attack on itself through physical vulnerability—and third, that it must be "cost-effective at the margin." Nitze meant by the last point that a defense must be cheap enough that an opponent would have "no incentive to add additional offensive capability to overcome the defense."[17] McFarlane agreed to Nitze's proposal, and it was eventually put before Reagan to approve, which he did.[18] Nitze introduced the criteria as official U.S. policy during a speech in February 1985.

Nitze's speech drew widespread attention. Critics of SDI claimed that a missile defense system was highly unlikely to meet all of the criteria. It appeared that Nitze was attempting to preclude, or at least temper, enthusiasm for any future deployment and that he put forth the criteria in order to position SDI as a bargaining chip for an offense-defense deal.[19] Nitze publicly denied any such motivation, stating that he was merely applying requirements to SDI that were normally de-

manded of other weapons systems and that there was no basis to believe that a future missile defense could not meet the criteria.[20] Yet sus-
picions ran high among those in the administration who opposed an
offense-defense trade-off. In his memoirs, Weinberger wrote that Nitze
was "one of the strongest opponents of SDI in the State Department"
and that Nitze had set out the criteria "in order to get a treaty."[21] Weinberger later said that there was "no question" that Nitze and his State
Department colleagues were not committed to developing SDI but
rather sought to use it as a bargaining chip. He remarked that they
"threw one obstacle after another at it" in order to achieve that aim,
specifically mentioning the "Nitze criteria" as one of those obstacles.[22]

In his February speech on SDI, Nitze also laid out a proposal for
SDI's future role in arms control and nuclear strategy that drew on the
strategic concept established in NSDD 153. He declared that the deployment of an effective missile defense would take place during a
long-term "transition period," which might last for decades, during
which the United States would maintain its offensive forces. During
that period, the United States would work with the USSR and then
with the other nuclear powers to reduce offensive nuclear weapons.
"Given the right technical and political conditions," Nitze added, "we
would hope to be able to continue the reduction of nuclear weapons
down to zero." Yet he concluded that, "quite frankly," the elimination
of nuclear weapons "may prove impossible to obtain; and, even if we
do eventually reach it, it will not be for many, many years—perhaps
well into the next century." Nitze emphasized that Reagan's rhetoric
regarding the elimination of nuclear weapons was not merely "lip service." "As you can see," Nitze said, "the United States is going beyond"
mere rhetoric; "the President has initiated a serious effort to see how it
can be accomplished."[23]

In the speech, Nitze himself paid lip service to the president's beliefs in missile defense and nuclear abolition while simultaneously trying to mitigate the impact of them on U.S. policy. He stated that any
deployment of missile defense would occur alongside the retention of
offensive nuclear forces; nowhere did he mention sharing a missile defense with the Soviets (a bugbear to all of Reagan's advisers, regardless

of their views on SDI or the abolition of nuclear weapons); and he took care to point out that a defense system could be deployed only "if defensive technologies prove feasible and we decide to move in that direction."[24] Nitze was maneuvering to create conditions in which he could attain what had preoccupied him since the 1960s: the negation, through arms control, of the Soviets' advantage in destabilizing offensive missiles. To Nitze, SDI was a bargaining chip to that end.

Time and again during early 1985, Reagan explicitly rejected the concept of using SDI as a bargaining chip in arms negotiations.[25] He continued to espouse his vision for SDI, in which a shared missile defense would catalyze the abolition of nuclear weapons and ensure against cheating in a nuclear-free world. "SDI is arms control," he declared. He addressed the critics of SDI by stating that they feared departing from conventional patterns of thought: "The truth is, I believe that they find it difficult to embrace any idea that breaks with the past, that breaks with consensus thinking and the common establishment wisdom. In short, they find it difficult and frightening to alter the status quo."[26]

During an interview with *Newsweek* in March, Reagan deflected criticism of the cost and feasibility of SDI by citing a cartoon he had recently seen. The cartoon had depicted a husband and wife watching a television report claiming that SDI could never work; the wife is turned toward her husband, wondering, as Reagan described it, " 'Well, then why don't the Russians want us to have it?'" Reagan's interviewers asked him directly whether an arms race in defensive technologies would "be so onerous on [the Soviets'] tottering economy that it could hasten the day of putting them on the ash heap of history?" The president demurred, saying that "there's the potential of them not having to create it," and then reiterated that prior to U.S. deployment of a missile defense, an agreement could be reached by which all nuclear weapons would be eliminated and by which the defensive system would then be "internationalized." Later in the interview, however, Reagan returned to his notion that the Soviet Union would not be able to keep up with the overall U.S. military buildup and would therefore be forced by necessity to seek arms reductions. He stated that "you'll get an agreement when it is in their practical interest": "They know they cannot match us industrially. . . . They're already pretty much up to full capacity with how far down their people's subsistence level is and all—that they could now see the practical value in saying, well, there is another way—if we start reducing [nuclear weapons] instead of increasing them."[27]

Following the January Shultz-Gromyko meeting, the United States and the USSR agreed to inaugurate the umbrella Nuclear and Space Talks (NST), consisting of START, INF, and defense and space negotiations, on March 12 in Geneva. Nitze and General Edward Rowny, the former INF and START negotiators, respectively, remained in Washington as advisers to the president and Shultz, although Shultz had effectively removed the hard-line Rowny from a position of influence. In their place, the United States sent Mike Glitman, Nitze's former deputy, to head INF, and recently retired Senator John Tower, a conservative and McFarlane's former boss, for START. To head the defense and space group, the administration chose Max Kampelman, a Democrat and Cold War hawk, who was also selected as head of the overall delegation. According to Shultz, Weinberger had argued for choosing Edward Teller as the leader of the delegation, worrying that "no one else could be trusted to be totally committed to SDI."[28]

U.S. PERCEPTIONS OF GORBACHEV AND SOVIET VULNERABILITIES

On the day before the NST negotiations began, Moscow announced that Konstantin Chernenko had died and that Mikhail Gorbachev had succeeded him as general secretary. In contrast to his predecessors, Gorbachev was young, articulate, and energetic. The Reagan administration knew that Gorbachev had been a protégé of Andropov, who had apparently realized the need for some economic reforms, and expected that the new leader might favor taking some limited steps to revitalize the Soviet economy.[29]

The administration had made careful note of a report on Gorbachev from British Prime Minister Margaret Thatcher, who had hosted Gorbachev in London in December 1984. On that occasion she had famously remarked that Gorbachev was "a man one could do business with," adding that "there is no doubt that he is completely loyal to the Soviet system, but he is prepared to listen and have a genuine dialogue and make up his own mind."[30]

According to McFarlane, Thatcher sent a letter to Reagan following her meeting with Gorbachev stating that "the overriding impression left was that the Russians are genuinely fearful of the immense cost of having to keep up with a further American technological advance" and thus were willing to negotiate serious arms reductions. She repeated that same theme in person to Reagan during a meeting at Camp David later that month. McFarlane later summarized her comments as saying that "[t]he Soviets were seriously worried about SDI."[31]

While the Reagan administration was cautiously optimistic that Gorbachev would be less rigid than his predecessors, it was not confident that his policies would prove more amenable to U.S. interests.[32] Reagan summed up this view during a press conference on March 14, during which he declared that while he did not think "there was any evidence that [Gorbachev] is less dominated by their system and their philosophy than any of the others . . . he has spoken out there to his own people about improvements in the economy." Reagan then immediately shifted into a familiar theme: "And now that [the Soviets] know that they have to compete with us with regard to security needs, I think they've got a healthy respect for our technology and our industrial capacity and that they, I believe, are really going to try and, with us, negotiate a reduction of armaments."[33]

Reagan agreed to a suggestion from Shultz that Vice President Bush, heading the U.S. delegation to Chernenko's funeral, carry a letter from Reagan to Gorbachev inviting him to a summit in the United States. Shultz joined Bush in Moscow to attend the funeral and to meet Gorbachev. In him they observed at first hand a leader who was vigorous and intelligent but who displayed defensiveness concerning American policy and Soviet competitiveness: "The two countries,"

Gorbachev remarked, "have now reached a point in their arms buildup when any new breakthroughs resulting from the scientific and technological revolution—not to mention shifting the arms race into space—could set in motion irreversible and uncontrollable processes." The new general secretary added that it would be "nothing but a pipe dream, nothing but adventurism, for the United States to follow the advice of experts about wearing down and weakening the USSR economically, reducing its role in the world."[34]

During the spring of 1985, officials in the Reagan administration began to anticipate that the weakness of the Soviet economy could force the Kremlin to moderate its own Cold War approach in the near term in the face of a heightened competition with the United States. For example, Andrew Marshall, head of the Pentagon's internal policy unit, sent a memo to Donald Fortier, then policy development chief on the NSC staff, in which he summarized a report to the effect that "[t]here has been a change in one faction of the [Soviet Communist] Party. They are very worried about the economy and want to do something about it. A pause in the competition with the U.S. may be required and, as in past cases, they may offer us something." Marshall emphasized that this "basic message" was "very important."[35] Arthur Hartman, the U.S. ambassador to the USSR, reported to Shultz that "the new mood under Gorbachev was of Soviet preoccupation with their domestic problems." He underscored the Soviets' determination to stop SDI. Shultz grew increasingly confident that the USSR's economic straits would soon necessitate considerable attention to domestic affairs and an altering of Soviet international behavior.[36]

However, Gorbachev chose not to agree immediately to Reagan's invitation to a summit, responding only that he took a "positive attitude" toward such a meeting.[37] Thereafter, the two sides engaged in diplomatic maneuvers over the timing and nature of the summit. This exacerbated divisions among Reagan's senior advisers over when and how to talk with the Soviets. Weinberger and Casey, in particular, worried that the administration might be moving too quickly toward a closer relationship with the USSR. They were especially wary of the possibility that Shultz, McFarlane, and Nitze might initiate an arms control deal that would place restrictions on SDI in exchange for reductions in offensive nuclear weapons. Reagan, meanwhile, continued to pursue his own vision of SDI, sending a letter to Gorbachev in which he declared that defensive systems could "provide the means of moving to the total abolition of nuclear weapons."[38]

In May, Shultz and McFarlane traveled to Vienna to meet with Gromyko. After a long, acrimonious series of meetings, Gromyko quietly pulled Shultz aside to discuss the summit. Informally, the two men agreed to a Reagan-Gorbachev summit in a European city in November. Reporting on that progress to Reagan in Washington, however, Shultz was dismayed at the lack of enthusiasm on the part of the president, who believed that the United States should "think about it some more, play hard to get." Shultz went away and worked up a full proposal for a summit, to which Reagan eventually acceded, thus setting into motion a lengthy effort to prepare for the event.[39]

An Attempt at an Offense-Defense Trade-off

In the spring, Nitze heard from Kampelman in Geneva that Soviet negotiators had expressed interest in securing an agreement that would bar either side from withdrawing from the ABM Treaty for ten years. The treaty, as it existed, allowed either side to withdraw after six months' notice; the Soviets sought a nonwithdrawal clause as "a form of breakout insurance against an SDI deployment for ten years."

With this information, Nitze embarked on a plan to bring about an offense-defense trade-off at the arms talks. He linked a ten-year nonwithdrawal clause for the ABM Treaty to a 50 percent reduction in offensive nuclear missiles over the same ten-year period. "Needing a completely innocuous title" for the proposed deal, Nitze labeled it the Monday Package, after the day on which he finalized it.[40]

In Shultz and McFarlane, Nitze found willing cohorts in the plan; both men saw a potential arms control coup. To them, it represented exactly the kind of use of SDI as a bargaining chip that they both desired and that McFarlane had hoped for since he had worked on the inception of SDI.[41] Nitze, Shultz, and McFarlane made a deliberate decision to exclude the civilian leadership of the Pentagon—namely Weinberger and Perle—from discussion of the package. In his memoirs, Nitze wrote that it was the hope of the three men "that we could achieve decisive progress as a fait accompli. Otherwise, the howls and leaks from Weinberger and Perle and their supporters would have made the project impossible."[42] McFarlane told the author that, in the thinking of Weinberger and Perle, "it was wrong to cast that proposal [for 50 percent offensive reductions] in tandem with a restriction on SDI. And it was that linkage that would not have gone down well in DoD."[43]

Nitze, Shultz, and McFarlane did seek the approval of the Joint Chiefs of Staff, however. Securing the backing of the Joint Chiefs for controversial ideas is a recurring theme in the story of SDI. The Chiefs were seen as relatively objective arbiters of what was in the nation's security interests and what was not; their institutional influence within the structure of defense and foreign policy decision making was considerable.

Nitze went to the Chiefs with an "outline" of the deal, carefully casting it as his "own idea." The military leaders reacted noncommittally, neither rejecting nor supporting the plan. Nitze later noted that McFarlane was supposed to fill in the details of the package to the Chiefs and acquire their support but in the end never did so.[44]

In his memoirs, Shultz wrote that he "discussed fully" with the president the idea "that if offensive strategic weapons were drastically reduced, the needs for defenses against them would be far less."[45] Nitze stated that Shultz and McFarlane "presented the President with the idea of negotiations with the Soviets to bring about a compromise along the lines of the Monday Package."[46] The language employed by both men lends itself to loose construction; it suggests that the three did not acquire—or seek—Reagan's approval for the specific plan they were proposing, which tied an important limitation on SDI to offensive arms reductions and which they knew conflicted with Reagan's convictions.[47] There are some accounts that McFarlane purposefully kept his comments to Reagan on the subject of the deal vague, brief, and seemingly routine.[48]

During a mid-July meeting with Ambassador Dobrynin, with McFarlane and Nitze in attendance, Shultz discussed the idea of secret U.S.-Soviet negotiations leading to a possible offense-defense compromise. Dobrynin seemed to ignore the proposal. A little over two weeks later, he brought Shultz word that Moscow's reply to the plan was negative; Shultz concluded from this that "Moscow wanted to stop SDI in its tracks, not just moderate it."[49]

Shultz, McFarlane, and Nitze thus failed in their effort that summer to place restrictions on SDI in exchange for reductions of offensive forces. Yet they were undeterred from seeking an offense-defense trade-off along the basic lines of the Monday Package. Both of the elements that made up the deal—50 percent reductions in offensive forces and a ten-year nonwithdrawal clause from the ABM Treaty—would turn up in later negotiations between the United States and the USSR.

EARLY PREPARATIONS FOR THE SUMMIT

On June 1, the Soviets agreed to a Reagan-Gorbachev summit, to be held November 19 to 21 in Geneva. The following day, Moscow announced that Eduard Shevardnadze would replace Gromyko as Soviet foreign minister. The Reagan administration had little idea of what to expect from Shevardnadze, who had been first secretary of the Communist Party in Georgia; he was "a question mark to U.S. officials."[50] It was evident, however, that Shevardnadze's move to the Foreign Ministry represented a step by Gorbachev to place his allies in positions of influence. The fact that Gromyko no longer held sway over Soviet foreign policy was seen as a boon.[51]

The new Soviet foreign minister was due to meet Shultz and other counterparts in Helsinki at the end of July to mark the tenth anniversary of the Helsinki Final Act. In preparation for that meeting, the State Department's Bureau of Intelligence and Research (INR) sent Shultz a memo and a separate intelligence briefing paper that focused on a possible Soviet need for arms control, and in doing so addressed the impact of SDI on Soviet perceptions and behavior. The memo from INR stated that "some intelligence reporting and our analysis suggest the possibility that [Gorbachev] may have elevated [arms control] on his priorities because SDI could require a costly response that would draw on the same sectors of the economy that he had intended to use in his economic retooling. Thus, there is at least some possibility that Gorbachev may have in mind a 'fast track' on arms control." The memo noted that evidence of such a "fast track" approach could come from Shevardnadze in Helsinki and might include an attractive offer on START and suggestions that a START agreement could be worked out in tandem with a halt to any testing of "space weapons" for a given period of time.[52]

The longer intelligence briefing paper from INR to Shultz reinforced this and reported:

> Gorbachev is apparently interested in devoting more resources to his domestic economic needs. Controlled defense spending is one important factor. The keynote here is *not* defense *savings*; it is *controlled* defense *growth*. The other crucial economic factor is those types of high technology resources most likely to be in scarce supply overall, and especially during competition between economic reinvigoration and strategic defense. Thus, SDI represents a threat to this Soviet preference on two levels. The first is the high technology competition already mentioned. Second, on a military level SDI would require an increase in strategic forces to overcome the defensive system and a comparable Soviet system to reestablish strategic parity, or both. Intelligence reports from Moscow have indicated that the Soviet military is pressuring Gorbachev to follow both of these avenues in response to SDI.

The briefing paper then pointed to the possibility that the Soviets might offer a "quick-fix" proposal for START, and allow INF to proceed separately, in exchange for a limit or ban on SDI testing for a specific time period. Yet it emphasized that "such an agreement would not 'solve' the Soviet problem re SDI; it would largely postpone it. Nonetheless, this is as much as they can realistically hope to achieve at this time given the inchoate nature of US SDI."[53]

The INR memo and intelligence briefing paper provide revealing evidence both of how the State Department interpreted the USSR's perceptions of SDI and of the information that Shultz was receiving on the topic. The documents highlighted that SDI and Soviet economic reinvigoration were in direct conflict—literally in "competition." The intelligence paper did not overtly discuss whether SDI was directly contributing to Gorbachev's perceived need to undertake domestic economic reforms; this was outside its purview. Significantly, however, the paper revealed that U.S. intelligence thought the Soviet military regarded the threat from SDI as extremely serious. Given the influence of the military within the power and decision-making structures of the USSR, its demand for a massive response to the American program would have been seen by the Reagan administration as placing a considerable burden on Gorbachev's economic resources and planning. The paper left no doubt that Soviet concern over SDI might drive changes in Soviet foreign policy, at the least.

However, Shevardnadze did not unveil a new "fast-track" package at his meetings with Shultz in Helsinki, although he adopted a "far less polemical" tone from that of Gromyko. Shultz found that to be a hopeful sign.[54] The Shultz-Shevardnadze meetings in Helsinki were notable in another respect. Nitze, over dinner with his former INF negotiating counterpart, Yuli Kvitinsky, who was now the head of the Soviet defense and space group at the NST talks in Geneva, "tried out a version of the Monday Package." Kvitinsky was not impressed, and the dinner ended without "useful discussion."[55] Two months after that dinner in Helsinki, Nitze again outlined the Monday Package to Kvitinsky, in Moscow. He was similarly rebuffed.

In mid-July, Gorbachev sent a sharply worded letter to Reagan that lashed out at SDI, focusing on its potential to expand and destabilize the arms race. In an August interview with *Time* magazine, Gorbachev reiterated that "the broad-scale introduction of new achievements" in science and technology could lead to "an entirely new phase in the arms race." He made clear that in the absence of an agreement to prevent an arms race in space, the USSR would not join any effort to limit or reduce offensive nuclear arms.[56] Gorbachev could not escape early speculation among some in the U.S. media that his efforts to restrain the arms race, especially with regard to SDI, grew out of a sense of desperation. In July, the Moscow correspondent of *The Washington Post* reported having a "clear impression" that "Gorbachev wants to reach some sort of accommodation with the United States that would limit the scope of the arms race" and that "Gorbachev's interest in foreign affairs at this point is primarily linked to his domestic policies as the continued arms buildup and other foreign commitments would inevitably interfere with his plans to modernize Soviet society and improve living standards."[57]

Preparations for the Reagan-Gorbachev summit occupied much of the Reagan administration's attention during the autumn of 1985.[58] At the heart of the administration's deliberations lay differences among Reagan's principal advisers regarding SDI. Shultz and Nitze, with McFarlane in general agreement, argued that the United States should exchange restrictions on SDI—likely in the form of adherence to the ABM Treaty for a given time period—for reductions in offensive nuclear arms. They viewed it as a virtual certainty that the Soviets would not agree to a deal on offensive weapons *unless* SDI was curtailed. Shultz later wrote that "I wanted to make SDI a part of, and reason for, an agreement with the Soviets for massive arms reductions."[59]

Neither Shultz nor Nitze harbored any substantial expectations for missile defense, particularly in the near term.[60] They certainly did not perceive the costs of limiting but not killing SDI as outweighing the gains to be won from an agreement that sharply reduced offensive arms.[61] To Reagan, however, the elimination of nuclear arms, which was his ultimate goal, would result from a realized SDI, not from limitations placed upon the initiative. In promoting their view, Shultz, Nitze, and McFarlane had to be thoroughly cautious to not run afoul of Reagan's own conception of SDI.[62] In a memo to Reagan on the subject, Shultz cast his ideas in delicately worded language. The "choices being set up in the current debate," he wrote—of pursuing SDI full speed ahead or bargaining it away—were "false choices"; while ensuring that the United States retained the full benefit of SDI's potential, the administration should position SDI "as the key to implementation of the offensive nuclear reductions."[63]

Meanwhile, Weinberger and Perle held firmly to the notion that the United States should not accept any restrictions, limitations, or alterations to the program. McFarlane told the author that Perle and his colleagues at the Pentagon "felt more strongly about the actual technological development of it—at least that's what [Perle] said—and that this really was to become the foundation of our future strategic policy." "At State," noted McFarlane, "I think there it was entirely just a bargaining chip—get all you can for it."[64]

Yet Reagan reiterated, both within the administration and publicly, that SDI was not a bargaining chip. During a September news conference, the president's questioners demonstrated an intense interest in whether the United States would agree to an offense-defense trade-off at the upcoming Geneva summit ("Mr. President, as you head toward the summit, one of the big questions is whether you would be willing to explore the possibility of a tradeoff on the space weapons [for] big cuts in the Soviet arsenal."). Reagan responded that SDI "is too important to the world to have us be willing to trade that off for a different number of nuclear missiles when there are already more than enough to blow both countries out of the world."

The president did allow that there was "a great deal of room for negotiation" concerning the actual deployment of a missile defense system. Yet this was not because of a willingness on his part to accept a delay or limitation on deployment in order to strike a deal with the Soviets; it was, rather, due to his determination to follow through on abolishing nuclear weapons. As Reagan explained it, "The room would be if and when such a [defensive] weapon does prove feasible, then prior to any deployment, to sit down with the other nations of the world and say, 'Here. Now, isn't this an answer?' . . . I see it as the time then that you could say, 'Isn't this the answer to any of us having nuclear weapons?'" Later in the same press conference, the president returned to that theme: "I stop short of deployment because, as I said . . . I'm willing to talk to our allies, talk to them, and talk to the Soviets—to anyone about the meaning of it, if it could be used in such a way as to rid the world of the nuclear threat."[65] Reagan's statements illustrated the direct connection he drew between SDI and the elimination of all nuclear weapons. In Reagan's view, a realized missile defense would provide "the answer" to nuclear weapons; the "meaning" of SDI, if it was not in fact the abolition of nuclear arms, certainly included approaching that prospect. Reagan stated that view explicitly during an exchange with reporters in October. He said, "[W]e're not going to retreat from the research that could deliver to the world a defense against these nuclear weapons and finally bring us to the realization that we should eliminate the nuclear weapons entirely."[66] A week later, he declared,

> What I'm speaking of is a balance of safety, as opposed to a balance of terror. This is not only morally preferable, but it may result in getting rid of nuclear weapons altogether. It would be irresponsible and dangerous on our part to deny this promise to the world. And so, we're dealing with the real issue of how to free the entire world from the nuclear threat.[67]

EVOLVING U.S. PERCEPTIONS OF GORBACHEV AND THE SOVIET RESPONSE TO SDI

During a series of appearances and interviews in September, Reagan continued to emphasize his belief that the USSR's economy could not withstand an effort to keep up with a heightened Cold War challenge from the United States and that the Soviets could be forced to initiate reforms in their foreign and domestic policy. The terms and tone of his statements suggested a particular immediacy. The president implied that Gorbachev, in the near future, could be pressured into undertaking serious reforms in order to avert an internal crisis.[68]

During the late summer and early autumn of 1985, as the Reagan administration continued its preparations for the November summit in Geneva, the CIA began issuing its first assessments of Gorbachev's record and his possible policy courses in the future. In August, the agency issued a secret report entitled "Gorbachev's Approach to Societal Malaise: A Managed Revitalization." That paper stated that a "deep social malaise" had pervaded Soviet society since the mid-1970s, resulting in a population that "has become more demanding, less believing, and less pliable" vis-à-vis the ruling regime. It identified a number of interrelated sources of this malaise, particularly economic stagnation, unfulfilled official promises, and a growing sense that life in the Soviet Union compared less favorably to that in the West.

The CIA paper judged that Gorbachev "has articulated an assessment that social problems are serious and that they require immediate attention."[69] Yet it stated that while he had pledged not to reduce social spending, "economic resources are stretched to the limit, and there are powerful competing claimants for resource allocations, including heavy industry and the military establishment." The study concluded that Gorbachev, in the near term, would focus his efforts where he thought he could "effect change without major commitment of resources." However, for the Soviet leader to counter social malaise effectively "would require a major redirection of resources." Limited measures would not work and might both undermine Gorbachev's interests and pose a challenge to the economic stability of the USSR.[70]

Another CIA intelligence assessment, entitled "Gorbachev's Economic Agenda: Promises, Potentials, and Pitfalls," issued in September, stated the problem bluntly:

> Gorbachev faces an economy that cannot simultaneously maintain rapid growth in defense spending, satisfy demand for greater quantity and variety of consumer goods and services, invest the amounts required for economic modernization and expansion, and continue to support client-state economies. Gorbachev, in our view, has a clear understanding of these limitations; he is obviously extremely impatient that they be addressed now.[71]

The September report emphasized that the Soviet defense buildup was not only taxing the USSR's economy but actively undermining it. It also asserted that the Soviet Union's capacity to produce advanced technology was markedly inferior to the West's, and that the Soviet Union's relative inability to develop advanced technologies affected its comparative military standing, specifically in the area of high-technology weapons systems.

The assessment stated that Soviet military leaders were pressuring Gorbachev to increase the growth rates for defense spending in response to "the US defense modernization and the long-term implications of the Strategic Defense Initiative."[72] The CIA felt that, in Gorbachev's view, the overall U.S. arms buildup, and SDI in particular, represented an economic threat to the Soviet Union; those initiatives demanded a Soviet response in the form of increased resources for defense that the USSR could ill afford.

The paper raised the possibility that Gorbachev might attempt to reallocate some resources away from defense to the civilian domestic economy. This went a step beyond the State Department's intelligence bureau report to Shultz in the summer, which had stated that Gorbachev was seeking to control the growth of the Soviet defense burden. The CIA report judged it possible that Gorbachev might strive to enact "far-reaching proposals that he has only hinted at to date." Among the signals that would demonstrate his resolve to follow such a course, according to the CIA, would be "[n]ew dramatic initiatives to reach an accord at Geneva and concrete proposals for reduced tensions at the November meeting between the US President and the General Secretary, which might signal a willingness and desire to reduce the Soviet resource commitment to defense."[73]

While Reagan administration policy makers were being informed of this possibility by the CIA, the first hint from the Soviets themselves came during a late-September meeting between Reagan and Soviet Foreign Minister Shevardnadze at the White House. During that meeting, Shevardnadze brought a proposal from Moscow that put forth a 50 percent reduction in the two sides' strategic nuclear arsenals. Those cuts would be conditional upon a complete ban on SDI.[74]

While many within the Reagan administration thought the package served Soviet propaganda purposes, they also regarded it as a measure of progress for U.S. interests; this was the first time that the Soviets had submitted a real plan for significant cuts in nuclear weapons.[75] Shultz viewed it as a "breakthrough of principle."[76] The package strengthened the belief within the administration that the Soviets were genuinely worried about the state of their economy and about the implications of SDI and that those fears were affecting the USSR's approach to the United States. Shultz later wrote that the "Soviet preoccupation with our SDI program was obviously a prime motivation for their desire to reach an agreement with us"; McFarlane felt that Shevardnadze conveyed an almost "desperate" underlying concern for the USSR's economy at the meeting with Reagan.[77]

REAGAN AS "AN IMMOVABLE OBJECT" WITH RESPECT TO SDI

Shultz and McFarlane traveled to Moscow during the first week of November for meetings with Gorbachev and Shevardnadze in preparation for the Geneva summit. They found Gorbachev in a combative mood. At a session that included Shevardnadze, Dobrynin, Shultz, McFarlane, and U.S. Ambassador to the USSR Hartman, Gorbachev launched into a wide-ranging criticism of the Reagan administration's policy toward the Soviet Union. He defended the USSR's economic and technological capabilities and attacked what he characterized as a deliberate plan on the part of the Reagan administration to exert pressure on the USSR in these areas. "Does the United States think that its present policies of exercising pressure and strength, that these policies have brought the Soviet Union back to the negotiating table?" he asked. "If that is the kind of thinking that motivates those around the President, then no success is possible."[78]

After a discussion by Shultz on the subject of the dawning information age and the ability of open societies to take advantage of this—an attempt by Shultz to encourage Gorbachev to see it as being in his own interest to change the Soviet system—the meeting turned to the topic of SDI. Gorbachev grew passionate:

We know what's going on. We know why you're doing this. You're inspired by illusions. You think you're ahead of us in information. You think you're ahead of us in technology and that you can use these things to gain superiority over the Soviet Union. But this is an illusion. . . . You can rest assured that we will not help the United States get out of its ABM Treaty obligations. We will not assist you with the politics of it or in a technical way so that you can take the arms race into space.

Shultz responded by stating that the United States saw nothing wrong with defending itself and that the Soviet Union had worked on missile defense for many years.[79] This set the Soviet leader on another criticism of the "illusions" that underpinned U.S. policy toward the USSR, including SDI:

You are full of illusions. First, you believe that the Soviet Union is less economically powerful and therefore it would be weakened by an arms race. Second, that you have the higher technology and therefore SDI would give you superiority over the Soviet Union in weapons. Third, that the Soviet Union is more interested in negotiations in Geneva than you are. Fourth, that the Soviet Union only thinks of damaging U.S. interests in regions around the world. And fifth, that it would be wrong to trade with the Soviet Union because this would just raise its capability. These are all illusions. . . . The Soviets know how to meet their challenges.[80]

After accusations from Gorbachev that the U.S. economy depended heavily on a military-industrial complex, which prompted rebuttals from Shultz and McFarlane, the U.S. national security adviser stressed the importance that the Reagan administration placed on SDI and its intention to discuss the introduction of defenses.[81] At that, Gorbachev reiterated the Soviet position that any prospect for a strategic arms deal rested upon the United States' ceasing the development of SDI. He strongly implied that any real progress in the overall U.S.-Soviet relationship, especially at the upcoming summit, would depend upon that caveat as well. "The Soviet Union will only compromise on the condition that there is no militarization of space," he declared. Referring to the Reagan administration's insistence on pursuing SDI, the

Soviet leader stated, "I hope that this is not your last word. If so, nothing will result from the negotiation."[82] Gorbachev asserted that in the
absence of an agreement curtailing SDI, the Soviets would engage in
a buildup of offensive arms aimed at overwhelming any defense; at the
same time, he insinuated that the USSR might be willing to eliminate
all nuclear arms if the United States abandoned SDI. Shultz offered
no reply to either comment.[83]

In the wake of the four-hour session in Moscow, the U.S. delegation reported back to Washington that Gorbachev's foremost priority
was to negotiate an end to SDI. That objective seemed to be heavily
influencing Moscow's approach to the United States across a range of
issues, and Gorbachev clearly intended to hold the summit hostage to
Soviet demands for limitations on SDI.[84]

After returning to Washington, Shultz wrote Reagan a long memo
in preparation for the Geneva summit. He emphasized that Gorbachev wanted "[a]bove all, to stop the SDI program. Gorbachev
made this clear in Moscow. He will press you hard on this issue. He
may not have made up his mind on how to handle other questions—
bilateral, regional and human rights issues—absent agreement on
SDI."[85] In his diary, Reagan wrote, "Gorbachev is adamant we must
cave in on SDI. Well, this will be a case of an irresistible force meeting
an immovable object."[86]

The U.S. delegation to the Moscow meeting brought back reports
to Washington that Gorbachev was conscious of his nation's economic
and technological difficulties and that this was affecting his foreign
policy. McFarlane later commented, "when we came home, we told
the president that [Gorbachev was] interested, genuinely interested, in
making some progress to bring greater stability to the relationship so
that he could get on with solving the enormous problems inside the
Soviet Union, and that that seemed to us to be a genuine agenda."[87] At
a secret White House briefing for senior staff a few days after his return
from Moscow, McFarlane said that "the stresses they face on their side
are very, very grave now."[88]

Reagan's long-standing beliefs about the strain that military ex-
penditure was putting on the Soviet economy took on increasing im-

mediacy. He engaged in public diplomacy to pressure Gorbachev to alter Soviet priorities. In a radio address, Reagan stated that "since the 1970's the Soviet Union has been engaged in a military buildup which far exceeds any rational definition of its defensive needs. These policies have inflicted bitter costs upon the Soviet peoples. . . . Mr. Gorbachev can change this; he can set in train a policy of arms reductions and lasting peace. By shifting resources from armaments to people, he can enable his nation to enjoy far more economic growth."[89] During a speech before the U.N. General Assembly in October, Reagan declared that he welcomed "enthusiastically" an ideological, economic, and scientific competition between the United States and the USSR. He added that he was seeking a race between the nations in missile defense technology: "If we're destined by history to compete, militarily, to keep the peace, then let us compete in systems that defend our societies rather than weapons which can destroy us both."[90] In an interview with the BBC a few days later, Reagan reiterated his advocacy of a "peaceful competition." Asked about his optimism that Gorbachev might moderate the USSR's foreign policy, Reagan responded that Gorbachev "has some practical problems in his own country, some problems of how long can they sustain an economy that provides for their people under the terrific cost of building up and pursuing this expansionist policy and this great military buildup."[91]

In early November, Reagan privately set out his thoughts on Gorbachev's general approach to foreign policy and on the Soviet leader's reaction to SDI. He wrote this assessment by hand on yellow legal paper:

> I believe Gorbachev is a highly intelligent leader, totally dedicated to traditional Soviet goals. He will be a formidable negotiator and will try to make Soviet foreign and military policy more effective.
>
> He is (as are all Soviet General Secretaries) dependent on the Soviet Communist hierarchy and will be out to prove to them his strength and dedication to Soviet traditional goals.
>
> If he really wants an arms control agreement, it will only be because he wants to reduce the burden of defense spending that is stagnating the Soviet economy. This could contribute to his opposition to

our SDI. He doesn't want to face the cost of competing with us. . . . Any new move on our part, such as SDI, forces them to revamp, and change their plan at great cost.[92]

Reagan's private views of Gorbachev's inclinations and intentions were thus more or less in accord with what he was saying publicly in 1985. The last paragraph of Reagan's handwritten assessment also revealed an important aspect of the president's thinking that he was *not* declaring in public. It confirmed that, by 1985 at the latest, Reagan believed that the Soviets viewed the cost of responding to SDI to be a significant, and perhaps unacceptable, threat to the USSR's economy.

Reagan shied away from publicly identifying SDI as a specific means of applying economic and technological pressure on the Soviet system.[93] Yet by November 1985, he perceived that the Soviet leadership viewed SDI as having exactly that effect. Reagan was sophisticated enough to recognize that public declarations that SDI was pressuring the Soviet Union's economy and technological base would muddle the message of a program that promised to "threaten no one."[94]

While avoiding public comment concerning SDI's impact on Soviet perceptions of economic vulnerability, as the Geneva summit approached Reagan continuously elaborated upon his notion of how SDI could lead to the abolition of nuclear weapons. In September, he declared that after development of a missile defense he anticipated the United States and the USSR "verifiably eliminating [nuclear] weapons, and then being able to turn to . . . other nations that maybe have some, and saying, 'Look, we've done this now. Come on, get in line. You do it, too. Let's rid the world of this nightmare and this threat.'"[95] In late October, Reagan called SDI "probably one of the most momentous things in a century." He reiterated that the United States would share a missile defense system with the USSR if nuclear weapons were eliminated entirely.[96] Yet he warned that in the event the USSR did not agree to total nuclear disarmament, the United States would proceed with deploying the defense; he was not "giving anyone a veto over this defensive system."[97]

In November 1985, just a few days before the Reagan-Gorbachev summit, the director of central intelligence issued a classified, twenty-page National Intelligence Estimate (NIE) entitled "Domestic Stresses on the Soviet Union." NIEs were regularly scheduled studies, prepared on an interagency basis by various intelligence services within the U.S. government, which addressed a particular topic, usually relating to one foreign nation, and analyzed likely future outcomes.[98] Noting that domestic stresses within the USSR had been accumulating for "many years," the document was the "first attempt to assess the impact of these internal Soviet problems." It also estimated Gorbachev's probable response to those challenges.

The report stated that "during the rest of the 1980s and well beyond, the domestic affairs of the USSR will be dominated by the efforts of the regime to grapple with" its economic and social problems, "which will also have an influence on Soviet foreign and national security behavior."[99] It estimated that the Soviet Union's internal shortcomings would not immediately threaten the ruling regime's political control or precipitate outright economic collapse, but that the situation would only worsen in the future. It also added that "we do not exclude the possibility that these tensions could eventually confront the regime with challenges that it cannot effectively contain without systemic change and the risks to control that would accompany such change." In setting forth its outlook for the long-term prospects of internal trends within the USSR, the study pointed to what it called "the essential dilemma of the Soviet system":

> The Soviet system of rule is optimized for maintaining tight central control over political and economic life. While this system served to drive the country through forced-draft industrialization in the era of steel and coal, it is highly unsuited to achieving the desired pace of technological advances throughout the economy under modern conditions. Unless the system is reformed in fundamental ways, it will hamper the growth its leaders seek because it stifles the innovation on which technological and social progress depends. But the liberalization that would permit and encourage innovation on the scale the system seeks would be unacceptable to the regime because it would inevitably entail reductions in centralized political power.[100]

The paper judged that while "a sense that the system's survival is on the line in the very long term" pervaded the Soviet leadership, Gorbachev's approach to addressing domestic problems was "mixed, but essentially conservative."[101] It did note, however, that Gorbachev could be forced to take "some steps along the lines of the liberal option . . . not so much as a deliberate strategy of the new regime, but rather as responses to new pressures deriving from the achievements and failures of the much more conservative strategy it is likely to pursue."[102]

The intelligence paper stated that the Soviet leadership's concern with domestic issues would lead in the near future to changes in the USSR's international behavior, although not in its ultimate goals. The NIE asserted that the high priority given to the military at the expense of other demands was producing particularly deleterious effects on the Soviet economy: "The military-industrial complex absorbs vast resources directly and indirectly, constituting a heavy burden on other social goals."[103] The study drew special attention to the fact that the USSR's overall difficulty in introducing high technology directly affected the Soviet military's competitiveness, claiming that "technological backwardness constrains Soviet ability to compete in high-technology weapons development."[104] It judged that Soviet military technology was unlikely to stay "fully competitive" if the United States and its allies continued to sustain a high level of commitment to advanced-technology programs such as SDI.[105]

The NIE asserted that the Soviet leadership felt particularly threatened by what it perceived as pressure on its internal system from its adversaries. "Soviet domestic problems," the paper stated, "have heightened the regime's sense of vulnerability to various foreign influences."[106] Furthermore, it claimed that "Soviet leaders have probably believed to some extent their own propaganda to the effect that the United States was seeking to undermine the Soviet system by breaking its economy in a renewed arms competition, use of economic sanctions, and increased subversive measures."[107] The NIE concluded that Gorbachev wanted "a breathing space to ease the task of managing Soviet internal problems."[108]

Reagan administration officials throughout the various national security branches would have paid attention to the NIE.[109] It was the first to look at the overall impact of internal Soviet problems on that nation's domestic and foreign policy; that it was released shortly before the Geneva summit would undoubtedly have spurred interest. That the Soviets felt economically pressured by military competition with the United States was echoed elsewhere within the Reagan administration during the run-up to the Geneva summit. According to Adelman, the State Department briefing book prepared for Reagan prior to the summit stated that the president should emphasize to Gorbachev that reducing defense spending would relieve pressure on the Soviet economy.[110]

While many Reagan administration officials believed by late 1985 that the Soviet leadership viewed SDI as a source of economic and technological threat to the Soviet internal system, they continued to disagree over how to approach the initiative in the context of arms control negotiations. Despite Reagan's constant declarations as the Geneva summit approached that he would not allow restrictions on SDI in exchange for reductions in offensive nuclear missiles, groups of his principal advisers opposed each other on that issue. Weinberger and Perle maintained that SDI must proceed without impediments. Shultz, Nitze, and McFarlane wanted at least the possibility of a trade-off. McFarlane hoped that the basis for a START deal could be worked out at the summit; he figured that it would require from the U.S. side a commitment to adhere to the ABM Treaty for a set period of time, as sketched out in Nitze's Monday Package.[111]

The U.S. delegation to the Geneva summit consisted of a large number of officials, including Shultz, McFarlane, Matlock, Nitze, Adelman, and Perle. Weinberger was not among them. He later stated that his exclusion "was largely McFarlane's doing"; McFarlane thought he would be "disruptive" and "didn't think my views should be before the president."[112]

A few days before the summit began, Weinberger sent a letter to Reagan in which he called on the president not to accept restrictions on SDI and to hold a hard line on an array of arms control issues. The text of the letter was immediately leaked to *The Washington Post*, prompting the media to report extensively on schisms within the administration.[113] In Geneva, McFarlane was publicly critical of Weinberger's missive, implying that it was intended preemptively to block progress toward arms control at the summit. McFarlane later stated that Weinberger, in writing the letter, was expressing "genuine concern" that Reagan would not have the defense secretary's advice at the summit, while "on the other hand he would be listening to me and to Shultz," with whom Weinberger "did not agree." McFarlane went on to say, "I think it accomplished its purpose. And frankly, although I was kind of dismissive of it in public at the time, it kind of helped us. In the sense that for Gorbachev to see that Reagan is being pressured from the right—to be tougher—was a very good signal to send."[114] Meanwhile, Reagan concurred with the substance of Weinberger's letter. In his diary, he wrote, "I agree with Cap."[115]

THE GENEVA SUMMIT

The U.S. memoranda of conversation (memcons) of the Reagan-Gorbachev summit in Geneva, held November 19 to 21, 1985, were declassified and released by the U.S. government in 2000.[116] The memcons reveal much about Reagan himself and the role of SDI in American policy during his tenure. One startling fact is the extent of the interaction and dialogue between the two leaders. Virtually no one else spoke during the plenary meetings, and the two men spent a significant amount of time in one-on-one conversations. This interaction famously established a level of familiarity, if not warmth, that set the pattern for later meetings and itself was an important factor in U.S.-Soviet relations during the denouement of the Cold War.

A second point is that the issue of SDI dominated the sessions between Reagan and Gorbachev. The latter made it clear that blocking SDI was a principal aim of the Soviet Union and that this was the sole condition on which he would agree to arms reductions and even an improvement in relations overall. Underlying Gorbachev's insistence on limiting SDI was a persistent defensiveness concerning the USSR's economic and technological circumstances. Reagan, for his part, continually pushed his personal vision of SDI, laying out for the Soviet leader the same conception of the program as a means of achieving a way out of the nuclear terror and abolishing nuclear weapons that he had espoused since the program's announcement.

By the time of the Geneva summit, Reagan also believed that SDI constituted an economic threat in the eyes of the Soviet leadership, in a way that he may or may not have intended when he first announced the program. That Reagan so passionately defended SDI and attempted to convince his Soviet counterpart of the rightness of that cause at Geneva manifested the combination of idealistic visions and hardheadedness that characterized his worldview and approach.

Following an introductory one-on-one meeting that opened the summit, Gorbachev denounced American "delusions" regarding the USSR. The Soviet leader claimed that he knew that the U.S. "ruling class" held a set of "delusions." The delusions listed by Gorbachev were that the Soviet economy was in a perilous state and was vulnerable to pressure from an arms race that would generate leverage for the United States; that the USSR was lagging behind America in high technology such that the United States could achieve military superiority; and that the Soviet Union itself desired military superiority. Gorbachev then abruptly shifted into an extended discussion on how military spending hampered economic growth, claiming that both the United States and the USSR would "do better if they could release [defense] resources to the civilian economy." The Soviet leader returned again to his theme that the Reagan administration thought it "should use the arms race to frustrate Gorbachev's plans, to weaken the Soviet Union." He asserted that in fact the USSR "is an enormous country that will take care of its problems."

In his presentation, Gorbachev made clear that "the central question" for the USSR was arms control and curtailing the arms race. He declared that negotiations would come to nought, however, if the Reagan administration believed that the USSR desired improved relations because of weakness.[117] Such moments of unprompted querulousness on the part of the Soviet leader recurred throughout the summit.

Reagan finished the first plenary meeting with a discourse of his own (during which he noted that U.S. defense spending accounted for a relatively small percentage of the nation's gross national product). At the end of that discussion, Reagan broached the topic of SDI directly, asserting that it was a long-term research project and that he was not sure if it would work, but that if it did, the United States would "make it available to everyone."[118]

During the second plenary meeting, disagreements over SDI crowded out other topics. Discussing the Soviets' opposition to SDI, Gorbachev said, "Even now, due to computer technology, one side could get ahead in space. But we can match any challenge, though you might not think so." The Soviet leader then claimed that SDI would lead to an all-out arms race in space, in both defensive and offensive weapons, and that because many scientists had stated that any shield could be pierced, the system would make sense only to guard against a retaliatory strike. Gorbachev was adamant that if the United States went ahead with SDI, the USSR would respond. At one point he stated that such a response would take the form of a buildup of missiles to overwhelm the defense, at another that the Soviets would field their own system that would be both simpler and more effective than the American version.

Gorbachev was clear, however, that without a ban on space weapons (i.e., SDI), there would be no reductions in offensive arms. This attempt to pressure Reagan was not subtle. Gorbachev implied that Moscow would be forced to "rethink" its approach to the entire U.S.-Soviet relationship if no agreement could be reached to stop SDI.[119]

In response, Reagan stated his belief that the MAD doctrine was "uncivilized." He reiterated that if strategic defenses proved feasible, "we would prefer to sit down and get rid of nuclear weapons, and with them, the threat of war."[120]

Reagan and Gorbachev then tangled over whether the two sides should move ahead with reductions of offensive arms in the absence of an agreement to limit SDI. That discussion spilled over into the famous one-on-one "fireside" session at the end of the summit's first day.

At that private meeting, Reagan handed Gorbachev a set of proposals outlining 50 percent cuts in strategic weapons and a plan to eliminate INF arsenals. Gorbachev responded that the agreement concluded by Shultz and Gromyko in January 1985 dictated that reductions in offensive weapons must be resolved in their interrelationship with space weapons. Reagan countered that missile defense did not constitute a space weapon inasmuch as it was defensive in nature, and that in any case such a system would be shared with the USSR; he again emphasized that he sought negotiations to see how SDI could bring about the elimination of nuclear weapons.[121] He commented that "all this could be covered by an agreement under which we as well as others could agree that no country would have a monopoly" on missile defense. Gorbachev asked Reagan why he should believe the president's claims that the United States would share a defensive system. Reagan asserted that negotiators could draft a formal agreement to that effect that both leaders could sign.

Gorbachev, with emotion, went on to criticize SDI as opening an arms race in "a new sphere," arguing that the ensuing weapons might not be construed as purely defensive. Toward the end of the one-on-one session, Gorbachev stated that "the Soviet Government had really carefully considered everything that had been said by the President with regard to SDI, especially all his arguments in favor of SDI." The general secretary understood that the "idea of strategic defense had captivated the President's imagination." But "as a political leader," Gorbachev "could not possibly agree with the President with regard to this topic."[122]

With the private meeting winding down, Reagan asked Gorbachev to think further about the possibility of agreeing to share a missile defense. The Soviet leader then embarked on a passionate statement that constituted a virtual plea. He "appealed to the President to recognize the true signal he was conveying to him" that the Soviet Union "did indeed wish to establish a new relationship with the United States." "The Soviet Union had conducted a deep analysis of the entire situation," Gorbachev continued, "and had come to the conclusion that it was necessary precisely now to proceed on the basis of the actual situation; later it would be too late." This conclusion "was why the Soviet Union had tabled serious and comprehensive" arms control proposals, Gorbachev said. It was "the result of a thorough assessment and profound understanding of where the two countries stood today." He concluded this appeal by asking the president not to regard the USSR's sincere desire for an improved relationship "as weakness on the part of Gorbachev and the Soviet leadership." Reagan did not reply.[123]

Over the course of the first day, Reagan and Gorbachev developed a functional relationship that allowed them to discuss issues largely without acrimony. Walking back from their "fireside" one-on-one, the leaders agreed to meet twice during the next two years, in Washington and then in Moscow; this in and of itself had been an important objective for each side heading into the meeting.

The relatively calm atmosphere that the two leaders had established at Geneva was severely tested during the third plenary session, held on the second day of the summit, when they engaged in a heated exchange of views on SDI, and when tensions at the summit reached a climax. During this session, Gorbachev declared that he "did not know what lay at the bottom of the U.S. position" concerning SDI. He stated that he "was concerned that the position was fed by an illusion that the U.S. was ahead in the technology and information transfer systems on which space systems would be based, and that a possibility therefore existed to obtain military superiority over the USSR." The Soviet leader went on to reiterate that he intended to hold to the Shultz-Gromyko January framework to stop the arms race on Earth and prevent it in space; if the United States departed from that by seeking offensive cuts without restrictions on SDI, he did not know when they could meet on such issues again, and "everything at the Geneva NST talks would come to a halt."[124]

Reagan countered that SDI was defensive only, that it would not lead to an arms race in space, and that the United States would share any missile defense technology. "If defensive systems could be found," the president stated, "they would be made available to all. This would end the nuclear nightmare for the U.S. people, the Soviet people, all people."

In response, Gorbachev declared that he "understood the President's arguments but found them unconvincing." Dispensing with diplomatic niceties, the Soviet leader stated that Reagan's arguments "contained many emotional elements, elements which were part of one man's dream." Gorbachev asserted that SDI would "open a new arms race in space" and that the president "would be held responsible."[125] In an atmosphere of growing antagonism and frustration, Reagan asked whether he was not unjustified in suspecting a threat to the United States from Soviet missiles. He added that the United States "was trying simply to see if there was a way to end the world's nightmare about nuclear weapons." Gorbachev then badgered Reagan, asking him three times why the president would not accept his assurances that the Soviet Union "would never attack." Gorbachev interrupted Reagan's answer each time to repeat the question. When he was able to respond, Reagan stated that "no individual could say to the U.S. people that they should rely on his personal faith rather than on sound defense."

Gorbachev replied by casting aspersions on the sincerity of Reagan's claims that the United States would share SDI. He then engaged in a second monologue on the motives behind the differing policies of the United States and the USSR. "The Soviet Union," Gorbachev said, "was prepared to compromise. But the U.S. had the impression that the USSR was weak and could be painted into a corner." Then he again blasted SDI as opening a new sphere in the arms race. Gorbachev declared:

> The Soviet Union had said it would agree to a separate INF agreement, to deep cuts [in START]. These had not been easy decisions. The Soviets had their concerns. But they felt that if steps were not taken in the next year to 18 months, the consequences would be grave. The President wanted to catch the "Firebird" of SDI by using the U.S. technological advantage. There would be disillusionment, but it would come too late, as the "infernal" train would already be moving.

Immediately after dubbing SDI "the infernal train," however, the Soviet leader backed off. Gorbachev acknowledged that "perhaps his remarks had grown a bit heated." He had "meant only to convey to the President the depth of Soviet concern on that issue."[126]

U.S. officials later referred to that moment as a turning point in the summit. They perceived that Gorbachev had come to Geneva determined to end SDI but that, faced with Reagan's fervent adherence to the cause of missile defense, the Soviet leader had realized that his counterpart would not waver.[127] According to Shultz, Gorbachev arrived at the conclusion that "there was no way in any negotiation he was going to talk the President out of that research program."[128]

The two continued to skirmish over SDI, however, with Reagan sticking to his message that missile defense would serve as a catalyst for, and guarantor of, the elimination of nuclear weapons and that the United States would share a system that it devised. Gorbachev stated that he wanted to emphasize the Soviet position on missile defense to Reagan because it was "the key question of their meeting." The question of SDI, he declared, "would define the future political dialogue between the two countries, the nature of the Geneva negotiations, the outcome of important decisions on domestic policy in both countries." Having overtly expressed that the American pursuit of SDI would directly affect Soviet domestic policy, Gorbachev continued, in a manner both resigned and threatening, that it "appeared that the President was very committed to the development, testing, and deployment of space weapons. The Soviets would have to consider and base their policy on this fact." Gorbachev then remarked that he felt that Reagan's advisers feared the president would lose prestige if he abandoned SDI, claiming that in fact Reagan would benefit from such a move.

Reagan was displeased by these last comments. He told Gorbachev that he thought the conversation had gone "too far" and suggested "a more reasonable approach."[129] The president reiterated his position that arms cuts should proceed without limitations on SDI. Gorbachev countered that the Soviets "wanted to lock the door against space weapons—to bar it or even drive in nails—and then begin reductions." Reagan replied to Gorbachev that reductions of nuclear arsenals "would make it possible to save considerable expenditures, e.g., for modernization." Gorbachev did not respond.

As the discussion of SDI and arms reductions wound down, Gorbachev expressed disappointment that the two sides could not reach agreement on a deal that would block SDI and cut offensive weapons.

He explained that the Soviets had expected that "when the two leaders met, after months of preparation, it would be possible to reach solutions and to clarify what had been agreed to in January." For his part, Reagan expressed his inability "to comprehend how, in a world full of nuclear weapons, it was so horrifying to seek to develop a defense against this awful threat, how an effort to reduce nuclear weapons could break down because of such an attempt."[130]

With no agreement possible on SDI or on reductions in offensive nuclear weapons, the two leaders turned for the few remaining sessions of the summit to settling on a concluding joint statement for public release. In the end, that document, in addition to outlining a variety of minor bilateral initiatives, announced the intention of the two leaders to meet again in Washington and Moscow and declared that both sides had agreed in principle to both 50 percent reductions in strategic nuclear arms and an interim INF arrangement. The statement avoided specific mention of SDI, instead reaffirming the ambiguous and contested framework set out by Shultz and Gromyko in January.[131]

THE AFTERMATH OF THE GENEVA SUMMIT

Reagan's advisers noted after the summit that the president felt he had developed a good working relationship with Gorbachev. The president saw his counterpart as someone who was different from previous Soviet leaders and with whom he could deal constructively. Reagan mentioned to his advisers that he felt that Gorbachev, though a devoted Marxist-Leninist, was possibly open to making changes and taking new approaches. He also believed, based on his interpretation of some casual comments by the Soviet leader, that deep down, Gorbachev believed in God. This was a "big deal" for Reagan, Adelman later said. It contributed to his belief that Gorbachev could possibly depart from past Soviet policies and practices, if encouraged.[132]

In his public comments following the summit, the president struck an optimistic tone, declaring that the U.S.-Soviet relationship was "headed in the right direction" and referring frequently to the "fresh start" in the two countries' relations that he and Gorbachev had catalyzed at their meetings.[133] He left little doubt as to why he thought such a fresh start was possible. "If there is one conclusion to draw from [the summit]," he said, "it's that America's policies are working. . . . American strength has caught the Soviets' attention . . . we are in the forefront of a powerful, historic tide for freedom."[134]

Reagan emphasized that one of the successes of the summit lay in his demonstrating to Gorbachev that he would not budge on SDI. During a radio address two days after the summit, he stated, "I think it's fair to point out that the Soviets' main aim at Geneva was to force us to drop SDI. I think I can also say that after Geneva Mr. Gorbachev understands we have no intention of doing so—far from it."[135] In the wake of the summit, the president reiterated his vision of SDI as an enabler of the eventual elimination of nuclear weapons. In an address to a joint session of Congress that met immediately upon the president's return from Geneva, Reagan declared that an effective missile defense would mean that "nations could defend themselves against missile attack and mankind, at long last, [could] escape the prison of mutual terror. And this is my dream."[136]

The president had tried to bring Gorbachev to agree to this vision during the Geneva summit. Reagan's insistence in that regard had clearly frustrated Gorbachev, for whom stopping SDI was—by his own admission—of the highest importance to the Soviet leadership.

Gorbachev's appeals to Reagan at Geneva were rooted in his circumstances. Gorbachev obviously wanted to convey to Reagan that he genuinely desired better relations and arms control agreements with the United States and that the Soviet leadership felt it could not delay achieving those objectives. At the same time as Gorbachev asked or warned Reagan—depending on whether other Soviet officials were present—not to perceive this new approach as deriving from a sense of vulnerability, his appeals indicated that the Soviet leadership did in fact fear the economic and technological consequences of a heightened arms race with the United States, particularly with respect to SDI.

As will be seen in the next chapter, Gorbachev's comments at Geneva validated the growing sense among Reagan administration officials that Moscow was seeking to reduce Cold War tensions and to address its internal problems. No one in the U.S. administration was more attuned to this than Reagan himself. In early December, he stated:

> I believe that, for the first time, [the Soviets] recognize, with some of their problems, that the arms race has helped create those problems for them. They have dwelt so much on military buildup that they've had to deny their people many of the things that you and I think are just everyday—in our ability to go down to the store and buy them. Well, they don't have such privileges. And we hope that with that as a help that maybe we can begin a reduction [of nuclear weapons].[137]

As in his previous remarks on the topic, Reagan claimed that the Soviet leadership feared the economic ramifications of an arms race in general. He did not publicly point to the effect of SDI on the Soviets' perceptions of their economic vulnerability, despite his belief, by November 1985, that Gorbachev "doesn't want to face the cost of competing with us" in the initiative. By the end of 1985, both Reagan and many of his advisers had come to see SDI as a useful and powerful strategic tool for furthering the administration's policy goals with respect to the Soviet Union. Intelligence reports, Soviet actions, and Soviet leaders' statements provided evidence that the leadership of the USSR perceived SDI as an economic and technological threat at a time of considerable strain on the Soviet system. It appeared that the economic and technological pressure building on the Soviet system could contribute to a possible need for foreign and domestic policy changes in the USSR.

AN IMPORTANT CHANGE

On December 4, 1985, a few weeks after the summit in Geneva, McFarlane resigned as national security adviser, citing family financial responsibilities.[138] He was replaced by his deputy, Poindexter. McFarlane soon came to regret his resignation. He later called it an "error" and a "cop-out." In the wake of his resignation, McFarlane worried that the administration would be less effective at sustaining funding and momentum for SDI and thus that the United States would begin to lose a crucial source of pressure on the USSR. He had long held a very particular view of SDI: that its principal benefit lay in forcing Moscow to agree to reduce its nuclear arsenal, particularly its ICBMs, and that limits on SDI could be part of an offense-defense deal. McFarlane regretted that he could no longer seek to guide the administration toward that end.[139]

To Shultz and Nitze, the replacement of McFarlane with Poindexter represented an unwelcome development; McFarlane tended to side with them on matters of U.S.-Soviet relations and arms control.[140] On the whole, Poindexter remained more neutral on substantive issues and at the same time provided Weinberger with greater direct access to Reagan than McFarlane had done.[141]

Unlike McFarlane, Poindexter had no particular personal agenda for SDI or for arms control generally. Poindexter did not see SDI as a bargaining chip to be traded away, and would not attempt to manage the program toward that end, as McFarlane had done. Among Reagan's advisers, Poindexter was also one of the least inclined to try to restrain Reagan from radically changing the status quo.

CHAPTER

VI

1986

B Y PRIOR agreement between Reagan and Gorbachev, a televised
message from each of the two leaders was broadcast in the other's
country on New Year's Day 1986. In his message to the people of the
USSR, Reagan emphasized his desire to see all nuclear weapons abolished and linked nuclear abolition to the creation of a defense against
missiles. After discussing U.S. goals for reducing offensive nuclear
arms, Reagan stated that it was his

> hope that one day we will be able to eliminate these [nuclear] weapons
> altogether and rely increasingly for our security on defense systems
> that threaten no one. Both the United States and Soviet Union are
> doing research on the possibilities of applying new technologies to the
> cause of defense. If these technologies become a reality, it is my dream
> that, well, to one day free us all from the threat of nuclear destruction.[1]

Gorbachev, in his message to Americans, attacked SDI. He declared that it was "senseless to seek greater security for oneself through

new types of weapons. At present, every new step in the arms race increases the danger and the risk for both sides and for all humankind." He reiterated the Soviet position that the joint goals of arms negotiations were "cutting back nuclear arsenals and keeping outer space peaceful"—the latter being Soviet terminology for stopping SDI. Gorbachev also stated that he urgently sought to reach agreement on offensive arms and SDI: "We would very much like" to reach a deal, he said, "this year."[2]

On the morning of January 15, 1986, two weeks after the exchange of the New Year's messages, Reagan released a statement on the ongoing U.S.-Soviet nuclear and space negotiations in Geneva. Again Reagan underscored his desire to abolish all nuclear weapons, declaring that it was his "hope that we can one day eliminate them altogether."[3] Later on that same morning of the fifteenth, Reagan received a letter from Gorbachev in which the Soviet leader proposed the elimination of all nuclear weapons by the year 2000. That elimination of nuclear weapons, Gorbachev wrote, would be conditional upon the United States' forswearing any "development, testing, and deployment" of SDI.[4]

Reagan's advisers did not believe that Gorbachev genuinely wanted to abolish nuclear weapons. They considered the proposal a propaganda ploy. Several, including Matlock, Adelman, and Nitze, noted that it resembled Soviet general and complete disarmament proposals from the Khrushchev era. Administration officials' belief that the letter was meant for propaganda purposes was deepened by the Soviets' making the proposal public, with much fanfare, on the same day it was sent to Reagan.[5] Reagan's aides also feared that Gorbachev's proposal would encourage the president in his own belief about abolition. In his memoirs, Matlock wrote, "In contrast to most of his advisers, Reagan believed nuclear weapons could and should be abolished, and now, for the first time, a Soviet leader was making concrete proposals to that end."[6] "This is going to give us great problems," Poindexter told Matlock as they reviewed the letter.[7]

As the president's advisers anticipated, Reagan "was quite taken" by the proposal.[8] Meeting with Shultz and Nitze to discuss the letter on the afternoon of the fifteenth, Reagan expressed the view that Gorbachev's plan for the abolition of nuclear arms was not ambitious enough: "Why wait until the end of the century for a world without nuclear weapons?"[9]

Although Reagan was "enthusiastic," according to Shultz and Nitze, about Gorbachev's plan to abolish nuclear weapons, he resolutely opposed giving up SDI.[10] Gorbachev's letter made a nuclear-free world dependent upon the United States' abandoning SDI; in Reagan's mind, the abolition of nuclear weapons and a defense against missiles were inextricably linked. Matlock told the author in an interview, "The fact is that Reagan did like the idea of elimination [of nuclear weapons]. He wanted it, but he wanted elimination to be coupled with a strategic defense. As he repeatedly told Gorbachev, 'You cannot erase from men's minds how to make these weapons, and even if we eliminate them, and the current powers eliminate them, some madman may develop them in the future; we'll need a defense against them if we're going to eliminate them.'" Matlock continued, "For that reason, he coupled elimination with SDI. But Gorbachev wanted to kill SDI and still get a commitment to elimination. That just wasn't going to work with Reagan."[11]

Reagan responded immediately to Gorbachev's letters by issuing two brief statements, one on the fifteenth and a slightly longer one the next day. Both statements emphasized his own support for the abolition of nuclear weapons, welcomed Gorbachev's move toward that goal, and promised "careful study" of the Soviet proposal.[12] While both statements avoided specifics, the longer one explicitly rejected Gorbachev's making nuclear abolition dependent upon a ban on SDI, declaring, "We believe strategic defenses can make a significant contribution to a world free from nuclear weapons."[13]

The Reagan administration's deliberations over how to respond more fully to Gorbachev's proposal sparked debate among the president's aides as to how to cope with Reagan's nuclear abolitionism. Poindexter maintained that the best approach was to "finesse" it. Poindexter, who as national security adviser interacted frequently with Reagan, was fascinated by him. He told the author in an interview that "the president was an introvert. He was a quiet, thoughtful guy. In the

Oval Office, he was an introvert; when he left it, he became an extrovert." According to Poindexter, Reagan thought about eliminating nuclear weapons—and about SDI as a means of catalyzing and guaranteeing that elimination—"a lot. Not in any great detail, but the fundamental principles." He also recognized that Reagan was not idly wishing for a world without nuclear weapons but was actively and quite seriously trying to bring it about.[14]

While Poindexter opposed Reagan's nuclear abolitionism, he did not do so because he thought it a bad idea in principle, as most of his colleagues did. Poindexter was not a strategic specialist by training, and at times he was happily willing to depart from what many others, both in and out of government, viewed as strategic orthodoxy (for example, his compunction-free involvement in the announcement of SDI). Though Poindexter held no illusions that the United States and the USSR could agree to abolish all nuclear weapons, much less carry out such an agreement, in principle he was "generally . . . in favor of eliminating all nuclear weapons, as the president always wanted to do."[15] As a "tactical issue," however, Poindexter thought Reagan's nuclear abolitionism disastrous. In Poindexter's opinion, seeking the elimination of nuclear weapons was "a very, very difficult position to support [at] home." He judged that the military and the Congress would never go along with it and that if Reagan were seen to be seriously pursuing a world without nuclear weapons, he would be "open to severe criticism."[16]

In "finessing" the president's nuclear abolitionism, Poindexter refrained from trying to persuade Reagan to drop the idea, which appeared impossible. He sought rather to ensure that eliminating all nuclear weapons would never become anything other than a distant goal of Reagan administration policy, to prevent the president from acting upon his nuclear abolitionism—such as in serious arms proposals or negotiations—or even to be perceived as doing so. Poindexter's approach was essentially similar to how other senior Reagan administration officials—Weinberger, for example—treated Reagan's nuclear abolitionism (although Weinberger did not share Poindexter's agreement in principle with nuclear abolitionism).[17]

During the administration's discussions of Gorbachev's letter, a number of sub-Cabinet-level officials at the State and Defense Departments, including Nitze, Hartman, and Perle, as well as representatives from the Joint Chiefs, tried to head off Reagan's nuclear abolitionism and to back away from "the institutionalization and acceptance" of it as U.S. policy. In a series of interagency meetings and less formal discussions, they argued that abolishing nuclear weapons was a foolish idea, one that ran counter to the interests of the United States and its allies, whose conventional military forces were far less powerful than the Soviets'. Even the broad objective of Gorbachev's proposal to abolish nuclear weapons should not be accepted, they claimed; the proposal was not serious but was intended as a means of pressuring the Reagan administration to give up SDI. Perle, in particular, made the case that the administration should not consider a positive response to Gorbachev's plan of working toward a world without nuclear weapons, for fear that Reagan would direct his advisers to develop a specific program to achieve that end.[18]

Shultz moved to block those officials—many of them from his own department—who tried to head off Reagan's nuclear abolitionism. His rebuttal to their arguments was that the president had "wanted to get rid of nuclear weapons all along," thought it was "a hell of a good idea," and had made his position clear in public "both before and since the last election." Shultz stated that administration officials, rather than setting out reasons why not to seek a nuclear-free world, should study how the United States could work toward it: what political, economic, and strategic changes would have to take place along with it, and so on.[19] This was characteristic of Shultz, who, as noted previously, had asked for similar studies since 1983. In a kind of unorganized passive resistance, those who would have been expected to produce these studies—such as Adelman—either did nothing at all about it or wrote up reasons why abolishing nuclear weapons was an awful idea.[20]

There was more to Shultz's aiding and abetting of Reagan's nuclear abolitionism than mere deference to the president's objectives. In the first place, Shultz genuinely thought the elimination of all nuclear weapons to be desirable; as described in previous chapters, he sympathized, both in principle and in practice, with Reagan's view. He also had a more calculating reason: he believed it might be useful in generating movement toward START and INF deals.[21] He sought to "convert the idea into an asset on which we could build a solid first phase of negotiations."[22]

So instead of considering Reagan's nuclear abolitionism to be a danger, Shultz viewed it as a means of providing impetus from the top of the U.S. government for arms reduction agreements. Yet he had to proceed carefully and ensure that negotiations remained focused solely on reaching START and INF deals rather than dissipating into debates over how to reach a nuclear-free world.

Shultz wanted the administration to respond to Gorbachev's letter by accepting the notion of an approach in stages toward eliminating nuclear weapons but to make the achievement of START and INF deals the first stage, thereby "front-end load[ing] our program in the first stage." The "fulfillment of key preconditions" for a world without nuclear weapons, such as redressing asymmetries in conventional forces, would be part of a second stage, conditional upon completion of the first.[23]

Shultz was largely successful in tamping down efforts by Perle and others within the administration to stop the president from moving toward his aim of abolition. Shultz held the stronger hand from the start. The elimination of nuclear weapons as "an ultimate objective" of the United States had been established as official administration policy at least since NSDD 153 in January 1985.[24] Given the strength of Reagan's conviction on the matter, the general U.S. posture was almost foreordained. Reagan wrote in his diary on the day he received Gorbachev's letter that "We'd be hard put to explain how we could turn it down."[25]

Still, some within the administration persisted in trying to dissuade Reagan from any kind of positive response to Gorbachev's letter. General Edward Rowny, a senior arms control adviser at the State Department, had been "alarmed" by Reagan's reaction to Gorbachev's letter.[26] He met with the president in an attempt to change his mind on the subject and in the process discovered what Poindexter, Shultz, and Weinberger already knew: that "anyone trying to talk [Reagan] out of his vision of a world without nuclear weapons was wasting his breath" (as Shultz later put it).[27] When Rowny told Reagan that a deal abolishing nuclear weapons would be impossible to verify and that the Soviets could not be trusted to live up to such a deal, Reagan responded, "Well, don't worry, this will all work out." Rowny urged the president not to "go soft on this," to which Reagan replied that he was not going soft. Then—"almost like Martin Luther King," Rowny later noted—Reagan said, "I have a dream. I have a dream of a world without nuclear weapons. I want our children and grandchildren particularly to be free of these weapons." Rowny left the meeting feeling anxious about Reagan's antinuclearism, and he grew increasingly "uncomfortable" with it over the course of the year. Rowny suspected that "if [Reagan] got a chance, he would agree to give up our nuclear weapons and go to zero."[28]

On February 4, Reagan met with his foreign and defense policy principals to consider a formal response to Gorbachev's letter. Excerpts from Reagan's diary for that day stated that some officials present "wanted to tag it a publicity stunt."[29] Reagan rejected this, telling his advisers that the United States would reply to the Soviet proposal by saying that "we share their overall goals and now want to work out the details. If it is a publicity stunt this will be revealed by them." The president directed his administration to engage the USSR in a serious process with the aim of eliminating nuclear weapons. If Gorbachev sincerely wanted this, Reagan would work with him to bring it about. If not, Reagan would call his bluff. The president also told his advisers that he would "announce we are going forward with SDI but if research reveals a defense against missiles is possible, we'll work out how it can be used to protect the whole world not just us."[30] His comments on SDI reflected both his refusal to give up SDI and his fixed adherence to the vision he had held since the inception of the initiative.

Following the meeting on the fourth, Reagan signed an NSDD that set out his administration's formal response to Gorbachev's letter. It generally followed the terms proposed by Shultz during the earlier interagency deliberations. The NSDD stated that the United States was "pleased" that the USSR "agrees with our ultimate goal of moving to the total elimination of nuclear weapons when possible." The first steps toward that goal would be START and INF agreements, on which negotiating efforts should focus exclusively until their completion. After START and INF had been completed, the United States could then "envision subsequent steps which could involve the United Kingdom, France, and the People's Republic of China so that all can move to zero nuclear weapons in a balanced and stable manner." The United States "would make it clear that, in its view, the total elimination of nuclear weapons requires conditions that include correcting conventional and other force imbalances and problems, full compliance with existing and future treaty obligations, peaceful resolution of regional conflicts in ways that allow free choice without outside interference, and a demonstrated commitment by the Soviet leadership to peaceful competition."[31]

That sentence of the NSDD stands as a preeminent example of Reagan administration officials attempting to "finesse" the president's nuclear abolitionism. By making its realization conditional upon a set of highly unlikely developments (at least during Reagan's three remaining years in office), the president's advisers meant to ensure that his goal of the elimination of nuclear weapons would be unattainable in practice.[32]

The NSDD did affirm Reagan's position that "the U.S. would also make clear its view that the elimination of nuclear weapons would not obviate the need for defenses against such weapons, particularly against cheating or breakout by any country."[33]

After the administration consulted with U.S. allies on its response to Gorbachev's letter as set forth in the NSDD (following which no major changes were made), Reagan sent a letter to Gorbachev conveying that response.[34] In the letter, which was drafted by the State Department, Reagan stated, "I am encouraged that you have suggested steps leading toward a world free from nuclear weapons, even though my view regarding the steps necessary differs from yours in certain respects. However, having agreed on the objective and on the need for taking concrete steps to reach that goal, it should be easier to resolve differences in our viewpoints as to what those steps should be." After emphasizing that negotiations should focus on "initial moves"—START and INF—the letter went on to list preconditions for the total elimination of nuclear weapons similar to those set out in the NSDD, such as adjustment of conventional forces, progress in human rights, solutions to regional conflicts, and the evolution of a peaceful, non-threatening U.S.-Soviet competition. After that litany, the letter declared Reagan's hope "that this concept provides a mutually acceptable route to a goal all the world shares. The goal would be to complete the process as soon as the conditions for a nonnuclear world have been achieved."[35]

In the end, then, the administration adopted as official U.S. policy, in the NSDD and in the letter to Gorbachev, the notion of working by steps toward a world without nuclear weapons—although Reagan's aides had tried to bury the prospects for the realization of a nuclear-free world beneath numerous conditions that were unlikely to be fulfilled. Reagan's aides, who had been playing various different angles and agendas during their deliberations over a response to Gorbachev's letter, may well have felt that they had successfully "finessed" the president's unorthodox views.[36] And in a sense, they had; they prevented him from formally proposing to Gorbachev the immediate elimination of all nuclear arms and the sharing of SDI.

Yet the overall effect was to further Reagan's goals. The NSDD and letter to Gorbachev established that the United States planned to work toward the abolition of nuclear weapons in specific stages. That constituted a significant change in U.S. policy. The "finessing" had done little to impede Reagan's determination to see all nuclear weapons abolished or his progress toward that objective. As Reagan saw it, developments were unfolding promisingly: the confluence of the U.S. arms buildup and the terrible state of the Soviet economy was forcing the leadership of the USSR to seek agreements on deep reductions in nuclear arms; SDI, which he had intended from the start as a catalyst for and guarantor of the abolition of all nuclear weapons, was under way; Gorbachev had taken up Reagan's notion of a world without nuclear weapons; and the United States had responded positively.[37] In July, Reagan stated that he was encouraged by the fact that here is, to my knowledge, the first Russian leader who has actually proposed reducing the number of weapons and who has also voiced the opinion that our goal should be the total elimination of nuclear weapons. Well, that's been our goal for years. In fact, I was campaigning on that in 1980—that I supported and would support and hoped that we could see the end of nuclear weapons—total elimination. So, obviously there's more reason for optimism in this.[38]

Reagan emphasized his vision of the role missile defense would play in the abolition of nuclear weapons. He said that he saw SDI "as a defense for all of mankind and as something that could really make it possible and practical for the elimination of nuclear weapons every place." "If we can develop an idea that shows that these ballistic missiles can be rendered obsolete," Reagan stated,

> that is the time then when Mr. Gorbachev's idea of total elimination of those weapons—that we could both have it. And frankly, I have said publicly a number of times [that] whichever one of us can come up, or if both of us come up, with such a defensive weapon, as far as we're concerned we'd be happy to make ours available worldwide in return for the elimination of those weapons.[39]

U.S. Intelligence on Gorbachev and Differing Interpretations within the Administration

In the late winter and spring of 1986, one year after Gorbachev became Soviet leader, the CIA issued another set of intelligence assessments outlining future prospects for his foreign and domestic policies. One of those assessments stated that the Soviet economy was "beset by worsening resource constraints, wide-spread technological backwardness, and low production standards."[40] Gorbachev's existing efforts were not likely to improve that performance even modestly and might result in backward movement.[41] However, "[s]hould this package of measures prove insufficient to achieve a sustained improvement in economic performance and impart momentum to his drive for industrial modernization, he may be prepared to try additional measures now under consideration."[42]

Another CIA paper investigated the implications of Gorbachev's industrial modernization program on Soviet defense spending and capabilities. It reported that Gorbachev's plans for industrial modernization "call for boosting economic growth through massive replacement of outdated plant and equipment and an emphasis on high-technology industries"; yet those plans "will, of necessity, involve more heated competition with defense for many of the resources involved in the production of weapons."[43] According to the CIA paper, there would be "intense" competition in the near term—over the ensuing two or three years—for materials, high-technology goods, and skilled labor that would result in trade-offs and some postponements in Soviet defense production. Nonetheless, the USSR would probably be able to meet its existing targets for defense outputs. After that period, however, the

> battle between civilian and defense interests will probably become more severe. . . . At that juncture, the objectives of industrial modernization could increase pressures to postpone certain major defense initiatives—an option almost certain to be unpalatable to a significant portion of the military and political leadership. The crunch could be aggravated if a reescalation of tensions in the US-Soviet relationship were to increase military pressures for additional resources. The seeds of the problem that could flare up for Gorbachev are illustrated by reports that he ran into skepticism from his Politburo colleagues regarding the meager results of the Geneva summit.[44]

Gorbachev, the paper noted, "appears to have settled on a foreign policy course designed to support his domestic economic agenda."[45] "By promoting a more relaxed atmosphere and a perception of arms control opportunities, Gorbachev almost certainly hopes to encourage downward pressure on US defense spending." The paper estimated that a "comprehensive arms control agreement, especially an accord that included sizable reductions in strategic forces and prevented or delayed deployment of a U.S. SDI program, would provide substantial economic benefits in the USSR. Reductions in deployed forces would enable the Soviets to save material and labor, and even greater savings would accrue if the agreements allowed the Soviets to forgo or post-pone the investment in plant and equipment for production of new weapon systems."[46]

A CIA paper in April analyzed the changes made to the Communist Party program at the Twenty-seventh Party Congress, which had been held the previous month. The changes made in 1986 constituted the first time that the program had been revised since 1961. Gorbachev had run into resistance from elements within the party during "long and often difficult negotiations and debate directly involving the top party leadership" and had been forced to compromise in areas but "clearly won some key points during the redrafting process."[47]

According to the paper, the new party program

> effectively opens up new options to Gorbachev. . . . The program makes clear that new policies are needed to get the country moving again, but it does not provide a specific plan of action. Instead, it opens the door to a wide range of options by removing some ideological bar-riers to reform and by calling for a thorough reassessment of the poli-cies inherited from the Brezhnev era. The program's general language on both domestic and foreign policy appears to have been crafted to give the regime flexibility as it hammers out more specific policies in the years ahead.[48]

The paper noted that while the new party program "retains the same ultimate goals of Soviet foreign and domestic policy—the worldwide victory of Communism and a life of material abundance for Soviet cit-izens—[it] reflects a major rethinking of how and when they are to be achieved," founded upon "a more sober view of Soviet prospects for the future, both at home and abroad" than the 1961 version it re-placed.[49] And the program "makes clear that revitalizing the domestic economy is the regime's top priority." In a reversal of the 1961 version, the order of the foreign and domestic policy sections had been switched, with domestic policy moving to first position. The foreign policy section of the new program, the paper pointed out, "opens with the pronouncement that the main goal of the USSR in the interna-tional sphere is to 'ensure favorable conditions' for domestic develop-ment."

The CIA paper asserted that the changes to the economic portion of the program enhanced "the new leadership's ability to explore . . . unorthodox options," such as expanding the role of market forces and the private sector, "should the leadership decide to move in that direction." It noted that Gorbachev's economic strategy was probably "still being worked out"; the changes to the program had been intended to allow him as much room for future maneuver as possible.[50] The paper reported that "the program adds to other indications . . . that the new leadership may be open to more substantial measures over the long term, should its ambitious goals require them. Indeed, well-placed Soviet economists have [said] that far-reaching economic reforms are being drawn up for possible introduction within two or three years."[51]

In terms of foreign policy, the paper judged that the "1986 program's scaled-down expectations for the international scene further indicate the Gorbachev regime's focus is on its domestic agenda." It noted that Gorbachev "appears to be keeping his options open" concerning his future approach to foreign policy but pointed out that the program "avoids harsh rhetoric and focuses instead on resolving specific bilateral issues." The paper highlighted the fact that arms control in particular had been given "high priority" in the program.[52]

It concluded that the discussion surrounding the program

papers over two different philosophical approaches to solving the problems facing the Soviet Union. Without challenging the basic assumptions on which the Communist system is based, Gorbachev appears to be willing to consider a broad range of political and economic options to strengthen the Soviet state. He seems to be meeting resistance from powerful conservative forces in the party, who oppose major innovations on ideological grounds, apparently because they fear that reforms could upset a delicate balance that allows the regime to maintain control . . . [they] argue that any significant relaxation of central control runs the risk of unleashing an uncontrollable process that could undermine the foundations of the system.

Despite the influence of entrenched conservatism, the paper added, the prospects for Gorbachev undertaking bold initiatives "should not be underestimated." He was seeking to undermine conservative arguments against reform, and was putting the party "on record as seeking new solutions to chronic problems." The paper noted that "most major policy shifts in Russian and Soviet history have not reflected the prevailing views of the political elite; instead, change has been initiated by a strong and determined leader. Gorbachev seems to be the kind of leader who could take such initiative."[53]

Throughout early 1986, the principal foreign policy and defense officials of the Reagan administration engaged in debate over Gorbachev's intentions and the future course of his tenure. One of the forums in which those debates aired was a series of high-level sessions hosted by Shultz that included Weinberger, Perle, Poindexter, Matlock, Casey, and CIA Deputy Director for Intelligence Robert Gates. Reagan did not attend the sessions, although he was aware of them.[54]

Shultz later wrote that he believed at the time that the USSR was "a declining power": its leadership and society "seemed increasingly to be in disarray," its society was "demoralized" and its economy "unresponsive," its strength—aside from its nuclear missiles—was "questionable," and its geopolitical expansionism had been halted and in some cases reversed.[55] Shultz thought that Gorbachev and Shevardnadze "were more knowledgeable than their predecessors about what was really going on in the Soviet Union. They were aware that it was a bad scene."[56] As Shultz viewed it, although Gorbachev "saw that the condition of the Soviet state was terrible," as yet he had "stopped short of what was needed" to alter it dramatically.[57] Shultz believed, however, that Gorbachev and Shevardnadze "were quite different people from their predecessors."[58] In them he perceived the potential for radical change; what he had seen of their shifts in Soviet foreign and domestic policy thus far suggested "the possibility of real change."[59]

Shultz felt that what would cause Gorbachev "to alter course" was "U.S. determination and strength combined with persuasive arguments that the Soviet Union would benefit from a different approach to its own people and to its foreign relations."[60] He told his colleagues at one of the sessions he hosted that Gorbachev's "goals could be met if he would change the system. So we need to keep trying to influence Gorbachev in that direction."[61]

Shultz's comments reflected the objectives of NSDD 75, the Reagan administration's statement of policy toward the Soviet Union. As described in Chapter 2, that document, issued in January 1983, stated that "Soviet aggressiveness has deep roots in the internal system" and established as official policy that the United States would "promote, within the narrow limits available to us, the process of change in the Soviet Union toward a more pluralistic political and economic system."[62] Shultz believed that a process of fundamental, systemic change within the USSR could unfold sooner rather than later. Shultz wanted to keep applying pressure on the Soviets—geopolitically, economically, politically, and in other spheres—and simultaneously to engage with them broadly, both in dialogue and in negotiations. The aim was to compel the Soviet leadership to conclude that it must of necessity move toward the U.S. agenda and undertake serious, thorough reforms. Shultz frequently noted during this period that that movement—on arms control in particular—had already begun.[63]

Shultz felt that the message of the top CIA officials was that "Gorbachev was simply putting a new face on the same old Soviet approach to the world and to their own people." Shultz wrote in his memoirs that Casey and Gates "would say that CIA intelligence analysis revealed that Gorbachev had done nothing new, only talked a different line."[64] He thought that the viewpoint of Casey and Gates was reinforced by Weinberger, who dismissed the changes in Gorbachev's rhetoric and policies as propaganda and emphasized the ongoing Soviet military buildup.[65]

Gates later said that Shultz "discerned in Gorbachev's rhetoric and proposals much more potential for fundamental change in Soviet direction than we [Casey and Gates] did."[66] Gates told Shultz that "all we have seen since Gorbachev took over leads us to believe that on fundamental objectives and policies he *so far* remains generally as inflexible as his predecessors."[67] The views Gates expressed did not necessarily reflect those of the CIA as a whole, various elements of which, as both Shultz and Gates later acknowledged, encompassed and expressed different outlooks.[68] That is evident from the intelligence assessments excerpted above. Particularly when compared to the intelligence reports from 1985 described in the previous chapter, those issued over the course of 1986 demonstrated an evolution toward the judgment that while Gorbachev hoped to avoid major changes, he was giving himself the widest possible room for maneuver in the future, and that the possibility that he might consider himself forced to make striking departures from past patterns "should not be underestimated."

Regardless, by all later accounts Shultz was ahead of the rest of his colleagues in the senior ranks of the Reagan administration in his conviction by early 1986 that Gorbachev could soon undertake radical changes in Soviet foreign and domestic policy. In an interview, Iklé stated that while there were not sharp differences within the administration over what was actually happening in the Soviet Union at the time, there was "quite a division between optimists and pessimists," with the former "more optimistic that Gorbachev was really a change." Iklé said that Shultz, who "felt a sense of change," was an optimist. (Iklé himself was "skeptical.")[69] Adelman also told the author that he was "very skeptical" of Gorbachev early on.[70] Later comments by Nitze, Shultz's right-hand man on arms control issues, indicated that he, too, was deeply wary of Gorbachev and did not share Shultz's early optimism.[71]

As described in previous chapters, Matlock had been instrumental in establishing, in 1983 and 1984, a plan and framework for negotiating with the Soviets. Matlock held that the USSR had to change internally in order for the U.S.-Soviet relationship to improve fundamentally and thus for the Cold War to wind down. "If the Soviet Union stayed as it was, we could only hope to manage the mutual hostility."[72] Matlock felt that sustained U.S. pressure, such as maintaining a military buildup that would force the USSR to confront the ruinous effects its defense spending was having on its economy, and supplying aid to forces fighting against Soviet occupation or clients abroad, could demonstrate to the Soviet leadership that it could not carry on as it was, either at home or internationally. At the same time, he wanted the United States to engage the Soviets in a broad, open-ended dialogue that went beyond arms control to include issues that reached to the heart of the internal nature of the Soviet system, such as human rights. That approach to U.S.-Soviet dialogue was first outlined as administration policy in a speech Reagan delivered in January 1984 (see Chapter 4).

Matlock told the author in an interview that "the way you get them to change substantially is to get to deal with them."[73] Matlock was convinced that if the United States handled a broadened dialogue skillfully enough, it could encourage the Soviet leadership toward the conclusion that pursuing greater "openness and democratization" was in its own best interests, that it was necessary to ensure a decently functioning economy and society in the future. Once changes in that direction started to take place in the USSR—which Matlock felt would beget a self-sustaining, long-term process—it would thereby address the "causes" of the Cold War. The two sides would then be able to resolve in a meaningful way what he called the "symptoms" of the Cold War, such as the arms race and regional conflicts. "Basically," Matlock believed, "you're not going to get anything important happening until they start changing internally." Matlock perceived Gorbachev to be the kind of Soviet leader who could come to see that it was in his own interests to begin a process of internal change toward greater political and economic openness. Yet he later acknowledged that he did not have any confidence that such a process had actually begun within the USSR, or was even in the works, until 1987.[74] In 1986, Matlock was interested in Gorbachev's rhetorical shifts but "wanted something more tangible than words."[75]

Reagan himself saw Gorbachev as a new and different Soviet leader in a welcome sense. Administration officials later stated that in 1986, the president and his secretary of state held similarly optimistic views of Gorbachev as a real change compared to his predecessors.[76] Reagan had long believed that he could help induce change in the Soviet Union through his own personal persuasion and negotiation with the Soviet leadership. His interaction with Gorbachev during the summit in Geneva had convinced the president that Gorbachev, unlike the previous Soviet leaders during Reagan's tenure, was someone with whom he could deal constructively, and this "encouraged the president to think that we could really bring about change."[77] Reagan told his advisers that he thought Gorbachev was "a different type of Soviet leader." Most of them remained skeptical, as described above. (Adelman, for one, considered the president's judgment of Gorbachev "quite nuts" and believed it to be another of Reagan's "funny ideas."[78] Reagan, Adelman thought, had gotten "carried away" with Gorbachev.)[79]

Reagan was genuinely impressed and encouraged by Gorbachev's January proposal to proceed toward the abolition of nuclear arms, and that contributed to his view of the Soviet leader as capable of pursuing new approaches. In July, Reagan stated that "[f]or the first time . . . we're not only pointed in the right direction—toward reduction and eventual elimination of nuclear weapons—we have begun to move, both sides, down that road." He declared that he "was hopeful that we have reached a stage where misunderstanding or suspicion in themselves will no longer keep us from our goal" of reducing and ultimately eliminating nuclear weapons, and spoke of "a possible moment of opportunity in our relations with the Soviet Union."[80]

Zero Ballistic Missiles

Beginning soon after the Geneva summit and continuing throughout early 1986, Reagan tried to fix a date for the next summit with Gorbachev, which they had agreed would take place in Washington at some time in the summer of 1986. Gorbachev refused, declaring that he would not agree to set a summit date unless he could be sure that the summit would produce tangible results in arms control. He made clear that by that he meant an agreement that would constrain SDI in exchange for reductions in strategic arms. This irritated Reagan, who resented Gorbachev's stalling on the summit as a means of trying to pressure the United States to give up SDI.[81]

In late May, while the two sides continued to quibble over the date of the Washington summit, the Soviets presented a new proposal at the Geneva NST negotiations. They set forth measures that would "strengthen" the ABM Treaty as preconditions for a START agreement that would reduce strategic nuclear arms by 30 percent. To "strengthen" the ABM Treaty, the Soviets proposed that both sides agree that deploy-

ment of weapons in space that could strike Earth, such as lasers and par-
ticle beams, should be banned indefinitely, and the testing of them severely limited; that both sides agree not to withdraw from the ABM
Treaty for fifteen to twenty years, followed by an indefinite period of
negotiations on how to proceed; that specific definitions of the "development" of missile defense and what constituted missile defense "components" be negotiated and added to the ABM Treaty; that research be
frozen at levels reached at the time of agreement; and that all work on
missile defense be confined to the "laboratory."[82] (The Soviets kept on
the table their earlier position that a 50 percent reduction in strategic
weapons was conditional upon a ban on research of a "purposeful" nature as well as a total ban on the development, testing, and deployment
of a defense.) The United States rejected the new proposal.

Meanwhile, Shultz, aided by Nitze, tried to convince Reagan to
agree to a deal that linked U.S. acceptance of limitations on SDI to
deep reductions in strategic arms. In his memoirs, Shultz wrote that he
judged that support for SDI "would not increase but decrease from
now on, especially when people started to face up to the enormous
costs of the program."[83] He thought that the United States should
move quickly to secure a START agreement in exchange for restrictions on SDI that did not require the United States to forgo research on
the initiative or the possibility of deployment in the long term, which
he knew Reagan would flatly reject.[84] Shultz and Nitze essentially revived the Monday Package that they had championed with McFarlane
the year before, proposing that the United States agree not to withdraw
from the ABM Treaty for five to eight years (down from ten in the
Monday Package), in order to reach agreement on 50 percent reductions in strategic weapons.[85] Shultz told the president that since it was
virtually impossible that the United States would have a missile defense ready to deploy within eight years, he could give the Soviets "the
sleeves from our vest on SDI and make them think they got our over-
coat," while still attaining massive cuts in strategic arms.[86]

Weinberger and Perle fiercely resisted any such offer, just as they
had fought similar ideas of using SDI as a bargaining chip in offensive
arms negotiations over the previous two years. Perle argued that "any

constraints on deployment of SDI would be a slippery slope to oblivion for the whole program."[87] In his memoirs, Reagan wrote that Weinberger asserted that if the Soviets "decided I was wavering on the SDI, it would send the wrong signals to Moscow and weaken our bargaining position." Reagan added that he thought Weinberger "was also worried that I might be persuaded by those advocating possible concessions on the SDI, but he needn't have worried." The president turned down Shultz's plan.[88]

At the same time, Reagan insisted that the United States formally propose to the Soviets that the two sides sign a new treaty guaranteeing that a missile defense, if it proved feasible, would be shared.[89] None of Reagan's advisers thought that the United States should, or even could, share a missile defense with the Soviets, and many of them tried to dissuade the president.[90] Reagan held firm. Adelman later said that Reagan "would cling to . . . this idea of sharing SDI, and this was an idea that we could not dislodge with a crowbar or any other way out of his mind."[91] Matlock recalled that "the specialists would say, 'You can't do that, you can't do that,' but [Reagan] said, 'Yeah, we can.'"

Reagan directed Matlock to include in a letter to Gorbachev his proposal to sign a treaty committing the United States to share SDI. Matlock tried to "satisfy the bureaucracy and weasel-word the sharing." Reagan "kept sending it back to me and said, 'Tell them we want to share.' And I changed the wording a bit, cleared it with our arms control people, and finally he came back with it and said, 'Damn it, Jack'—he had a little note—'Damn it, Jack, it's my letter. This is what it's going to say. I'll commit us to share, and I'll do it in a treaty.'"[92]

Weinberger found himself in a difficult position. There did not seem to be any way to finesse Reagan's intention to share SDI, and pressure—both from the Soviets and from within the administration— to strike a deal that would limit SDI was reaching a high point. Weinberger's response was a radical one. During a meeting in early June with Reagan and only the principal national security policy makers in attendance, Weinberger suggested that the administration propose the elimination of all ballistic missiles. He pointed out "that it made little sense to commit to share the benefits of advanced defenses with the

Soviet Union if the Soviet Union insisted on continuing to retain large numbers of offensive ballistic missiles which would, in turn, attempt to defeat our defenses."[93] The United States would share a defense if both sides agreed to eliminate all ballistic missiles; there would be vastly fewer reasons to oppose sharing SDI with the Soviets if they had no ballistic missiles than if they had many, or even some.

The idea of abolishing ballistic missiles—independent of any consideration of it as a precondition for sharing SDI—had originated with Iklé, who had asserted as early as 1973 that getting rid of the fast-flying, highly accurate weapons would lead to greater stability in the nuclear competition. Iklé had discussed the idea informally with a few administration officials, both in the Pentagon and in the State Department, in 1985 and early 1986.[94] Weinberger and Perle both signed on to the concept. Perle said that he liked the notion because it had "a powerful heuristic effect": not only did he agree with Iklé that the elimination of ballistic missiles, if it could be realized, would be beneficial to U.S. security, but he also felt that proposing the concept would strike at the heart of the Soviet argument against SDI. In the absence of ballistic missiles, it would be difficult for the Soviets to charge that a missile defense would provide the United States with a military advantage.[95] While Weinberger approved of the idea before the June meeting, it was Reagan's determination to share SDI that spurred him to propose it then.

Poindexter, who heard the idea for the first time at the June meeting, "was very much in favor of it." He had always disliked ballistic missiles, which he felt posed a "hair-trigger kind of problem," and particularly ICBMs, which were "too vulnerable and provided a target in the continental United States" and in which the USSR held a considerable advantage over the United States. As described in Chapter 3, Poindexter's involvement in the inception of SDI had been driven largely by his frustration with the ICBM imbalance and the difficulties faced by the United States in redressing it. He considered the elimination of ballistic missiles "a good objective." Poindexter later said that he "would not have been willing to eliminate all ballistic missiles if we were going to eliminate SDI," however, "because we simply had to have an insurance policy that was effective if they decided to cheat." He, like the civilian leadership of the Pentagon, saw a symbiotic relationship between the abolition of ballistic missiles and the deployment of a missile defense. A missile defense would protect against Soviet cheating or attacks by rogue nations if the superpowers eliminated ballistic missiles, while at the same time it would be easier to build a system that would defend against relatively small numbers of missiles. Poindexter also thought Weinberger's idea of zero ballistic missiles to be "the best alternative in terms of moving toward" Reagan's goal of abolishing all nuclear weapons.[96] Eliminating ballistic missiles, he felt, was both desirable and "manageable."[97]

Shultz thought the idea of abolishing ballistic missiles a good one in principle. Although he had doubts as to whether the Soviets would seriously negotiate on the matter, given their strategic advantage over the United States in ICBMs and relative disadvantage in bombers and cruise missiles, he liked the boldness of Weinberger's proposal and supported it.[98]

Reagan was highly enthusiastic. Eliminating ballistic missiles accorded with his nuclear abolitionism. As Adelman later wrote, Reagan saw the abolition of ballistic missiles as "a mighty step toward his personal penchant for a nuclear-free world."[99] Notably, Weinberger's setting forth the concept of zero ballistic missiles was the second occasion on which he introduced a dramatic arms control proposal that drew on and appealed to Reagan's desire to eliminate all nuclear weapons—the first being the zero-zero option for the INF negotiations. In each case, critics within and outside the administration suspected that Weinberger had come up with the proposal because he believed the Soviets would never agree to it. As it happened, the United States and the USSR ended up negotiating seriously over both positions, with the zero-zero option becoming ensconced in the INF Treaty of 1987.

Poindexter determined that with Reagan, Shultz, Weinberger, and himself all in agreement on the zero ballistic missiles idea, it should be developed into a formal proposal with the least possible interference by those at lower levels of the bureaucracy. He and Robert Linhard, his chief arms control specialist on the NSC staff, worked with Weinberger and Shultz to put together a proposal for Reagan to include in a letter to Gorbachev, as Reagan wanted.[100]

During that process, Shultz pressed for the administration to agree to some sort of limitation on the future deployment of SDI. Without it, he argued, the Soviets would not consider negotiating reductions in strategic arms, much less the elimination of ballistic missiles.[101] Weinberger and Perle, after initial resistance, finally acceded on this point. Perle later said that an agreement to eliminate ballistic missiles would have had such a positive and transformative effect on U.S. security that allowing the deployment of SDI to be temporarily delayed was "conceivable" in his view. He was "aware [that] there might be deals we should consider," and this was one.[102] Reagan, too, probably arrived at a similar conclusion, for he accepted a link between eliminating ballistic missiles and nonwithdrawal from the ABM Treaty for a limited time, although there is little evidence to reveal his reasoning for doing so.

The final proposal that was approved by Reagan and included in a letter sent to Gorbachev on July 25 stated that both sides should agree not to withdraw from the ABM Treaty, and thus not to deploy an advanced missile defense, through 1991. In the meantime, the United States "would be prepared to sign a treaty now" that mandated that if either party intended to deploy a defense at any time after 1991, it would be required to "share the benefits of such a system with the other providing there is mutual agreement to eliminate the offensive ballistic missiles of *both* sides." After one side had submitted a specific plan to the other for eliminating ballistic missiles and sharing the benefits of the defense, the details of those steps would be negotiated for no more than two years. Following those two years, either side would be free to deploy the defense after giving its required six months' notice of withdrawal from the ABM Treaty.[103]

The Reagan administration did not announce the proposal publicly until September 22, when the president enunciated it during a speech at the United Nations. This followed the administration's practice over the previous few years of introducing proposals privately, often in letters to Gorbachev, before making them publicly known, for the purpose of facilitating negotiations.[104] In this case, this policy was adhered to strictly, with few leaks.[105]

Reagan believed, as he wrote in his diary, that the proposal was "a good one and should open the door to some real arms negotiations if [Gorbachev] is really interested."[106]

Putting forth a serious, near-term plan for the elimination of ballistic missiles was a radical step in U.S. policy. Reagan was working assiduously toward his objectives of using SDI as a catalyst for the abolition of nuclear arms and then sharing a defense as insurance. His views on nuclear weapons and missile defense and his determination to pursue them placed considerable pressure on his advisers to follow along. In this case, Weinberger responded with the zero ballistic missiles proposal—the idea being to mitigate the impact of sharing a missile defense—and the rest of the president's senior aides signed on.

While his advisers sought to prevent him from actually trying to abolish nuclear arms and share SDI, Reagan steadily pursued his goals. The frequent result, as here, was a new and highly unorthodox U.S. policy. The president was pulling U.S. policy in his own direction.

Toward Reykjavík

By the summer of 1986, many officials in the Reagan administration had concluded that the confluence of the U.S. military buildup and the struggling Soviet economy was forcing Gorbachev to seek to lower the Soviet defense burden through a more cooperative international approach generally and arms control specifically. Gates later wrote that even by the end of 1985,

> [e]veryone knew . . . that Gorbachev desperately needed improved relations with the West, especially with the United States. Because of multiple crises at home, he needed to constrain the arms race, and new U.S. strategic programs in particular, to avoid new Soviet military expenditures and perhaps even allow some reductions in spending. Domestic crises compelled Soviet initiatives to relax tensions.[107]

Reagan later wrote that in early 1986, he was "getting more and more evidence that the Soviet economy was in dire shape."[108] In his public comments, Reagan declared that Gorbachev was entering into serious arms negotiations with the United States because he needed to reach agreements for economic reasons.[109] Reagan said in July that Gorbachev "believes that, for the sake of their economy, that it might be in their own interest and practical for them to join in reducing these great stores of arms and ending an arms race, which has been so costly to them that it has been the principal cause of their economic problems."[110] He declared in August that the Soviet Union was "an economic basket case because of the massive arms buildup that it's been conducting over the last few decades" and that it was consequently seeking to reduce nuclear weapons.[111]

He also spoke more broadly of an ascendant West and a declining, and increasingly backward, Soviet Union. He pointed to setbacks faced by the Soviets and Soviet clients abroad, claiming that a "democratic revolution" was engulfing Communist countries.[112] He particularly emphasized the economic and technological strength of the United States. "America," he said, "leads the world in a technological revolution."[113] In March, Reagan stated, "Ours is a time of enormous social and technological change everywhere, and one country after another is discovering that only free peoples can make the most of this change. Countries that want progress without pluralism, without freedom, are finding that it cannot be done."[114] Reagan, who often spoke of SDI in the same breath as he described the United States leading a technological revolution, noted on several occasions that in his view, SDI had been influential in bringing the Soviets to negotiate deep cuts in the two sides' nuclear arsenals.[115]

Most of Reagan's advisers believed by mid-1986 that the Soviets perceived SDI as a technological and economic threat to the USSR. As Reagan administration officials saw it, stopping SDI had become a preeminent issue for the Soviets to the point of preoccupation. Soviet concerns about SDI were driving much of the changes in the USSR's approach to arms control, Reagan administration officials thought, and were exacerbating a sense within the Soviet leadership of falling behind the United States economically and technologically. Bush later said that he thought the Soviets "were scared of SDI."[116] Weinberger noted that the Soviets saw "that while they might not be able to do it, we almost certainly could."[117] Poindexter commented that the Soviets "were very, very concerned about it. They held our technology in very high regard and felt that if we set our minds to it, we could do it."[118] In an interview with the author, Matlock stated that "they understood very well they probably couldn't afford to keep up in a major crash program to develop strategic defenses."[119] Gorbachev, Nitze noted, "took [SDI] very seriously"; it had "a large effect" upon the Soviet leader.[120]

Adelman later wrote that it was obvious to the Reagan administration that SDI was "the engine driving [the Soviets] to negotiate over deep reductions in categories of strategic arms."[121] Matlock believed that the Soviet military had insisted on attempting to match SDI, while the civilian leadership had decided, "No, we can't afford it, we have to find another way," and tried to restrain it via arms control.[122]

It was not lost upon officials in the Reagan administration, whether they thought an advanced defense was ultimately feasible or not, that it would take many years to come to fruition and that in many ways the Soviets' reaction to the initiative reflected more their perceptions of the difficulties posed by a high-technology, expensive competition in general with the United States than with an objective assessment of SDI as an actual program. Perle later told the author that "we were gaining quite extraordinary leverage from a system that was a long way from being operational. It was just wonderful."[123] During an interview, the author asked Iklé if he had seen the apparent Soviet obsession with stopping SDI as a sign of Soviet economic and technological weakness. "Yes," he responded, "and their exaggerated imagination of a very successful second Manhattan Project in the U.S." Iklé said that he thought the Soviets believed "that we could do more with [SDI] than we actually did" and noted that this point was discussed within the Reagan administration at the time.[124]

Adelman later stated, "None of us . . . could have imagined SDI's impact" when Reagan launched the initiative in March 1983.[125] SDI, he said, "became tremendous leverage in the arms control talks" and in a larger sense affected the way the Soviets approached the overall competition with the United States.

Adelman told the author that he had concluded, particularly after discussions with Soviet officials and scientists at the Geneva summit, that "they were convinced . . . that the United States technologically could do almost anything, that technologically they could do almost nothing, that there must be a lot to it if we were going to do it, and it would totally leave them behind." Reagan administration officials thought that the Soviets believed "they could not get the high technology to be successful, and therefore their society was not technologically sophisticated, so they were going to be left in the dust in things that counted." Whether SDI would work in the form Reagan desired—Adelman had his doubts—"certainly the Soviets [thought] there's a lot to it." "They were scared to death of American technology." SDI, Adelman asserted, played "into our strength of high tech. So it was a really, really new ball game, and they saw it as such."[126] SDI, he concluded, had become a "symbol" for the Soviets of U.S. technological superiority and their own relative weakness.[127]

Reagan and nearly all of his advisers thus saw SDI as an increasingly effective means of adding economic and technological pressure on the Soviet system in the eyes of the Soviet leadership. In that sense, Reagan and his aides viewed SDI as a significant strategic tool with which the United States applied pressure on the Soviet system in a way that furthered the administration's overall policy objectives. The Soviet leadership's perception of SDI as an economic and technological threat, Reagan administration officials believed, was contributing to shaping a decision-making environment in Moscow that encouraged changes in Soviet foreign policy. Reagan, in particular, joined by Shultz, viewed these changes as welcome. Intelligence reports and Soviet statements indicated a possibility that this process could soon extend to domestic policy within the USSR.

On September 19, Reagan received a letter from Gorbachev that proposed a meeting between the two leaders in advance of the Washington summit (and also rejected Reagan's zero ballistic missiles proposal). The point of the meeting would be to lay the groundwork for a "productive and fruitful" summit in Washington.[128] Reagan accepted the idea and, after haggling with the Soviets over a date, announced on September 30 that the two leaders would meet on October 11 and 12 in Reykjavík, Iceland.

Indications prior to the meeting continued to suggest that the highest priority for the Soviets was to stop SDI, and that they would seek to do so through linking that to a strategic arms reduction agreement. Casey said at an NSC meeting a few days before the summit that Gorbachev "will press hardest on limiting SDI. . . . [H]e will have to use the appeal of nuclear reductions to get you to agree to constraints that would effectively block SDI and eventually kill the program."[129] The briefing book prepared for Reagan prior to the meeting reported that Shevardnadze had made clear that "'strengthening' of the ABM Treaty as suggested by Soviets is essential for progress on offensive reductions."[130]

However, the Reagan administration apparently did not intend, or even expect, to engage in detailed negotiations on SDI and START at Reykjavík. The Soviets did not signal that Gorbachev was bringing a major new package to Reykjavík to be negotiated then and there—in retrospect it is clear that he purposely avoided any signal to that effect—and the Reagan administration evidently did not foresee that this might happen.[131] An NSDD issued prior to the Reykjavík meeting stated that the Reagan administration did not "anticipate signing any agreements in Reykjavik." Its goals for the meeting were "[i]dentifying issues with reasonable prospects of solution, and accelerating efforts to resolve them." The NSDD added that the United States would engage the Soviets "in substantive and serious discussions on the entire range of issues on the US agenda" and would "not permit the meeting to focus exclusively or disproportionately on arms control."[132]

REYKJAVÍK

Reagan arrived at Reykjavík with essentially the same group of advisers he had taken to Geneva (except that Poindexter had replaced McFarlane). Weinberger, who had not been at Geneva, did not go to Reykjavík, either. Weinberger later said that the letter he had written Reagan before Geneva warning against concessions on SDI—which had been promptly leaked—meant that he was then "considered banned" from attending Reykjavík.[133]

Reykjavík was meant to be a brief working meeting, with three sessions between Reagan and Gorbachev scheduled over two days and no extraneous social events. Reagan and Gorbachev, together with their aides, descended upon Hofdi House, a small and isolated structure looking out over the sea, on October 11, 1986.

The following account of the Reagan-Gorbachev sessions at Reykjavík is based upon the recently declassified and released official U.S. memcons of the meeting.

On the morning of the eleventh, the two leaders met alone, with only interpreters and note takers present. In his opening remarks, Reagan told Gorbachev that he was especially interested in reducing strategic arms and that he thought that both the United States and the USSR "would like to see a world without nuclear missiles." Gorbachev responded that arms control was the main issue for the meeting, and after a brief discussion of when and how to talk later about human rights, Gorbachev went on to say that although the U.S.-Soviet relationship overall "had been improving," he was concerned over the lack of progress in arms control.[134]

Gorbachev explained that he had proposed the meeting as a means of adding impetus to arms control negotiations so that agreements could be signed in Washington. He told Reagan that he "was in favor of proposals which were aimed at total elimination of nuclear arms, and on the way to this goal there should be equality and equal security" for both sides. The two sides, he stated, "were now at the stage where they could begin a concrete process aimed at arriving at agreements." The Soviets believed that the Washington summit "should be marked by concrete results on important issues, primarily those concerning halting the arms race," and that achieving that result "could not be permitted to fail." At that point, Gorbachev and Reagan brought Shevardnadze and Shultz into the session; from then on, all of the Reagan-Gorbachev sessions at Reykjavík included the two foreign ministers.

Gorbachev then introduced a set of new arms proposals. He stated that the Soviets, as a first step toward the elimination of nuclear weapons, would agree to reduce strategic arms by 50 percent, and that in so doing they would be willing to accept deep cuts in their heavy ICBMs, which they had resisted previously, and would agree to redefine the term "strategic" in a way that represented a concession to the American negotiating position. On INF, he relented from the previous Soviet stance that British and French missiles were to be included with U.S. weapons and offered to eliminate all INF missiles in Europe and negotiate over reducing INF missiles in Asia. He told Reagan that the United States should "appreciate these significant" concessions. Gorbachev said that the Soviets insisted on a deal by which both sides would agree not to withdraw from the ABM Treaty for ten years at least, "followed by a 3–5 year period for negotiations on how to proceed subsequently," and would also agree that all research and testing throughout those years be confined to the laboratory. Gorbachev suggested that he and Reagan give instructions to their staffs to produce a draft agreement for signature in the United States based upon the "package" of Soviet proposals that he had just introduced.[135]

Reagan responded that the proposals "were very encouraging" but first noted a difference between the Soviet and U.S. position on INF missiles in Asia before saying that the "main issue" was strategic arms, which he wanted to reduce "to zero." He added that he could not accept the ABM provisions of the Soviet package. SDI, he stated, "was born as an idea which would give a chance to all of us to completely eliminate strategic weapons." The United States "proposed to go forward in reducing the number of strategic weapons and to sign a treaty which would supersede the ABM Treaty." Reagan tried to convince Gorbachev to sign a new treaty committing each side to share a defense. With a shared defense deployed to protect against cheating or "a madman," the two sides "could rid the world of strategic nuclear arms."

Gorbachev, dismissing Reagan's comments, suggested that the U.S. side study the new Soviet package further. Reagan insisted that Gorbachev did not understand the point of SDI. He again proposed that he would agree to share SDI with the Soviets and that it would be deployed after the "complete elimination of nuclear weapons."[136]

With that the two leaders adjourned the morning session and consulted with their waiting advisers. During the afternoon session, Reagan led off with a lengthy response to Gorbachev's package that had obviously been constructed by his aides, pointing out the differences between U.S. positions and the new Soviet proposals. After arguing over the specifics of START and INF, he and Gorbachev returned to SDI. Reagan claimed that SDI was "the best possibility for ensuring peace in this century" and reiterated that he would agree to share a missile defense. Mutual assured destruction, he argued, was "an uncivilized situation." "I think that the world will be much more civilized," he continued, "if we, the two great powers . . . create defensive systems and eliminate terrible modern armaments. I think that we would then be able to look proudly into the eye of the entire world."

Gorbachev told Reagan that he wanted to take the discussion in a more practical direction and repeated his proposal from that morning regarding the ABM Treaty. Reagan again stated that he would share SDI. Gorbachev then told Reagan that he did not take his "idea of sharing SDI seriously. You don't want to share even petroleum equipment, automatic machine tools or equipment for dairies, while sharing SDI would be a second American revolution. And revolutions do not occur all that often. Let's be realistic and pragmatic."[137] With the session winding down, Reagan and Gorbachev agreed that two negotiating groups from each side would meet that evening, one to discuss arms control issues and the other to go over regional disputes, human rights, and bilateral issues.

The working group negotiations on arms control, which extended all night, ended with considerable further Soviet movement toward the U.S. positions on strategic arms; most significantly, the Soviets agreed to 50 percent cuts in a manner that arrived at equal end limits in the various categories of the two sides' arsenals, as opposed to 50 percent cuts across the board, which had long been the Soviet position. By morning, most of the Reagan team believed it might be possible to structure an agreement to reduce strategic arms and felt both surprise and excitement that the meeting had produced such a result. Nitze, who chaired the U.S. arms control working group, later wrote in his memoirs that Soviet concessions during the overnight negotiations had "opened up a significant prospect for real progress" toward a comprehensive START agreement. On SDI, however, the two sides had remained apart, and the Soviets continued to link a START deal, and an INF deal as well, with blocking SDI.[138]

During their morning session on October 12, which was scheduled to be their last, Reagan and Gorbachev reviewed the work accomplished overnight by the negotiating groups. After they did so, Gorbachev asked when "the U.S. will start making concessions of its own." He reiterated his insistence that Reagan accept the proposals for the ABM Treaty that he had set forth the previous morning.

Reagan countered that he would agree to share SDI and that the initiative would "facilitate the elimination of nuclear weapons." He said that he "failed to see the magic of the ABM regime," which enshrined MAD. He emphasized that he wanted "to eliminate missiles so that our populations could sleep in peace" and that a shared missile defense would "give the world a means of protection that would put the nuclear genie back in his bottle." Gorbachev replied firmly that "[n]o one in the Soviet leadership," nor he personally, "could agree to steps which would undercut" the ABM Treaty.

After Reagan and Gorbachev traded long statements about why each nation had historically mistrusted the other, Shultz, looking toward statements to issue at the conclusion of the session, interjected to say that "it appeared there was the beginning of a joint statement on strategic weapons," and perhaps on INF as well, but that on SDI "there had been no agreement." Gorbachev noted dryly that the meeting had convinced him that Reagan did not like to make any concessions whatsoever, particularly with respect to SDI.

Shevardnadze then pushed the discussion toward focusing on nonwithdrawal from the ABM Treaty for a given period of time, suggesting that the two sides work to find an agreement built around that concept. He and Gorbachev made clear again that such an agreement was a precondition for reductions in offensive systems. Gorbachev said that the Soviets "had proposed a package, and the individual elements of their proposals must be regarded as a package."

Reagan rejected that linkage. Gorbachev declared that with that the meeting could end, but that "it had not produced the results that had been expected in the Soviet Union, and that Gorbachev had personally expected." After an argument over human rights and bilateral negotiations, Gorbachev then suggested to Reagan that Shultz and Shevardnadze "might see what they could come up with" on arms control questions "while the two leaders took a brief break." Reagan agreed, and thus the two leaders extended the length of the meeting.[139]

Shultz gathered a group of U.S. advisers, including Nitze, Poindexter, Perle, and Linhard, and met with Shevardnadze and a corresponding group of Soviet officials. Shevardnadze told the U.S. side in no uncertain terms that there was only one issue to discuss, and that was SDI. "Without the resolution of this issue," Shevardnadze warned, "nothing is agreed."[140]

While Shultz and Shevardnadze debated, Linhard and Perle quickly wrote up a proposal that they then passed to the rest of the U.S. side for approval. Their proposal was that the United States and the USSR should agree not to withdraw from the ABM Treaty for ten years. During the first five years, both sides would reduce their strategic arms by 50 percent; during the second, all remaining ballistic missiles would be eliminated. Perle later told the author that he and Linhard put forward the new proposal in large part because of the "exigency" of the moment. "We were in a negotiating situation," Perle said, and the new proposal seemed to be "a way out of the deadlock."[141]

The other Reagan administration officials at the table quickly endorsed the proposal. Poindexter was both surprised and relieved by the Linhard-Perle initiative. At dinner with Reagan and Shultz the night before, he had suggested that they might consider recasting the zero ballistic missiles idea and proposing it at Reykjavík. Poindexter believed that Reagan was eager to propose, and agree to, the total elimination of all nuclear weapons then and there at the Reykjavík meeting and felt that "we really needed to lay on the table something that was not quite as drastic" and "that we could support back home" in order to preempt Reagan's nuclear abolitionism. Poindexter judged "that if the Soviets by chance agreed to [the elimination of ballistic missiles], we could support that and get that agreed to" in the United States.[142]

Shultz read out the new proposal to Shevardnadze, while duly noting that Reagan had not yet approved it. Shevardnadze expressed concern that the proposal allowed deployment of SDI after ten years. The session then broke up so that each of the leaders could be briefed. Reagan was pleased with the Linhard-Perle offer and took it into his next session with Gorbachev. That session began hours after the Reykjavík meeting was supposed to have ended; by this time both sides were vigorously negotiating an actual arms reduction agreement.

Gorbachev opened the session on the afternoon of the twelfth by presenting a new proposal of his own. Both sides would agree to a ten-year nonwithdrawal period from the ABM Treaty, during which research and testing would be confined to the laboratory. During the first five years, 50 percent of all strategic arms would be eliminated, and during the second, all of the remaining strategic arms would be eliminated. Reagan countered by reading out the Linhard-Perle proposal, to which Gorbachev responded that the U.S. side's formula "does not satisfy Soviet requirements." The Soviets' "main objective, for the period when we are pursuing deep reductions, is to strengthen the ABM Treaty and not undermine it." He thus "once again ask[ed] the U.S. side to meet this minimal requirement": SDI must be confined to the laboratory.

The two then disputed the issue of confining SDI to the laboratory. Reagan stated that he "thought the two sides were very close to an agreement"; he could not see why, if both sides had "completely eliminated all nuclear weapons," there could be concern "if one side built a safeguard, a defensive system against non-existent weapons, in case there might be a need for it in the future?" Reagan claimed that with nuclear weapons eliminated and a defense deployed, ten years from now he and Gorbachev could return to Iceland, each of them bringing "the last nuclear missile" from his country, and "give a tremendous party for the whole world." Gorbachev replied that he thought the two sides were close to agreement as well, which prompted Reagan to continue describing the scene in Iceland ten years hence.

After Gorbachev confirmed that they had agreed to eliminate missiles, Reagan said that they had gotten "good results": 50 percent reduction in the first five-year stage and elimination in the second (he did not distinguish among ballistic, strategic, or all nuclear weapons); Gorbachev would get his ten-year restriction on SDI deployment; and Reagan would be allowed to proceed with the initiative. He said that he thought the U.S. and Soviet people "would cheer that they had gotten rid of nuclear missiles."

Gorbachev repeated that SDI needed to be confined to the laboratory. Reagan countered that the question of research, development, and testing should be left for the Washington summit. Gorbachev stated that without a commitment to confine SDI to the laboratory, "there was no package." Reagan said that they were not getting anywhere and suggested a break to consult with their advisers. Gorbachev said that Reagan "could go out and fix everything in ten minutes."[143]

During the hour-long break, Reagan expressed disappointment to his advisers that Gorbachev was not coming around to see the benefits of strategic defense. When the discussion turned to the ramifications of confining SDI to the laboratory, as Gorbachev was insisting, Perle and Adelman stated categorically that restricting SDI to the laboratory would effectively kill the program, which reinforced Reagan's determination not to agree to that restriction.[144]

For much of the rest of the break, Reagan's aides focused on trying to impress upon him and Shultz (who did not seem clear on the matter) the difference between ballistic missiles and strategic weapons, which Reagan had muddled throughout the talks. The United States, Reagan's advisers said, did not want to give up its bombers and cruise missiles; eliminating all strategic weapons would come close to eliminating all nuclear arms, leaving only weapons that could not reach directly from the United States to the USSR. Adelman later wrote that Reagan did not seem interested in such a distinction. While the president's aides were "trying to go over our next move with care," Reagan "was picturing himself racing downfield like mad." Reagan wanted to eliminate as many nuclear weapons as possible, and hopefully all.[145]

Reagan's aides prepared another version of the Linhard-Perle offer that did not change any of the specifics, and Reagan read it out to Gorbachev when their session resumed. Gorbachev noted that the United States had agreed neither to confine SDI to the laboratory nor to eliminate all strategic weapons.

At the end of a long discussion on the various categories of weapons being negotiated on, in which he seemed either not to have known or not to have cared about the difference between ballistic and strategic arms, Reagan declared that it would be fine with him "if we eliminated all nuclear weapons." Gorbachev replied, "We can do that. We can eliminate them." Shultz was not a silent spectator; he interjected to say, "Let's do it."[146]

Reagan told Gorbachev that they could turn over to the Geneva negotiators the task of preparing the details of an agreement on eliminating nuclear weapons that the two leaders could then sign in Washington. Gorbachev agreed.

Gorbachev then returned to the central dispute over SDI. He declared that he had to limit SDI to the laboratory. Reagan replied that he "would not destroy the possibility of proceeding with SDI"; he "could not confine work to the laboratory." Gorbachev asked him if that position was final. Reagan said yes; one "must go outdoors to try out what has been done in the lab."

Gorbachev declared that if they did not agree to confine SDI to the laboratory, they could "forget everything they had discussed." Shevardnadze stepped in to say that the two sides "were so close" to accomplishing a historical feat "that if future generations read the minutes of these meetings, and saw how close we had come but how we did not use these opportunities, they would never forgive us."

Reagan asked Gorbachev to "do this one thing," not to constrain SDI to the laboratory: "It is a question of one word. This should not be turned down over a word." Gorbachev responded that "it is not just a question of one word, it is a question of principle." If he signed something "that gave the U.S. the opportunity to conduct SDI-related research and testing in broad tests, and to go into space, the testing of space weapons in space," he "could not go back to Moscow"; he "would be called a dummy and not a leader." Gorbachev emphasized that he could not allow the "development of a space-based ABM system, which would permit the U.S. to destroy the Soviet Union's offensive nuclear potential." Reagan replied that "there would be no offensive weapons left to destroy." He asked Gorbachev to "change his mind" on the issue of confining SDI to the laboratory so that they could "go on and bring peace to the world" with the abolition of nuclear weapons and a shared defense. Gorbachev declared that he could not, at which point the session—and the Reykjavík meeting—ended.[147]

THE AFTERMATH

At the conclusion of the meeting, Reagan was "madder than hell" at Gorbachev, Adelman later said, for refusing to cut nuclear arms unless he could stop SDI.[148] Reagan genuinely believed, then and later, that he had been close to attaining his goal of abolishing all nuclear weapons. He wrote in his memoirs that at Reykjavík, "my hopes for a nuclear-free world soared briefly, then fell during one of the longest, most disappointing—and ultimately angriest—days of my presidency."

Though Reagan was convinced that he and Gorbachev had almost reached an agreement to eliminate all nuclear weapons, he felt that Gorbachev "had brought me to Iceland with one purpose": to "kill" SDI. In his diary, Reagan wrote on the night of October 12 that the "price was high but I wouldn't sell and that's how the day ended."[149]

The outcome of the meeting at Reykjavík has puzzled journalists and scholars. Yet Reagan's actions at Reykjavík—his proposal that the United States and the USSR abolish all nuclear weapons, and his eventual refusal to agree to a nuclear-free world without a missile defense to guarantee it—were entirely consistent with, and grew directly out of, his ideas regarding nuclear weapons and missile defense.[150] Reagan was unwilling to accept the demise of SDI, even when he thought that Gorbachev was offering to give up all nuclear weapons in return, for he believed that a missile defense was necessary to protect a nuclear-free world. At the meeting he pursued his own, singular agenda.

Officials from the two sides spoke to the press immediately after the meeting ended. Both on the day and afterward, various Reagan administration officials presented conflicting accounts of what Reagan and Gorbachev had each proposed and agreed to, or almost agreed to. Shultz explained the Linhard-Perle proposal to the press but noted that Reagan "was ready to agree" to the elimination of "all offensive strategic arms and ballistic missiles" during the last five years of non-withdrawal from the ABM Treaty.[151] Shultz did not say that Reagan had proposed the abolition of nuclear weapons but noted that Reagan and Gorbachev had "contemplate[d] it."[152] (On another occasion soon after the meeting, however, he commented that "the peace movement should become the biggest fans of Ronald Reagan," because he "is trying in a creative and increasingly effective way to eliminate all these weapons.")[153]

Poindexter publicly stated that Reagan had proposed only the Linhard-Perle plan to eliminate ballistic missiles in ten years.[154] However, Donald Regan, then Reagan's chief of staff, whose influence on foreign policy was minimal but with whom the president had spoken immediately after the meetings, told reporters correctly that Reagan had "volunteered that we should give up all [nuclear] weapons. . . . Everything was on the table."[155] The rest of Reagan's advisers maintained, and have continued to maintain, that on the last day the United States formally proposed and supported only the Linhard-Perle plan.

The question of what exactly had taken place during the last sessions was complicated by the fact that Poindexter, who as national security adviser controlled the official U.S. memoranda of conversation of the sessions, tightly restricted their distribution within the administration. When he read the memcons days after the meeting (the memcons were prepared by Thomas Simons, a U.S. note taker, and Matlock), he was appalled that Reagan had proposed the abolition of all nuclear weapons, that Shultz had gone along with it enthusiastically, and that it had been agreed upon by Reagan and Gorbachev. Poindexter did not want any of this to be known either within or outside the administration, so he held the memcons close, barring their distribution even at the highest levels of the administration.[156] Adelman, for example, never saw the memcons before the author showed them—now declassified—to him in 2001.[157] Few within the administration knew what had really been discussed at Reykjavík.

In his public comments after Reykjavík, Reagan avoided mention of his discussions with Gorbachev on abolishing strategic, and indeed all, nuclear weapons, focusing instead on his formal proposal to eliminate ballistic missiles. That Reagan had formally proposed the abolition of ballistic missiles at Reykjavík in itself caused a huge uproar among U.S. allies, particularly Margaret Thatcher, and strategic specialists. Ironically, Reagan's determination to pursue SDI, which the allies feared would lead to the decoupling of the U.S. extended nuclear deterrent, had become the reason he had not given up ballistic missiles—which they saw as an even greater peril.

In the wake of Reykjavík, almost all of the officials who accompanied Reagan to the meeting continued to approve generally of seeking the abolition of ballistic missiles with the Soviets. Poindexter was particularly keen to keep the idea extant.[158] However, Admiral William Crowe, the new chairman of the Joint Chiefs of Staff, who had signed off on the proposal in the July 25 letter only reluctantly, argued during an NSC meeting in late October that abolishing ballistic missiles would significantly damage U.S. national security.[159] Still, Reagan signed an NSDD calling for the Pentagon to prepare studies showing what the effects of eliminating ballistic missiles would be and how the United States could work toward it.[160] The Reagan administration finally ended up retreating from the idea, however, when Frank Carlucci, Weinberger's former deputy, who thought the idea was a terrible one, took over from Poindexter as a result of the Iran-*contra* scandal that fall and pushed it to the side.[161]

After Reykjavík, everyone in the Reagan administration, including the president, concluded that Gorbachev had come to the meeting with the intention of killing SDI and that this had spurred his willingness to accept deep reductions in nuclear arms.[162] The meeting demonstrated to administration officials the extent to which the Soviets feared the initiative. Reagan administration officials were convinced, too, that in terms of end results the meeting had been a success; Gorbachev had made a series of important concessions that the United States felt would be difficult for him to take back.[163] Reagan and Shultz repeated time and again in the aftermath of the meeting that SDI had brought the Soviets to the negotiating table, had led them to agree to deep cuts in offensive arms, and would lead them to continue to do so.[164]

There was another reason why the meeting was judged to be both a success and a turning point in the U.S.-Soviet relationship. Matlock, in particular, felt that up to that time, Gorbachev had tried to rely on improved relations with the United States generally, and arms control specifically, to alleviate Soviet economic problems by lowering the Soviet defense burden. Gorbachev, Matlock felt, had now gone as far as he could to stop SDI in particular, and also to cut nuclear weapons, and had been unable to succeed. Matlock concluded that Gorbachev would be forced to look at more radical, systemic changes at home and abroad.[165]

As the next chapter illustrates, in Reagan's last years as president the importance of SDI receded somewhat as the range of issues in the U.S.-Soviet relationship expanded and as the initiative faced problems at home. Yet the administration believed that SDI still served to further overall U.S. policy goals, and Reagan continued his efforts to see his vision of it realized.

DENOUEMENT AND CONCLUSION

DENOUEMENT: 1987–1989

After reaching the peak of his popularity and political power in the middle of 1986, Ronald Reagan confronted a difficult political situation by the end of 1986 and throughout the first half of 1987. The Republican Party lost control of the U.S. Senate to the Democrats during the midterm elections of 1986. The Democrats' control of both houses of Congress during Reagan's last two years in office meant a decidedly less favorable environment on Capitol Hill regarding SDI. The Iran-*contra* scandal also erupted in the fall of 1986. The scandal engulfed the Reagan administration for the rest of that year and the first half of the next (although Reagan then regained much of his previous popularity for the rest of his term) and led to personnel changes that brought Carlucci to the White House as national security adviser to replace Poindexter. The experienced, pragmatic Carlucci had been brought in specifically to provide steady leadership after the turmoil of Iran-*contra*.

Carlucci disapproved of what had taken place at Reykjavík, believing that Reagan had gone too far in his discussions with Gorbachev and that the process of dealing with the Soviets had been too unstructured. He sought a gradual, stable improvement of relations with the Soviets. With respect to arms control specifically, he played an important role in causing the administration to back away gradually from the zero ballistic missiles idea and instead focus on a START deal that would accomplish 50 percent cuts. Carlucci was wary of Reagan's nuclear abolitionism. After he became national security adviser, he told the president many times, and wrote numerous memos, that the United States should not eliminate nuclear weapons; they had kept the peace between the superpowers for forty years. Carlucci's arguments had little effect on Reagan, who constantly brought up the connection he saw between nuclear war and the Apocalypse, emphasized his conviction that MAD was "appalling," and insisted that abolishing nuclear weapons was "a good thing to do." Carlucci recognized that Reagan believed SDI to be the catalyst for a world without nuclear weapons. While he himself was not an SDI enthusiast, he viewed the initiative as "useful" in the context of drawing concessions from the Soviets, and he also understood the intensity of Reagan's devotion to it. Carlucci argued with Reagan that he should not persist in his attempts to share SDI with the Soviets, but the president refused to back away from the notion. Carlucci told the author that Reagan's commitment to his "firmly held views" of abolishing nuclear weapons and sharing SDI "was absolutely unshakeable," and that throughout the remainder of his presidency, Reagan "never gave up" his efforts to realize those aims.[1]

In early 1987, Weinberger pushed for Reagan to approve the start of a process that would lead to deployment of some initial elements of SDI—apparently a layered system comprising space-based kinetic kill vehicles and ground-based interceptors—in two years.[2] Shultz, Carlucci, and Crowe suspected that Weinberger was seeking approval for "early deployment" to bolster political support for the initiative and argued that near-term deployment was unfeasible.[3] As Carlucci later said, deploying a space-based defense by 1989 was "just unimaginable from a technical point of view."[4] Reagan concurred. He signed an NSDD in

February that stated that "the SDI program has not yet progressed to the point that it has generated options involving advanced defenses which meet our criteria," and thus that an early deployment decision "is not appropriate at this time."[5] However, Weinberger's intention to pursue early deployment, and the ensuing intra-administration dispute, were promptly leaked to the media and inflamed the already tense relations between the administration and Congress over SDI. In Congress, many Democrats and some Republicans grew increasingly bold in their skepticism of the progress of SDI and increasingly hostile to funding it at the levels sought by the administration. That autumn, Congress cut the administration's request by a third. Finding it difficult both to answer persistent questions about the program's technical prospects and to obtain the desired levels of funding from Congress, the administration was struggling at home with SDI.[6]

Reagan continued to pursue his vision of SDI, at one point raising the idea of a special international organization to oversee the abolition of nuclear weapons and the sharing of missile defense reminiscent of his approach to nuclear arms immediately after World War II. During a meeting with his advisers over how to deal with SDI in arms negotiations with the Soviets, he asked, "Why not . . . develop the idea of sharing SDI technology, combine it with the total elimination of nuclear weapons, and do this through an international body?" "That way," Reagan continued, "SDI would exist for everyone, not just for us and the Russians. No one would want or need nuclear weapons any longer. We could turn a page of history." Adelman countered that nuclear weapons had kept the peace, to which the president "responded rather firmly" that that "wasn't clear." Reagan continued that the U.S. negotiators in Geneva should "change what they're doing and present this scheme. That way we might get somewhere." Adelman reacted negatively, as did others present (except for Shultz, who expressed support for the idea).[7] Reagan's advisers avoided following up on his plan in the wake of the meeting, while some, including Carlucci, continued their efforts to move Reagan off of his desire to abolish nuclear weapons and share SDI.

In late February 1987, Gorbachev announced that the USSR

would no longer link an INF treaty to deals on SDI and START. That step paved the way for an INF treaty to be signed at the Washington summit later in the year, and resulted in a series of trips by Shultz to meet with Gorbachev and Shevardnadze in Moscow, and by Shevardnadze to meet with Reagan and Shultz in Washington, to hammer out the details of an INF agreement and set the rest of the agenda for the as-yet-unscheduled summit in Washington.[8]

Gorbachev's INF announcement proved to be the first of a series of significant changes in Soviet policy that unfolded over the course of Reagan's last two years. In 1987, Gorbachev spoke of "reasonable sufficiency" as the guiding principle behind Soviet defense policy; while he did not initially spell out the meaning of this, it was clearly meant to provide him an ideological rationale for curtailed growth in defense expenditures and deployments, or even cuts.[9] In September, Shevardnadze privately told Shultz that the Soviets would withdraw from Afghanistan in the immediate future. The apparent sincerity of his statement—Reagan administration officials had been skeptical of previous public comments on the subject by Gorbachev and Shevardnadze—constituted, as Shultz wrote in his memoirs, "a development of immense importance."[10] By the time of Shevardnadze's September visit to the United States, the Soviets had agreed to sign an INF treaty that would completely eliminate all medium-range ballistic missiles worldwide—the Reagan administration's zero-zero option, first set forth in 1981—and all short-range missiles as well.

Yet the two sides made little progress toward reducing strategic weapons, which the Soviets continued to link to curtailing SDI. Stopping SDI, Carlucci later commented, "was an obsession of the Soviets."[11] During an October meeting with Shultz and Carlucci in Moscow that was supposed to finalize the INF Treaty and set a date for the Washington summit, Gorbachev attacked the Reagan administration's stance on SDI. SDI, Gorbachev said, was "this central problem," and together with strategic arms reductions constituted "the most important issues for the United States and the Soviet Union." Gorbachev insisted that the two sides agree not to withdraw from the ABM Treaty for ten years and negotiate what development and testing would be allowed.[12] Carlucci replied, "Mr. Secretary General, what you've just said is totally unacceptable to the president. He's not going to compromise SDI." A highly agitated Gorbachev "threw down his pencil," recalled Carlucci, "and said, 'Then we won't have a summit.' And Shultz said, 'Fine, we won't have the summit.'"[13] Before leaving the session, Shultz warned Gorbachev "to weigh carefully the advisability of tying the entire relationship with the United States to SDI."[14]

Just over a week later, Shevardnadze came to Washington with a letter from Gorbachev. Gorbachev proposed a summit in early December in Washington, at which the INF Treaty would be signed. He also wanted to work toward a START treaty, paired with an agreement on nonwithdrawal from the ABM Treaty, to be signed during a Moscow summit in the first half of 1988. While Gorbachev stated that the ABM Treaty should be "strictly observed," he dropped his insistence that provisions be negotiated and added to "strengthen" it.[15] The two sides agreed on a December summit in Washington, while leaving unresolved the issue of pairing a START deal to nonwithdrawal from the ABM Treaty.

Reagan emphasized publicly that his aim with respect to arms control extended beyond merely reducing nuclear weapons. He sought to abolish them and saw the INF and START negotiations as the beginning of that process. "What we're doing right now," he said, was "negotiating, even piecemeal, in trying to get a reduction and start on the path leading to ultimate elimination of nuclear weapons."[16] He left no doubt that SDI had an important role to play in nuclear abolition: "SDI truly serves the purposes of offensive weapons reduction. SDI can help us move toward a safer world. . . . And it has been a singularly effective instrument for bringing the Soviets to the bargaining table."[17]

Over the course of 1987, Carlucci occasionally brought in experts from outside the administration to provide Reagan with additional insights into how to proceed with the Soviets. One of those he invited later in the year was Perle, who had voluntarily left the Pentagon in the spring. Perle went "expressly to dissuade" Reagan of his nuclear abolitionism, which worried him deeply. Perle asked the president how he could be sure that the Soviets wouldn't cheat and keep some nuclear weapons, to which Reagan replied, "That's why we need SDI." (Perle "didn't find that convincing.") Reagan, Perle recalled, "was fixed in his ways on a nuclear-free world."[18] Carlucci and others, including his deputy, Colin Powell, worked to keep Reagan's nuclear abolitionism in check. They were concerned about what Reagan would try to negotiate with Gorbachev. Carlucci, in particular, did not want a Reykjavík redux.[19] Abraham Sofaer, the State Department's legal adviser, later told the author that "everyone [in the administration] understood [Reagan's] passionate commitment to his conviction to mutually reduce to zero. It was a vision that a lot of people who claim to admire Ronald Reagan didn't share." Reagan, Sofaer noted, was "different from" most of his aides; "he really meant it. No question about it."[20]

In November, Weinberger stepped down as secretary of defense, for personal reasons. Carlucci replaced him, and Powell moved up to become national security adviser. They remained in those positions, and Shultz in his, until the end of Reagan's tenure in January 1989. (Matlock had replaced Hartman as ambassador to Moscow earlier in the year and would stay there until 1991.)

By the autumn of 1987, then, SDI's two principal champions at the Pentagon, Weinberger and Perle, had left government, and the administration was losing support in the Congress for SDI amid political tensions and technical doubts. Yet the administration continued to receive indications both from the Soviets' words and actions and from intelligence reports that SDI was having a significant effect on Soviet policy. A CIA paper issued in November stated that the Soviets feared SDI for three primary reasons. First, there were the strategic implications: a defense would create uncertainty as to the ability of Soviet strategic forces to accomplish their targeting missions in war and their deterrence missions in times of crisis. And it would shift the technological competition from ballistic missiles, "which the Soviets have acquired at great cost," to advanced defensive technologies, in which the United States "has many advantages that would fundamentally change the dynamics of US-Soviet strategic competition." Second, there were the opportunity costs in the military and civilian sector that would result from a response, as the Soviets already faced stiff competition for resources. Third, there was the technological challenge posed by the initiative: the Soviets were worried that they could not compete with the United States in advanced defense technologies and also feared that the technological spinoffs from defense research would benefit other U.S. military capabilities and perhaps create new ones.[21]

The report estimated that the Soviets had four basic options in responding to SDI: saturating a defense by dramatically building up their strategic ballistic missile arsenal; circumventing it by building up cruise missiles and bombers; suppressing it with antisatellite (ASAT) weapons and space mines; or trying to match the initiative. The Soviets, the paper noted, would want to respond to SDI with some combination of these options. Yet it judged that they believed that trying to match the initiative was "prohibitive," both economically and technologically, while anything other than small, incremental increases in ICBMs, cruise missiles, and ASAT systems, which even then they were seeking to avoid, "would lead to unprecedented expenditures and greatly increased military demand for a variety of scarce resources."[22]

The paper emphasized that the threats posed to the USSR by SDI were affecting Gorbachev's approach toward resource allocation "at a crucial juncture." It asserted that the Soviets simply could not allow SDI to proceed unchallenged, as it could potentially reshape the U.S.-Soviet military and technological competition. At the same time, they could not mount a major response to it—even by producing more offensive strategic weapons—without cutting other military programs and diverting substantial resources both from the military and from Gorbachev's industrial modernization efforts. Those steps would, in turn, "inhibit the Soviets' ability to compete effectively with the West in the development and deployment of advanced technology weapons systems" in the long run. SDI, the assessment concluded, uniquely "exacerbates" Soviet "uncertainties about the outcome of the industrial modernization program and its effect on the country's ability to meet future military requirements"; those uncertainties "complicated" Soviet planning for long-term economic growth and weapons modernization.[23]

The paper judged that the Soviets had not yet committed themselves to any of the options listed above and would not do so until they were certain they could not stop SDI by arms control. It added that Gorbachev's claims that the Soviets would respond to SDI cheaply and effectively—which he often repeated to Reagan when they met— were purposely false, or at least exaggerated. "The prospect of near term trade-offs" that would result from a response to SDI, the report noted, "provides the Soviets a strong incentive to try to stop or delay U.S. development and especially deployment of BMD systems," and their goal was to do so through arms control, particularly by continuing to link curtailing SDI to reductions in strategic arms.[24]

A CIA intelligence assessment from the summer that focused on the implications of Gorbachev's domestic economic policy reported that the USSR's economic difficulties were worsening, that Gorbachev's reforms to that point had not succeeded in achieving his economic goals, and that he was likely to "push through more radical reforms" that would change the Soviet economic system. (The assessment also asserted that he would try to expand glasnost and foster controlled democratization.)[25]

The report emphasized that "external developments impinge on all of the decisions Gorbachev might make. The connection is direct in matters of resource allocation, but even progress on political and cultural reforms depends on the General Secretary's authority, which can be strengthened or eroded by what happens to his foreign policy initiatives." It stated that "Gorbachev's linkage of 'new thinking' on defense to his economic strategy suggests . . . that he is trying not only to affect Western opinion, but also to bring Soviet defense and foreign policies in line with his perception of the USSR's economic capabilities and priorities."

While Gorbachev was attempting to restrain or cut the Soviet defense burden, "it would be difficult if not impossible for him to resist for long the political and military demands for more resources for defense that would result from continuing improvements in U.S. strategic capabilities and conventional force technologies. SDI, in particular, confronts the Soviets with an extreme form of competition they wish to avoid." The assessment noted that Gorbachev "must man-age the military competition with the United States politically in order to avoid having to deal with it in ways that could subvert his economic agenda." It added that the imminent INF Treaty "very likely reflects this strategy." While the resource implications of the treaty were in themselves minimal, "the larger process of arms control is seen by Gor-bachev as his principal avenue for politically constraining external pressures for enlarging the USSR's overall resource commitment to the military." Gorbachev, it judged, wanted to provide momentum toward a more substantial agreement on strategic defensive and offen-sive forces.[26]

The CIA papers provided further evidence to the administration that Soviet leaders' perceptions of SDI were affecting their decision-making environment and their approach to foreign and domestic pol-icy, and even contributing to serious policy changes. The papers also went beyond previous intelligence assessments in judging that Gor-bachev was likely to turn to dramatic, systemic change in the near future.

In an NSDD issued in November that laid out Reagan's objec-tives for the Washington summit, the administration stated that the signing of the INF Treaty "represents a triumph and vindication for the policy that this Administration has followed toward the Soviet Union from the start." It added that the USSR was "changing slowly," al-though the nature of its regime still set "limits on what we can achieve with Moscow by negotiation and diplomacy." It underscored that Rea-gan and his advisers should ensure that the Washington summit did not focus solely or even mainly on the INF Treaty and accomplishing a START agreement, directing that "[p]rior to and at the Summit, we should create political pressure for the Soviets to take positive steps on our human rights, regional, and bilateral concerns."[27] By this stage, the administration believed that it would be able to follow through on its long-term goal of encouraging change in Soviet policies and in the Soviet system itself through pressure and through discourse with Gor-bachev, whom many in the administration—Reagan, Shultz, and Mat-lock, for example—viewed as taking steps toward greater economic and political openness within the USSR. The administration sought to keep issues related to the internal nature of the USSR, as well as its geopolitical behavior, at the front of the agenda.

It succeeded in that respect at the Washington summit, during which, in addition to signing the INF Treaty, Reagan and Gorbachev worked through bilateral relations, human rights, and regional issues, such as Afghanistan, Central America, and southern Africa. On SDI, there remained little progress (Carlucci recalled that Gorbachev "ranted about SDI at some length" during the summit), and although the two sides drew closer to mutually acceptable terms for a START treaty, the Soviets' continued linkage of reductions in strategic weapons to blocking SDI limited the prospects for START.[28]

By the end of the summit, however, Reagan and Gorbachev had further developed the comfortable working relationship and interaction that they had initiated at Geneva but that had been impeded at the end of Reykjavík. Carlucci later stated that Reagan "was very taken by Gorbachev"; he "understood that this was a new figure in the Soviet Union" and "that this was a historical moment." Reagan, Carlucci told the author, "grew to like Gorbachev, and he thought Gorbachev was making changes." Carlucci, however, urged caution, saying to Reagan that Gorbachev was "trying to save communism, not get rid of it, Mr. President, we've got to be very careful." Reagan, Carlucci noted, "would take that on board, but he was very positive on the things Gorbachev was doing."[29] Both Reagan and Shultz were optimistic that Gorbachev was moving toward major changes, even if only because he felt compelled to do so, and they sought to encourage him in that direction. Shultz later noted that Reagan had "confidence and willingness to appraise things as changeable and changing" while others around him expressed "nervousness."[30] Iklé told the author that Reagan "pushed cooperation with a seemingly changing Soviet Union more boldly than many of us did who worked for him." (He added that, in retrospect, "some of us, including myself, were skeptical that [changes in the USSR] would go very far for probably a bit too long.")[31]

In early February 1988, Gorbachev announced that Soviet forces would begin to withdraw from Afghanistan in May and would be out within a year. Throughout the early months of 1988, Shultz and Shevardnadze continued their Washington-Moscow circuit for meetings with Reagan and Gorbachev. Increasingly, the agendas of those meetings focused on working toward solutions to regional disputes, principally Afghanistan, and issues related to internal changes in the USSR, such as human rights, as well as the START negotiations. SDI gradually receded as other aspects of the expanding range of discussions and negotiations between the two nations came to the fore.[32]

To Reagan, SDI remained a means of achieving his long-held dream. During a speech in March 1988, he said:

> The fact is that many Americans are unaware that at this moment the United States has absolutely no defenses against a ballistic missile attack. If even one missile were to be accidentally fired at the United States, the President would have no way of preventing the wholesale destruction of American lives. All he could do is retaliate—wipe out millions of lives on the other side. This is the position we find ourselves in; to perpetuate it forever is simply morally untenable.
>
> . . . It can be said that the old discredited policy of MAD is like two adversaries holding loaded guns to each other's head. It may work for a while, but you sure better hope you don't make a slip. People who put their trust in MAD must trust it to work 100 percent—forever, no slip-ups, no madmen, no unmanageable crises, no mistakes—forever.
>
> For those who are not reassured by such a prospect, and I count myself among their number, we must ask: Isn't it time we invented a cure for the madness? Isn't it time to begin curing the world of this nuclear threat? . . . I believe that, given the gravity of the nuclear threat to humanity, any unnecessary delay in the development and deployment of SDI is unconscionable.
>
> . . . [T]he world is changing rapidly, and technology won't stop here. All we can do is make sure that technology becomes the ally and protector of peace, that we build better shields rather than sharper and more deadly swords. In so doing, maybe we can help to bring an end to the brutal legacy of modern warfare. We can stop the madness from continuing into the next century. We can create a better, more secure, more moral world, where peace goes hand in hand with freedom from fear—forever.[33]

In the meantime, Carlucci, having taken over at the Pentagon, "wanted some reassurance" that SDI "could be done." He commissioned a group of experts from outside the administration, most of them scientists, to provide an independent and objective report solely to him. Carlucci later told the author that "they concluded it could be done, but at a big price." He "called in Jim Abrahamson, who was the project manager, and told him he should stop being a salesman and get the costs down." Carlucci then put SDI into the standard Pentagon budgeting and programming system—it had been outside the system since its inception—"so it could be weighed against other priorities."[34]

Both Reagan and Shultz pushed hard for a START treaty to be prepared for the Moscow summit, which was scheduled for the spring of 1988, even though Carlucci and the Joint Chiefs emphasized the difficulties of that undertaking.[35] With the substance of the treaty far from finalized, the two sides still in dispute over the terms of the Soviets' linkage of strategic arms reductions to restrictions on SDI, and both the Soviets and the United States looking toward the presidential election in the fall of 1988 and a new administration, the prospects for a START treaty during Reagan's term in office faded as the year progressed.

A CIA paper on Gorbachev's approach to arms control issued before the Moscow summit reiterated that the Soviet leader's arms control objectives were being "driven in large measure by domestic economic imperatives," noting that the Soviet economy was "foundering" and that Gorbachev himself had referred to it as reaching a "pre-crisis" stage.[36] (A separate CIA paper in April had reported that the Soviet economy had grown at its lowest rate in ten years during 1987, that "[d]ifficulties were encountered in practically all sectors of the economy," that the poor performance was likely to continue in 1988, and that Gorbachev's efforts to reform the economy were "off to an unimpressive start.")[37] The paper suggested that Gorbachev sought to prevent the United States from withdrawing from the ABM Treaty as "a guarantee against being dragged into a full-scale technological competition with the US in SDI" and, together with reductions in strategic arms, as a means of "free[ing] his hand to pursue his highest priority economic goal, the modernization of the Soviet economy." Nonetheless, Gorbachev might believe that a new U.S. administration would build on the work already achieved in START and provide "a fresh opportunity to break the impasse."[38]

Setting out its objectives for the Moscow summit in an NSDD, the administration stated that a primary aim was "to consolidate the gains made by the Administration on the four-part agenda with the Soviet Union and to press for further progress" on a START agreement, "significant improvement in the Soviet Union's human rights performance, and resolution of regional conflicts beyond Afghanistan." The president should encourage the Soviet Union to move toward democratization, the NSDD added.[39]

Reagan pursued those objectives at the summit, held in May. In his public speeches in Moscow and his meetings with Gorbachev, Reagan tried to promote greater openness and freedom in the Soviet Union. He and Gorbachev worked, for the most part, in an amicable way. Notably, during a walk with Gorbachev in Red Square, a reporter asked Reagan what had become of the "evil empire." "I was talking about another time, another era," Reagan responded.[40]

The CIA issued another assessment in June that stated that the ongoing "debate in the USSR on the precepts that guide decisions on the size and composition of Soviet military forces . . . derive[d] much of its impetus from the need to manage defense requirements under conditions of increasing economic stringency." It noted, "The doctrine of sufficiency appears designed to provide a theoretical justification for shifting resources away from the defense sector."[41] In a section on high technology, the assessment noted that while "the intensity of the Soviets' earlier alarm over SDI seems to have moderated somewhat as they have gained a clearer appreciation of the technical and political obstacles to deployment of an effective system," they "remained concerned that even a partially effective SDI has the potential to change the strategic balance to the Soviets' serious disadvantage," that matching SDI "promises to severely strain Soviet economic and technological capacities," that overwhelming SDI through fielding more nuclear weapons "would still add unwelcome costs to the Soviet defense budget," and that "[r]egardless of the ultimate success or failure of SDI as an ABM system, the program may produce spinoffs that could lead to other threatening US advances in space-based or ground-launched weapons systems."[42] The administration thus received information in its last months that while SDI's importance was slipping, it still played a part in creating conditions within the USSR that encouraged changes in both Soviet foreign and domestic policy.

By the autumn, attention within the United States had turned almost entirely to the presidential election, and the Soviets now viewed the Reagan administration as a lame duck. Reagan and Gorbachev met one last time, however, after the election, in New York. After Gorbachev gave a speech at the United Nations during which he announced significant reductions in Soviet conventional forces in Eastern Europe, he met with Reagan and President-elect Bush for lunch. Reagan told Gorbachev that "we all" were on his side concerning his attempts to reform the Soviet system. Gorbachev replied that his country "had become a different one" and "would never go back to what it had been three years before."[43]

CONCLUSION

Ronald Reagan harbored an intense dislike of nuclear weapons and the concept of mutual assured destruction. That antinuclearism was based on his deeply rooted personal beliefs and religious views. Reagan was convinced that it was his personal mission to avert nuclear war. His goals were to eliminate the threat posed by nuclear weapons—particularly those in the hands of the Soviet Union—and ultimately to abolish nuclear weapons altogether.

Before becoming president, Reagan had also developed his own approach to Cold War policy. That approach centered on his views that the Soviet system was inherently flawed, that it was straining under Soviet foreign and defense policy generally and the Soviet arms buildup specifically, and that the leadership of the USSR could be compelled to change its policies and even the internal system of that country if confronted with U.S. pressure paired with skillful negotiations. Those views, which he developed on his own and which departed from the conventional wisdom of the time, later became the basis of the Reagan administration's Cold War policy. They were tied closely to his nuclear abolitionism; Reagan believed that if faced with strong competition from the United States, particularly in the form of an arms race, the Soviet leadership would be forced to agree to deep reductions in nuclear weapons.

After an initial period of disorganization and turmoil during his first year as president, Reagan exerted personal control over his administration's national security policy-making process by reorganizing the bureaucracy and by shifting personnel so that those who followed his lead and adhered to his approach occupied positions of influence, particularly on the NSC staff. In 1982, the Reagan administration established an unprecedentedly ambitious and assertive U.S. Cold War policy that was founded upon the president's beliefs. NSDD 75 sought to encourage change in Soviet policy and within the USSR's internal system by applying "pressure on the USSR to weaken the sources of imperialism" so as to promote a "more pluralistic political and economic system." The administration's policy documents were purposefully vague as to *how* the United States would pressure the Soviet system to encourage both international restraint and fundamental changes from within, however.

In his first two years in office, Reagan's long-standing desire to undertake a missile defense effort grew based upon personal and political experiences. He sought to gather information on the economic and technological feasibility of such an effort.

In late 1982 and early 1983, Reagan exploited his presidential power to control and expedite the inception and announcement of SDI. He waited briefly but then seized upon what seemed to him an opportune moment. He carefully organized support for the notion of expanded research and development in missile defense among certain key elements within the bureaucracy, in particular the Joint Chiefs of Staff and the NSC staff, without which he felt the project could not proceed. He then acted discreetly and rapidly to avoid interference by other elements within the administration, such as the Defense and State Departments, and by Congress.

Reagan saw SDI as a means of accomplishing his objective of a nuclear-free world. An effective missile defense, he believed, could render ballistic missiles "impotent and obsolete." In his eyes, such a defense would make not just ballistic missiles but all nuclear weapons negotiable and would spur negotiations that would result in the elimination of all nuclear arms. He thought that the United States could then share a defense, and that an "internationalized" defense would serve to guarantee security in a nuclear-free world. From the inception of the initiative throughout the rest of his presidency, Reagan held unwaveringly to that vision of SDI.

Few of Reagan's advisers initially knew what to make of SDI in the context of U.S.-Soviet relations, in part because of the sudden way the president had created the initiative. Largely because of the vehement and sustained negative Soviet reaction to SDI, it soon came to occupy a central role in U.S.-Soviet relations. Reagan's principal advisers disagreed over how to approach and pursue SDI. All of them, however, and Reagan himself, saw it as a source of leverage over the Soviets in arms control negotiations. It appeared that Soviet fears of the economic and technological ramifications of SDI led the Soviet Union to engage seriously in arms reduction negotiations in order to constrain the initiative.

Some of Reagan's advisers, especially Shultz and Nitze, who were skeptical regarding the feasibility of SDI, sought to use it as an actual bargaining chip in arms control talks, to be traded away for reductions in Soviet offensive strategic forces. This accorded with the view of McFarlane, who had played a major role in the inception of the initiative in the belief that it could later be traded away. Others, including Weinberger and Perle, intended to develop the initiative steadily so that if an advanced strategic defense proved feasible, it could be deployed and improve deterrence of nuclear attack.

Reagan resolutely adhered to pursuing his particular vision of SDI, which constrained what his advisers could do by way of shaping and using the initiative to achieve their goals for it. In serving as an arbiter of the various views within the administration, Reagan adopted those that seemed to him to advance his own objectives and rejected those that did not. In particular, while Reagan allowed SDI to be used to bring the Soviets to the negotiating table, he refused to allow it to be traded away as a bargaining chip.

None of Reagan's advisers thought that all elements of his vision of SDI were feasible or desirable, especially the abolition of nuclear weapons and the sharing of a defense system, and many of them tried to dissuade him or "finesse" Reagan's objectives by rendering them unattainable. Yet Reagan worked assiduously to realize his concept. At crucial junctures, enough of Reagan's advisers supported various elements of it for him to proceed as he wanted; and when they did not, he kept to his view but sought to bring it about at a different time.

Based for the most part on their perceptions and interpretation of the Soviets' reaction to SDI, almost all senior officials in the Reagan administration, including the president himself, came to the conclusion during Reagan's second term that SDI constituted a unique and powerful strategic tool in pursuing the administration's policy aims with respect to the Soviet Union. They believed that Soviet fears of SDI were a principal factor driving the Soviets' increasing willingness to negotiate deep cuts in offensive nuclear forces and, in the years after Gorbachev took power in the USSR, judged that the Soviet leadership's concern over SDI contributed to some of the changes Gorbachev made in both foreign and domestic policy.

Reagan, alone with Gorbachev and their foreign ministers in meetings at Reykjavík, proposed to his Soviet counterpart that they eliminate all nuclear arms. Gorbachev agreed but insisted that SDI would have to be curtailed. The negotiations foundered on the disagreement over the future of SDI. Reagan was deeply disappointed at the outcome, believing that he had come close to achieving his goal of nuclear abolition. But he and many of his aides also interpreted Reykjavík as a turning point after which Gorbachev was more inclined to pursue change in Soviet policies, having failed to secure downward pressure on defense spending through arms control.

Reagan continued to push for the realization of his concept of SDI during his last two years in office, even as the significance of the initiative waned in the overall context of U.S.-Soviet relations as the range of issues and cooperation broadened and as SDI faced mounting troubles in the United States. While the administration noted that the Soviets recognized some of those troubles, SDI remained, in the view of Reagan and his advisers, a strategic tool through the end of the administration.

Reagan was a thoughtful man of bold, original ideas. He was also a skillful wielder of power. He employed the inherent power of the U.S. presidency to direct the administration toward his goals. He did so both through direct action and by arbitrating the advice of his advisers in such a way as to advance his own views. It is notable that several of Reagan's former aides later stated that he was smarter and more adept than they thought at the time, that he was constantly working to achieve his own ends whether they agreed or not—and in many cases when they could not even see that that was what he was doing.[44]

Reagan's dream of a nuclear-free world protected by an internationalized missile defense is of course unrealized. Yet in many important respects Reagan's goals have been accomplished, and in others progress has been made toward those goals.

Reagan successfully negotiated the INF Treaty, which eliminated an entire category of nuclear weapons for the first time. The INF Treaty as signed in 1987 corresponded almost exactly with the zero-zero proposal that the Reagan administration had set out in its first year, which critics had assailed as being nonnegotiable. Reagan laid the groundwork for his successor to complete the START Treaty, the first agreement to reduce strategic nuclear weapons.

Under Gorbachev the Soviet leadership did undertake reforms that changed the Soviet system—and eventually instigated the collapse of the Soviet empire and the Soviet Union itself. The United States and Russia, no longer enemies, have concluded several agreements to make vast cuts in their respective nuclear arsenals. The Soviet Union is no more, the direct nuclear threat from Russia to the United States is small, and Russian and U.S. nuclear forces are greatly reduced.

Despite persistent controversy, plans to build an extensive missile defense continue in the United States. The present U.S. missile defense effort derives from Reagan's initiative, although recent administrations have changed the strategic rationale for it as the international environment has changed.

We live in a world that Ronald Reagan did much to bring about. There is a great deal to be gained by exploring what it was that he actually sought to do, and why.

NOTES

CHAPTER I: ORIGINS

1. Notice bill for "Atomic Power and Foreign Policy," mass meeting sponsored by the Hollywood Independent Citizens Committee of Arts, Sciences and Professions, Hollywood Legion Stadium, December 12, 1945 (notice bill undated), from the University of Southern California, School of Cinema-Television, Warner Bros. Archives, Los Angeles, Calif. (hereafter USC-WB); letter from Edmund Morris to the author (hereafter the author will be cited as "PL"), November 12, 2001. Morris's letter draws on his research at USC-WB. In 1985, President Reagan appointed Morris to be his authorized biographer. Morris's book *Dutch: A Memoir of Ronald Reagan* (London: HarperCollins, 1999) appeared fourteen years later. Morris does not mention the December 1945 rally in *Dutch*, but he raised it during an interview with PL, August 21, 2001, Washington, D.C. (hereafter all interviews with the author will be cited as "PL interview"). He discussed it further during a telephone conversation with PL on September 4, 2001, and in the November 12, 2001, letter.
2. Stephen Vaughn, *Ronald Reagan in Hollywood: Movies and Politics* (Cambridge, U.K.: Cambridge University Press, 1994), pp. 121–132; Morris, *Dutch*, pp. 232–234; Anne Edwards, *Early Reagan: The Rise of an American Hero* (London: Hodder & Stoughton, 1987), pp. 293–312; Lou Cannon, *President Reagan: The Role of a Lifetime*, 2nd ed. (New York: PublicAffairs, 2000), pp. 243–244.
3. Reagan, quoted in Cannon, *President Reagan*, p. 244.
4. Vaughn, *Ronald Reagan in Hollywood*, pp. 121–122; "Three Discuss Atomic Power," *Los Angeles Times*, December 13, 1945, p. 10.
5. S. David Broscious, "Longing for International Control, Banking on American Superiority: Harry S Truman's Approach to Nuclear Weapons," in John Lewis Gaddis, Philip H. Gordon, Ernest R. May, and Jonathan Rosenberg, eds., *Cold War Statesmen Confront the Bomb: Nuclear Diplomacy Since 1945* (Oxford: Oxford University Press, 1999), pp. 25, 20. "U.N.O. Atomic Control Seen by January," *Los Angeles Times*, December 10, 1945, p. 6, provides an indication of the seriousness with which the proposals to internationalize atomic power were taken during late 1945.
6. Edward Teller with Judith L. Shoolery, *Memoirs: A Twentieth Century Journey in Science and Politics* (Cambridge, Mass.: Perseus Publishing, 2001), pp. 233–235.
7. Morris, *Dutch*, pp. 735 (note 221), 221, 229.
8. Notice bill for "Atomic Power and Foreign Policy" mass meeting, from USC-WB; Morris, letter to PL, November 12, 2001; Vaughn, *Ronald Reagan in Hollywood*, p. 122. On Corwin and "Set Your Clock at U-235," see R. LeRoy Bannerman, *Norman Corwin and Radio: The Golden Years* (University, Ala.: University of Alabama Press, 1986), especially pp. 176–177; and Norman Corwin, *Untitled and Other*

Radio Dramas (New York: Henry Holt and Company, 1947), pp. 509–518, 547–548 (for the text of the poem, pp. 511–515).

9. Norman Corwin, "Set Your Clock at U-235," in Corwin, Untitled *and Other Radio Dramas*, pp. 511, 513.

10. Telegram from R. J. Obringer, Warner Bros., to Reagan, c/o MCA Artists, December 6, 1945, from USC-WB; handwritten note on same; telegram from Lew Wasserman, MCA Artists, to Obringer, December 7, 1945, USC-WB; Morris, letter to PL, November 12, 2001; Vaughn, *Ronald Reagan in Hollywood*, pp. 121–122.

11. Truman, quoted in Broscious, "Longing for International Control," p. 36.

12. Ronald Reagan, *An American Life: The Autobiography* (New York: Pocket Books, 1990), pp. 105–115; Lou Cannon, *Reagan* (New York: Perigree Books, 1982), pp. 79–85; Cannon, *President Reagan*, pp. 242–246; Vaughn, *Ronald Reagan in Hollywood*, passim; Morris, *Dutch*, pp. 218–273.

13. Alexander L. George, "Assessing Presidential Character," in Alexander L. George and Juliette L. George, *Presidential Personality and Performance* (Boulder, Colo.: Westview Press, 1998), pp. 154–156. On the suddenness with which Reagan became a dedicated anti-Communist in 1946–1947, see Morris, *Dutch*, pp. 246, 271, 288, 750 (note 287).

14. Reagan, *An American Life*, p. 550.

15. Ibid., pp. 21–33; Cannon, *Reagan*, pp. 22–32; Morris, *Dutch*, pp. 11–51.

16. Reagan, *An American Life*, pp. 21–33; Cannon, *Reagan*, pp. 22–32; Morris, *Dutch*, pp. 11–51. See in particular Morris, *Dutch*, pp. 26, 28.

17. Cannon, *Reagan*, p. 28; Morris, *Dutch*, pp. 24–43.

18. Reagan, *An American Life*, p. 31.

19. Ibid. See also Morris, *Dutch*, pp. 25, 29; Cannon, *Reagan*, p. 28; and Adriana Bosch, *Reagan: An American Story* (New York: TV Books, 2000), p. 26.

20. Reagan, quoted in Cannon, *Reagan*, pp. 18, 19.

21. Trude Feldman, "Neil Reagan: Memories of the President's Mother," *The San Antonio Sunday Express-News*, May 10, 1981, p. 2-E, from the Miscellaneous Collection (also called "Vertical File") of the Ronald Reagan Presidential Library, Simi Valley, Calif. (hereafter RRPL-MC/VF).

22. David Nyhan, "'Born-Again' Run the Race for President," *The Boston Globe*, May 26, 1980, p. 11.

23. Reagan, *An American Life*, pp. 20–21.

24. Ronald Reagan with Richard G. Hubler, *Where's the Rest of Me? The Ronald Reagan Story* (New York: Duell, Sloan and Pearce, 1965), p. 21; Cannon, *President Reagan*, p. 180; Morris, *Dutch*, p. 61.

25. Morris, *Dutch*, p. 703 (note 91); see also Cannon, *President Reagan*, p. 181.

26. Reagan with Hubler, *Where's the Rest of Me?* p. 21; see also Joseph Roddy, "Ronnie to the Rescue," *Look*, November 1, 1966, p. 52, from RRPL-MC/VF.

27. Morris, *Dutch*, p. 662.

28. William P. Clark, "Ronald Reagan, Lifeguard," p. 8, Foreword to Ronald Reagan, "Abortion and the Conscience of the Nation" (Sacramento, Calif.: New Regency Publishing, 2000). (Reagan's essay was first published in 1983.) Courtesy of Clark.

29. Cannon, *President Reagan*, pp. 181–182. On the relationship between Reagan's lifeguarding and his political career, see Cannon's book review of Morris's *Dutch*. Cannon, "To Tell the Truth: Will the Real Ronald Reagan Please Stand Up?" *Los Angeles Times Book Review*, October 3, 1999, pp. 1, 6–7.

30. Morris, quoted in Bosch, *Reagan: An American Story*, p. 35.

31. Michael K. Deaver, *A Different Drummer: My Thirty Years with Ronald Reagan* (New York: HarperCollins, 2001), pp. 14–15; Morris, *Dutch*, p. 667; Bosch, *Reagan: An American Story*, p. 34.

32. Reagan, *An American Life*, pp. 44–56; Cannon, *Reagan*, pp. 33–41.

33. Cannon, *Reagan*, pp. 36–37; Reagan with Hubler, *Where's the Rest of Me?* p. 43.

34. Morris, *Dutch*, pp. 80–83; Edna St. Vincent Millay, *Aria da Capo: A Play in One Act* (New York: Harper & Brothers, 1920). Morris and PL discussed the possible link between this play and Reagan's later dislike of mutual assured destruction during an interview on August 21, 2001, the former expressing regret that he had never asked Reagan about the connection.

35. Reagan, *An American Life*, pp. 56–59; Cannon, *Reagan*, pp. 36–37; Morris, *Dutch*, p. 108. See R. C. Sherriff, *Journey's End: A Play in Three Acts* (New York: Brentano's, 1929).

36. Morris, *Dutch*, pp. 99–100. The longer of the two pieces, entitled "Killed in Action" (written May 7, 1931), is published in its entirety in Kiron K. Skinner, Annelise Anderson, and Martin Anderson, eds., *Reagan, in His Own Hand: The Writings of Ronald Reagan That Reveal His Revolutionary Vision for America* (New York: Free Press, 2001), pp. 430–433.

37. Cannon, *Reagan*, p. 37; Morris, *Dutch*, pp. 111, 122–133; Reagan, *An American Life*, p. 75.

38. In the summer of 1943, Reagan was "the top box-office draw in Hollywood." Morris, *Dutch*, p. 209.

39. Ibid., pp. 157–217; Edwards, *Early Reagan*, pp. 292–293; Doug McClelland, *Hollywood on Ronald Reagan: Friends and Enemies Discuss Our President, The Actor* (Winchester, Mass.: Faber and Faber, 1983), pp. 45, 46, 166, 188.

40. Of his politics during those years, Reagan later wrote, "Probably because of my dad's influences and my experiences during the Depression, I had loved the Democratic Party." Reagan, *An American Life*, p. 119.

41. Cannon, *Reagan*, p. 80.

42. Reagan, quoted in Morris, *Dutch*, p. 227. "I really wanted a better world and I think I thought what I was saying would help bring it about." Reagan, *An American Life*, p. 106.

43. Reagan, *An American Life*, pp. 106, 111–113.

44. Morris, *Dutch*, pp. 222, 232; Vaughn, *Ronald Reagan in Hollywood*, p. 123. See also Edwards, *Early Reagan*, p. 302.

45. Cannon, *Reagan*, p. 79; Cannon, *President Reagan*, p. 243. See also Vaughn, *Ronald Reagan in Hollywood*, pp. 123–132.

46. Reagan, quoted in Vaughn, *Ronald Reagan in Hollywood*, p. 130, and in Edwards, *Early Reagan*, p. 300.

47. Morris, *Dutch*, pp. 230, 231.

48. Reagan, *An American Life*, pp. 106–107. See also Vaughn, *Ronald Reagan in Hollywood*, p. 130, and Edwards, *Early Reagan*, p. 302.

49. Ronald Reagan, "How Do You Fight Communism?" *Fortnight*, January 22, 1951, p. 13, from RRPL-MC/VF; Reagan, *An American Life*, pp. 112–113; Vaughn, *Ronald Reagan in Hollywood*, pp. 125, 130–132; Morris, *Dutch*, pp. 232, 233–234; Cannon, *Reagan*, p. 79. Reagan later claimed that he had resigned at the same time as the other members of the Roosevelt-led group. Reagan, *An American Life*,

p. 113. He may not have, however. One of the group maintained that Reagan stayed on with HICCASP for a while to act as an "observer" for the FBI. Morris, *Dutch*, pp. 234, 739–740 (notes). See also Vaughn, *Ronald Reagan in Hollywood*, p. 132.

50. Reagan, quoted in Vaughn, *Ronald Reagan in Hollywood*, p. 132.
51. Cannon, *Reagan*, p. 72; Reagan, *An American Life*, p. 103.
52. Reagan, *An American Life*, pp. 107–110; Cannon, *Reagan*, pp. 73–76; Cannon, *President Reagan*, p. 244; Morris, *Dutch*, pp. 222–226, 237–246.
53. Morris, *Dutch*, p. 288; Reagan, *An American Life*, p. 111.
54. Reagan, *An American Life*, p. 111.
55. Morris, *Dutch*, p. 246.
56. Reagan, *An American Life*, pp. 114, 115.
57. For a similar conclusion, see Cannon, *Reagan*, pp. 86–87; and Morris, *Dutch*, pp. 246, 247, 261. Reagan later wrote that during those years he had come to conclude that "Joseph Stalin had set out to make Hollywood an instrument of propaganda for his program of Soviet expansionism aimed at communizing the world." Reagan, *An American Life*, p. 110.
58. In 1981, then-President Reagan stated that his perception of communism was still fundamentally shaped by his Hollywood experiences from the late 1940s: "I had my earliest experience with communism, and it is still pretty much the same. I know that it sounds kind of foolish maybe to link Hollywood, an experience there, to the world situation, and yet, the tactics seemed to be pretty much the same." Reagan, press conference, December 23, 1981, in *Public Papers of the Presidents, 1981* (Washington, D.C.: U.S. Government Printing Office, 1982), p. 1197.
59. Fred Iklé, PL interview, July 24, 2001, Washington, D.C.; Jack Matlock, PL interview, September 5, 2001, Princeton, N.J.
60. Reagan, *An American Life*, pp. 119–120.
61. Reagan, "How Do You Fight Communism?" p. 13.
62. Morris, *Dutch*, pp. 304–305; Cannon, *Reagan*, pp. 92–94.
63. Reagan, *An American Life*, pp. 127–129.
64. "I have been making these tours for eight years and not once has General Electric suggested a subject, read a speech I have prepared, offered one opinion for me to use." Reagan, quoted in Larry Lawrence, "There Are No Strangers in a Crowd with Reagan," *Amarillo Daily News*, March 3, 1962, p. 5, from RRPL-MC/VF. See also Reagan, *An American Life*, pp. 128–130; and Cannon, *Reagan*, pp. 93, 95.
65. Reagan, *An American Life*, pp. 128–130. During a speech in 1962, Reagan stated, "I am a sort of 'Johnny One-Note.' I continue more or less hammering away at the same subject. The music is always the same, now and then a little re-wording of the lyrics, but it still comes out sounding the same way." Reagan, "Losing Freedom by Installments," address to the Rotary Club of Long Beach, Calif., June 6, 1962, p. 1, from RRPL-MC/VF.
66. Reagan, "A Time for Choosing," *Monitor*, March 1963, p. 1; Reagan, "A Time for Choosing" (undated, 1961–1963), p. 2, both from RRPL-MC/VF.
67. See, e.g., Reagan, "A Time for Choosing," *Monitor*, March 1963, p. 1; Reagan, "Losing Freedom by Installments," *Qualified Contractor*, November 1961, p. 1; Reagan, quoted in "Liberalism Lambasted by Reagan," *The Dallas Morning News*, February 28, 1962, p. 1; Reagan, speech in *Executives' Club News* (Chicago: Executives' Club, March 26, 1965), p. 3, all from RRPL-MC/VF.

68. Reagan, "Encroaching Control," speech at the Evanston Chamber of Commerce, Evanston, Ill.: May 8, 1961, p. 12, from RRPL-MC/VF.

69. Reagan, "No Place to Escape To," *Monitor*, September 1964, p. 32, from RRPL-MC/VF.

70. Reagan, address to employees of Forest Lawn, November 2, 1961, p. 3; Reagan, "Losing Freedom by Installments," *Qualified Contractor*, November 1961, p. 1, both from RRPL-MC/VF.

71. See especially Reagan, "Losing Freedom by Installments," *Qualified Contractor*, November 1961, p. 1; and Reagan, "A Time for Choosing" (undated, 1961–1963), p. 2, both from RRPL-MC/VF.

72. "Speech to Engineers: Actor Reagan Hurls Blast at Liberals," *Corpus Christi Caller*, February 23, 1962, p. 12; Reagan, "Losing Freedom by Installments," *Qualified Contractor*, November 1961, p. 6, both from RRPL-MC/VF.

73. Reagan, "Losing Freedom by Installments," address to the Rotary Club of Long Beach, Calif., June 6, 1962, p. 6; see also Reagan, "A Time for Choosing" (undated, 1961–1963), p. 3, both from RRPL-MC/VF.

74. Reagan, "Are Liberals Really Liberal?" (1963), in Skinner, Anderson, and Anderson, eds., *Reagan, in His Own Hand*, pp. 438–442.

75. Barry Goldwater, *The Conscience of a Conservative* (Washington, D.C.: Regnery Gateway, 1990 [originally published 1960]), pp. 88, 95, 96, 104, 112, 117.

76. Ibid., pp. 114, 117. See also Barry Goldwater, *Why Not Victory? A Fresh Look at American Foreign Policy* (New York: McGraw-Hill, 1962).

77. Goldwater, *Why Not Victory?* p. 163.

78. For more early instances of Reagan stating that the Soviet economy was a source of comparative weakness and potential vulnerability relative to that of the United States, see Reagan, "A Time for Choosing" (undated, 1961–1963), p. 15; and Reagan, speech printed in *The Shreveport Times*, March 1, 1964, p. B3, both from RRPL-MC/VF.

79. Skinner, Anderson, and Anderson make a similar point in their comments introducing the 1963 document in *Reagan, in His Own Hand*, p. 438.

80. Reagan, speech printed in *The Shreveport Times*, March 1, 1964, p. B3, from RRPL-MC/VF.

81. Reagan, "No Place to Escape To," *Monitor*, September 1964, p. 32; Reagan, speech printed in *Executives' Club News* (Chicago: Executives' Club, March 26, 1965), p. 8; Reagan, "Freedom Is Not Spelled with an 'S,'" *Proceedings of the International Newspaper Advertising Executives and the California Newspaper Advertising Executives Association 1965 Joint Meeting*, p. 12; Reagan, "Freedom Has No 'S,'" August 1965, pp. 1, 7, all from RRPL-MC/VF.

82. There would be a further precedent for his "evil empire" speech of March 1983: in 1978, Reagan called the USSR an "evil influence throughout the world." Kiron K. Skinner, "Reagan's Plan," *The National Interest*, 56 (Summer 1999), p. 139.

83. Lou Cannon, *Ronald Reagan: The Presidential Portfolio* (New York: PublicAffairs, 2001), p. 33.

84. See, e.g., "Liberalism Lambasted by Reagan," *The Dallas Morning News*, February 28, 1962, p. 1; and "'Loopholes' in Tax Structure Attacked," *Amarillo Daily News*, March 3, 1962, p. 1, both from RRPL-MC/VF.

85. Reagan, *An American Life*, pp. 132–136; Cannon, *Reagan*, pp. 96–97.

86. Reagan, "A Time for Choosing," nationally televised address, October 27, 1964, in

Ronald Reagan, *A Time for Choosing: The Speeches of Ronald Reagan, 1961–1982* (Chicago: Regnery Gateway, 1983), pp. 41–57.

87. Cannon, *Reagan*, p. 98; see also pp. 13–14, 98–103.

88. Teller with Shoolery, *Memoirs*, p. 509.

89. Ibid., pp. 224, 467, 525–526.

90. Agenda for November 22, 1967, Reagan visit from archives of the Lawrence Livermore National Laboratory, Livermore, Calif. (hereafter LLNL).

91. Donald R. Baucom, *The Origins of SDI, 1944–1983* (Lawrence: University Press of Kansas, 1992), pp. 19, 92; Donald R. Baucom, "The U.S. Missile Defense Program: 1944–1997" (unpublished paper, courtesy of Baucom), p. 2; Teller with Shoolery, *Memoirs*, pp. 508–509.

92. Teller with Shoolery, *Memoirs*, p. 509. There appears to be no documentary evidence that Reagan wrote or spoke of missile defense before 1967. In interviews, those who were closest to him and later worked with him on missile defense knew of no occasion earlier than 1967 that had stimulated Reagan's interest in missile defense. Anderson, PL interview, July 10, 2000, by telephone; General James Abrahamson, quoted in Deborah Hart Strober and Gerald S. Strober, *Reagan: The Man and His Presidency, The Oral History of an Era* (Boston: Houghton Mifflin, 1998), p. 231. Both Cannon and Morris, who briefly mention the Livermore visit, concur. Cannon, *President Reagan*, p. 276; Morris, *Dutch*, p. 470.

93. Teller with Shoolery, *Memoirs*, p. 509.

94. Teller, PL interview, August 16, 2000, Stanford, Calif.

95. Teller, quoted in Strober and Strober, *Reagan*, p. 232.

96. Abrahamson, quoted in Strober and Strober, *Reagan*, p. 232.

97. Letter from Earl C. Bolton to Michael M. May, November 27, 1967, from LLNL.

98. "Predict Fight by Reagan for G.O.P. Bid," *Chicago Tribune*, March 3, 1968. U.S. Secretary of Defense Robert McNamara publicly announced in November 1966 that the Soviets were building an ABM system. Baucom, *The Origins of SDI*, pp. 27–30.

99. Reagan, speech in Amarillo, Tex., July 19, 1968, from RRPL-MC/VF.

100. Reagan, speech to California Institute of Technology banquet, Los Angeles, November 8, 1967, p. 2, from RRPL-MC/VF.

101. Cannon, *President Reagan*, pp. 247–250; Morris, PL interview, August 21, 2001, Washington, D.C. See also Bosch, *Reagan: An American Story*, pp. 219–220.

102. Meese, PL interview, August 3, 2000, Washington, D.C.

103. Caspar Weinberger, *Fighting for Peace: Seven Critical Years in the Pentagon* (London: Michael Joseph, 1990), pp. 206, 216, 229, 240.

104. Weinberger, PL interview, August 1, 2001, Washington, D.C.

105. Weinberger, quoted in Strober and Strober, *Reagan*, p. 233.

106. Weinberger, PL interview, August 1, 2001, Washington, D.C.

107. Weinberger, interview with Don Oberdorfer, May 23, 1990, p. 10, from Don Oberdorfer papers at the Seeley G. Mudd Manuscript Library, Princeton University, Princeton, N.J. (hereafter DO-NJ).

108. Deaver, PL interview, August 3, 2001, Washington, D.C.

109. Lawrence Freedman, *The Evolution of Nuclear Strategy*, 2nd ed. (London: Macmillan, 1989), pp. 246–256, 340. See also Baucom, *The Origins of SDI*, pp. 20–24.

110. Freedman, *The Evolution of Nuclear Strategy*, pp. 251–256.

111. Ibid., pp. 246–248, 255, 340.
112. Reagan, speech in Amarillo, Tex., July 19, 1968, from RRPL-MC/VF.
113. Reagan, *An American Life*, p. 547. On Reagan's MAD/ Old West simile, see also Martin Anderson, *Revolution: The Reagan Legacy*, 2nd ed. (Stanford, Calif.: Hoover Institution Press, 1990), p. xxxiii; Cannon, *President Reagan*, p. 276; and Meese, PL interview, August 3, 2000, Washington, D.C.
114. Deaver, PL interview, August 3, 2001, Washington, D.C.; Meese, PL interview, August 3, 2000, Washington, D.C.; Weinberger, PL interview, August 1, 2001, Washington, D.C.
115. Weinberger, PL interview, August 1, 2001, Washington, D.C.
116. Meese, PL interview, August 3, 2000, Washington, D.C.
117. Reagan, quoted in Anderson, *Revolution*, p. xxxiii.
118. Cannon, *President Reagan*, p. 249.
119. Deaver, PL interview, August 3, 2001, Washington, D.C.
120. Freedman, *The Evolution of Nuclear Strategy*, pp. 249–261; Baucom, *The Origins of SDI*, pp. 25–38.
121. Paul H. Nitze, *From Hiroshima to Glasnost: At the Centre of Decision, A Memoir* (London: Weidenfeld and Nicolson, 1989), pp. 293–299; and Baucom, *The Origins of SDI*, pp. 39–50.
122. Nitze, *From Hiroshima to Glasnost*, pp. 294–295; Nitze, quoted in *Foreign Policy in the Reagan Presidency: Nine Intimate Perspectives*, ed. Kenneth W. Thompson (Lanham, Md.: University Press of America, 1993), pp. 151–153.
123. Treaty between the United States of America and the Union of Soviet Socialist Republics on the Limitation of Anti-Ballistic Missile Systems (plus Agreed Statements, etc.), in *Arms Control and Disarmament Agreements: Texts and Histories of Negotiations* (Washington, D.C.: U.S. Arms Control and Disarmament Agency, 1982), pp. 139–147.
124. Interim Agreement between the United States of America and the Union of Soviet Socialist Republics on Certain Measures with Respect to the Limitation of Strategic Offensive Arms (plus Protocol, Agreed Statements, etc.), in *Arms Control and Disarmament Agreements*, pp. 148–157.
125. The treaty did contain a unilateral withdrawal clause, however, which the George W. Bush administration exercised in 2001.
126. Baucom, "The U.S. Missile Defense Program: 1944–1997," pp. 3–4. See Protocol to the Treaty Between the United States of America and the Union of Soviet Socialist Republics on the Limitation of Anti-Ballistic Missile Systems, in *Arms Control and Disarmament Agreements*, pp. 161–163.
127. John Lewis Gaddis, *Strategies of Containment: A Critical Appraisal of Postwar American National Security Policy* (Oxford: Oxford University Press, 1982), p. 283.
128. Reagan, "The Obligations of Liberty," speech to the World Affairs Council, October 12, 1972, in Reagan, *A Time for Choosing: The Speeches of Ronald Reagan, 1961–1982*, pp. 103–104.
129. Weinberger, PL interview, August 1, 2001, Washington, D.C.
130. Deaver, PL interview, August 3, 2001, Washington, D.C.
131. Cannon, *Reagan*, pp. 198–200.
132. Reagan, quoted in ibid., p. 216 (see also p. 219).
133. Reagan, quoted in "Where Reagan Stands: Interview on the Issues," *U.S. News & World Report*, May 31, 1976, p. 20.

134. Reagan, speech to the Merchants and Manufacturers Association Annual Banquet, Los Angeles, Calif., May 16, 1967, p. 1, from RRPL-MC/VF.
135. Reagan, "Communism, the Disease," May 1975, in Skinner, Anderson, and Anderson, eds., *Reagan, in His Own Hand*, p. 12. Reagan used abbreviations and occasionally sloppy spelling and punctuation in the handwritten scripts of his radio commentaries, from which these quotes are taken.
136. Reagan, "The Russian Wheat Deal," October 1975, in Skinner, Anderson, and Anderson, eds., *Reagan, in His Own Hand*, pp. 30, 31.
137. Reagan, quoted in "Where Reagan Stands: Interview on the Issues," *U.S. News & World Report*, May 31, 1976, p. 20.
138. Cannon, *Reagan*, pp. 210–226.
139. For descriptions of the scene in Kansas City and Reagan's speech, see Anderson, *Revolution*, pp. 63–72; Morris, *Dutch*, pp. 401–405; and Cannon, *President Reagan*, p. 253.
140. Reagan, "Will They Say We Kept Them Free?" August 19, 1976, p. 3, from RRPL-MC/VF.
141. Anderson, PL interview, August 15, 2000, Stanford, Calif.
142. Deaver, PL interview, August 3, 2001, Washington, D.C.
143. Cannon, *President Reagan*, pp. 253–254.
144. Carter, quoted in Gaddis, *Strategies of Containment*, p. 345.
145. Strobe Talbott, *Deadly Gambits: The Reagan Administration and the Stalemate in Nuclear Arms Control* (London: Picador, 1984), pp. 215, 220.
146. See Charles Tyroler, II, ed., *Alerting America: The Papers of the Committee on the Present Danger* (Washington, D.C.: Pergamon-Brassey's, 1984).
147. Reagan, official announcement speech, November 13, 1979, p. 10, from RRPL-MC/VF.
148. Reagan, nomination acceptance address before the Republican National Convention, Detroit, July 17, 1980, in Reagan, *A Time for Choosing: The Speeches of Ronald Reagan, 1961–1982*, pp. 229, 220.
149. Reagan, speech to the Veterans of Foreign Wars Convention, Chicago, August 18, 1980, pp. 1–4, from RRPL-MC/VF.
150. Cannon, *Reagan*, pp. 279, 282, 283–287, 291, 296, 298; Anderson, PL interview, August 15, 2000, Stanford, Calif.; Deaver, PL interview, August 3, 2001, Washington, D.C.
151. Carter and Reagan (in September 1980), quoted in Cannon, *Reagan*, p. 283.
152. Iklé, quoted in "The Cold War: Ten Years Later," video recording of conference at the RRPL, November 13, 1995 (Simi Valley, Calif.: Ronald Reagan Center for Public Affairs).
153. Freedman, *The Evolution of Nuclear Strategy*, pp. 390–393; Paul P. Craig and John A. Jungerman, *Nuclear Arms Race: Technology and Society*, 2nd ed. (New York: McGraw-Hill, 1990), p. 4.
154. Reagan, speech to the American Legion National Convention, Boston, August 20, 1980, p. 1, from RRPL-MC/VF.
155. Reagan, quoted in "Reagan: 'It Isn't Only Washington That Has a Compassionate Heart,'" *National Journal*, March 8, 1980, p. 392.
156. Cannon, *President Reagan*, p. 255.
157. Lou Cannon, "Arms Boost Seen as Strain on Soviets," *The Washington Post*, June 19, 1980, p. A3.
158. Cannon, *President Reagan*, p. 255.

159. Reagan, quoted in Steven F. Hayward, *The Age of Reagan: The Fall of the Old Liberal Order, 1964–1980* (Roseville, Calif.: Prima Publishing, 2001), pp. 692, 693.

160. Anderson, *Revolution*, p. 74. Iklé told the author that Reagan said this to his advisers "many times" during the campaign. Iklé, PL interview, July 24, 2001, Washington, D.C.

161. Anderson, PL interview, August 15, 2000, Stanford, Calif.

162. Hayward, *The Age of Reagan*, p. 693.

163. Reagan, "Russians," May 25, 1977, in Skinner, Anderson, and Anderson, eds., *Reagan, in His Own Hand*, p. 34.

164. Anderson, *Revolution*, pp. 81–83.

165. Anderson, PL interview, August 15, 2000, Stanford, Calif.

166. Anderson, *Revolution*, p. 83.

167. Anderson, PL interview, August 15, 2000, Stanford, Calif.

168. Anderson, *Revolution*, p. 83. Following his trip with Anderson to NORAD, Reagan wrote a letter of thanks to General James E. Hill, the commanding officer of the facility and Reagan's host during the visit, in which he stated, "All the way to Los Angeles we were talking about the briefing and what we had learned. I can assure you it will be most valuable to all of us in the days ahead. . . . thank you for an enjoyable, interesting and exciting experience." Letter from Reagan to Hill, c. August 1979, in Skinner, Anderson, and Anderson, eds., *Reagan: A Life in Letters*, p. 423.

169. Anderson, PL interview, August 15, 2000, Stanford, Calif.

170. "Foreign Policy and National Security," Policy Memorandum no. 3, Reagan for President, August 1979, included as appendix in Anderson, *Revolution*, p. 471.

171. Anderson, PL interview, August 15, 2000, Stanford, Calif.

172. Anderson, *Revolution*, p. 86; David Hoffman and Lou Cannon, "President Overruled Defense Advisers in Announcing Defense Plan," *The Washington Post*, March 26, 1983, p. A7.

173. Anderson, *Revolution*, p. 86.

174. Anderson, PL interview, August 15, 2000, Stanford, Calif.

175. Lou Cannon, "Interview on the Issues" with Reagan, October 15, 1979, *Political Profiles: Ronald Reagan*, 1980, pp. 7, 10, from RRPL-MC/VF.

176. Reagan, interview with Scheer, 1980, in Robert Scheer, *With Enough Shovels: Reagan, Bush and Nuclear War* (London: Secker and Warburg, 1983), pp. 232–234.

177. "Reagan: 'It Isn't Only Washington That Has a Compassionate Heart,'" *National Journal*, March 8, 1980, p. 392.

178. *Official Report of the Proceedings of the Thirty-Second Republican National Convention Held in Detroit, Michigan, July 14, 15, 16, 17, 1980* (Republican National Committee: 1980), p. 299.

179. The interviewee wished not to have his comments attributed directly to him. Anderson told the author that Allen had "played a major role in writing the 1980 platform on missile defenses." Anderson, PL interview, August 15, 2000, Stanford, Calif.

Chapter II: 1981–1982

1. Alexander M. Haig, Jr., *Caveat: Realism, Reagan, and Foreign Policy* (London: Weidenfeld and Nicolson, 1984), pp. 1–19.

2. Cannon, *Reagan*, p. 308.

3. Haig, *Caveat*, p. 65. See also Cannon, *President Reagan*, p. 157.
4. Laurence I. Barrett, *Gambling with History: Ronald Reagan in the White House* (Garden City, N.Y.: Doubleday & Co., 1983), pp. 327–328.
5. Ibid., pp. 330–335; Morris, *Dutch*, pp. 455–456; Cannon, *Reagan*, pp. 396–397.
6. Cannon, *Reagan*, pp. 396–397.
7. Haig, *Caveat*, p. 66.
8. McFarlane, PL interview, August 22, 2000, Washington, D.C.; Robert C. McFarlane and Zofia Smardz, *Special Trust* (New York: Cadell & Davies, 1994), pp. 168–169.
9. Caspar W. Weinberger with Gretchen Roberts, *In the Arena: A Memoir of the 20th Century* (Washington, D.C.: Regnery, 2001), pp. 73–75, 149–150, 173, 177.
10. Iklé, PL interview, July 24, 2001, Washington, D.C.
11. Robert M. Gates, *From the Shadows: The Ultimate Insider's Story of Five Presidents and How They Won the Cold War* (New York: Touchstone, 1996), p. 199.
12. Reagan, "A Strategy of Peace for the '80s," televised address, October 19, 1980, p. 2, from RRPL-MC/VF.
13. Cannon, *President Reagan*, p. 155. See also Allen, quoted in "The Role of the National Security Adviser," transcript of Oral History Roundtable presented by the National Security Project (College Park, Md.: Center for International Security Studies at Maryland, School of Public Affairs, University of Maryland, and Washington, D.C.: Brookings Institution, 2000), p. 3.
14. Ivo H. Daalder and I. M. Destler, introduction to "The Role of the National Security Adviser."
15. Ibid.
16. Others included Henry "Scoop" Jackson (D-Wash.), for whom Perle had worked, John Tower (R-Tex.), for whom McFarlane had worked, and Malcolm Wallop (R-Wyo). *BusinessWeek*, May 19, 1980. See also Baucom, *The Origins of SDI*, pp. 122–129.
17. Gilbert Lewthwaite, "Reagan Tells Schmitt He Wants to Develop ABM for Mutual Protection," *Baltimore Sun*, December 13, 1980, p. 8.
18. Weinberger, *Fighting for Peace*, pp. 209, 216.
19. Weinberger, interview with Oberdorfer, May 23, 1990, p. 9, from DO-NJ.
20. Weinberger, quoted in Strober and Strober, *Reagan*, p. 233.
21. Weinberger, interview with Oberdorfer, May 23, 1990, p. 9, from DO-NJ.
22. Hedrick Smith, "U.S. Might Consider Reviving the ABM's," *The New York Times*, January 16, 1981, p. A11.
23. Weinberger, PL interview, August 21, 2001, Washington, D.C.
24. Smith, "U.S. Might Consider Reviving the ABM's," *The New York Times*, January 16, 1981, p. A11.
25. Reagan, *An American Life*, p. 279.
26. Anderson, PL interview, August 15, 2000, Stanford, Calif.
27. *Public Papers of the Presidents: Ronald Reagan, 1981* (Washington, D.C.: U.S. Government Printing Office, 1982).
28. Dennis S. Ippolito, "Defense, Budget Policy, and the Reagan Deficits," in Eric J. Schmertz, Natalie Datlof, and Alexej Ugrinsky, eds., *President Reagan and the World* (Westport, Conn.: Greenwood Press, 1997), p. 220. For the Reagan administration's justification of its first defense budgets, see Weinberger, "U.S. Defense Policy Requirements," speech before the American Newspaper Publishers Associ-

ation Meeting, Chicago, May 5, 1981, in *American Foreign Policy Current Documents, 1981* (hereafter *AFPCD 1981*) (Washington, D.C.: Department of State, 1984), p. 38; and Weinberger, "We Must Make America Strong Again," speech before the Council on Foreign Relations, New York, June 17, 1981, in *AFPCD 1981*, pp. 45–49. See also Weinberger, *Fighting for Peace*, pp. 28–55. Historically, Reagan's defense budgets were not remarkable. On average, U.S. defense spending during the early 1950s constituted 10.8% of the country's gross national product; during the late 1950s, 10.4%; during the early 1960s, 9.3%; during the late 1960s, 8.6%; and during the early 1970s, 6.9%. It fell under Ford and Carter to 5.1% of GNP. During Reagan's eight years in office, defense spending never exceeded 6.5% of GNP. The numbers with respect to defense spending as percentage of total U.S. federal budget outlays form a similar pattern. On average, during the 1950s, defense spending constituted 58% of total budget outlays; during the 1960s, between 45% and 49%; during the early 1970s, 35%; and during the late 1970s, 24%. Under Reagan, defense spending as share of total budget outlays peaked at 28.1% in 1987. Table 11-1, "Defense Outlays, Fiscal Years 1950–1990," in Ippolito, "Defense, Budget Policy, and the Reagan Deficits," p. 220. See also Table 541, "National Defense Outlays and Veterans Benefits: 1960–1990," in *Statistical Abstract of the United States, 1991* (Washington, D.C.: U.S. Department of Commerce, 1991), p. 336. See also Ippolito, "Defense, Budget Policy, and the Reagan Deficits," pp. 218, 220, 222, 224–225; Cannon, *Ronald Reagan: The Presidential Portfolio*, pp. 128, 130; and "Reagan's Legacy," transcript of online interview with Lou Cannon, www.washingtonpost.com, February 6, 2001.

29. Morris, *Dutch*, p. 450; Deaver, *A Different Drummer*, p. 154.
30. Anderson, PL interview, August 15, 2000, Stanford, Calif.
31. Reagan, question-and-answer session with reporters, August 13, 1981, in *Public Papers of the Presidents: Ronald Reagan, 1981*, pp. 708, 711.
32. Reagan, *An American Life*, pp. 237–238, 267–268. Also Adelman, PL interview, August 13, 2001, Arlington, Va.; Poindexter, PL interview, August 16, 2001, Arlington, Va.; and Michael Beschloss, introduction to Cannon, *Ronald Reagan: The Presidential Portfolio*, p. viii.
33. Morris, *Dutch*, pp. 428–432.
34. Ibid., p. 432; Reagan, *An American Life*, p. 263.
35. Deaver, *A Different Drummer*, p. 146.
36. Reagan, *An American Life*, p. 269.
37. Ibid., pp. 258, 265, 269.
38. Morris, *Dutch*, pp. 436, 790 (notes); quoted from Reagan, *An American Life*, p. 270.
39. Reagan, *An American Life*, p. 270.
40. Richard Pipes, *Vixi: Memoirs of a Non-Belonger* (New Haven: Yale University Press, 2003), p. 148; Cannon, *President Reagan*, pp. 157, 161–163; Morris, *Dutch*, p. 437.
41. Reagan, *An American Life*, p. 270.
42. Morris, *Dutch*, p. 790 (note).
43. Reagan, *An American Life*, p. 271.
44. Pipes, PL interview, September 20, 2000, Cambridge, Mass.
45. Cannon, *President Reagan*, p. 259.
46. The latter scenario is less plausible, given that Pipes very specifically remembered

the letter he discussed as one that Reagan had written while recovering from his wounds and that had eventually been sent.

47. Handwritten letter from Reagan to Brezhnev, April 24, 1981, pp. 1, 2, from RRPL, Collection: National Security Affairs, Assistant to the President for: Records: Head of State File, File Folder: USSR (hereafter RRPL-NS/HS/USSR), General Secretary Brezhnev, Box 38, Lettercase 8190204. The author was unable to find the original draft of the letter.

48. Ibid., p. 4.

49. Ibid., p. 2.

50. Typewritten letter from Reagan to Brezhnev, April 24, 1981, p. 1, from RRPL-NS/HS/USSR, General Secretary Brezhnev, Box 38, Lettercase 8190203.

51. Letter from Brezhnev to Reagan, May 25, 1981, from RRPL-NS/HS/USSR, General Secretary Brezhnev, Box 38, Lettercase 8190205; letter from Brezhnev to Reagan, May 27, 1981, from RRPL-NS/HS/USSR, General Secretary Brezhnev, Box 38, Lettercase 8190206.

52. Letter from Brezhnev to Reagan, May 25, 1981, p. 1, from RRPL-NS/HS/USSR, General Secretary Brezhnev, Box 38, Lettercase 8190205.

53. Reagan, *An American Life*, p. 273.

54. Reagan, news conference, January 29, 1981, in *Public Papers of the Presidents: Ronald Reagan, 1981*, p. 57.

55. Reagan, Commencement Address at the University of Notre Dame, May 17, 1981, in *Public Papers of the Presidents: Ronald Reagan, 1981*, pp. 434, 435.

56. Reagan, news conference, June 16, 1981, in *Public Papers of the Presidents: Ronald Reagan, 1981*, p. 520. See also Reagan, Speech to the World Affairs Council of Philadelphia, October 15, 1981, in *Public Papers of the Presidents: Ronald Reagan, 1981*, p. 939.

57. Reagan, Speech to the Illinois Forum Reception in Chicago, September 2, 1981, in *Public Papers of the Presidents: Ronald Reagan, 1981*, p. 746.

58. Reagan, question-and-answer session with out-of-town editors, October 16, 1981, in *Public Papers of the Presidents: Ronald Reagan, 1981*, pp. 957, 958.

59. Raymond L. Garthoff, *The Great Transition: American-Soviet Relations at the End of the Cold War* (Washington, D.C.: Brookings Institution, 1994), p. 30.

60. Matlock, PL interview, September 5, 2001, Princeton, N.J.; McFarlane, quoted in Nina Tannenwald, ed., "Understanding the End of the Cold War," provisional transcript of oral history conference at Brown University, May 7–10, 1998 (Providence, R.I.: Watson Institute for International Studies, Brown University, 1999), pp. 31–32; Perle, PL interview, September 27, 2000, by telephone.

61. Haig, interview with *The Wall Street Journal*, July 6, 1981, *AFPCD 1981*, p. 589. See also Haig, quoted in "The Soviet Union Shows Clear Signs of Economic Decline," *U.S. News & World Report*, May 18, 1981, p. 29.

62. Matlock, PL interview, September 5, 2001, Princeton, N.J.; McFarlane, quoted in Tannenwald, ed., "Understanding the End of the Cold War," pp. 31–32; Perle, PL interview, September 27, 2000, by telephone.

63. Garthoff, *The Great Transition*, p. 30.

64. Weinberger, television interview, March 29, 1981, p. 153; see also Weinberger, television interview, March 8, 1981, p. 150, both from *AFPCD 1981*.

65. Reagan, Remarks on the Announcement of the U.S. Strategic Weapons Program, October 2, 1981, in *Public Papers of the Presidents: Ronald Reagan, 1981*, p. 878.

66. National Security Decision Directive (NSDD) 12, "Strategic Forces Moderniza-tion Program," October 1, 1981, from RRPL, Records Declassified and Released by the National Security Council, National Security Decision Directives (hereafter RRPL-NSC/NSDD).

67. NSDD 1, "National Security Council Directives," February 25, 1981, p. 1, from RRPL-NSC/NSDD.

68. See overview of *Presidential Directives on National Security from Truman to Clin-ton*, National Security Archive (Alexandria, Va.: Chadwyck-Healey, 1994); and the U.S. National Archives Web page, www.nara.gov.

69. Inventory of Records Declassified and Released by the National Security Council, from RRPL.

70. NSDD 12, "Strategic Forces Modernization Program," October 1, 1981, pp. 1–3, from RRPL-NSC/NSDD.

71. Reagan, Remarks on the Announcement of the U.S. Strategic Weapons Program, October 2, 1981, in *Public Papers of the Presidents: Ronald Reagan, 1981*, p. 879.

72. Weinberger, press briefing, October 2, 1981, AFPCD 1981, pp. 140, 141, 144.

73. John Quirt, "Washington's New Push for Missile Defense," *Fortune*, October 19, 1981, pp. 142–148.

74. Perle told the author that there was no "intense, serious look going on" regarding missile defense in the Defense Department during 1981 and 1982. Perle, PL inter-view, September 27, 2000, by telephone. Iklé later noted that Undersecretary of Defense for Research and Engineering Richard DeLauer was "very skeptical" re-garding the feasibility of national missile defense. Iklé took part in discussions both with technical experts who doubted the feasibility of an advanced national de-fense and with missile defense enthusiasts and "wondered who was right," but he took no action. Iklé, PL interview, July 24, 2001, Washington, D.C. McFarlane later maintained that in 1981 or early 1982, Weinberger asked the Joint Chiefs if an advanced missile defense was feasible, and they responded in the negative. (Sev-eral of the Joints Chiefs from that time, including the chairman, had retired and been replaced when Reagan discussed missile defense with the Joint Chiefs prior to announcing SDI as described in the next chapter.) McFarlane, interview with Oberdorfer, p. 8, from DO-NJ. Also McFarlane, quoted in Tannenwald, ed., "Un-derstanding the End of the Cold War," p. 59; McFarlane, PL interview, August 22, 2000, Washington, D.C. In his memoirs, Weinberger wrote that in early 1981, he asked for a briefing on the status of existing missile defense efforts and discussed with his staff the possibility of establishing a commission to investigate the feasi-bility of a missile defense. His memoirs did not elaborate on the outcome, if any, of either. Weinberger, *Fighting for Peace*, p. 300.

75. Anderson, *Revolution*, pp. 89–92.

76. Anderson, PL interview, August 15, 2000, Stanford, Calif.

77. Anderson, *Revolution*, p. 91; Anderson, PL interview, August 15, 2000, Stanford, Calif.

78. Keyworth, interview with Baucom, September 28, 1987, pp. 1, 6, 17, from RRPL, Oral History Transcripts 35–39, Box 8, Oral History Interviews: Strategic Defense Initiative Organization (hereafter RRPL-OH/SDIO).

79. Ibid., pp. 1–17; Anderson, PL interview, August 15, 2000, Stanford, Calif.; Meese, PL interview, August 3, 2000, Washington, D.C.; Anderson, *Revolution*, pp. 92–96; Baucom, *The Origins of SDI*, pp. 149–155.

80. Joseph Coors, interview with Baucom, July 31, 1987, pp. 2–3, 8–9, from RRPL-OH/SDIO; Jaquelin Hume, interview with Baucom, October 28, 1987, pp. 4, 8–9, from RRPL-OH/SDIO; Baucom, *The Origins of SDI*, pp. 150–166.

81. Anderson, *Revolution*, pp. 92–96; Keyworth, interview with Baucom, September 28, 1987, pp. 1–17, from RRPL-OH/SDIO.

82. Anderson, *Revolution*, pp. 95–96; Baucom, *The Origins of SDI*, pp. 153–154; Keyworth, interview with Baucom, September 28, 1987, pp. 9–11, from RRPL-OH/SDIO.

83. Anderson, *Revolution*, p. 96.

84. Keyworth, interview with Baucom, September 28, 1987, pp. 1–5, 8, 10, 13–14, 26–28, from RRPL-OH/SDIO.

85. Talbott, *Deadly Gambits*, pp. 61–75.

86. Reagan, Remarks to Members of the National Press Club on Arms Reduction and Nuclear Weapons, November 18, 1981, in *Public Papers of the Presidents: Ronald Reagan, 1981*, pp. 1062–1067.

87. Weinberger, interview with Oberdorfer, May 23, 1990, pp. 6–7, from DO-NJ. See also Weinberger, *Fighting for Peace*, p. 240.

88. Iklé, quoted in "The Cold War: Ten Years Later."

89. Reagan, *An American Life*, pp. 550–551.

90. This applied especially to the zero-zero proposal: "He really liked the idea of, rather than just kind of stabilizing the competition in different categories of arms, that you could actually do away with a whole category of arms." Burt, PL interview, July 31, 2001, Washington, D.C.

91. Carlucci, PL interview, July 17, 2001, Washington, D.C.; Carlucci, quoted in Cannon, *President Reagan*, p. 250.

92. Carlucci, quoted in Strober and Strober, *Reagan*, p. 234.

93. John Newhouse, "Annals of Diplomacy: Reagan and the Nuclear Age—Part I, The Abolitionist," *The New Yorker*, January 9, 1989, p. 39.

94. Weinberger, *Fighting for Peace*, p. 240; Weinberger, PL interview, August 1, 2001, Washington, D.C.

95. Weinberger, interview with Oberdorfer, May 23, 1990, p. 9, from DO-NJ.

96. Weinberger, PL interview, August 1, 2001, Washington, D.C.

97. Weinberger, interview with Oberdorfer, May 23, 1990, p. 9, from DO-NJ. See also Oberdorfer, *From the Cold War to a New Era*, p. 26.

98. Carlucci, PL interview, July 17, 2001, Washington, D.C.

99. Kimmitt, PL interview, January 27, 1999, Washington, D.C.

100. Allen, quoted in "The Role of the National Security Adviser," p. 7.

101. Poindexter, quoted in Strober and Strober, *Reagan*, p. 116.

102. Poindexter, PL interview, August 16, 2001, Arlington, Va.; Cannon, *President Reagan*, pp. 156–157. See also Reagan, interview with the *Los Angeles Times*, January 20, 1982, in *Public Papers of the Presidents: Ronald Reagan, 1982*, Book 1 (Washington, D.C.: U.S. Government Printing Office, 1983), p. 58.

103. Ibid.

104. McFarlane, PL interview, August 22, 2000, Washington, D.C. Other former Reagan administration officials made similar comments in interviews with PL: Burt, PL interview, July 31, 2001, Washington, D.C.; Dobriansky, PL interview, December 18, 2000, Washington, D.C.; Pipes, PL interview, September 20, 2000, Cambridge, Mass.; Poindexter, PL interview, August 16, 2001, Arlington, Va.

105. Anderson, PL interview, August 15, 2000, Stanford, Calif.

106. Poindexter, PL interview, August 16, 2001, Arlington, Va. According to Weinberger, Clark "innately understood the way Reagan thought and operated" and "was totally devoted and loyal to the cause of Mr. Reagan's success." Weinberger with Roberts, *In the Arena*, p. 149.

107. Morris, *Dutch*, p. 663.

108. Poindexter, PL interview, August 16, 2001, Arlington, Va.

109. McFarlane, PL interview, August 22, 2000, Washington, D.C.

110. Meese, PL interview, August 3, 2000, Washington, D.C. The development and adoption of the NSDDs that ensued "was pretty clearly traceable back to [Clark]," Weinberger later told the author, "and to his concern and desire that we did have a consistent, thought-out strategic approach." Weinberger, PL interview, August 1, 2001, Washington, D.C.

111. Morris, PL interview, August 21, 2001, Washington, D.C.

112. Clark, PL interview, August 1, 2001, by telephone.

113. Anderson added that not only was Clark "doing what Reagan wanted, but . . . Clark agreed with Reagan." Anderson, PL interview, August 15, 2000, Stanford, Calif. This was confirmed by another former Reagan administration official (who was not a supporter of Clark) in off-the-record comments to the author.

114. McFarlane, PL interview, August 22, 2000, Washington, D.C.

115. NSSD 1-82, "U.S. National Security Strategy," February 5, 1982, pp. 1, 2, from RRPL, Records Declassified and Released by the National Security Council, National Security Study Directives (hereafter RRPL-NSC/NSSD).

116. Gaddis, *Strategies of Containment*, provides an excellent guide to the Cold War approach of each postwar presidential administration.

117. "U.S. National Security Strategy," April 1982, pp. 8, 4, from RRPL, Records Declassified and Released by the National Security Council, Related Documents, System II (hereafter RRPL-NSC/RD).

118. Gaddis, *Strategies of Containment*, passim.

119. Ibid., p. 155. See also Freedman, *The Evolution of Nuclear Strategy*, p. 77.

120. "U.S. National Security Strategy," April 1982, p. 5, from RRPL-NSC/RD.

121. Clark, PL interview, August 1, 2001, by telephone.

122. In addition to the ones described, the study also included the objectives of the United States in each of the world's regions and some not specifically related to the Cold War.

123. "U.S. National Security Strategy," April 1982, p. 8, from RRPL-NSC/RD.

124. Ibid., pp. 23, 10.

125. Ibid., pp. 11, 84–85.

126. Ibid., pp. 13, 9.

127. Ibid., pp. 84, 21.

128. Ibid., pp. 73, 13.

129. Ibid., pp. 14, 52, 83.

130. Clark, PL interview, August 1, 2001, by telephone.

131. Ibid.; Weinberger, PL interview, August 1, 2001, Washington, D.C.; Meese, PL interview, August 3, 2000, Washington, D.C.; and Anderson, PL interview, August 15, 2000, Stanford, Calif.

132. Poindexter, PL interview, August 16, 2001, Arlington, Va.

133. NSDD 32, "U.S. National Security Strategy," May 20, 1982, pp. 1, 8, from RRPL-NSC/NSSD.

134. The speech was a rarity for Clark, who usually avoided making public addresses.

135. Clark, "National Security Strategy," address before the Center for Strategic and International Studies, Georgetown University, May 21, 1982, in *American Foreign Policy Current Documents, 1982* (hereafter *AFPCD 1982*) (Washington, D.C.: Department of State, 1985), pp. 89, 90, 91, 93. During his remarks on the defense section of the study and NSDD 32, Clark mentioned that one of the administration's goals was to "improve strategic defenses," without elaborating further.

136. Meese, PL interview, August 3, 2000, Washington, D.C.; Pipes, PL interview, September 20, 2000, Cambridge, Mass.

137. Inventory of Records Declassified and Released by the National Security Council, from RRPL.

138. Reagan, "A Five-Point Program for Peace with the Soviet Union," address at Eureka College, Eureka, Ill., May 9, 1982, in *AFPCD 1982*, p. 134.

139. Letter from Brezhnev to Reagan, probably late December 1981, pp. 2, 5, from RRPL-NS/HS/USSR, General Secretary Brezhnev, Box 38, Lettercase 8190211.

140. Handwritten marginal notes by Reagan on letter from Brezhnev to Reagan, May 20, 1982, pp. 1–5, from RRPL-NS/HS/USSR, General Secretary Brezhnev, Box 38, Lettercase 8190342.

141. Reagan's marginal notes were passed on to the NSC staff, who fretted over whether he might want them incorporated into any reply. Memo from "dsm" to "Carol," citing instructions from Poindexter, May 26, 1982, from RRPL-NS/HS/USSR, General Secretary Brezhnev, Box 38, Lettercase 8190342.

142. Poindexter, PL interview, August 16, 2001, Arlington, Va. According to Poindexter, there was a "strong feeling" among the White House senior staff, including Clark, that Reagan's own ideas "should see the light of day" and that Haig was trying to block this.

143. Reagan, *An American Life*, pp. 360, 361.

144. Anderson, PL interview, August 15, 2000, Stanford, Calif.

145. Shultz, *Turmoil and Triumph*, p. 10.

146. Reagan, Remarks to the People of Foreign Nations, television address, January 1, 1982, in *Public Papers of the Presidents: Ronald Reagan, 1982*, Book 1, p. 2. See also Reagan, interview with the *Los Angeles Times*, January 20, 1982, in ibid., p. 62.

147. Reagan, interview with the *New York Post*, March 23, 1982, in *Public Papers of the Presidents: Ronald Reagan, 1982*, Book 1, p. 368. See also Reagan, news conference, June 30, 1982, in ibid., pp. 831–832.

148. Reagan, news conference, March 31, 1982, in *Public Papers of the Presidents: Ronald Reagan, 1982*, Book 1, pp. 402–403.

149. Reagan, "A Five Point Program," in *AFPCD 1982*, pp. 131–133.

150. Reagan, interview with Western European publications, May 21, 1982, in *Public Papers of the Presidents: Ronald Reagan, 1982*, Book 1, pp. 692, 696, 698. See also similar comments by Reagan in an interview on June 1, 1982, in ibid., p. 714.

151. He later described the address as "one of the most important speeches I gave as president." Reagan, Introduction to Address to the British Parliament, June 8, 1982, in Reagan, *Speaking My Mind*, p. 107.

152. Reagan, "Promoting Democracy and Peace," address to the British Parliament, June 8, 1982, in *AFPCD 1982*, pp. 16–19.

153. Reagan, interview with the *Los Angeles Times*, January 20, 1982, in *Public Papers of the Presidents: Ronald Reagan, 1982*, Book 1, p. 59. See also Reagan, news conference, January 19, 1982, p. 43; interview with the Iowa Daily Press Association,

February 9, 1982, pp. 150–151; and news conference, May 13, 1982, p. 619, all in *Public Papers of the Presidents: Ronald Reagan, 1982*, Book 1.

154. Reagan, Remarks at the White House for members of the Newspaper Association, March 11, 1982, in *Public Papers of the Presidents: Ronald Reagan, 1982*, Book 1, p. 285.

155. Reagan, radio address to the nation on nuclear weapons, April 17, 1982, p. 487. See also Reagan, news conference, March 31, 1982, p. 398; Reagan, news conference, May 13, 1982, p. 623; and Reagan, interview, June 1, 1982, p. 715, all in *Public Papers of the Presidents: Ronald Reagan, 1982*, Book 1.

156. Reagan, question-and-answer session with reporters, April 20, 1982, in *Public Papers of the Presidents: Ronald Reagan, 1982*, Book 1, p. 499.

157. Reagan, Radio Address to the Nation on Nuclear Weapons, April 17, 1982, p. 488; Reagan, question-and-answer session with high school students in Chicago, May 10, 1982, p. 605; and Reagan, Speech to United Nations General Assembly, New York, June 17, 1982, p. 786, all in *Public Papers of the Presidents: Ronald Reagan, 1982*, Book 1.

158. Reagan, question-and-answer session with high school students in Chicago, May 10, 1982, *Public Papers of the Presidents: Ronald Reagan, 1982*, Book 1, p. 605. This statement inaugurated a curious habit of Reagan throughout his presidency to expound on the abolition of nuclear weapons during unscripted sessions with high schoolers. See also Reagan, interview with the *New York Post*, March 23, 1982, in *Public Papers of the Presidents: Ronald Reagan, 1982*, Book 1, pp. 368–369. Using similar language to that of his session with Chicago high school students, Reagan wrote to Jill Conway, the president of Smith College, "But let me assure you I share your view that our ultimate goal must be the elimination of nuclear weapons." Letter from Reagan to Conway, October 25, 1982, in Kiron K. Skinner, Annelise Anderson, and Martin Anderson, eds., *Reagan: A Life in Letters* (New York: Free Press, 2003), p. 390.

159. Reagan, interview with the *Daily Oklahoman*, March 16, 1982, in *Public Papers of the Presidents: Ronald Reagan, 1982*, Book 1, p. 309.

160. Meese, PL interview, August 3, 2000, Washington, D.C. Poindexter told the author that the point was to devise a "multi-pronged, integrated approach." Poindexter, PL interview, August 16, 2001, Arlington, Va.

161. NSSD 11-82, "U.S. Policy Toward the Soviet Union," August 21, 1982, pp. 1–4, from RRPL-NSC/NSSD.

162. Pipes, *Vixi*, pp. 198–199.

163. Pipes, PL interview, September 20, 2000, Cambridge, Mass. In November 1981, Pipes had sent a memo to Reagan that made four main points: (1) Communism was inherently expansionistic. (2) The Soviet system was confronting a crisis, primarily due to economic failures and overexpansion. (3) There were elements within the Soviet leadership that would potentially seek systemic reform. (4) It was in the interest of the United States both to encourage internal reform in the USSR and to raise the costs of Soviet expansionism. Notes by PL of an account by Pipes at a dinner and reunion conference held by former Reagan NSC staff officials at the University Club, Washington, D.C., September 26, 2000, organized by the Potomac Foundation. For more on Pipes's approach to Soviet policy and his involvement in preparing the NSDD: Pipes, PL interview, September 20, 2000, Cambridge, Mass.; Pipes, *Vixi*, pp. 188–202; Richard Pipes, *Survival Is Not Enough: Soviet Realities and America's Future* (New York: Simon & Schuster,

1984); Richard Pipes, "Soviet Strategy and American Response," in Craig Snyder, ed., *The Strategic Defense Debate: Can Star Wars Make Us Safe?* (Philadelphia: University of Pennsylvania Press, 1986), pp. 43–48; Richard Pipes, "Can the Soviet Union Reform?" *Foreign Affairs* 63, no. 1 (Fall 1984), pp. 47–61; Richard Pipes, "Misinterpreting the Cold War: The Hard-Liners Had It Right," *Foreign Affairs* 74, no. 1 (January–February 1995), pp. 154–160.

164. Pipes, "Misinterpreting the Cold War: The Hard-Liners Had It Right," p. 157.
165. Poindexter, PL interview, August 16, 2001, Arlington, Va.
166. Clark, PL interview, August 1, 2001, by telephone.
167. NSDD 75, "U.S. Relations with the USSR," January 17, 1983, p. 1, from RRPL-NSC/NSDD.
168. Ibid., pp. 2–8.
169. Pipes, PL interview, September 20, 2000, Cambridge, Mass. Pipes thought that with a fundamentally changed USSR, "we would still have a Communist regime to cope with, but it would be much more amenable to agreements and so on."
170. Ibid; and Pipes, *Vixi*, pp. 200–201.
171. Memo from Clark to Reagan, December 16, 1982, p. 1, from RRPL, Executive Secretariat, NSC: NSDDs collection (hereafter RRPL-ES/NSC/NSDDs), file folder: NSDD 75 [2 of 4] box 91287.
172. Talking points for Clark for December 16, 1982, NSC meeting, from same location as above. Pipes told the author that the objective of encouraging reform in the USSR through pressure was "revolutionary. That was never part of American policy [before]. It goes way beyond Kennan's containment," which, Pipes said, stated that "if we contain the Soviet Union territorially, there will be an implosion." Pipes, PL interview, September 20, 2000, Cambridge, Mass. See also Pipes, *Vixi*, p. 201.

CHAPTER III: THE ANNOUNCEMENT OF SDI

1. Teller with Shoolery, *Memoirs*, p. 530; Keyworth, interview with Baucom, September 28, 1987, p. 5, from RRPL-OH/SDIO.
2. Teller with Shoolery, *Memoirs*, pp. 529–530; Teller, interview with Baucom, July 6, 1987, pp. 5–6, from RRPL-OH/SDIO.
3. Keyworth, interview with Baucom, September 28, 1987, pp. 6–7, from RRPL-OH/SDIO.
4. Teller, interview with Baucom, July 6, 1987, p. 6, from RRPL-OH/SDIO.
5. Keyworth, interview with Baucom, September 28, 1987, pp. 5–8, from RRPL-OH/SDIO.
6. Teller with Shoolery, *Memoirs*, pp. 527–528; Teller, interview with Baucom, July 6, 1987, p. 4, from RRPL-OH/SDIO.
7. Teller, PL interview, August 16, 2000, Stanford, Calif. See also Teller with Shoolery, *Memoirs*, p. 530.
8. Keyworth, interview with Baucom, September 28, 1987, pp. 6–7, from RRPL-OH/SDIO.
9. Herken, *Cardinal Choices*, p. 333 (note 61); Keyworth, interview with Baucom, September 28, 1987, pp. 6–8, from RRPL-OH/SDIO.
10. Keyworth, interview with Baucom, September 28, 1987, pp. 6–8, 16–18, from RRPL-OH/SDIO; Herken, *Cardinal Choices*, p. 210. Keyworth was familiar with Teller's preference.

11. Teller, interview with Baucom, July 6, 1987, p. 6, from RRPL-OH/SDIO; Teller with Shoolery, *Memoirs*, p. 530.
12. Teller, interview with Baucom, July 6, 1987, p. 6, from RRPL-OH/SDIO; Teller, PL interview, August 16, 2000, Stanford, Calif.; Teller, quoted in Strober and Strober, *Reagan*, p. 232. See also note from Reagan to Clark, July 29, 1982, in Skinner, Anderson, and Anderson, eds., *Reagan: A Life in Letters*, p. 408.
13. Teller, interview with Baucom, July 6, 1987, p. 1, from RRPL-OH/SDIO.
14. Teller, PL interview, August 16, 2000, Stanford, Calif. In retrospect, Teller told the author, Reagan "had a real point" in asserting that SDI should focus on nonnuclear technologies. He implied that this was the case both politically and technologically. Ibid. After Teller understood Reagan's nonnuclear conviction, he championed other technologies that were being pursued in SDI research. Teller with Shoolery, *Memoirs*, pp. 532–533.
15. Reagan, *An American Life*, p. 547.
16. Many of those who were close to Reagan at the time have since emphasized this. Keyworth stated that the initiative was "entirely [Reagan's] idea." "I don't know of anything that was more clearly Ronald Reagan's than SDI was." Keyworth, interview with Baucom, September 28, 1987, pp. 5, 28, from RRPL-OH/SDIO. Shultz recalled that the "truth of SDI's origin was simple: the vision came from Ronald Reagan." Shultz, *Turmoil and Triumph*, p. 261. He noted that SDI "was very much driven by Ronald Reagan. It was personal." Shultz, quoted in William C. Wohlforth, ed., *Witnesses to the End of the Cold War* (Baltimore: Johns Hopkins University Press, 1996), p. 35. Weinberger wrote in his memoirs that it was "the President's proposal." Weinberger, *Fighting for Peace*, p. 216. According to Carlucci, SDI "was very much Ronald Reagan's program." Carlucci, quoted in Wohlforth, ed., *Witnesses to the End of the Cold War*, p. 43. Meese asserted that "you would never have had the Strategic Defense Initiative" without Reagan. Meese, PL interview, August 3, 2000, Washington, D.C.
17. Keyworth, quoted in David Hoffman and Lou Cannon, "President Overruled Advisers on Announcing Defense Plan," *The Washington Post*, March 26, 1983, p. A7.
18. Table 3-2, "The Evolution over Time of the Three Legs of the United States Strategic Triad," and Table 3-3, "The Evolution over Time of the Soviet Union's Nuclear Arsenal," in Craig and Jungerman, *Nuclear Arms Race: Technology and Society*, pp. 55, 56.
19. Ibid.
20. Table 557, "Intercontinental Ballistic Missiles, Submarines, and Bombers—U.S. and Soviet Union Balance: 1980 to 1989," in *Statistical Abstract of the United States*, 1991, p. 343. By 1983, the ratio had expanded to exactly three to one.
21. See Freedman, *The Evolution of Nuclear Strategy*, pp. 387–394. The advent of multiple independently targeted reentry vehicles (MIRVs) made it possible for multiple warheads released from one launched ICBM to destroy more than one of the opposing side's ICBMs—and thus all of those missiles' own multiple warheads—in their silos. It was thus conceivable that if the number of ICBMs and the number of MIRVs on each ICBM were roughly evenly matched between the two sides, one side could destroy the other's entire ICBM fleet and still have ICBMs of its own to spare if it struck first with ICBMs (depending on the number of warheads considered sure to destroy one ICBM in its silo, and assuming that the attacked side did not launch its ICBMs before they were hit). If the two sides were

not in balance, the relative numbers of ICBMs and warheads on each side would obviously affect both the perceived and probable outcomes of such a scenario.

22. Ibid., pp. 387–394.

23. Cannon, *President Reagan*, p. 133.

24. Baucom, *The Origins of SDI*, pp. 172–176; Freedman, *The Evolution of Nuclear Strategy*, p. 411; Cannon, *President Reagan*, pp. 133–135.

25. Reagan, Address to the Nation on Strategic Arms Reduction and Nuclear Deterrence, November 22, 1982, in *Public Papers of the Presidents: Ronald Reagan, 1982*, Book 2 (Washington, D.C.: U.S. Government Printing Office, 1983), pp. 1507–1508.

26. Baucom, *The Origins of SDI*, p. 180.

27. Ibid.; Hartmann, *Naval Renaissance*, p. 251.

28. Photographs C12095-7A and C12095-15A, December 22, 1982, from RRPL, Audio-Visual Collection (hereafter RRPL-AV).

29. Schedule proposal from Clark to William Sadleir, November 17, 1982; memorandum from Clark to Deaver, November 17, 1982, from RRPL, Collection: WHORM [White House Office of Records Management]: Subject File (hereafter RRPL-WHORM/SF), File Location FG013-06 Joint Chiefs of Staff, Lettercase 050690. A May 1983 White House memo lists the dates of Reagan's sessions with the Chiefs until then, including the meetings on December 22, 1982, and February 11, 1983 (discussed later in this chapter). Memo from "Ellen" to "Fred," May 11, 1983, from same location as above.

30. Memo from Allan Myer to Clark, December 6, 1982; memo from Clark to Weinberger, December 13, 1982, both from RRPL-NS, Records, Chron File 8207713; memo from Weinberger to Clark, December 20, 1982, with "Highlights of JCS Presentation" attachment, from RRPL, Executive Secretariat, NSC: Rcds, System File (hereafter RRPL-ES/NSC/SF), File Folder 8291013.

31. No minutes or other notes from the December 22, 1982, meeting have yet been declassified and released.

32. Anderson, *Revolution*, p. 97. Anderson wrote that the meeting between Reagan and the Joint Chiefs during which Reagan asked this question had taken place in the White House in "December 1982." The documents cited in notes 28–30 above show that the meeting on December 22, 1982, was the only one between Reagan and the Joint Chiefs during that month. Anderson concurred that the meeting on December 22, 1982, must have been the one he described. Anderson, PL interview, August 15, 2000, Stanford, Calif. An item listed by the Air Force chief of staff on the agenda for the December 22 meeting was "Strategic Offensive and Defensive Forces," which could have prompted Reagan's question. "Highlights of JCS Presentation," p. 2, from RRPL-ES/NSC/SF, File Folder 8291013. McFarlane and Watkins do not remember Reagan specifically asking the Joint Chiefs of Staff to investigate missile defense during the December 22, 1982, meeting. McFarlane, PL interviews, August 22 and September 28, 2000, Washington, D.C.; Watkins, PL interview, July 31, 2000, Washington, D.C.

33. Anderson, PL interview, August 15, 2000, Stanford, Calif. Anderson stated that in Reagan's leadership style, asking a question in that manner "meant he wanted to do it." Anderson, conversation with PL, July 14, 2000, by telephone. See also Morris, *Dutch*, p. 468.

34. Anderson, *Revolution*, p. 97. Reiterated by Anderson in PL interview, August 15, 2000, Stanford, Calif.

35. Clark, PL interview, August 1, 2001, by telephone.

36. Anderson, PL interview, August 15, 2000, Stanford, Calif.

37. Clark, letter to PL, November 13, 2001. Clark stated that, looking back on the December 1982 meeting, he could "almost see [Reagan's] hands in the air," gesticulating for emphasis, as he asked the Joint Chiefs, "Gentlemen, what if . . ." Clark, PL interview, August 1, 2001, by telephone.

38. Weinberger, PL interview, August 1, 2001, Washington, D.C. In his second volume of memoirs, Weinberger included a photograph of the December 22, 1982, meeting and noted in the caption, "Missile defense was on the agenda." Weinberger with Roberts, *In the Arena*, photograph plate between p. 210 and p. 211.

39. Meese, PL interview, August 3, 2000, Washington, D.C. Meese "definitely remembered" the December 22 meeting. See also Meese, *With Reagan*, pp. 193–194.

40. Memo from Clark to Deaver, January 3, 1983. See also memo from Allan Myer to Clark, December 28, 1982, and memo from Clark to William Sadlier, January 3, 1983. All from RRPL-WHORM/SF, File Location FG013-06 Joint Chiefs of Staff (116000-180999).

41. Note (dated 1/5/83) on memo from Clark to Sadlier, January 3, 1983.

42. Reagan, quoted in Anderson, *Revolution*, pp. xxxiii–xxxiv. Prefacing Reagan's remarks, Anderson wrote that the first meeting Reagan referred to had occurred in December 1982. The account Reagan provided in his presidential memoir is more vague. Reagan, *An American Life*, pp. 547–548, 571. See also Reagan, quoted in Cannon, *President Reagan*, p. 285.

43. Poindexter, PL interview, August 16, 2001, Arlington, Va.

44. McFarlane, PL interview, August 22, 2000, Washington, D.C. In his memoirs, McFarlane wrote that he knew Reagan was "appalled" by MAD and was concerned "that we had no defense against attack." McFarlane continued that Reagan "had a strong and persistent sense of responsibility to protect Americans against attack. He had mentioned it on occasion, whenever we would be discussing some military program or other. . . . 'You know,' he would say, 'I just wish we could . . . protect Americans from this scourge of nuclear annihilation.'" McFarlane and Smardz, *Special Trust*, p. 228. See also Robert C. McFarlane, "Effective Strategic Policy," *Foreign Affairs* 67, no. 1 (Fall 1988), p. 37.

45. McFarlane, PL interview, August 22, 2000, Washington, D.C.

46. McFarlane, quoted in Baucom, *The Origins of SDI*, p. 181.

47. McFarlane, "Effective Strategic Policy," p. 40.

48. McFarlane, quoted in Smith, *The Power Game*, p. 606. See also McFarlane and Smardz, *Special Trust*, p. 226.

49. McFarlane, PL interview, August 22, 2000, Washington, D.C.

50. McFarlane, "Effective Strategic Policy," p. 41. See also Cannon's similar description of McFarlane's thinking on this point in *President Reagan*, p. 281.

51. McFarlane, PL interview, August 22, 2000, Washington, D.C.

52. McFarlane, "Effective Strategic Policy," p. 41.

53. McFarlane, PL interview, September 28, 2000, Washington, D.C.

54. McFarlane, PL interview, August 22, 2000, Washington, D.C.

55. McFarlane, PL interview, September 28, 2000, Washington, D.C.

56. Ibid.; see also Cannon, *President Reagan*, pp. 281–282; and McFarlane, quoted in Strober and Strober, *Reagan*, pp. 248–249.

57. Poindexter, PL interview, August 16, 2001, Arlington, Va.

58. McFarlane, PL interviews, August 22 and September 28, 2000, Washington, D.C.;

Cannon, *President Reagan*, p. 282; McFarlane, interview with Oberdorfer, p. 15, from DO-NJ.

59. Poindexter, PL interview, August 16, 2001, Arlington, Va.

60. Poindexter, quoted in Baucom, *The Origins of SDI*, p. 183. See also Poindexter, quoted in Hartmann, *Naval Renaissance*, p. 257.

61. Poindexter, PL interview, August 16, 2001, Arlington, Va.

62. It was literally "an in-house effort." Poindexter, PL interview, August 16, 2001, Arlington, Va. See also Baucom, *The Origins of SDI*, p. 183.

63. Poindexter, PL interview, August 16, 2001, Arlington, Va. Confirmed by McFarlane. McFarlane, PL interview, September 28, 2000, Washington, D.C. Poindexter said that "My group concluded that even though there were lots of problems, it was worth looking into." Poindexter, quoted in Strober and Strober, *Reagan*, p. 235.

64. McFarlane, PL interview, August 22, 2000, Washington, D.C. Also McFarlane, PL interview, September 28, 2000, Washington, D.C.

65. See Baucom, *The Origins of SDI*, p. 191; Cannon, *President Reagan*, pp. 282–283; and Smith, *The Power Game*, p. 607.

66. McFarlane, PL interview, August 22, 2000, Washington, D.C.

67. Ibid.; McFarlane and Smardz, *Special Trust*, p. 227; Poindexter, PL interview, August 16, 2001, Arlington, Va.; Poindexter, quoted in Hartmann, *Naval Renaissance*, pp. 257–258.

68. Watkins, PL interview, July 31, 2000, Washington, D.C.

69. Ibid.; Hartmann, *Naval Renaissance*, p. 252; Baucom, *The Origins of SDI*, p. 184.

70. Watkins, PL interview, July 31, 2000, Washington, D.C. See also McFarlane, quoted in Hartmann, *Naval Renaissance*, p. 256.

71. Watkins, quoted in Hartmann, *Naval Renaissance*, p. 253.

72. Watkins, PL interview, July 31, 2000, Washington, D.C.

73. Watkins, quoted in Cannon, *President Reagan*, p. 283. See also Baucom, *The Origins of SDI*, pp. 185–188, and Hartmann, *Naval Renaissance*, p. 252.

74. Watkins, PL interview, July 31, 2000, Washington, D.C. Watkins's colleagues later recalled that moral considerations derived from his religious beliefs and ethical principles played an important part in motivating him to support missile defense. Keyworth, interview with Baucom, September 28, 1987, pp. 24–25, from RRPL-OH/SDIO; McFarlane, PL interview, August 22, 2000, Washington, D.C.; McFarlane and Smardz, *Special Trust*, p. 227; McFarlane, quoted in Hartmann, *Naval Renaissance*, p. 256.

75. Watkins, PL interview, July 31, 2000, Washington, D.C.

76. McFarlane, PL interview, August 22, 2000, Washington, D.C. See also McFarlane and Smardz, *Special Trust*, p. 227.

77. Watkins, PL interview, July 31, 2000, Washington, D.C.

78. McFarlane, PL interview, August 22, 2000, Washington, D.C.

79. McFarlane and Smardz, *Special Trust*, p. 227.

80. Watkins, PL interview, July 31, 2000, Washington, D.C. Watkins commented that Teller "has this good mind. Does he always convert it to useful, politically acceptable practices? No—that's Teller. But you've got to listen to Teller, because Teller has a fascinating bank of knowledge that very few other people have."

81. Baucom, *The Origins of SDI*, p. 189; Hartmann, *Naval Renaissance*, pp. 253–254; Smith, *The Power Game*, p. 607; Cannon, *President Reagan*, p. 284; Teller with Shoolery, *Memoirs*, pp. 530–531.

82. Baucom, *The Origins of SDI*, p. 189.

83. Hartmann, *Naval Renaissance*, p. 254; Baucom, *The Origins of SDI*, pp. 189–190; Smith, *The Power Game*, p. 607.

84. Watkins, PL interview, July 31, 2000, Washington, D.C.

85. Hartmann, *Naval Renaissance*, p. 254; Baucom, *The Origins of SDI*, p. 190.

86. Watkins, PL interview, July 31, 2000, Washington, D.C. See also Baucom, *The Origins of SDI*, p. 190; and Hartmann, *Naval Renaissance*, p. 254.

87. Watkins, PL interview, July 31, 2000, Washington, D.C.

88. Meese, *With Reagan*, pp. 193–194; Baucom, *The Origins of SDI*, pp. 190–191; Smith, *The Power Game*, p. 607; Cannon, *President Reagan*, pp. 283–285; Hartmann, *Naval Renaissance*, pp. 254–255; Keyworth, interview with Baucom, September 28, 1987, p. 24, from RRPL-OH/SDIO.

89. Cannon, *President Reagan*, p. 283. Also Watkins, PL interview, July 31, 2000, Washington, D.C.

90. Watkins, PL interview, July 31, 2000, Washington, D.C.; Cannon, *President Reagan*, p. 283.

91. Baucom, *The Origins of SDI*, p. 190. Vessey had a religious basis for his qualms, as did Watkins. Confirmed in a conversation with an individual who knew both Vessey and Watkins.

92. Vessey, quoted in Cannon, *President Reagan*, p. 284.

93. Watkins, PL interview, July 31, 2000, Washington, D.C.

94. Hartmann, *Naval Renaissance*, pp. 254–255.

95. Meese, PL interview, August 3, 2000, Washington, D.C.; "List of invitees to luncheon with the Joint Chiefs of Staff, Friday, February 11, 1983 — 12 noon — Cabinet Room," from Office of the President: Presidential Briefing Papers, January–June 1983, Box 3, RRPL; photograph C12954-28, February 11, 1983, from RRPL-AV; Clark, letter to the author, November 13, 2001.

96. Poindexter later said that Clark had "put [missile defense] on the agenda for the meeting." Poindexter, PL interview, August 16, 2001, Arlington, Va. Some secondary works have claimed that Weinberger was opposed to the Joint Chiefs' missile defense recommendation prior to and at the February 11 meeting, although he stated during the meeting that the president should hear it. Cannon, *President Reagan*, p. 284; Baucom, *The Origins of SDI*, p. 191. According to another account, Weinberger stated during the meeting, "We have not studied this. It's not something I can endorse at this time." Smith, *The Power Game*, p. 607. Cannon, Baucom, and Smith each cited an interview with Watkins as the source of information on the matter. When asked by the author, however, Watkins indicated that Weinberger had not been opposed to the Chiefs' proposal. Watkins responded that Weinberger "knew Reagan," had been aware for many years of Reagan's desire to pursue a missile defense, and recognized that Reagan was going to embrace the Chiefs' report enthusiastically. Watkins, PL interview, July 31, 2000, Washington, D.C. In his memoirs, Weinberger wrote that during the February 11 meeting, he discussed his "basic objections" to the ABM Treaty and "the vulnerable position in which I thought it had left us." Weinberger, *Fighting for Peace*, p. 212.

97. McFarlane, PL interview, August 22, 2000, Washington, D.C.; McFarlane and Smardz, *Special Trust*, p. 229; Poindexter, PL interview, August 16, 2001, Arlington, Va.

98. Hartmann, *Naval Renaissance*, p. 255.

99. Meese, PL interview, August 3, 2000, Washington, D.C. Meese added that Vessey

(and later Watkins, when he spoke; see text below) conveyed that he "felt that mutual assured destruction, as the president did, was the wrong doctrine: the idea that if you blow up our cities we're going to blow up your cities was not a very good defense."

100. Baucom, *The Origins of SDI*, p. 192.
101. Reagan, quoted in Morris, *Dutch*, p. 471.
102. Weinberger, PL interview, August 1, 2001, Washington, D.C.
103. General Edward Meyer, then chief of staff of the Army, quoted in Smith, *The Power Game*, p. 608.
104. Vessey, quoted in Smith, *The Power Game*, p. 608.
105. Watkins, PL interview, July 31, 2000, Washington, D.C.
106. McFarlane, PL interview, August 22, 2000, Washington, D.C. Watkins recalled that McFarlane said, "Mr. President, what you've heard here is a very significant watershed in deterrence that we're talking about." Watkins, PL interview, July 31, 2000, Washington, D.C. See also McFarlane and Smardz, *Special Trust*, p. 229; Smith, *The Power Game*, p. 608; Hartmann, *Naval Renaissance*, pp. 255–256; Baucom, *The Origins of SDI*, pp. 191–192; and Cannon, *President Reagan*, p. 285.
107. McFarlane, PL interview, August 22, 2000, Washington, D.C.
108. McFarlane and Smardz, *Special Trust*, p. 229; McFarlane, PL interview, August 22, 2000, Washington, D.C.
109. Smith, *The Power Game*, p. 608.
110. Reagan, quoted in Smith, *The Power Game*, p. 609, and Morris, *Dutch*, p. 471.
111. Morris, *Dutch*, p. 799 (note).
112. Smith, *The Power Game*, p. 609; Weinberger, interview with Oberdorfer, May 23, 1990, p. 7, from DO-NJ.
113. Smith, *The Power Game*, p. 609.
114. Shultz sent the memo, entitled "U.S.–Soviet Relations in 1983," to Reagan on January 19. Shultz, *Turmoil and Triumph*, p. 162.
115. Ibid., p. 164; Oberdorfer, *From the Cold War to a New Era*, pp. 15–17.
116. Shultz, *Turmoil and Triumph*, p. 246.
117. Poindexter, PL interview, August 16, 2001, Arlington, Va.
118. Shultz, *Turmoil and Triumph*, p. 246. See also Oberdorfer, *From the Cold War to a New Era*, p. 27.
119. McFarlane, PL interview, August 22, 2000, Washington, D.C.
120. Weinberger, *Fighting for Peace*, pp. 212–213.
121. Cannon, *President Reagan*, p. 286; McFarlane and Smardz, *Special Trust*, pp. 230–231; Herken, *Cardinal Choices*, p. 211; Smith, *The Power Game*, pp. 609–610.
122. McFarlane and Smardz, *Special Trust*, p. 230. See also Herken, *Cardinal Choices*, p. 211, and Oberdorfer, *From the Cold War to a New Era*, p. 28.
123. Morris, PL interview, August 21, 2001, Washington, D.C.
124. McFarlane and Smardz, *Special Trust*, p. 230.
125. McFarlane, PL interview, August 22, 2000, Washington, D.C. "To do anything, ever, dramatically different is bound to encounter huge opposition. And hence the reason for it [the initiative] being done in secret," McFarlane noted. He added that the uniformed military had been the "key people" whose support the president needed to "protect" himself. With their support, the initiative could be prepared within the White House, without much input from the departments or agencies. See also McFarlane and Smardz, *Special Trust*, p. 235.

126. McFarlane, PL interview, August 22, 2000, Washington, D.C.; Poindexter, PL interview, August 16, 2001, Arlington, Va.; McFarlane and Smardz, *Special Trust*, pp. 231–232; Smith, *The Power Game*, p. 610; Baucom, *The Origins of SDI*, pp. 192–194; Cannon, *President Reagan*, p. 286.

127. Poindexter, PL interview, August 16, 2001, Arlington, Va.

128. Poindexter, quoted in Hartmann, *Naval Renaissance*, p. 258.

129. Poindexter, PL interview, August 16, 2001, Arlington, Va.

130. McFarlane, PL interview, August 22, 2000, Washington, D.C.

131. Meese, PL interview, August 3, 2000, Washington, D.C.

132. Weinberger, *Fighting for Peace*, p. 213. Also Weinberger, PL interview, August 1, 2001, Washington, D.C.

133. Gilbert Rye, an NSC staff member who worked on the insert, later stated that he and his colleagues had asked themselves, "How can the president go on the tube directing a major high-technology initiative and tell his science adviser nothing?" Rye, quoted in Herken, *Cardinal Choices*, p. 334 (note 74).

134. Keyworth, interview with Baucom, September 28, 1987, pp. 16–22, from RRPL-OH/SDIO. See also Baucom, *The Origins of SDI*, pp. 194; Herken, *Cardinal Choices*, pp. 211–212; and Smith, *The Power Game*, pp. 610–611. Herken wrote that the report had been commissioned at the request of Meese, who urged Keyworth to follow up on the information that Teller and the "kitchen Cabinet" group supporting missile defense (see Chapter 2) had provided to the White House in 1981 and 1982. Herken, *Cardinal Choices*, p. 334 (note 75).

135. Keyworth, interview with Baucom, September 28, 1987, pp. 16–22, from RRPL-OH/SDIO. See also Baucom, *The Origins of SDI*, pp. 194; Herken, *Cardinal Choices*, pp. 211–212; and Smith, *The Power Game*, pp. 610–611.

136. Herken, *Cardinal Choices*, p. 212.

137. Keyworth, interview with Baucom, September 28, 1987, pp. 1–29, from RRPL-OH/SDIO. During his conversation with Reis, Keyworth argued, "Neither of us was the President of the United States, neither of us had been elected, and so on." Ibid., p. 21.

138. Ibid., pp. 21, 22.

139. Keyworth, quoted in Herken, *Cardinal Choices*, p. 334 (note 80).

140. Keyworth, interview with Baucom, September 28, 1987, p. 22, from RRPL-OH/SDIO. See also Baucom, *The Origins of SDI*, pp. 194–195; and Smith, *The Power Game*, pp. 611–612.

141. Keyworth, interview with Baucom, September 28, 1987, pp. 1–29, from RRPL-OH/SDIO.

142. In 1987, after he had left the White House, Keyworth reflected on his doubts about the technical feasibility of missile defense prior to the announcement of SDI: "In retrospect, I think it is easier than I thought at the time." Keyworth, interview with Baucom, September 28, 1987, p. 26, from RRPL-OH/SDIO.

143. Reis, quoted in Herken, *Cardinal Choices*, p. 335 (note 81).

144. Keyworth, quoted in FitzGerald, *Way Out There in the Blue*, p. 206.

145. Watkins, PL interview, July 31, 2000, Washington, D.C.; Cannon, *President Reagan*, p. 286; Smith, *The Power Game*, p. 613; Hartmann, *Naval Renaissance*, p. 258.

146. Watkins, quoted in Smith, *The Power Game*, p. 613. Watkins told PL that he would have preferred further study prior to the announcement. Watkins, PL interview, July 31, 2000, Washington, D.C.

147. Vessey, quoted in Smith, *The Power Game*, p. 613. General Meyer later remarked that the Chiefs had been "shocked" by the insert. "The issue needed to be debated at the very highest levels by people concerned with policy and people concerned with technology." He added, "I would have preferred six or seven months to study it internally. We could have started out in a more organized way." Meyer, quoted in ibid., pp. 608–609, 613. Carlucci recalled that the Joint Chiefs "did not expect to happen what happened." Carlucci, quoted in Wohlforth, ed., *Witnesses to the End of the Cold War*, p. 45.

148. Watkins, PL interview, July 31, 2000, Washington, D.C.

149. A draft of the insert marked "3/22/83–0930" was heavily edited and revised by Reagan. Draft text with Reagan's handwritten revisions, from RRPL-WHORM/SF, File Location: SP 735, Address to the Nation on Defense and National Security 3/23/83 (8 of 8). On the evening of March 22, Reagan wrote in his diary, "On my desk was a draft of the speech on defense to be delivered tomorrow night on TV. This was one hassled over by N.S.C., State and Defense. Finally I had a crack at it. I did a lot of rewriting." Reagan, *An American Life*, p. 571. Reagan's diary entry indicated that at least some officials from State and Defense had already been notified of the announcement, and had begun attempts to alter it, by the twenty-second. It is exceptionally difficult to establish a precise chronology of when each of the relevant State and Defense officials first learned of the announcement and received the insert text, as their later recollections varied widely and were often contradictory. See Shultz, *Turmoil and Triumph*, pp. 249–250; Burt, PL interview, July 31, 2001, Washington, D.C.; McFarlane and Smardz, *Special Trust*, p. 232; Weinberger, *Fighting for Peace*, pp. 213–214. Smith, *The Power Game*, p. 613; Poindexter, PL interview, August 16, 2001, Arlington, Va.

150. Poindexter, PL interview, August 16, 2001, Washington, D.C. See also Poindexter, quoted in Strober and Strober, *Reagan*, pp. 235–236. Keyworth later said, "I have never seen such opposition to anything, as that which I saw to the strategic defense idea during those few days in the White House." Keyworth, interview with Baucom, September 28, 1987, p. 26, from RRPL-OH/SDIO. See also Keyworth, quoted in Baucom, *The Origins of SDI*, pp. 247–248 (note 85).

151. Perle, PL interview, September 27, 2000, by telephone.

152. Perle, quoted in Smith, *The Power Game*, p. 613.

153. Perle, PL interview, September 27, 2000, by telephone. Perle expressed his displeasure at the "great secrecy" with which the NSC staff prepared the announcement.

154. Poindexter, quoted in Baucom, *The Origins of SDI*, p. 248 (note 85). See also Oberdorfer, *From the Cold War to a New Era*, pp. 28–29; Poindexter, PL interview, August 16, 2001, Washington, D.C.; Keyworth, interview with Baucom, September 28, 1987, p. 25, from RRPL-OH/SDIO; Smith, *The Power Game*, p. 614; Shultz, *Turmoil and Triumph*, pp. 254–255; and Winik, *On the Brink*, p. 315. Winik wrote, "At the outset, Perle had been skeptical [of SDI], but more because of how SDI surfaced—the allies and the Congress were not informed in advance, nuances and niceties that mattered—and less because he didn't see benefits to the policy."

155. Keyworth, interview with Baucom, September 28, 1987, p. 25, from RRPL-OH/SDIO; also Poindexter, PL interview, August 16, 2001, Washington, D.C., and Baucom, *The Origins of SDI*, p. 248 (note 85). Richard DeLauer, undersecretary of defense for research and engineering, opposed the announcement. "That's nonsense. That can't be so," he reportedly told Keyworth when he first saw the in-

sert. DeLauer, quoted in Smith, *The Power Game*, p. 612. DeLauer subsequently asked not to be involved with SDI. Iklé, PL interview, July 24, 2001, Washington, D.C.

156. Perle, PL interview, September 27, 2000, by telephone. See also Perle, quoted in Strober and Strober, *Reagan*, pp. 233–234, 243. Iklé's approach to Reagan's speech before it was given was similar to Perle's. Iklé told the author that he was "pleased with the idea" of moving toward a missile defense, but "concerned how it would come across with the congressional reaction and so on and how [we] would accommodate cost." He was "happy" to support it after the announcement. Iklé, PL interview, July 24, 2001, Washington, D.C. A *Washington Post* article from March 26 reported that Iklé was supportive of "the general idea of a defensive system" but "was doubtful about the timing and format of Reagan's proposal." Hoffman and Cannon, "President Overruled Advisers on Announcing Defense Plan," *The Washington Post*, March 26, 1983, pp. A1, A7.

157. Perle, PL interview, September 27, 2000, by telephone.

158. Weinberger, PL interview, August 1, 2001, Washington, D.C. See also Weinberger, *Fighting for Peace*, pp. 213–214.

159. Perle told PL that Weinberger "agreed" with his criticisms. Perle, PL interview, September 27, 2000, by telephone; McFarlane and Smardz, *Special Trust*, pp. 232–233; Smith, *The Power Game*, p. 614.

160. On his lobbying to inform his fellow NATO defense ministers, see Weinberger, PL interview, August 1, 2001, Washington, D.C.; and Weinberger, *Fighting for Peace*, pp. 214–215. Poindexter later stated that Weinberger had "agreed" with the announcement. Hartmann, *Naval Renaissance*, p. 258. See also Baucom, *The Origins of SDI*, p. 248 (note 85). In his memoirs of his time at the Pentagon, Weinberger wrote that he had noted an account "to the effect that I was opposed to SDI and tried to block the inclusion of it in the President's speech. This is quite false." Weinberger, *Fighting for Peace*, pp. 231–232 (note 7).

161. Shultz, *Turmoil and Triumph*, pp. 249–264; Keyworth, interview with Baucom, September 28, 1987, p. 25, from RRPL-OH/SDIO; Burt, PL interview, July 31, 2001, Washington, D.C.; Poindexter, PL interview, August 16, 2001, Arlington, Va.; Morris, *Dutch*, pp. 474–477; Oberdorfer, *From the Cold War to a New Era*, p. 29.

162. Shultz, *Turmoil and Triumph*, pp. 251, 770.

163. Ibid., pp. 249–256; Smith, *The Power Game*, p. 614. Burt, then the assistant secretary of state for European affairs (he had moved from the State Department's Political-Military Bureau), later noted that U.S. relations with its European allies were then in a crucial and tense phase, as the deployment of American intermediate-range missiles in Western Europe was to commence that autumn. In Burt's view, "we needed a big debate over the basics of deterrence and defense at that point like a hole in the head." Burt first learned of the insert when he received a telephone call from Perle (with whom Burt constantly differed during intra-administration debates over arms control). Perle told Burt that if it made him "feel any better," Perle himself had neither known about nor been involved in the drafting of the insert. At the time of the call, Burt was with Vice President Bush. Burt later said that Bush appeared to be "very uncomfortable about the whole thing" when Burt informed him of the imminent announcement. Burt, PL interview, July 31, 2001, Washington, D.C. Poindexter, however, remembered that Bush had favored the announcement. Baucom, *The Origins of SDI*, p. 248 (note 85).

164. Shultz, *Turmoil and Triumph*, pp. 249–264; Keyworth, interview with Baucom,

September 28, 1987, p. 25, from RRPL-OH/SDIO; Burt, PL interview, July 31, 2001, Washington, D.C.

165. Shultz, *Turmoil and Triumph*, pp. 249–250.
166. Smith, *The Power Game*, p. 614.
167. Shultz, *Turmoil and Triumph*, pp. 249–256.
168. Morris, *Dutch*, p. 477; Smith, *The Power Game*, pp. 614–615.
169. Poindexter, PL interview, August 16, 2001, Arlington, Va.
170. Keyworth, interview with Baucom, September 28, 1987, pp. 25–26, from RRPL-OH/SDIO.
171. "Reagan for the Defense," *Time*, April 4, 1983, p. 10.
172. Weinberger, PL interview, August 1, 2001, Washington, D.C. See also Weinberger, *Fighting for Peace*, pp. 8, 206, 208, 215, and Weinberger, quoted in Strober and Strober, *Reagan*, pp. 237, 246–247.
173. Reagan wrote the last eight words here into the draft. Draft text with Reagan's handwritten revisions, March 22, 1983, p. 3, from RRPL-WHORM/SF, File Location: SP 735, Address to the Nation on Defense and National Security 3/23/83 (8 of 8).
174. In the draft of the insert from the morning of the twenty-second, this sentence was followed by one that read, "Let me emphasize again, such defense is no near-term panacea." Reagan deleted it. Ibid.
175. Ibid., p. 4. Cf. Reagan's diary entry from February 11, 1983, quoted earlier in this chapter.
176. Smith, *The Power Game*, p. 612; Morris, *Dutch*, p. 802 (note 477). DeLauer later said of the "impotent and obsolete" phrase that "those of us who knew what was really going on couldn't support that." DeLauer, quoted in *Star Wars Quotes: Statements by Reagan Administration Officials, Outside Experts, Members of Congress, U.S. Allies, and Soviet Officials on the Strategic Defense Initiative*, compiled by the Arms Control Association (Washington, D.C.: Arms Control Association, 1986), p. 29.
177. President Reagan, televised address on peace and national security, March 23, 1983, *American Foreign Policy Current Documents*, 1983 (hereafter AFPCD 1983) (Washington, D.C.: U.S. Department of State, 1985), pp. 56–62.
178. Reagan, *An American Life*, p. 571. See also Morris, *Dutch*, pp. 475, 477.
179. Reagan, *An American Life*, p. 571.
180. On the immediate negative reaction of scientists and strategic specialists, see Herken, *Cardinal Choices*, pp. 213–214; Michael Getler, "Speech Also Attacked on Anti-ICBM Issue," *The Washington Post*, March 25, 1983, pp. A1, A9; Charles Mohr, "Scientists Dubious over Missile Plan," *The New York Times*, March 25, 1983, p. A8; Michael Getler, "Science Adviser Sees Lasers and Mirrors As a Missile Defense," *The Washington Post*, March 26, 1983, p. A8; Richard L. Garwin, "Reagan's Riskiness," *The New York Times*, March 30, 1983, p. A31; "Reagan for the Defense," *Time*, April 4, 1983, pp. 13–14; Strobe Talbott, "The Risks of Taking Up Shields," *Time*, April 4, 1983, pp. 20–21; interview with Jan Lodal, *U.S. News & World Report*, April 11, 1983, pp. 24–25. According to Weinberger, "the academic community and the defense specialists all leaped on [SDI] and poured scorn on it, on the idea that it upset all of the conventional wisdom." Weinberger, quoted in Strober and Strober, *Reagan*, p. 237. See also Weinberger, *Fighting for Peace*, p. 215. Reagan's initiative did garner support among some scientists and strategists, inevitably including Teller. Edward Teller, "Reagan's Courage," *The New York*

Times, March 30, 1983, p. A31; Arnold Kramish, "Bundy Has It Wrong," *The Washington Post*, March 31, 1983; "The Old Lion Still Roars," *Time*, April 4, 1983, p. 12; "Reagan for the Defense," *Time*, April 4, 1983, p. 13; Daniel Southerland, "Top Scientist Defends 'Space Wars' Strategy," *The Christian Science Monitor*, April 4, 1983, p. 13.

181. "Reagan for the Defense," *Time*, April 4, 1983, p. 13; FitzGerald, *Way Out There in the Blue*, p. 211. Not all commentary in the national media was negative. One columnist in *Time* compared the initiative to the challenges of the Manhattan Project, the Apollo program, and the building of the Panama Canal. He noted that a "determined, skilled President who captures a nation's imagination, energy and know-how can work miracles." Hugh Sidey, "Turning Vision into Reality," *Time*, April 4, 1983, p. 19. A *Washington Post* editorial stated that the principles of mutual nuclear threat and vulnerability "were not written in stone" but rather represented "merely the best guesses made by harried men groping with the historically unprecedented circumstance—the capacity to end the world as we know it—that technology had put in their hands." It implied that Reagan might not have been amiss in challenging those principles. The *Post* editorial perceptively noted that the initiative was "pure Reagan." The idea of pursuing a missile defense, it observed, was "simple at first glance, complex at the second, running against the grain, sure to arouse a storm. It is the product of Ronald Reagan's peculiar knack for asking an obvious question, one that has moral as well as political dimensions and one that the experts assumed had been answered, or found not worth asking, long ago." "Mr. Reagan's New Defense Idea," *The Washington Post*, March 25, 1983, p. A22.

182. Deaver, quoted in "Reagan for the Defense," *Time*, April 4, 1983, p. 13. See also Russell Warren-Howe and Bill King, "Development to Be Ordered for Missile Defense in Space," *The Washington Times*, March 25, 1983, pp. 1A, 12A; excerpt from Reagan's diary in Reagan, *An American Life*, p. 572; and Shultz, *Turmoil and Triumph*, pp. 259–260. Deaver, PL interview, August 3, 2001, Washington, D.C.; and McFarlane, PL interviews, August 22 and September 28, 2000, Washington, D.C.

183. Weinberger, *Fighting for Peace*, pp. 214–215.

184. Larry Pressler, *Star Wars: The Strategic Defense Initiative Debates in Congress* (New York: Praeger, 1986), pp. 66–67; Lou Cannon, "President Seeks Futuristic Defense Against Missiles," *The Washington Post*, March 24, 1983, pp. A1, A13; Francis X. Clines, "Democrats Assert Reagan Is Using 'Star Wars' Scare to Hide Blunders," *The New York Times*, March 25, 1983; Getler, "Speech Also Attacked on Anti-ICBM Issue," *The Washington Post*, March 25, 1983, pp. A1, A9; Warren-Howe and King, "Development to Be Ordered for Missile Defense in Space," *The Washington Times*, March 25, 1983, pp. A1, A12; "'Star Wars' Defense Plan Hit," *The Washington Times*, April 4, 1983; "Reagan for the Defense," *Time*, April 4, 1983, pp. 9–13. See also Abrahamson, and Teller, quoted in Strober and Strober, *Reagan*, pp. 239–240; McFarlane and Smardz, *Special Trust*, pp. 233–234; and Weinberger, *Fighting for Peace*, pp. 215–216.

185. Poindexter, PL interview, August 16, 2001, Arlington, Va.; Poindexter, quoted in Strober and Strober, *Reagan*, p. 239. "We wanted a catchy name but couldn't come up with one," Poindexter told Strober and Strober, "so I finally said, 'Let's call it SDI.'"

186. Letter from Reagan to Patrick Mulvey, June 20, 1983, in Skinner, Anderson, and

Anderson, eds., *Reagan: A Life in Letters*, p. 425. See also letter from Reagan to Drs. Ivy Mooring and John Shelton, November 1, 1984, in ibid., p. 426.

187. Pressler, *Star Wars*, pp. 67–69, 106–111; letters of support received at the White House, from RRPL-WHORM/SF, File Location: SP 735, Address to the Nation on Defense and National Security 3/23/83; copies of remarks and speeches in Congress, from same location.

188. Letter from Goldwater to Reagan, March 24, 1983, from RRPL-WHORM/SF, File Location: SP 735, Address to the Nation on Defense and National Security 3/23/83 (1 of 8).

189. "Reagan for the Defense," *Time*, April 4, 1983, p. 13.

190. McFarlane and Smardz, *Special Trust*, p. 234.

191. Weinberger, PL interview, August 1, 2001, Washington, D.C.

192. Pressler, *Star Wars*, pp. 144–145.

193. Shultz, *Turmoil and Triumph*, p. 260; Weinberger, PL interview, August 1, 2001, Washington, D.C.

194. Shultz, *Turmoil and Triumph*, p. 256.

195. Dusko Doder, "Moscow Asserts Plan Would Violate Treaty," *The Washington Post*, March 25, 1983, pp. A1, A8.

196. Arthur Hartman, the U.S. ambassador to the USSR from 1981 to 1987, told PL that his analysis at the time was that "real thinkers" in the USSR knew that Reagan would not "push the button because he had a defense." The Soviet argument that Reagan was seeking SDI in order to launch a first strike with impunity was "not believable," he said; it was an example of the Soviets' use of manipulating and encouraging fear of nuclear war for their own propaganda purposes. Hartman, PL interview, August 1, 2001, by telephone.

197. Andropov, quoted in John F. Burns, "Andropov Says U.S. Is Spurring a Race for Nuclear Arms," *The New York Times*, March 27, 1983, pp. 1, 14. See also "Excerpts from Interview with Andropov on ABM Plan," *The New York Times*, March 27, 1983, p. 14; and Dusko Doder, "Andropov Accuses Reagan of Lying About Soviet Arms," *The Washington Post*, March 27, 1983, pp. A1, A13.

198. Shultz, *Turmoil and Triumph*, pp. 258, 264.

199. Getler, "Speech Also Attacked on Anti-ICBM Issue," *The Washington Post*, March 25, 1983, p. A9.

200. Weinberger, quoted in John Darnton, "Weinberger Says ABM Pact May Ultimately Need Amending," *The New York Times*, March 25, 1983.

201. Speech by Weinberger, April 11, 1983, excerpted in *Defense Science & Electronics*, May 1983, p. 21.

202. Darnton, "Weinberger Says ABM Pact May Ultimately Need Amending," *The New York Times*, March 25, 1983.

203. Interview with George Keyworth, *U.S. News & World Report*, April 11, 1983, pp. 24–25.

204. Speech by Weinberger, April 11, 1983, excerpted in *Defense Science & Electronics*, May 1983, p. 21.

205. Darnton, "Weinberger Says ABM Pact May Ultimately Need Amending," *The New York Times*, March 25, 1983.

206. Cannon, *President Reagan*, pp. 277–278; letter from Reagan to Lawrence W. Belienson, July 25, 1983, in Skinner, Anderson, and Anderson, eds., *Reagan: His Life in Letters*, pp. 425–426.

207. Interview with Keyworth, *U.S. News & World Report*, April 11, 1983, pp. 24–25.

208. Keyworth, quoted in Getler, "Science Adviser Sees Lasers and Mirrors As a Missile Defense," *The Washington Post*, March 26, 1983, p. A8.

209. Reagan, question-and-answer session with reporters, March 25, 1983, in *Public Papers of the Presidents: Ronald Reagan, 1983*, Book I (Washington, D.C.: U.S. Government Printing Office, 1984), p. 448.

210. See, for example, Keyworth, interview with Baucom, September 28, 1987, pp. 27–28, from RRPL-OH/SDIO; Cannon, *President Reagan*, p. 274; Morris, *Dutch*, p. 470.

211. In 1985, for example, Reagan stated, "It kind of amuses me that everyone is so sure I must have heard about it, that I never thought of it myself. The truth is, I did." Reagan, quoted in *Star Wars Quotes*, p. 26. He added, "At one of my regular meetings with the Chiefs of Staff, I brought up this subject about a defensive weapon. . . . And when they did not look aghast at the idea and instead said yes, they believed that such a thing offered a possibility and should be researched, I said, 'Go.'" Ibid. In 1988, Reagan wrote to a correspondent that SDI "was my idea to begin with." Letter from Reagan to Robert Dick, c. May 1988, from RRPL, Presidential Handwriting File, series II: Presidential Records 1/30/88–10/20/88. See Morris, *Dutch*, p. 470. He used similar language during an interview after he had left office: "SDI was my idea." Reagan, quoted in Cannon, *President Reagan*, p. 274.

212. Reagan, question-and-answer session with reporters, March 25, 1983, in *Public Papers of the Presidents: Ronald Reagan, 1983*, Book 1, pp. 448–449.

213. Reagan, question-and-answer session with reporters, March 29, 1983, in *Public Papers of the Presidents: Ronald Reagan, 1983*, Book 1, p. 465.

214. Handwritten draft of letter and typewritten final version of letter from Reagan to Roy Innis (National Chairman of the Congress of Racial Equality), June 20, 1983, from RRPL-WHORM/SF, File Location: SP 735, Address to the Nation on Defense and National Security 3/23/83 (8 of 8). See also similar letters in the same location.

215. Letter from Reagan to Patrick Mulvey, June 20, 1983, in Skinner, Anderson, and Anderson, eds., *Reagan: His Life in Letters*, p. 425.

216. Weinberger, interview with Oberdorfer, May 23, 1990, p. 7, from DO-NJ.

217. Weinberger, PL interview, August 1, 2001, Washington, D.C.

218. Poindexter, PL interview, August 16, 2001, Arlington, Va.

219. Deaver, PL interview, August 3, 2001, Washington, D.C. Also Iklé, PL interview, July 24, 2001, Washington, D.C.

220. Ronald Reagan, "It Was 'Star Wars' Muscle That Wrestled Arms Race to a Halt," *Los Angeles Times*, July 31, 1991.

CHAPTER IV: 1983–1984

1. Reagan, quoted in Cannon, *President Reagan*, p. 273.

2. Reagan, Address from Camp David, Md., January 8, 1983, in *American Foreign Policy Current Documents, 1983* (hereafter AFPCD 1983) (Washington, D.C.: U.S. Department of State, 1985), p. 498.

3. Reagan, Address to the American Legion, February 22, 1983, in *AFPCD 1983*, pp. 265, 270.

4. Reagan, press conference, March 25, 1983, in *Public Papers of the Presidents: Ronald Reagan, 1983*, Book 1, p. 448.

5. Reagan, statement, January 14, 1983, in *AFPCD 1983*, p. 107.

6. Reagan, question-and-answer session with reporters, January 20, 1983, in *Public Papers of the Presidents: Ronald Reagan, 1983*, Book 1, p. 76.

7. Reagan, question-and-answer session with high school students, March 25, 1983, in *Public Papers of the Presidents: Ronald Reagan, 1983*, Book 1, p. 455.

8. Reagan, speech before the World Affairs Council, Los Angeles, March 31, 1983, *AFPCD 1983*, p. 120; question-and-answer session with high school students, March 25, 1983, in *Public Papers of the Presidents: Ronald Reagan, 1983*, Book 1, p. 455.

9. "U.S.-Soviet Relations in 1983," memo from Shultz to Reagan, January 19, 1983, pp. 1–4, in Vladislav Zubok, Catherine Nielsen, and Greg Grant, eds., *Compendium of Declassified Documents*, for "Understanding the End of the Cold War: Reagan/Gorbachev Years," Oral History Conference, May 7–10, 1998, Brown University (Providence, R.I.: Watson Institute for International Studies, Brown University, 1998).

10. Shultz, *Turmoil and Triumph*, p. 162; Oberdorfer, *From the Cold War to a New Era*, pp. 34–35.

11. Shultz, *Turmoil and Triumph*, p. 162.

12. Ibid., pp. 163–165; Oberdorfer, *From the Cold War to a New Era*, pp. 15–20.

13. Shultz, *Turmoil and Triumph*, pp. 265–274.

14. Ibid., p. 268.

15. Matlock, PL interview, September 5, 2001, Princeton, N.J.

16. Jack F. Matlock, *Autopsy on an Empire: The American Ambassador's Account of the Collapse of the Soviet Union* (New York: Random House, 1995), p. 77. Confirmed by Poindexter, PL interview, August 16, 2001, Arlington, Va.

17. Matlock, PL interview, September 5, 2001, Princeton, N.J. See also Matlock, *Autopsy on an Empire*, pp. 11, 77–82, 88; and Matlock, quoted in Wohlforth, ed., *Witnesses to the End of the Cold War*, p. 76.

18. Oberdorfer, *From the Cold War to a New Era*, p. 35.

19. Morris, *Dutch*, pp. 481–500.

20. See, e.g., FitzGerald, *Way Out There in the Blue*, pp. 225–226, and Oberdorfer, *From the Cold War to a New Era*, p. 36.

21. Shultz, *Turmoil and Triumph*, p. 276; Shultz, "U.S.-Soviet Relations in the Context of U.S. Foreign Policy," statement before the Senate Foreign Relations Committee, June 15, 1983, in *AFPCD 1983*, p. 508.

22. Shultz, "U.S.-Soviet Relations in the Context of U.S. Foreign Policy," p. 508.

23. Ibid., p. 510.

24. Ibid., p. 511.

25. Ibid., p. 509.

26. Ibid., p. 514.

27. "Dimensions of Civil Unrest in the Soviet Union," Intelligence Report, CIA/National Intelligence Council, April 1983, pp. 16, 5, 22–23, 20, in *The Soviet Estimate: U.S. Analysis of the Soviet Union, 1947–1991*, National Security Archive (Alexandria, Va.: Chadwyck-Healey, 1995).

28. "U.S. Intelligence Estimates of the Soviet Union," essay in *The Soviet Estimate: U.S. Analysis of the Soviet Union, 1947–1991, Guide and Index*, pp. 21–22.

29. This point was made by Perle (though not with reference to this specific report) in PL interview, September 27, 2000, by telephone.

30. "Possible Soviet Responses to the US Strategic Defense Initiative," Interagency Intelligence Assessment, Director of Central Intelligence, September 1983, pp. 1–4, in *The Soviet Estimate: U.S. Analysis of the Soviet Union, 1947–1991*.

31. Poindexter, PL interview, August 16, 2001, Arlington, Va.
32. Adelman, PL interview, August 13, 2001, Arlington, Va.
33. Matlock, PL interview, September 5, 2001, Princeton, N.J. Hartman concurred. Hartman, PL interview, August 1, 2001, by telephone.
34. Matlock, PL interview, September 5, 2001, Princeton, N.J.
35. Reagan, handwritten draft letter to Andropov, July 1983, from DO-NJ.
36. Clark, memo to Reagan, July 9, 1983, from DO-NJ.
37. Reagan, handwritten letter to Andropov, July 11, 1983, from DO-NJ.
38. Adelman, PL interview, August 13, 2001, Arlington, Va.; Burt, PL interview, July 31, 2001, Washington, D.C.; Iklé, PL interview, July 24, 2001, Washington, D.C.; Matlock, PL interview, September 5, 2001, Princeton, N.J.
39. Adelman, PL interview, August 13, 2001, Arlington, Va.
40. Burt, PL interview, July 31, 2001, Washington, D.C.; Perle, PL interview, September 27, 2000, by telephone.
41. McFarlane, PL interviews, August 22 and September 28, 2000, Washington, D.C.; Cannon, *President Reagan*, pp. 280–283; Strobe Talbott, *The Master of the Game: Paul Nitze and the Nuclear Peace* (New York: Alfred A. Knopf, 1988), pp. 200–207.
42. McFarlane, PL interviews, August 22 and September 28, 2000, Washington, D.C.
43. Oberdorfer, *From the Cold War to a New Era*, p. 71.
44. Interview with McFarlane, November 1, 1999, Appendix B of "The Role of the National Security Adviser," pp. 43–44; Matlock, PL interview, September 5, 2001, Princeton, N.J.
45. McFarlane, PL interview, September 28, 2000, Washington, D.C.; Oberdorfer, *From the Cold War to a New Era*, p. 71; Shultz, *Turmoil and Triumph*, pp. 463–467.
46. Matlock, PL interview, September 5, 2001, Princeton, N.J.
47. Reagan, "The U.S.-Soviet Relationship," January 16, 1984, *American Foreign Policy Current Documents, 1984* (hereafter *AFPCD 1984*) (Washington, D.C.: U.S. Department of State, 1986), p. 407.
48. Matlock, PL interview, September 5, 2001, Princeton, N.J. See also Matlock, *Autopsy on an Empire*, pp. 11, 77–82, 88.
49. Reagan, "The U.S.-Soviet Relationship," p. 409.
50. Reagan, State of the Union Address, January 25, 1984, *AFPCD 1984*, p. 28.
51. Kimmitt, PL interview, January 27, 1999, Washington, D.C.
52. On the technology and strategy panels, see "Strategic Defense Initiative," Department of Defense Fact Sheet, March 9, 1984, *AFPCD 1984*, pp. 42–43; Weinberger, "Strategic Defense: A Possible Dream," Address to the National Press Club, May 1, 1984, *AFPCD 1984*, p. 53.
53. Weinberger, *Fighting for Peace*, pp. 216–217.
54. Weinberger, PL interview, August 1, 2001, Washington, D.C.
55. Ibid.
56. Ibid.
57. Reagan, *An American Life*, p. 665.
58. Colin Powell with Joseph E. Persico, *A Soldier's Way: An Autobiography* (London: Hutchinson, 1995).
59. "Strategic Defense Initiative," Department of Defense Fact Sheet, March 9, 1984, *AFPCD 1984*, pp. 42, 43.
60. See, e.g., Weinberger, "Strategic Defense: A Possible Dream," Address to the National Press Club, May 1, 1984, *AFPCD 1984*, p. 53.

61. Adelman, PL interview, August 13, 2001, Arlington, Va.
62. Shultz, *Turmoil and Triumph*, pp. 472–478.
63. Weinberger, PL interview, August 1, 2001, Washington, D.C.
64. Perle, PL interview, September 27, 2000, by telephone.
65. Memo from McFarlane to Matlock, January 28, 1984, from RRPL, Files of Jack Matlock, US-USSR 1984.
66. Memo from Matlock to McFarlane, April 6, 1984, from RRPL, Files of Jack Matlock, US-USSR 1984.
67. McFarlane with Smardz, *Special Trust*, p. 299; and Shultz, *Turmoil and Triumph*, p. 477.
68. NSDD 142, "Arms Limitation Talks," July 5, 1984, from RRPL-NSC/NSDD.
69. McFarlane, statement on the U.S. response to Soviet proposal for negotiations on outer space weapons systems, June 29, 1984, *AFPCD 1984*, pp. 103–104.
70. NSDD 142, "Arms Limitation Talks."
71. Weinberger, PL interview, August 1, 2001, Washington, D.C.; Perle, PL interview, September 27, 2000, by telephone.
72. McFarlane, PL interviews, August 22 and September 28, 2000, Washington, D.C.
73. Nitze, *From Hiroshima to Glasnost*, p. 402.
74. Nitze, quoted in Wohlforth, ed., *Witnesses to the End of the Cold War*, p. 38.
75. Strobe Talbott, *The Master of the Game: Paul Nitze and the Nuclear Peace* (New York: Alfred A. Knopf, 1988), p. 210.
76. McFarlane, e-mail to J[ohn] P[oindexter] and W[ilma] H[all], including text of memo from McFarlane to Reagan, September 17, 1984, from *White House Emails*, unpublished collection, National Security Archive, Washington, D.C. (hereafter NSA-WH).
77. Shultz, *Turmoil and Triumph*, p. 491.
78. Ibid.
79. Ibid., p. 498.
80. NSDD 148, "The U.S. Umbrella Talks Proposal," October 26, 1984, from RRPL-NSC/NSDD.
81. McFarlane, PL interviews, August 22 and September 28, 2000, Washington, D.C.
82. Lou Cannon, "Reagan Predicts Serious Talks on Arms Curbs in Next Term," *The Washington Post*, November 7, 1984, p. A38.
83. Shultz, *Turmoil and Triumph*, p. 498.
84. Reagan, letter to Lawrence W. Beilenson, December 10, 1984, in Skinner, Anderson, and Anderson, eds., *Reagan: A Life in Letters*, pp. 426–427.
85. Ibid.
86. McFarlane, PL interview, September 28, 2000, Washington, D.C.
87. Perle, PL interview, September 27, 2000, by telephone.
88. NSDD 153, "Instructions for the Shultz-Gromyko Meeting in Geneva," January 1, 1985, p. 5, from RRPL-NSC/NSDD.
89. Ibid., p. 4.
90. Ibid., pp. 2, 4.
91. Ibid., pp. 5, 9.
92. McFarlane, PL interview, September 28, 2000, Washington, D.C.
93. Oberdorfer, *From the Cold War to a New Era*, p. 102.

CHAPTER V: 1985

1. Shultz, *Turmoil and Triumph*, p. 513; Oberdorfer, *From the Cold War to a New Era*, p. 102.
2. Memorandum of conversation (memcon), Shultz-Gromyko meeting, afternoon session, Geneva, January 7, 1985, p. 3, in Zubok, Nielsen, and Grant, eds., *Compendium of Declassified Documents*, for "Understanding the Cold War: Reagan/Gorbachev Years."
3. Ibid., pp. 4, 11.
4. Ibid., pp. 1, 2.
5. Ibid., p. 10.
6. Ibid., p. 12.
7. Shultz, "U.S.-Soviet Agreement on the Structure of New Arms Control Negotiations," transcript of press conference, Geneva, January 9, 1985, *American Foreign Policy Current Documents, 1985* (hereafter *AFPCD 1985*) (Washington, D.C.: U.S. Department of State, 1986), p. 73.
8. Ibid., p. 75.
9. McFarlane and Smardz, *Special Trust*, p. 302.
10. McFarlane, PL interview, September 28, 2000, Washington, D.C.
11. Ibid.
12. Reagan, Inaugural Address, January 21, 1985, in *Public Papers of the Presidents: Ronald Reagan, 1985*, Book I, p. 57.
13. Reagan, interview with *The New York Times*, February 11, 1985, in *Public Papers of the Presidents: Ronald Reagan, 1985*, Book 1, p. 159.
14. Reagan, interview with *The Wall Street Journal*, February 7, 1985, in *Public Papers of the Presidents: Ronald Reagan, 1985*, Book 1, p. 144.
15. Reagan, Remarks at the National Space Club Luncheon, March 29, 1985, in *The Soviet Union Fights the Cold War: Official Documents of the Reagan Administration, 1981–1989* (Washington, D.C.: American Foreign Policy Council, 1999).
16. Nitze, *From Hiroshima to Glasnost*, pp. 406–407.
17. Nitze, Address before the World Affairs Council of Philadelphia, February 20, 1985, *AFPCD 1985*, pp. 77–78.
18. Nitze, *From Hiroshima to Glasnost*, p. 407.
19. FitzGerald, *Way Out There in the Blue*, p. 277.
20. Nitze, *From Hiroshima to Glasnost*, pp. 407–408.
21. Weinberger, *Fighting for Peace*, pp. 223–224.
22. Weinberger, PL interview, August 1, 2001, Washington, D.C.
23. Nitze, Address before the World Affairs Council of Philadelphia, February 20, 1985, *AFPCD 1985*, pp. 78–79.
24. Ibid., p. 79.
25. See, e.g., Reagan, news conference, January 9, 1985, p. 24; interview with *The New York Times*, February 12, 1985, pp. 158–159; interview with *Newsweek*, March 4, 1985, p. 259, all in *Public Papers of the Presidents: Ronald Reagan, 1985*, Book 1.
26. Reagan, Remarks at the Annual Dinner of the Conservative Political Action Committee Conference, March 1, 1985, in *Public Papers of the Presidents: Ronald Reagan, 1985*, Book 1, p. 229.
27. Reagan, interview with *Newsweek*, March 4, 1985, in *Public Papers of the Presidents: Ronald Reagan, 1985*, Book 1, pp. 259, 262.

28. Shultz, *Turmoil and Triumph*, p. 521.
29. Matlock, PL interview, September 5, 2001, Princeton, N.J.; Matlock, *Autopsy on an Empire*, pp. 50–52.
30. McFarlane, *Special Trust*, p. 301.
31. Ibid.
32. Matlock, *Autopsy on an Empire*, pp. 45–67.
33. Reagan, remarks at a question-and-answer session with members of the Magazine Publishers Association, March 14, 1985, in *Public Papers of the Presidents: Ronald Reagan, 1985*, Book 1, p. 285.
34. Shultz, *Turmoil and Triumph*, pp. 527, 530.
35. Memo from Marshall to Fortier, April 19, 1985, from RRPL, Donald R. Fortier files, Soviet Union—US Policy toward Soviet Union [1 of 3] OA 90706.
36. Shultz, *Turmoil and Triumph*, pp. 536, 564.
37. Oberdorfer, *From the Cold War to a New Era*, p. 114.
38. Shultz, *Turmoil and Triumph*, p. 537.
39. Ibid., p. 566.
40. Nitze, *From Hiroshima to Glasnost*, pp. 410–411.
41. Shultz, *Turmoil and Triumph*, p. 264; McFarlane, PL interview, September 28, 2000, Washington, D.C. McFarlane added that "part of the reason, and it's not a good reason," that he supported the venture was that he "knew that I was getting toward the end of my time [as national security adviser], and I wanted to get some more momentum into" negotiations with the Soviets.
42. Nitze, *From Hiroshima to Glasnost*, p. 412.
43. McFarlane, PL interview, September 28, 2000, Washington, D.C.
44. Nitze, *From Hiroshima to Glasnost*, p. 412.
45. Shultz, *Turmoil and Triumph*, p. 570.
46. Nitze, *From Hiroshima to Glasnost*, p. 411.
47. McFarlane later explained that he did not directly discuss the notion of using SDI as a bargaining chip with Reagan because he knew that Reagan opposed that. McFarlane, interview with Oberdorfer, October 9, 1989, p. 15, from DO-NJ.
48. See FitzGerald, *Way Out There in the Blue*, p. 280.
49. Shultz, *Turmoil and Triumph*, pp. 570, 571; Nitze, *From Hiroshima to Glasnost*, p. 412.
50. Matlock, *Autopsy on an Empire*, p. 72; and Shultz, *Turmoil and Triumph*, pp. 571–573.
51. McFarlane and Smardz, *Special Trust*, p. 313; Oberdorfer, *From the Cold War to a New Era*, p. 121.
52. Memo from C. Thomas Thorne, Acting Head, INR, to Shultz, "re: Arms Control and your Shevardnadze Meetings," July 26, 1985, p. 1, in Zubok, Nielsen, and Grant, eds., *Compendium of Declassified Documents*, "Understanding the Cold War: Reagan/Gorbachev Years."
53. INR Intelligence Brief, "Soviet Motivations for a 'Quick-Fix' Arms Control Agreement," July 25, 1985, pp. 1–3, attachment (Tab I) to Thorne memo to Shultz, July 26, 1985.
54. Shultz, *Turmoil and Triumph*, p. 574.
55. Nitze, *From Hiroshima to Glasnost*, pp. 408, 416.
56. Oberdorfer, *From the Cold War to a New Era*, p. 128.
57. Dusko Doder, "New Leader Shows Youth, Energy," *The Washington Post*, July 30, 1985, quoted in FitzGerald, *Way Out There in the Blue*, p. 286.

58. See McFarlane and Smardz, *Special Trust*, p. 312.

59. Shultz, *Turmoil and Triumph*, p. 576.

60. Shultz and Nitze, quoted in Wohlforth, ed., *Witnesses to the End of the Cold War*, pp. 57–58; John Whitehead, quoted in "Understanding the Cold War, 1980–1987," p. 185.

61. Nitze, *From Hiroshima to Glasnost*, p. 411.

62. McFarlane, interview with Oberdorfer, October 9, 1989, pp. 5, 15, from DO-NJ.

63. Shultz, *Turmoil and Triumph*, p. 575.

64. McFarlane, PL interview, September 28, 2000, Washington, D.C.

65. Reagan, news conference, September 17, 1985, in *Public Papers of the Presidents: Ronald Reagan, 1985*, Book 2, pp. 1103, 1104, 1106–1107.

66. Reagan, Informal Exchange with Reporters in St. Bernard, Ohio, October 3, 1985, in *The Soviet Union Fights the Cold War*.

67. Reagan, Radio Address to the Nation, October 12, 1985, in *The Soviet Union Fights the Cold War*.

68. See, e.g., Reagan, interview with representatives of college radio stations, September 9, 1985, in *Public Papers of the Presidents: Ronald Reagan, 1985*, Book 2, pp. 1068–1069.

69. "Gorbachev's Approach to Societal Malaise: A Managed Revitalization," Intelligence Assessment, Directorate of Intelligence, CIA, August 1985, pp. 1, 9, in Zubok, Nielsen, and Grant, eds., *Compendium of Declassified Documents and Chronology of Events*, for "Understanding the Cold War: Reagan/Gorbachev Years."

70. Ibid., p. 9.

71. "Gorbachev's Economic Agenda: Promises, Potentials, and Pitfalls," Intelligence Assessment, Directorate of Intelligence, CIA, September 1985, p. iii, from *The Soviet Estimate: U.S. Analysis of the Soviet Union, 1947–1991*.

72. Ibid., pp. 17–18.

73. Ibid., pp. 16–18.

74. Shultz, *Turmoil and Triumph*, pp. 576–577; and Oberdorfer, *From the Cold War to a New Era*, pp. 129–130.

75. Ibid.

76. Shultz, *Turmoil and Triumph*, p. 577.

77. Ibid.; and McFarlane and Smardz, *Special Trust*, p. 313.

78. Oberdorfer, *From the Cold War to a New Era*, p. 132. See also p. 497. The U.S. memcons from this meeting have not yet been declassified and released. Oberdorfer's account used direct quotes. PL has reason to know that Oberdorfer was given some access to official transcripts as a source.

79. Shultz, *Turmoil and Triumph*, p. 592.

80. Ibid., pp. 592–593. Oberdorfer, *From the Cold War to a New Era*, p. 135, corroborates this.

81. Oberdorfer, *From the Cold War to a New Era*, p. 136.

82. Shultz, *Turmoil and Triumph*, p. 593.

83. Oberdorfer, *From the Cold War to a New Era*, pp. 136–137.

84. Ibid, p. 139, note.

85. Memo from Shultz to Reagan, re: "Your Meetings with Gorbachev in Geneva," November 7, 1985, p. 4, from U.S. Department of State, Freedom of Information Act Reading Room, Washington, D.C. (hereafter DOS).

86. Oberdorfer, *From the Cold War to a New Era*, p. 139 (note). This is corroborated

by Morris, who had access to Reagan's diary, in *Dutch*, pp. 547–548 and p. 820 (notes). Morris wrote that Reagan used the same quip during an interview with Morris that day, November 5.

87. McFarlane, PL interview, September 28, 2000, Washington, D.C.
88. McFarlane, quoted in Morris, *Dutch*, p. 545. Morris attended the meeting. *Dutch*, p. 819 (note).
89. Reagan, Radio Address to the Nation on Foreign Policy, September 21, 1985, in *Public Papers of the Presidents: Ronald Reagan, 1985*, Book 2, p. 1126.
90. Reagan, Address to the United Nations General Assembly, October 24, 1985, in *Public Papers of the Presidents: Ronald Reagan, 1985*, Book 2, pp. 1286, 1287.
91. Reagan, interview with the BBC, October 29, 1985, in *Public Papers of the Presidents: Ronald Reagan, 1985*, Book 2, pp. 1310, 1313.
92. Morris, *Dutch*, pp. 543–544. Also quoted by Donald Regan in "The Cold War: Ten Years Later," videotape of conference at RRPL, November 13, 1985 (Simi Valley, Calif.: Ronald Reagan Center for Public Affairs, 1995).
93. See, e.g., Reagan, interview with *Newsweek*, March 4, 1985, cited in note 25 above.
94. Reagan, remarks at a question-and-answer session with regional editors and broadcasters, March 11, 1985, in *Public Papers of the Presidents: Ronald Reagan, 1985*, Book 2, p. 268.
95. Reagan, interview with representatives of college radio stations, September 9, 1985, in *Public Papers of the Presidents: Ronald Reagan, 1985*, Book 2, p. 1069.
96. Reagan, interview with the BBC, October 29, 1985, in *Public Papers of the Presidents: Ronald Reagan, 1985*, Book 2, pp. 1311, 1312. See also Reagan, interview with foreign broadcasters, November 12, 1985, p. 1374, ibid.
97. Reagan, interview with representatives of the wire services, November 6, 1985, in *Public Papers of the Presidents: Ronald Reagan, 1985*, Book 2, p. 1350.
98. *The Soviet Estimate: U.S. Analysis of the Soviet Union, 1947–1991*, Guide and Index, pp. 9, 17.
99. "Domestic Stresses on the Soviet System," NIE 11-18-85, Director of Central Intelligence, November 1985, pp. 1, 3, 18, from Central Intelligence Agency, Office of Information Management, Washington, D.C. (hereafter CIA).
100. Ibid., p. 19.
101. Ibid., pp. 4, 15–20.
102. Ibid., p. 16.
103. Ibid., p. 9.
104. "Soviet domestic problems are a constraint on Soviet capabilities for military technological competition with the West, especially with respect to mass production of high-technology items." Ibid., p. 20. "As military technologies become more complex and diffuse, Soviet military power is becoming more constrained by low technology levels in the society at large, a source of worry to Soviet military authorities." Ibid., p. 9.
105. Ibid., p. 20.
106. Ibid., p. 19.
107. Ibid., p. 14.
108. Ibid., p. 5.
109. Perle suggested that NIEs in general were taken very seriously within the administration. Perle, PL interview, September 27, 2000, by telephone.
110. Kenneth Adelman, *The Great Universal Embrace: Arms Summitry—A Skeptic's Account* (New York: Simon & Schuster, 1989), pp. 128–129.

111. McFarlane, PL interview, September 28, 2000, Washington, D.C.
112. Weinberger, interview with Oberdorfer, May 23, 1990, pp. 11–12, from DO-NJ.
113. Morris, *Dutch*, p. 820 (note). See also Oberdorfer, *From the Cold War to a New Era*, p. 151 (note). Who was responsible for the leak of the letter has never been established.
114. McFarlane, PL interview, September 28, 2000, Washington, D.C.
115. Morris, *Dutch*, p. 820 (notes).
116. The memcons are from RRPL-ES/NSC/SF, file folder 8510141 (1–3). They were prepared by the State Department interpreter present at each particular session, including the one-on-one meetings between Reagan and Gorbachev, and/or by other U.S. officials who spoke Russian and attended the plenary sessions as note takers. The memcons occasionally report in the third person the words of the participants.
117. Memcon, first plenary meeting, Geneva, November 19, 1985, pp. 3–6.
118. Ibid., pp. 7, 8.
119. Memcon, second plenary meeting, Geneva, November 19, 1985, pp. 4, 5.
120. Ibid., p. 6.
121. Memcon, second private meeting, Geneva, November 19, 1985, p. 2.
122. Ibid., pp. 4, 5.
123. Ibid., p. 7.
124. Memcon, third plenary meeting, Geneva, November 20, 1985, p. 4.
125. Ibid., p. 5.
126. Memcon, third plenary meeting, Geneva, November 20, 1985, pp. 6, 7.
127. Oberdorfer, *From the Cold War to a New Era*, pp. 149–150.
128. Ibid., p. 150. In his memoirs, Shultz wrote that on the second day of the summit, "Ronald Reagan had made an immense impression on Mikhail Gorbachev, who must have realized that he could not talk, con, bully, or in any other way manipulate Ronald Reagan into dropping his SDI research program." Shultz, *Turmoil and Triumph*, p. 603.
129. Memcon, third plenary meeting, Geneva, November 20, 1985, p. 8.
130. Ibid., pp. 9, 10.
131. Joint Soviet–United States Agreement on the Summit Meeting in Geneva, November 21, 1985, in *Public Papers of the Presidents: Ronald Reagan, 1985*, Book 2, pp. 1407–1410.
132. Adelman, PL interview, August 13, 2001, Arlington, Va.; Poindexter, PL interview, August 16, 2001, Arlington, Va.; Morris, PL interview, August 21, 2001, Washington, D.C.
133. Reagan, Remarks on Issuing the Joint Soviet–United States Statement on the Summit Meeting in Geneva, November 21, 1985, in *Public Papers of the Presidents: Ronald Reagan, 1985*, Book 2, p. 1411; and Reagan, Radio Address to the Nation on the Soviet–United States Summit Meeting in Geneva, November 23, 1985, ibid., p. 1417.
134. Reagan, Radio Address to the Nation on the Soviet–United States Summit Meeting in Geneva, November 23, 1985, in *Public Papers of the Presidents: Ronald Reagan, 1985*, Book 2, p. 1417.
135. Ibid.
136. Reagan, Address Before a Joint Session of the Congress Following the Soviet–United States Summit Meeting in Geneva, November 21, 1985, in *Public Papers of the Presidents: Ronald Reagan, 1985*, Book 2, p. 1413.

137. Reagan, question-and-answer session with high school students, Fallston, Md., in *Public Papers of the Presidents: Ronald Reagan, 1985*, Book 2, p. 1437.
138. McFarlane and Smardz, *Special Trust*, pp. 329–331. Weariness with bureaucratic battles provided another reason, as did the unfolding of what became Iran-*contra*.
139. McFarlane, PL interview, September 28, 2000, Washington, D.C.
140. Nitze, *From Hiroshima to Glasnost*, p. 420.
141. Oberdorfer, *From the Cold War to a New Era*, pp. 172–173.

CHAPTER VI: 1986

1. Reagan, New Year's Message, January 1, 1986, in *Public Papers of the Presidents: Ronald Reagan, 1986*, Book 1 (Washington, D.C.: U.S. Government Printing Office, 1988), p. 1.
2. Gorbachev, New Year's Message, January 1, 1986, in *Public Papers of the Presidents: Ronald Reagan, 1986*, Book 1, p. 2.
3. Reagan, Statement on Soviet–U.S. Nuclear and Space Negotiations, January 15, 1986, in *Public Papers of the Presidents: Ronald Reagan, 1986*, Book 1, p. 50.
4. The letter did not mention banning *research* on SDI. Although the ABM Treaty permitted missile defense research, the Soviets had maintained after the announcement of SDI that research on the program should be banned. The absence of such a statement in the January 15 letter did not signal a total Soviet retreat from the previous position; when Soviet negotiators put the January 15 proposal on the table in Geneva, they explained that "fundamental" research on missile defense should be allowed but "purposeful" research should not—the implication being that the United States, having declared its intention to seek a missile defense system, was pursuing "purposeful" research, while the USSR was not. Nitze, *From Hiroshima to Glasnost*, pp. 422–423.
5. Matlock, PL interview, September 5, 2001, Princeton, N.J.; Adelman, *The Great Universal Embrace*, pp. 64–65; Matlock, and Rowny, quoted in Tannenwald, ed., "Understanding the End of the Cold War, 1980–87," pp. 128–130, 132–133; Matlock, *Autopsy on an Empire*, pp. 93–94; Shultz, *Turmoil and Triumph*, pp. 699, 704; Nitze, *From Hiroshima to Glasnost*, p. 421.
6. Matlock, *Autopsy on an Empire*, pp. 93–94.
7. Matlock, quoted in Tannenwald, ed., "Understanding the End of the Cold War, 1980–87," p. 128.
8. Matlock, PL interview, September 5, 2001, Princeton, N.J.; Matlock, *Autopsy on an Empire*, p. 93. See also Adelman, *The Great Universal Embrace*, p. 65; Rowny, quoted in Tannenwald, ed., "Understanding the End of the Cold War, 1980–87," p. 132; Shultz, quoted in "High Noon at Reykjavik," transcript of conference at the RRPL, November 18, 1996 (Simi Valley, Calif.: Ronald Reagan Center for Public Affairs), p. 6.
9. Shultz, *Turmoil and Triumph*, p. 700; Nitze, *From Hiroshima to Glasnost*, p. 422.
10. Shultz, *Turmoil and Triumph*, p. 719; Nitze, *From Hiroshima to Glasnost*, p. 422.
11. Matlock, PL interview, September 5, 2001, Princeton, N.J.
12. Reagan, statement on the Soviet proposal on nuclear and space arms reductions, January 15, 1986, in *Public Papers of the Presidents: Ronald Reagan, 1986*, Book 1, p. 58; statement by Principal Deputy Press Secretary Speakes on the Soviet proposal on nuclear and space arms reductions, January 16, 1986, ibid., pp. 59–60.

13. Statement by Speakes, January 16, 1986, in *Public Papers of the Presidents: Ronald Reagan, 1986*, Book 1, pp. 59–60.
14. Poindexter, PL interview, August 16, 2001, Arlington, Va.
15. Poindexter, interview with Oberdorfer, November 1, 1990, p. 5, from DO-NJ.
16. Poindexter, PL interview, August 16, 2001, Arlington, Va.
17. On Weinberger disagreeing in principle with the desirability of abolishing nuclear weapons: Iklé, PL interview, July 24, 2001, Washington, D.C.; and Cannon, *President Reagan*, p. 259.
18. Shultz, *Turmoil and Triumph*, pp. 700, 702, 704–705.
19. Ibid., p. 701.
20. Adelman, *The Great Universal Embrace*, p. 69.
21. Shultz, *Turmoil and Triumph*, pp. 700, 701, 705, 720. Also Adelman, PL interview, August 13, 2001, Arlington, Va.; Perle, PL interview, September 27, 2000, by telephone.
22. Shultz, *Turmoil and Triumph*, p. 720.
23. Ibid., pp. 700, 701, 705.
24. NSDD 153, "Instructions for the Shultz-Gromyko Meeting in Geneva," January 1, 1985, p. 5, from RRPL-NSC/NSDD.
25. Reagan, *An American Life*, p. 651.
26. Rowny, quoted in Tannenwald, ed., "Understanding the End of the Cold War, 1980–87," p. 132.
27. Shultz, *Turmoil and Triumph*, p. 705.
28. Rowny, quoted in Tannenwald, ed., "Understanding the End of the Cold War, 1980–87," pp. 132–133.
29. Reagan, *An American Life*, p. 651. The diary excerpts do not state which advisers made that case, but Shultz would not have been among them; Poindexter, Weinberger, and Casey might have been.
30. Reagan, *An American Life*, p. 651.
31. NSDD 210, "Allied Consultations on the US Response to General Secretary Gorbachev's January 14, 1986, Arms Control Proposal," February 4, 1986, pp. 1–2, from RRPL-NSC/NSDD.
32. Adelman, *The Great Universal Embrace*, p. 69.
33. NSDD 210, "Allied Consultations on the US Response to General Secretary Gorbachev's January 14, 1986, Arms Control Proposal," February 4, 1986, p. 2, from RRPL-NSC/NSDD.
34. NSDD 214, "U.S. Response to Gorbachev's January Arms Control Proposals," February 21, 1986, from RRPL-NSC/NSDD.
35. Reagan, *An American Life*, pp. 656–658. On the State Department drafting the letter, see Shultz, *Turmoil and Triumph*, pp. 705–706, 708–709.
36. Adelman, *The Great Universal Embrace*, p. 69.
37. Adelman, PL interview, August 13, 2001, Arlington, Va.; Hartman, PL interview, August 1, 2001, by telephone; Matlock, PL interview, September 5, 2001, Princeton, N.J.
38. Reagan, interview with the New York *Daily News*, July 8, 1986, in *Public Papers of the Presidents: Ronald Reagan, 1986*, Book 1, p. 931.
39. Reagan, question-and-answer session for regional editors and broadcasters, June 13, 1986, in *Public Papers of the Presidents: Ronald Reagan, 1986*, Book 1, p. 770.
40. "The Soviet Experiment in Industrial Management: Status and Prospects," Re-

search Paper, Directorate of Intelligence, CIA, March 1986, p. 1, in *CIA's Analysis of the Soviet Union, 1947–1991*, vol. 2.

41. Ibid., pp. 9–12.
42. Ibid., pp. 12–13.
43. "Gorbachev's Modernization Program," Intelligence Assessment, Directorate of Intelligence, CIA, March 1986, p. iii, in Zubok, Nielsen, and Grant, eds., *Compendium of Declassified Documents*, for "Understanding the End of the Cold War: Reagan/Gorbachev Years."
44. Ibid., pp. iii–iv, 10.
45. Ibid., p. iv.
46. Ibid., pp. 10–11.
47. "The New CPSU Program: Charting the Soviet Future," Intelligence Assessment, Directorate of Intelligence, CIA, April 1986, pp. iii–v, 1–2, in *CIA's Analysis of the Soviet Union, 1947–1991*, vol. 2.
48. Ibid., p. iii.
49. Ibid., pp. 1, iii.
50. Ibid., pp. 3, 5–7.
51. Ibid., p. 15.
52. Ibid., pp. iii, 12.
53. Ibid., pp. 15–17.
54. Shultz, *Turmoil and Triumph*, pp. 702–703; Gates, *From the Shadows*, p. 376.
55. Shultz, *Turmoil and Triumph*, pp. 709, 711.
56. Shultz, quoted in Strober and Strober, *Reagan*, p. 335. Also Shultz, quoted in Wohlforth, ed., *Witnesses to the End of the Cold War*, p. 150.
57. Shultz, *Turmoil and Triumph*, p. 711.
58. Shultz, quoted in Strober and Strober, *Reagan*, p. 335.
59. Shultz, *Turmoil and Triumph*, pp. 704, 711.
60. Ibid., p. 702.
61. Ibid., p. 711.
62. NSDD 75, "U.S. Relations with the USSR," January 17, 1983, p. 1, from RRPL-NSC/NSDD.
63. Shultz, *Turmoil and Triumph*, p. 702; Gates, *From the Shadows*, p. 405.
64. Shultz, *Turmoil and Triumph*, pp. 703, 706–707. Also Shultz, quoted in Strober and Strober, *Reagan*, p. 335.
65. Shultz, *Turmoil and Triumph*, pp. 706, 711. Also Shultz, quoted in Strober and Strober, *Reagan*, p. 335.
66. Gates, *From the Shadows*, p. 378.
67. Ibid., p. 377.
68. Ibid., pp. 375–389; Shultz, *Turmoil and Triumph*, p. 708.
69. Iklé, PL interview, July 24, 2001, Washington, D.C.
70. Adelman, PL interview, August 13, 2001, Arlington, Va.
71. Nitze, quoted in Wohlforth, ed., *Witnesses to the End of the Cold War*, p. 111.
72. Matlock, *Autopsy on an Empire*, p. 80.
73. Matlock, PL interview, September 5, 2001, Princeton, N.J.
74. Matlock, quoted in Tannenwald, ed., "Understanding the End of the Cold War, 1980–87," pp. 272–273.
75. Matlock, *Autopsy on an Empire*, p. 94. The paragraphs above on Matlock's approach draw on Matlock, PL interview, September 5, 2001, Princeton, N.J.; Mat-

lock, *Autopsy on an Empire*, pp. 11, 16, 76–86, 88, 94, 670; Matlock, quoted in Tannenwald, ed., "Understanding the End of the Cold War, 1980–87," pp. 80–81, 94, 174, 272–273, 237–238; Matlock, quoted in Schmertz, Datlof, and Ugrinsky, eds., *President Reagan and the World*, pp. 122–124; Matlock, quoted in Wohlforth, ed., *Witnesses to the End of the Cold War*, pp. 53–54.

76. Iklé, PL interview, July 24, 2001, Washington, D.C.; Adelman, PL interview, August 13, 2001, Washington, D.C.; Gates, *From the Shadows*, p. 407.

77. Poindexter, PL interview, August 16, 2001, Arlington, Va.

78. Adelman, quoted in Schmertz, Datlof, and Ugrinsky, eds., *President Reagan and the World*, pp. 241, 240.

79. Adelman, PL interview, August 13, 2001, Arlington, Va.

80. Reagan, Remarks at a Briefing for Republican Student Interns, July 29, 1986, in *Public Papers of the Presidents: Ronald Reagan, 1986*, Book 2, pp. 1019–1020.

81. Reagan, *An American Life*, pp. 649, 661–662; Shultz, *Turmoil and Triumph*, p. 708; Matlock, *Autopsy on an Empire*, pp. 93–94; Matlock, quoted in Tannenwald, ed., "Understanding the End of the Cold War, 1980–87," p. 145; Ridgway, Oberdorfer, Nitze, and Matlock, quoted in Wohlforth, ed., *Witnesses to the End of the Cold War*, pp. 51–54; Nitze, *From Hiroshima to Glasnost*, p. 427; Oberdorfer, *From the Cold War to a New Era*, pp. 157, 158, 166, 184; Garthoff, *The Great Transition*, pp. 265–268; "Soviet Statements on Summit," in Background Book to President Reagan's Trip to Reykjavik, October 10–12, 1986, in Zubok, Nielsen, and Grant, eds., *Compendium of Declassified Documents*, for "Understanding the End of the Cold War: Reagan/Gorbachev Years."

82. "Defense and Space" and "ABM Treaty Interpretation," in Background Book to President Reagan's Trip to Reykjavik, October 10–12, 1986, in Zubok, Nielsen, and Grant, eds., *Compendium of Declassified Documents*, for "Understanding the End of the Cold War: Reagan/Gorbachev Years"; Nitze, *From Hiroshima to Glasnost*, p. 426; Shultz, *Turmoil and Triumph*, p. 718.

83. Shultz, *Turmoil and Triumph*, p. 690.

84. Ibid., pp. 690, 705–706, 710, 716–724.

85. Ibid.; Nitze, *From Hiroshima to Glasnost*, pp. 424–425.

86. Shultz, *Turmoil and Triumph*, p. 716.

87. Nitze, *From Hiroshima to Glasnost*, p. 425. Also Weinberger, PL interview, August 1, 2001, Washington, D.C.; Perle, PL interview, September 27, 2000, by telephone; Shultz, *Turmoil and Triumph*, p. 719.

88. Reagan, *An American Life*, pp. 665–666. Also Shultz, *Turmoil and Triumph*, pp. 718, 721.

89. Matlock, PL interview, September 5, 2001, Princeton, N.J.

90. Ibid.; Matlock and Shultz, quoted in Wohlforth, ed., *Witnesses to the End of the Cold War*, pp. 43–44, 36; Adelman, PL interview, August 13, 2001, Arlington, Va.; Iklé, PL interview, July 24, 2001, Washington, D.C.; Poindexter and Powell, quoted in Strober and Strober, *Reagan*, pp. 353–354; Shultz, *Turmoil and Triumph*, pp. 721, 761; Adelman, *The Great Universal Embrace*, p. 27; Poindexter, interview with Oberdorfer, November 1, 1990, p. 4, from DO-NJ.

91. Adelman, quoted in Schmertz, Datlof, and Ugrinsky, eds., *President Reagan and the World*, p. 241.

92. Matlock, PL interview, September 5, 2001, Princeton, N.J. Also Matlock, quoted in Wohlforth, ed., *Witnesses to the End of the Cold War*, pp. 43–44.

93. NSDD 250, "Post-Reykjavik Follow-Up," November 3, 1986, p. 4, from RRPL-NSC/NSDD.

94. Iklé, PL interview, July 24, 2001, Washington, D.C.; Oberdorfer, *From the Cold War to a New Era*, pp. 170–172.

95. Perle, PL interviews, September 27 and 29, 2000, by telephone.

96. Poindexter, interview with Oberdorfer, November 1, 1990, pp. 5, 15, from DO-NJ.

97. Poindexter, PL interview, August 16, 2001, Arlington, Va.

98. Shultz, *Turmoil and Triumph*, pp. 716, 719–720.

99. Adelman, *The Great Universal Embrace*, p. 30. See also Cannon, *President Reagan*, p. 684.

100. Poindexter, PL interview, August 16, 2001, Arlington, Va.; Adelman, *The Great Universal Embrace*, pp. 27–30; Oberdorfer, *From the Cold War to a New Era*, pp. 173–174.

101. Shultz, *Turmoil and Triumph*, pp. 720–723.

102. Perle, PL interview, September 27, 2000, by telephone.

103. The text of the proposal is included in NSDD 232, "Preparations for the Next NST Negotiating Round," August 16, 1986, and NSDD 233, "Consultations on a Response to General Secretary Gorbachev," July 31, 1986, from RRPL-NSC/NSDD.

104. Matlock had strongly advocated following that tack. Matlock, PL interview, September 5, 2001, Princeton, N.J.

105. Poindexter, PL interview, August 16, 2001, Arlington, Va. Also Poindexter, interview with Oberdorfer, November 1, 1990, p. 3, from DO-NJ.

106. Reagan, *An American Life*, p. 666.

107. Gates, *From the Shadows*, p. 404.

108. Reagan, *An American Life*, p. 660.

109. See Reagan, interview with *The Baltimore Sun*, March 13, 1986, in *Public Papers of the Presidents: Ronald Reagan, 1986*, Book 1, p. 330; Reagan, interview with *The New York Times*, March 23, 1986, ibid., p. 387.

110. Reagan, question-and-answer session with the American Legion Boys Nation, July 25, 1986, in *Public Papers of the Presidents: Ronald Reagan, 1986*, Book 2, p. 1008.

111. Reagan, Remarks at a Briefing for Supporters of SDI, August 6, 1986, ibid., p. 1058.

112. Reagan, Message to the Congress on Freedom, Regional Security, and Global Peace, March 14, 1986, in *Public Papers of the Presidents: Ronald Reagan, 1986*, Book 1, p. 344.

113. Reagan, Remarks to the Future Farmers of America, July 22, 1986, in *Public Papers of the Presidents: Ronald Reagan, 1986*, Book 2, p. 981; Reagan, Remarks at a High School in Va., February 7, 1986, in *Public Papers of the Presidents: Ronald Reagan, 1986*, Book 1, p. 178.

114. Reagan, Message to the Congress on Freedom, Regional Security, and Global Peace, March 14, 1986, in *Public Papers of the Presidents: Ronald Reagan, 1986*, Book 1, p. 344.

115. See, e.g., Reagan, Remarks at Senate Campaign Fundraiser in La., ibid., p. 411; and Reagan, Remarks to the American Legion Auxiliary's Girls Nation, July 18, 1986, in *Public Papers of the Presidents: Ronald Reagan, 1986*, Book 2, pp. 972–973.

116. Bush, quoted in Strober and Strober, *Reagan*, p. 245.

117. Weinberger, quoted in ibid., p. 245.

118. Poindexter, quoted in ibid., p. 358.

119. Matlock, PL interview, September 5, 2001, Princeton, N.J.

120. Nitze, quoted in Wohlforth, ed., *Witnesses to the End of the Cold War*, p. 38.

121. Adelman, *The Great Universal Embrace*, p. 304.
122. Matlock, PL interview, September 5, 2001, Princeton, N.J.
123. Perle, PL interview, September 29, 2000, by telephone.
124. Iklé, PL interview, July 24, 2001, Washington, D.C.
125. Adelman, quoted in Schmertz, Detlof, and Ugrinsky, eds., *President Reagan and the World*, p. 85.
126. Adelman, PL interview, August 13, 2001, Arlington, Va.
127. Adelman, quoted in "High Noon at Reykjavik," p. 59.
128. Reagan, *An American Life*, p. 672.
129. Gates, *From the Shadows*, p. 409.
130. "Defense and Space," in Background Book to President Reagan's Trip to Reykjavik, October 10–12, 1986, in Zubok, Nielsen, and Grant, eds., *Compendium of Declassified Documents*, for "Understanding the End of the Cold War: Reagan/Gorbachev Years."
131. Oberdorfer, *From the Cold War to a New Era*, pp. 186–189.
132. NSDD 245, "Reagan-Gorbachev Preparatory Meeting," October 7, 1986, pp. 1, 2, from RRPL-NSC/NSDD.
133. Weinberger, interview with Oberdorfer, May 23, 1990, pp. 11, 12, from DO-NJ.
134. Memcon, morning session, Reykjavík, October 11, 1986, pp. 1–4, from RRPL-ES/NSC/SF, File Folder 8690725. All of the other memcons cited below are from this location, with one noted exception.
135. Memcon, morning session, Reykjavík, October 11, 1986, pp. 4–9.
136. Ibid.
137. Transcript of Reagan-Gorbachev Talks, second session, October 11, 1986, from Gorbachev Archives (trans. from Russian), in Zubok, Nielsen, and Grant, eds., *Compendium of Declassified Documents*, for "Understanding the End of the Cold War: Reagan/Gorbachev Years." The U.S. memcon for this session is not available.
138. Nitze, *From Hiroshima to Glasnost*, pp. 429–432.
139. Memcon, morning session, Reykjavík, October 12, 1986, pp. 8–21.
140. Nitze, *From Hiroshima to Glasnost*, p. 433.
141. Perle, PL interview, September 29, 2000, by telephone.
142. Poindexter, PL interview, August 16, 2001, Arlington, Va.
143. Memcon, afternoon session, Reykjavík, October 12, 1986, pp. 1–8.
144. Adelman, PL interview, August 13, 2001, Arlington, Va.; Perle, quoted in Bosch, *Reagan: An American Story*, pp. 283–284.
145. Adelman, *The Great Universal Embrace*, pp. 72–73; Adelman, PL interview, August 13, 2001, Arlington, Va.
146. Memcon, afternoon session, Reykjavík, October 12, 1986, p. 11.
147. Ibid., pp. 8–16.
148. Adelman, PL interview, August 13, 2001, Arlington, Va.
149. Reagan, *An American Life*, p. 679.
150. A point made later by Abraham Sofaer and Max Kampelman. Abraham Sofaer, PL interview, December 4, 2003, by telephone; Max M. Kampelman, "The Ronald Reagan I Knew," *The Weekly Standard* 9, no. 11, November 24, 2003.
151. Shultz, press conference, October 12, 1986, Reykjavík, in *American Foreign Policy Current Documents, 1986* (Washington, D.C.: U.S. Department of State, 1987) (hereafter *AFPCD 1986*), p. 77.
152. Ibid., pp. 82–87.

153. Shultz, press conference, October 13, 1986, in *AFPCD 1986*, p. 86.
154. Poindexter, press briefing, October 13, 1986, in *AFPCD 1986*, pp. 87–90.
155. "Donald Regan: 'SDI Is Our Strong Card,'" *The Washington Post*, p. A32.
156. Poindexter, PL interview, August 16, 2001, Arlington, Va.; Matlock, PL interview, September 5, 2001, Princeton, N.J.
157. Adelman, PL interview, August 13, 2001, Arlington, Va.
158. Poindexter, PL interview, August 16, 2001, Arlington, Va.; Matlock, PL interview, September 5, 2001, Princeton, N.J.
159. Crowe, interview with Oberdorfer, November 16, 1989, pp. 5–15, from DO-NJ; Oberdorfer, *From the Cold War to a New Era*, pp. 207–208. Adelman also opposed the idea at the same meeting. Adelman, *The Great Universal Embrace*, pp. 84–87.
160. NSDD 250, "Post-Reykjavik Follow-Up," November 3, 1986, from RRPL-NSC/NSDD.
161. Matlock, PL interview, September 5, 2001, Princeton, N.J.
162. Unlike Reagan, however, many in the administration doubted that Gorbachev would have seriously carried out an agreement to eliminate all ballistic, strategic, or nuclear weapons.
163. Matlock, PL interview, September 5, 2001, Princeton, N.J.; Perle, PL interview, September 29, 2000, by telephone; Shultz, quoted in "High Noon at Reykjavik," p. 20; Shultz, quoted in Wohlforth, ed., *Witnesses to the End of the Cold War*, pp. 173–175; Shultz, press conference, Brussels, October 13, 1986, in *AFPCD 1986*, p. 84; Shultz, *Turmoil and Triumph*, pp. 775–776, 779–780; Adelman, quoted in "High Noon at Reykjavik," p. 70; Nitze, *From Hiroshima to Glasnost*, pp. 435–436; Weinberger, PL interview, August 1, 2001, Washington, D.C.
164. See, e.g., Shultz, press conference, October 12, 1986, in *AFPCD 1986*, p. 77; Reagan, Address to the Nation on the Meetings with Gorbachev in Iceland, p. 1370; question-and-answer session with journalists, October 14, 1986, p. 1379; Remarks at Senate Campaign Fundraising Luncheon, Baltimore, October 15, 1986, p. 1387; Remarks at Senate Campaign Rally, Ga., October 28, 1986, p. 1457, all from *Public Papers of the Presidents: Ronald Reagan, 1986*, Book II.
165. Matlock, PL interview, September 5, 2001, Princeton, N.J.; Matlock, *Autopsy on an Empire*, pp. 80, 86–88; Matlock, quoted in Strober and Strober, *Reagan*, p. 358; Matlock, quoted in Tannenwald, ed., "Understanding the End of the Cold War, 1981–87," pp. 160, 176–178.

DENOUEMENT AND CONCLUSION

1. Carlucci, PL interview, July 27, 2001, Washington, D.C.
2. On the type of system, see NSDD 261, "Consultations on the SDI Program," February 18, 1987, "Terms of Consultation," p. 1, from RRPL-NSC/NSDD.
3. Oberdorfer, *From the Cold War to a New Era*, pp. 212–213.
4. Carlucci, quoted in Wohlforth, ed., *Witnesses to the End of the Cold War*, p. 57.
5. NSDD 261, "Consultations on the SDI Program," "Terms of Consultation," p. 1.
6. Oberdorfer, *From the Cold War to a New Era*, p. 266; Carlucci, quoted in Wohlforth, ed., *Witnesses to the End of the Cold War*, p. 56.
7. Adelman, *The Great Universal Embrace*, pp. 317–319.
8. Oberdorfer, *From the Cold War to a New Era*, pp. 231–234.
9. Ibid.

10. Shultz, *Turmoil and Triumph*, p. 987.
11. Carlucci, PL interview, July 27, 2001, Washington, D.C.
12. Oberdorfer, *From the Cold War to a New Era*, pp. 248–249; Shultz, *Turmoil and Triumph*, p. 997.
13. Carlucci, PL interview, July 27, 2001, Washington, D.C.
14. Oberdorfer, *From the Cold War to a New Era*, p. 253.
15. Shultz, *Turmoil and Triumph*, p. 1002.
16. Reagan, question-and-answer session, Los Angeles World Affairs Council, April 10, 1987, in *The Soviet Union Fights the Cold War*.
17. Reagan, statement on the Strategic Defense Initiative, March 23, 1987, in *The Soviet Union Fights the Cold War*.
18. Perle, PL interview, September 27, 2000, by telephone.
19. Carlucci, PL interview, July 27, 2001, Washington, D.C.; Powell, quoted in Strober and Strober, *Reagan*, p. 232.
20. Abraham Sofaer, PL interview, December 4, 2003, by telephone.
21. "Soviet SDI Response Options: The Resource Dilemma," Research Paper, Directorate of Intelligence, CIA, November 1987, pp. 1–2, in *CIA's Analysis of the Soviet Union, 1947–1991*, vol. 2.
22. Ibid., pp. iv–vi, 2–3, 15–17, 19, 23–24.
23. Ibid.
24. Ibid., pp. v–vi, 23.
25. "Gorbachev: Steering the USSR into the 1990s," Intelligence Assessment, Directorate of Intelligence, CIA, July 1987, pp. iii–ix, 25, in *The Soviet Estimate: U.S. Analysis of the Soviet Union, 1947–1991*.
26. Ibid., pp. 19–20, 25.
27. NSDD 288, "My Objectives at the Summit," November 10, 1987, p. 1, from RRPL-NSC/NSDD.
28. Carlucci, PL interview, July 27, 2001, Washington, D.C.
29. Carlucci, quoted in Wohlforth, ed., *Witnesses to the End of the Cold War*, p. 102.
30. Shultz, quoted in ibid., p. 105.
31. Iklé, PL interview, July 24, 2001, Washington, D.C.
32. Oberdorfer, *From the Cold War to a New Era*, pp. 275–289.
33. Reagan, Remarks to the Institute for Foreign Policy Analysis, March 14, 1988, in *The Soviet Union Fights the Cold War*.
34. Carlucci, PL interview, July 27, 2001, Washington, D.C.
35. Shultz, *Turmoil and Triumph*, pp. 1085–1086; Oberdorfer, *From the Cold War to a New Era*, p. 289.
36. "Arms Control," Director of Central Intelligence, 1987, p. 1, in *CIA's Analysis of the Soviet Union, 1947–1991*, vol. 2.
37. "Annual Bulletin on Soviet Economic Growth," Directorate of Intelligence, CIA, April 1988, pp. i, 1, 19, in ibid.
38. "Arms Control," pp. 1, 2, 5, 12, 21, 22.
39. NSDD 305, "Objectives at the Moscow Summit," April 26, 1988, p. 1, from RRPL-NSC/NSDD.
40. Oberdorfer, *From the Cold War to a New Era*, p. 299.
41. "Soviet National Security Policy: Responses to the Changing Military and Economic Environment," Intelligence Assessment, Directorate of Intelligence, CIA, June 1988, pp. 1, 17, 20, in *CIA's Analysis of the Soviet Union, 1947–1991*, vol. 2.

42. Ibid., pp. 18–19.

43. Memcon, private meeting, New York, December 7, 1988, p. 5, from RRPL-ES/NSC/SF, File Folder 8890944.

44. See, e.g., Adelman, PL interview, August 13, 2001, Arlington, Va.; and Burt, PL interview, July 31, 2001, Washington, D.C.

BIBLIOGRAPHY

I. Primary Sources

Archives *(Acronyms below are used in the notes.)*

CIA . . . . Central Intelligence Agency, Office of Information Management, Washington, D.C.

DOD . . . . U.S. Department of Defense, Freedom of Information Act Reading Room, Washington, D.C.

DOS . . . . U.S. Department of State, Freedom of Information Act Reading Room, Washington, D.C.

LLNL . . . . Lawrence Livermore National Laboratory, Archives, Livermore, Calif.

NSA . . . . National Security Archive, Washington, D.C. (published collections of primary documents from NSA listed separately)

NSA-SDI . . . . The Strategic Defense Initiative (unpublished collection of primary and secondary documents)

NSA-WH . . . . White House e-mails (unpublished collection of primary documents)

RRPL . . . . Ronald Reagan Presidential Library, Simi Valley, Calif.

RRPL-AV . . . . Audio-Visual Collection

RRPL-ES/NSC/SF . . . . Executive Secretariat, NSC, Records, System File

RRPL-MC/VF . . . . Miscellaneous Collection, or "Vertical File"

RRPL-NSC/HS/USSR . . Assistant to the President for National Security Affairs Collection, Head of State File, USSR

RRPL-NSC/NSDD . . . . Records Declassified and Released by the National Security Council, National Security Decision Directives

RRPL-NSC/NSSD . . . . Records Declassified and Released by the National Security Council, National Security Study Directives

RRPL-NSC/RD . . . . . . Records Declassified and Released by the National Security Council, Related Documents, System II

RRPL-OH/SDIO . . . . . Oral History Transcripts 35–39, Box 8, Oral History Interviews: Strategic Defense Initiative Organization

RRPL-WHORM/SF . . . White House Office of Records Management, Subject File

USC-WB . . . . University of Southern California, School of Cinema-Television, Warner Bros. Archives, Los Angeles, Calif.

Personal Papers

DO-DC . . . . Don Oberdorfer Papers, Washington, D.C.

DO-NJ . . . . Don Oberdorfer Papers, Seeley G. Mudd Manuscript Library, Princeton University, Princeton, N.J.

Interviews with the Author (Only those positions and activities relevant to the narrative are listed. All interviews except the Kraemer interview and the interviews conducted by telephone were taped.)

KENNETH ADELMAN (U.S. Deputy Representative to the United Nations, 1981–1983; Director, U.S. Arms Control and Disarmament Agency, 1983–1988). August 13, 2001, Arlington, Va.

MARTIN ANDERSON (White House Domestic Policy Adviser, 1981–1982). July 10 and 14, 2000, by telephone; August 15, 2000, Stanford, Calif.

NORMAN BAILEY (Senior NSC Staff Official, Economic Affairs and Policy Planning, 1981–1984). December 22, 2000, McLean, Va.

DONALD BAUCOM (Official Historian, Strategic Defense Initiative Organization, now Missile Defense Agency, U.S. Department of Defense, 1987–present). December 28, 1999, Arlington, Va.

RICHARD BURT (Director, Bureau of Political-Military Affairs, U.S. Department of State, 1981–1983; U.S. Assistant Secretary of State for European Affairs, 1983–1985; U.S. Ambassador to West Germany, 1985–1989). July 31, 2001, Washington, D.C.

FRANK CARLUCCI (U.S. Deputy Secretary of Defense, 1981–1982; National Security Adviser, 1987; U.S. Secretary of Defense, 1987–1989). July 27, 2001, Washington, D.C.

WILLIAM CLARK (U.S. Deputy Secretary of State, 1981–1982; National Security Adviser, 1982–1983; U.S. Secretary of the Interior, 1983–1985). August 1, 2001, by telephone.

MICHAEL DEAVER (Deputy White House Chief of Staff, 1981–1985). August 3, 2001, Washington, D.C.

PAULA DOBRIANSKY (Senior NSC Staff Official, Soviet and Eastern European Affairs, 1980–1987). December 18, 2000, Washington, D.C.

ARTHUR HARTMAN (U.S. Ambassador to the USSR, 1981–1987). August 1, 2001, by telephone.

FRED IKLÉ (U.S. Undersecretary of Defense for Policy, 1981–1989). July 24, 2001, Washington, D.C.

ROBERT KIMMITT (Senior NSC Staff Official, 1978–1983; Executive Secretary and General Counsel, NSC, 1983–1985; General Counsel, U.S. Department of the Treasury, 1985–1987; U.S. Undersecretary of State for Political Affairs, 1988–1991). January 27, 1999, Washington, D.C.

SVEN KRAEMER (Senior NSC Staff Official, Defense and Arms Control, 1981–1989). September 2, 2000, Washington, D.C.

JACK MATLOCK (Senior NSC Staff Official, Soviet and Eastern European Affairs, 1983–1986; U.S. Ambassador to the USSR, 1987–1991). September 5, 2001, Princeton, N.J.

ROBERT MCFARLANE (Counselor, U.S. Department of State, 1981–1982; Deputy National Security Adviser, 1982–1983; National Security Adviser, 1983–1985). August 22 and September 28, 2000, Washington, D.C.

EDWIN MEESE (Counselor to the President, 1981–1985; U.S. Attorney General, 1985–1988). August 3, 2000, Washington, D.C.

EDMUND MORRIS (official biographer of Ronald Reagan from 1985). August 21, 2001, Washington, D.C.; September 4, 2001, by telephone.

DON OBERDORFER (Senior Diplomatic Correspondent, *The Washington Post*, throughout Reagan's presidency). August 2, 2001, Washington, D.C.

RICHARD PERLE (U.S. Assistant Secretary of Defense for International Security Policy, 1981–1987). September 27 and 29, 2000, by telephone.

RICHARD PIPES (Senior NSC Staff Official, Soviet and Eastern European Affairs, 1981–1982). September 20, 2000, Cambridge, Mass.

JOHN POINDEXTER (Military Assistant to the National Security Adviser, 1981–1983; Deputy National Security Adviser, 1983–1985; National Security Adviser, 1985–1986). August 16, 2001, Arlington, Va.

ABRAHAM SOFAER (Legal Adviser, U.S. Department of State, 1985–1990). December 4, 2003, by telephone.

EDWARD TELLER (physicist and member of several advisory boards to the U.S. government). August 16, 2000, Stanford, Calif.

JAMES WATKINS (Chief of Naval Operations, 1982–1986). July 31, 2000, Washington, D.C.

CASPAR WEINBERGER (U.S. Secretary of Defense, 1981–1987). August 1, 2001, Washington, D.C.

Correspondence with the Author

WILLIAM CLARK, letter to PL, November 13, 2001.

EDMUND MORRIS, letter to PL, November 12, 2001.

Published Primary Sources

A. A. Gromyko Interviewed by Soviet Political Analysts, January 13, 1985. Moscow: Novosti Press Agency Publishing House, 1985.

American Foreign Policy Current Documents (multiple years: 1981–1989). Washington, D.C.: U.S. Department of State, multiple years.

Arms Control and Disarmament Agreements: Texts and Histories of Negotiations. Washington, D.C.: U.S. Arms Control and Disarmament Agency, 1982.

CARTER, ASHTON B. "Directed Energy Missile Defense in Space." U.S. Congress Office of Technology Assessment Background Paper, April 1984. Washington, D.C.: U.S. Government Printing Office, 1984.

Cold War International History Project Bulletin (multiple numbers). Washington, D.C.: Woodrow Wilson International Center for Scholars, multiple years.

Discriminate Deterrence: Report of the Commission on Integrated Long-Term Strategy. Washington, D.C.: U.S. Government Printing Office, 1988.

Documents on Disarmament (multiple years: 1981–1989). Washington, D.C.: U.S. Arms Control and Disarmament Agency, multiple years.

Foreign Relations of the United States (multiple volumes). Washington, D.C.: U.S. Government Printing Office, multiple years.

GORBACHEV, MIKHAIL. The Results and Lessons of Reykjavík. Moscow: Novosti Press Agency Publishing House, 1986.

———. Reykjavík: Documents and Materials. Moscow: Novosti Press Agency Publishing House, 1986.

Official Report of the Proceedings of the Thirty-second Republican National Convention Held in Detroit, Michigan, July 14, 15, 16, 17, 1980. Republican National Committee, 1980.

Presidential Directives on National Security from Truman to Clinton. National Security Archive. Alexandria, Va.: Chadwyck-Healey, 1994.

The President's Strategic Defense Initiative. Washington, D.C.: White House, January 1985.

Public Papers of the Presidents of the United States: Ronald Reagan (multiple years: 1981–1989). Washington, D.C.: U.S. Government Printing Office, multiple years.

REAGAN, RONALD. *Abortion and the Conscience of the Nation.* Sacramento, Calif.: New Regency Publishing, 2000 (originally published 1983).

———. "It Was 'Star Wars' Muscle That Wrestled Arms Race to a Halt." *Los Angeles Times,* July 31, 1991.

———. *National Security Strategy of the United States.* Washington, D.C.: Pergamon-Brassey's, 1988.

———. *Speaking My Mind: Selected Speeches.* London: Hutchinson, 1990.

———. *A Time for Choosing: The Speeches of Ronald Reagan, 1961–1982.* Chicago: Regnery Gateway, 1983.

Realism, Strength, Negotiation: Key Foreign Policy Statements of the Reagan Administration. Washington, D.C.: U.S. Department of State, May 1984.

SDI: Strategic Defense Initiative—A Chronology. United States Information Agency, April 1988.

SIMPSON, CHRISTOPHER. *National Security Directives of the Reagan & Bush Administrations: The Declassified History of U.S. Political & Military Policy, 1981–1991.* Boulder, Colo.: Westview Press, 1995.

SKINNER, KIRON K., ANNELISE ANDERSON, and MARTIN ANDERSON, eds. *Reagan: A Life in Letters.* New York: Free Press, 2003.

———. *Reagan, in His Own Hand: The Writings of Ronald Reagan That Reveal His Revolutionary Vision for America.* New York: Free Press, 2001.

The Soviet Estimate: U.S. Analysis of the Soviet Union, 1947–1991. National Security Archive. Alexandria, Va.: Chadwyck-Healey, 1995.

Statistical Abstract of the United States (multiple years). Washington, D.C.: U.S. Department of Commerce, multiple years.

TYROLER, CHARLES, ed. *Alerting America: The Papers of the Committee on the Present Danger.* Washington, D.C.: Pergamon-Brassey's, 1984.

U.S. Military Uses of Space. National Security Archive. Alexandria, Va.: Chadwyck-Healey, 1991.

ZUBOK, VLADISLAV, CATHERINE NIELSEN, and GREG GRANT, eds. *Compendium of Declassified Documents and Chronology of Events,* and *Supplement,* from the National Security Archive, for "Understanding the End of the Cold War, Reagan/Gorbachev Years," Oral History Conference, May 7–10, 1998, Brown University. Providence, R.I.: Watson Institute for Advanced International Studies, Brown University, 1998.

Collections of Primary Sources on CD-ROM

CIA's Analysis of the Soviet Union 1947–1991, 2 vols. Washington, D.C.: Central Intelligence Agency.

The Soviet Union Fights the Cold War: Official Documents of the Reagan Administration, 1981–1989. Washington, D.C.: American Foreign Policy Council, 1999.

Memoirs

ADELMAN, KENNETH L. *The Great Universal Embrace: Arms Summitry—A Skeptic's Account.* New York: Simon & Schuster, 1989.

ANDERSON, MARTIN. *Revolution: The Reagan Legacy,* 2nd ed. Stanford, Calif.: Hoover Institution Press, 1990.

DEAVER, MICHAEL K. *A Different Drummer: My Thirty Years with Ronald Reagan.* New York: HarperCollins, 2001.

DEAVER, MICHAEL K., with MICKEY HERSKOWITZ. *Behind the Scenes: In Which the Author Talks About Ronald and Nancy Reagan . . . and Himself.* New York: William Morrow, 1987.

DOBRYNIN, ANATOLY. *In Confidence: Moscow's Ambassador to America's Six Cold War Presidents, 1962–1986.* New York: Times Books, 1995.

DOUGLAS, HELEN GAHAGAN. *A Full Life.* Garden City, N.Y.: Doubleday & Co., 1982.

FITZWATER, MARLIN. *Call the Briefing! Reagan and Bush, Sam and Helen: A Decade with Presidents and the Press.* Holbrook, Mass.: Adams Media Corporation, 1995.

GATES, ROBERT M. *From the Shadows: The Ultimate Insider's Story of Five Presidents and How They Won the Cold War.* New York: Touchstone, 1997.

GORBACHEV, MIKHAIL. *Memoirs.* London: Doubleday, 1995.

HAIG, ALEXANDER M. *Caveat: Realism, Reagan, and Foreign Policy.* London: Weidenfeld and Nicolson, 1984.

HOWE, GEOFFREY. *Conflict of Loyalty.* London: Macmillan, 1994.

MATLOCK, JACK F. *Autopsy on an Empire: The American Ambassador's Account of the Collapse of the Soviet Union.* New York: Random House, 1995.

McFARLANE, ROBERT C., and ZOFIA SMARDZ. *Special Trust.* New York: Cadell & Davies, 1994.

MEESE, EDWIN III. *With Reagan: The Inside Story.* Washington, D.C.: Regnery Gateway, 1992.

NITZE, PAUL H. *From Hiroshima to Glasnost: At the Centre of Decision, A Memoir.* London: Weidenfeld and Nicolson, 1989.

PALAZCHENKO, PAVEL. *My Years with Gorbachev and Shevardnadze: The Memoir of a Soviet Interpreter.* University Park, Pa.: Pennsylvania State University Press, 1997.

PIPES, RICHARD. *Vixi: Memoirs of a Non-Belonger.* New Haven: Yale University Press, 2003.

POWELL, COLIN, with JOSEPH E. PERSICO. *A Soldier's Way: An Autobiography.* London: Hutchinson, 1995.

REAGAN, NANCY, with WILLIAM NOVAK. *My Turn: The Memoirs of Nancy Reagan.* London: Weidenfeld and Nicolson, 1989.

REAGAN, RONALD. *An American Life: The Autobiography.* New York: Simon & Schuster, 1990.

REAGAN, RONALD, with RICHARD G. HUBLER. *Where's the Rest of Me? The Ronald Reagan Story.* New York: Duell, Sloan and Pearce, 1965.

REGAN, DONALD T. *For the Record: From Wall Street to Washington.* London: Hutchinson, 1988.

SHULTZ, GEORGE P. *Turmoil and Triumph: My Years as Secretary of State.* New York: Charles Scribner's Sons, 1993.

TELLER, EDWARD, with JUDITH SHOOLERY. *Memoirs: A Twentieth-Century Journey in Science and Politics.* Cambridge, Mass.: Perseus Publishing, 2001.

THATCHER, MARGARET. *The Downing Street Years.* New York: HarperCollins, 1993.

WALLISON, PETER J. *Ronald Reagan: The Power of His Conviction and the Success of His Presidency.* Boulder, Colo.: Westview Press, 2003.

WEINBERGER, CASPAR. *Fighting for Peace: Seven Critical Years in the Pentagon.* London: Michael Joseph, 1990.

WEINBERGER, CASPAR W., with GRETCHEN ROBERTS. *In The Arena: A Memoir of the 20th Century.* Washington, D.C.: Regnery, 2001.

Oral Histories

CHARLTON, MICHAEL. *The Star Wars History, From Deterrence to Defence: The American Strategic Debate.* London: BBC Publications, 1986.

"Cold War Endgame." Conference at Princeton University, Princeton, N.J., March 30, 1996. Organized by the Woodrow Wilson School of Public Affairs, Princeton University, and the James A. Baker III Institute for Public Policy of Rice University.

"The Cold War: Ten Years Later." Video recording of conference at the Ronald Reagan Presidential Library, Simi Valley, Calif., November 13, 1995. Simi Valley, Calif.: The Ronald Reagan Center for Public Affairs.

Dinner and reunion conference held by former Reagan administration National Security Council staff members at the University Club, Washington, D.C., September 26, 2000. Organized by the Potomac Foundation, McLean, Va.

"High Noon at Reykjavik." Transcript of conference at the Ronald Reagan Presidential Library, Simi Valley, Calif., November 18, 1996. Simi Valley, Calif.: The Ronald Reagan Center for Public Affairs.

"The Role of the National Security Adviser." Transcript of Oral History Roundtable, The National Security Council Project, October 25, 1999. College Park, Md.: Center for International and Security Affairs at Maryland, School of Public Affairs, University of Maryland, 2000.

STROBER, DEBORAH HART, and GERALD S. STROBER. *Reagan: The Man and His Presidency, The Oral History of an Era.* Boston: Houghton Mifflin, 1998.

TANNENWALD, NINA, ed. "Understanding the End of the Cold War, 1980–1987." Provisional transcript of Oral History Conference, Brown University, Providence, R.I., May 7–10, 1998. Translated and transcribed by Jeffrey W. Dillon. Providence, R.I.: Watson Institute for International Studies, Brown University, May 1999.

THOMPSON, KENNETH W., ed. *Foreign Policy in the Reagan Presidency: Nine Intimate Perspectives.* Lanham, Md.: University Press of America, 1993.

WOHLFORTH, WILLIAM C., ed. *Witnesses to the End of the Cold War.* Baltimore: Johns Hopkins University Press, 1996.

II. SECONDARY SOURCES

Articles and Shorter Works

ALGER, CHADWICK F. "Did Hiroshima Signal the Beginning or the End? The World Nuclear Disarmament's Efforts to Influence the Answer." *Diplomatic History* 19, no. 3 (Summer 1995), pp. 499–505.

BAILEY, NORMAN A. "The Strategic Plan That Won the Cold War: National Security Decision Directive 75," 2nd ed. McLean, Va.: Potomac Foundation, 1999.

BAUCOM, DONALD R. "Hail to the Chiefs: The Untold History of Reagan's SDI Decision." *Policy Review* (U.S.), Summer 1990, pp. 66–73.

———. "Reflections on the U.S. Military and Research and Development: Command Technology and the End of the Cold War." Paper presented at University of Maryland, College Park, Md., February 9, 1996.

———. "The U.S. Missile Defense Program: 1944–1997," unpublished paper, 1997.

BECKER, ABRAHAM S. *Sitting on Bayonets: The Soviet Defense Burden and the Slowdown of Soviet Defense Spending.* Santa Monica, Calif.: RAND/UCLA Center for the Study of Soviet International Behavior, 1986.

BELL, CORAL. "From Carter to Reagan." *Foreign Affairs* 63, no. 3 (1985), pp. 490–510.

BERKOWITZ, BRUCE, and JEFFREY RICHELSON. "The CIA Vindicated: The Soviet Collapse *Was* Predicted." *The National Interest*, no. 41 (Fall 1995), pp. 36–47.

BESCHLOSS, MICHAEL. Introduction to Cannon, Lou, *Ronald Reagan: The Presidential Portfolio*. New York: Public Affairs, 2001.

BILLINGTON, JAMES H. "The Foreign Policy of President Ronald Reagan." Speech, September 25, 1997. Text at RRPL-MC/VF.

BLANK, STEPHEN. *SDI and Defensive Doctrine: The Evolving Soviet Debate*. Kennan Institute for Advanced Russian Studies Occasional Paper #240. Washington, D.C.: Kennan Institute for Advanced Russian Studies, 1990.

BRODY, RICHARD I. *Strategic Defences in NATO Strategy*. International Institute for Strategic Studies Adelphi Paper 225. Oxford: Oxford University Press, 1987.

BROOKS, STEPHEN G., and WILLIAM C. WOHLFORTH. "Power, Globalization, and the End of the Cold War: Reevaluating a Landmark Case for Ideas." *International Security* 25, no. 3 (Winter 2000–01), pp. 5–53.

BROSCIOUS, S. DAVID. "Longing for International Control, Banking on American Superiority: Harry S. Truman's Approach to Nuclear Weapons." In Gaddis, John Lewis, Philip H. Gordon, Ernest R. May, and Jonathan Rosenberg, eds., *Cold War Statesmen Confront the Bomb: Nuclear Diplomacy Since 1945*. Oxford: Oxford University Press, 1999.

BYMAN, DANIEL L., and KENNETH M. POLLACK. "Let Us Now Praise Great Men: Bringing the Statesman Back In." *International Security* 25, no. 4 (Spring 2001), pp. 107–146.

CANNON, LOU. "Arms Boost Seen as Strain on Soviets." *The Washington Post*, June 19, 1980, p. A3.

———. "To Tell the Truth: Will the Real Ronald Reagan Please Stand Up?" *Los Angeles Times Book Review*, October 3, 1999, pp. 1, 6–7.

CLARK, WILLIAM P. "Ronald Reagan, Lifeguard." Foreword to Reagan, Ronald, "Abortion and the Conscience of the Nation." Sacramento, Calif.: New Regency Publishing, 2000. (Reagan's essay first published 1983.)

COLACELLO, BOB. "Ronnie and Nancy." *Vanity Fair*, no. 455 (July 1998), pp. 76–89, 134–142.

DAALDER, IVO H., and I. M. DESTLER. Introduction, "The Role of the National Security Adviser." Transcript of Oral History Roundtable, The National Security Council Project, October 25, 1999. College Park, Md.: Center for International and Security Affairs at Maryland, School of Public Affairs, University of Maryland, 2000.

DAVIES, PHILIP H. J. "Spies as Informants: Triangulation and the Interpretation of Elite Interview Data in the Study of the Intelligence and Security Services." *Politics* 21, no. 1 (February 2001), pp. 73–80.

DAVIS, WILLIAM A. *Asymmetries in U.S. and Soviet Strategic Defense Programs: Implications for Near-Term American Deployment Options*. Special Report, Institute for Foreign Policy Analysis. Washington, D.C.: Pergamon-Brassey's, 1986.

DESCHAMPS, LOUIS. *The SDI and European Security Interests*. Atlantic Paper no. 62. The Atlantic Institute for International Affairs. London: Croon Helm, 1987.

DOENECKE, JUSTUS D. "The Peace Movement: A Necessary Corrective." *Diplomatic History* 25, no. 4 (Fall 2001), pp. 701–705.

EVANGELISTA, MATTHEW. "Norms, Heresthetics, and the End of the Cold War." *Journal of Cold War Studies* 3, no. 1 (Winter 2001), pp. 5–35.

FARNHAM, BARBARA. "Reagan and the Gorbachev Revolution: Perceiving the End of Threat." *Political Science Quarterly* 116, no. 2 (Summer 2001), pp. 225–252.

FITZGERALD, MARY C. *Soviet Views on SDI*. Carl Beck Papers in Russian and East European Studies no. 601. Pittsburgh: University of Pittsburgh, 1987.

"Former Cold War Leaders Spar over Old SDI." *BMD Monitor*, October 20, 1995, p. 372.

FREEDMAN, LAWRENCE. *The Revolution in Strategic Affairs*. International Institute for Strategic Studies Adelphi Paper 318. Oxford: Oxford University Press, 1998.

———. *Strategic Defence in the Nuclear Age*. International Institute for Strategic Studies Adelphi Paper 224. Oxford: Oxford University Press, 1987.

GADDIS, JOHN LEWIS. "International Relations Theory and the End of the Cold War." *International Security* 17, no. 3 (Winter 1992–93), pp. 5–58.

———. "The Landscape of History: Explorations in Methodology." Lecture Series, Oxford University, Hilary Term 2001.

———. "NSC 68 and the Soviet Threat Reconsidered." *International Security* 4, no. 4 (Spring 1980), pp. 164–170.

———. "The Tragedy of Cold War History." *Foreign Affairs* 73, no. 1 (January–February 1994), pp. 142–154.

GEORGE, ALEXANDER L. "Assessing Presidential Character." In George, Alexander L., and Juliette L. George, *Presidential Personality and Performance*. Boulder, Colo.: Westview Press, 1998.

———. "The 'Operational Code': A Neglected Approach to the Study of Political Leaders and Decision-Making." *International Studies Quarterly* 13, no. 2 (June 1969), pp. 190–222.

GEYELIN, PHILIP. "The Reagan Crisis: Dreaming Impossible Dreams." *Foreign Affairs* 65, no. 3 (1987), pp. 447–457.

GREEN, JOSHUA. "Reagan's Liberal Legacy." *The Washington Monthly*, January–February 2003.

GREENSTEIN, FRED I. Foreword to George, Alexander L., and Juliette L. George. *Presidential Personality and Performance*. Boulder, Colo.: Westview Press, 1998.

———. "The Impact of Personality on Politics: An Attempt to Clear Away Underbrush." *The American Political Science Review* 61, no. 3 (September 1967), pp. 629–641.

———. "Reckoning with Reagan: A Review Essay on Edmund Morris's *Dutch*." *Political Science Quarterly* 115, no. 1 (2000), pp. 115–122.

HARTLEY, ANTHONY. "After the Thatcher Decade." *Foreign Affairs* 68, no. 5 (1989–90), pp. 102–118.

HENRY, DAVID, and KURT RITTER. "Ronald Reagan: Conservative Spokesman for the American Dream." In Koester, Susan H., ed., *Western Speakers: Voices of the American Dream*. Manhattan, Kans.: Sunflower University Press, 1988.

HERMANN, MARGARET G. "Leaders and Foreign Policy Decision-making." In Caldwell, Dan, and Timothy J. McKeown, eds., *Diplomacy, Force, and Leadership: Essays in Honor of Alexander L. George*. Boulder, Colo.: Westview Press, 1993, pp. 77–94.

———. "When Leader Personality Will Affect Foreign Policy: Some Propositions." In Rosenau, James N., ed., *In Search of Global Patterns*. New York: Free Press, 1976, pp. 326–333.

"History of the Strategic Defense Initiative Organization Systems Deputate 1 January 1987–31 January 1989." Washington, D.C.: Strategic Defense Initiative Organization, U.S. Department of Defense, March 20, 1989.

HOUSE, ROBERT J., and MARY L. BAETZ. "Leadership: Some Empirical Generalizations and New Research Directions." In Cummings, L. L., and Barry M. Staw, eds., *Leadership, Participation, and Group Behavior*. Greenwich, Conn.: JAI Press Inc., 1990, pp. 1–83.

HOWARD, MICHAEL. "A European Perspective on the Reagan Years." *Foreign Affairs* 66, no. 3 (1988), pp. 479–493.

IPPOLITO, DENNIS S. "Defense, Budget Policy, and the Reagan Deficits." In Schmertz, Eric J., Natalie Datlof, and Alexej Ugrinsky, eds., *President Reagan and the World*. Westport, Conn.: Greenwood Press, 1997.

JACKSON, WILLIAM D. "Soviet Reassessment of Ronald Reagan, 1985–1988." *Political Science Quarterly* 113, no. 4 (1998–99), pp. 617–644.

JOHNSON, PAUL. "Europe and the Reagan Years." *Foreign Affairs* 68, no. 1 (1989), pp. 28–38.

KAMPELMAN, MAX M. "The Ronald Reagan I Knew." *The Weekly Standard* 9, no. 11 (November 24, 2003).

KAVANAGH, DENNIS. "Why Political Science Needs History." *Political Studies* 39, no. 3 (September 1991), pp. 479–495.

KOTKIN, STEPHEN. "What They Knew (Not!): 44 Years of C.I.A. Secrets." *The New York Times*, March 17, 2001.

LAMBETH, BENJAMIN S. *The Strategic Defense Initiative in Soviet Planning and Policy*. Santa Monica, Calif.: RAND Corporation, 1988.

LEBOW, RICHARD NED. "We Still Don't Know!" *Diplomatic History* 22, no. 4 (Fall 1998), pp. 627–632.

MAY, ERNEST R. "History—Theory—Action." *Diplomatic History* 18, no. 4 (Fall 1994), pp. 589–603.

MCFARLANE, ROBERT C. "Effective Strategic Policy." *Foreign Affairs* 67, no. 1 (Fall 1988), pp. 33–48.

——. "His Faith in U.S. Altered the World." *Los Angeles Times*, October 4, 1999.

MCMAHON, ROBERT J. "Making Sense of American Foreign Policy During the Reagan Years." *Diplomatic History* 19, no. 2 (Spring 1995), pp. 367–384.

MORRIS, EDMUND. "A Celebration of Reagan: What the Presidential Library Reveals About the Man." *The New Yorker*, February 16, 1998, pp. 50–57.

——. "In Memoriam: Christina Reagan." *The American Spectator*, August 1993, pp. 18–19.

——. "Push and Shove in a Cold Climate." *Forbes FYI*, May 6, 1996, pp. 117–124.

NEWHOUSE, JOHN. "Annals of Diplomacy: Reagan and the Nuclear Age—Part I, The Abolitionist." *The New Yorker*, January 2, 1989, pp. 37–52.

——. "Annals of Diplomacy: Reagan and the Nuclear Age—Part II, The Abolitionist." *The New Yorker*, January 9, 1989, pp. 51–72.

"One on One: Edward Teller." *Defense News* (U.S.), May 25–31, 1992, p. 30.

PIPES, RICHARD. "Can the Soviet Union Reform?" *Foreign Affairs* 63, no. 1 (Fall 1984), pp. 47–61.

——. "Misinterpreting the Cold War: The Hard-Liners Had It Right." *Foreign Affairs* 74, no. 1 (January–February 1995), pp. 154–160.

——. "Soviet Strategy and American Response." In Craig Snyder, ed., *The Strategic Defense Debate: Can Star Wars Make Us Safe?* Philadelphia: University of Pennsylvania Press, 1986, pp. 43–48.

PODHORETZ, NORMAN. "The Reagan Road to Détente." *Foreign Affairs* 63, no. 3 (1985), pp. 447–464.

POWASKI, RONALD. "The Antinuclear Movement Was Effective—But Not Completely." *Diplomatic History* 23, no. 4 (Fall 1999), pp. 711–714.

"SDI and the End of the Cold War Quotations as of February 4, 1997." Compiled by the Office of the Historian, Ballistic Missile Defense Organization, U.S. Department of Defense, 1997.

The Strategic Defense Initiative and American Security. Aspen Strategy Group Report. Lanham, Md.: University Press of America, 1987.

REARDEN, STEVEN L. "Paul H. Nitze: Last of the Cold Warriors." *Diplomatic History* 17, no. 1 (Winter 1993), pp. 143–146.

REYNOLDS, DAVID. "The Special Relationship: Rethinking Anglo-American Relations." *International Affairs* 65, no. 1 (Winter 1988–89), pp. 89–111.

RISEN, JAMES. "Documents Shed New Light on C.I.A.'s View of Soviets." *The New York Times*, March 10, 2001.

"The Road to Ballistic Missile Defense, 1983–2007." Prepared by the Ballistic Missile Defense Organization, U.S. Department of Defense, 1999.

SCHROEER, DIETRICH. *Directed-Energy Weapons and Strategic Defence: A Primer.* International Institute for Strategic Studies Adelphi Paper 221. Oxford: Oxford University Press, 1987.

"Scientist Urges U.S. Foundation for Research." *Los Angeles Times*, December 11, 1945, p. 2.

SKINNER, KIRON K. "Reagan's Plan." *The National Interest*, no. 56 (Summer 1999), pp. 136–140.

TAUBMAN, PHILIP. "How the C.I.A.'s Judgments Were Distorted by Cold War Catechisms." *The New York Times*, March 18, 2001.

"Three Discuss Atomic Power." *Los Angeles Times*, December 13, 1945, p. 10.

TUCKER, ROBERT. "Reagan's Foreign Policy." *Foreign Affairs* 68, no. 1 (1989), pp. 1–27.

"U.N.O. Atomic Control Seen by January." *Los Angeles Times*, December 10, 1945, p. 6.

WENDT, ALEXANDER E. "The Agent-Structure Problem in International Relations Theory." *International Organization* 41, no. 3 (Summer 1987), pp. 335–370.

WENDT, JAMES C., and PETER A. WILSON. "Post-INF: Toward Multipolar Deterrence." Unclassified Technical Report distributed by the Defense Technical Information Center, U.S. Department of Defense. Santa Monica, Calif.: RAND Corporation, February 1988.

Books

AMBROSE, STEPHEN E., and DOUGLAS G. BRINKLEY. *Rise to Globalism: American Foreign Policy Since 1938.* New York: Penguin Books, 1997.

ANDREW, CHRISTOPHER. *For the President's Eyes Only: Secret Intelligence and the American Presidency from Washington to Bush.* London: HarperCollins, 1996.

ANDREW, CHRISTOPHER, and OLEG GORDIEVSKY. *KGB: The Inside Story.* New York: HarperCollins, 1990.

ANDREW, CHRISTOPHER, and VASILI MITROKHIN. *The Mitrokhin Archive: The KGB in Europe and the West.* London: Penguin Press, 1999.

ANZOVIN, STEVEN, ed. *The Star Wars Debate.* New York: H. W. Wilson Co., The Reference Shelf, vol. 58, no. 1, 1986.

ARBATOV, ALEXEI G. *Lethal Frontiers: A Soviet View of Nuclear Strategy, Weapons, and Negotiations.* Trans. Kent D. Lee. New York: Praeger, 1988.

BANNERMAN, R. LEROY. *Norman Corwin and Radio: The Golden Years.* University, Ala.: University of Alabama Press, 1986.

BARRETT, LAURENCE I. *Gambling with History: Ronald Reagan in the White House.* Garden City, N.Y.: Doubleday & Co., 1983.

BAUCOM, DONALD R. *The Origins of SDI, 1944–1983.* Lawrence, Kans.: University Press of Kansas, 1992.

BELL, CORAL. *The Reagan Paradox: American Foreign Policy in the 1980s.* Aldershot, U.K.: Edward Elgar, 1989.

BIALER, SEWERYN, and MICHAEL MANDELBAUM, eds. *Gorbachev's Russia and American Foreign Policy.* Boulder, Colo.: Westview Press, 1988.

BOBBITT, PHILIP, LAWRENCE FREEDMAN, and GREGORY F. TREVERTON, eds. *US Nuclear Strategy: A Reader.* London: Macmillan, 1989.

BOFFEY, PHILIP, et al. *Claiming the Heavens:* The New York Times *Complete Guide to the Star Wars Debate.* New York: Times Books, 1988.

BOSCH, ADRIANA. *Reagan: An American Story.* New York: TV Books, 2000.

BRAUCH, HANS GÜNTER, ed. *Star Wars and European Defence.* New York: St. Martin's Press, 1987.

BROAD, WILLIAM J. *Teller's War: The Top-Secret Story behind the Star Wars Deception.* New York: Simon & Schuster, 1992.

BROWN, ARCHIE. *The Gorbachev Factor.* Oxford: Oxford University Press, 1996.

BRZEZINSKI, ZBIGNIEW, ed. *Promise or Peril: The Strategic Defense Initiative, Thirty-Five Essays by Statesmen, Scholars, and Strategic Analysts.* Washington, D.C.: Ethics and Public Policy Center, 1986.

CANNON, LOU. *Governor Reagan: His Rise to Power.* New York: PublicAffairs, 2003.

———. *President Reagan: The Role of a Lifetime,* 2nd ed. New York: PublicAffairs, 2000.

———. *Reagan.* New York: Perigree Books, 1982.

———. *Ronald Reagan: The Presidential Portfolio.* New York: PublicAffairs, 2001.

COLTON, TIMOTHY J. *The Dilemma of Reform in the Soviet Union.* New York: Council on Foreign Relations, 1986.

CORWIN, NORMAN. Untitled *and Other Radio Dramas.* New York: Henry Holt and Company, 1947.

COWEN, REGINA, PETER RAJCSANYI, VLADIMIR BILANDRIC. *SDI and European Security.* Boulder, Colo.: Westview Press, 1987.

CRAIG, PAUL P., and JOHN A. JUNGERMAN. *Nuclear Arms Race: Technology and Society,* 2nd ed. New York: McGraw-Hill, 1990.

DAALDER, IVO. *The SDI Challenge to Europe.* Cambridge, Mass.: Ballinger Publishing Co., 1987.

D'AGOSTINO, ANTHONY. *Gorbachev's Revolution, 1985–1991.* London: Macmillan, 1998.

DALLMEYER, DORINDA G., ed. *The Strategic Defense Initiative: New Perspectives on Deterrence.* Boulder, Colo.: Westview Press, 1986.

Department of Defense Dictionary of Military and Associated Terms. Washington, D.C.: Joint Chiefs of Staff, 1987.

DOUGHERTY, JAMES E., and ROBERT L. PFALTZGRAFF, JR. *American Foreign Policy: FDR to Reagan.* New York: Harper & Row, 1986.

DUMBRELL, JOHN. *American Foreign Policy: Carter to Clinton.* London: Macmillan, 1997.

DUNBABIN, J. P. D. *The Cold War: The Great Powers and Their Allies.* London: Longman, 1994.

EDWARDS, ANNE. *Early Reagan: The Rise of an American Hero.* London: Hodder & Stoughton, 1987.

FISCHER, BETH A. *The Reagan Reversal: Foreign Policy and the End of the Cold War.* Columbia, Mo.: University of Missouri Press, 1997.

FITZGERALD, FRANCES. *Way Out There in the Blue: Reagan, Star Wars and the End of the Cold War.* New York: Simon & Schuster, 2000.

FREEDMAN, LAWRENCE. *The Evolution of Nuclear Strategy,* 2nd ed. London: Macmillan, 1989.

———. *U.S. Intelligence and the Soviet Strategic Threat,* 2nd ed. London: Macmillan, 1986.

GADDIS, JOHN LEWIS. *Russia, the Soviet Union and the United States: An Interpretive History.* Boston: McGraw-Hill, 1990.

———. *Strategies of Containment: A Critical Appraisal of Postwar American National Security Policy.* Oxford: Oxford University Press, 1982.

———. *The United States and the End of the Cold War: Implications, Reconsiderations, Provocations.* Oxford: Oxford University Press, 1992.

GADDIS, JOHN LEWIS, PHILIP H. GORDON, ERNEST R. MAY, and JONATHAN ROSENBERG, eds. *Cold War Statesmen Confront the Bomb: Nuclear Diplomacy Since 1945.* Oxford: Oxford University Press, 1999.

GARTHOFF, RAYMOND L. *The Great Transition: American-Soviet Relations and the End of the Cold War.* Washington, D.C.: Brookings Institution, 1994.

GEORGE, ALEXANDER L., and JULIETTE L. GEORGE. *Presidential Personality and Performance.* Boulder, Colo.: Westview Press, 1998.

GOLDWATER, BARRY. *The Conscience of a Conservative.* Washington, D.C.: Regnery Gateway, 1990 (originally published 1960).

———. *Why Not Victory? A Fresh Look at American Foreign Policy.* New York: McGraw-Hill, 1962.

GREENSTEIN, FRED I. *The Presidential Difference: Leadership Style from FDR to Clinton.* Princeton, N.J.: Princeton University Press, 2000.

HALEY, P. EDWARD, and JACK MERRITT, eds. *Strategic Defense Initiative: Folly or Future?* Boulder, Colo.: Westview Press, 1986.

HARTMANN, FREDERICK H. *Naval Renaissance: The U.S. Navy in the 1980s.* Annapolis, Md.: Naval Institute Press, 1990.

HAYWARD, STEVEN F. *The Age of Reagan: The Fall of the Old Liberal Order, 1964–1980.* Roseville, Calif.: Prima Publishing, 2001.

HERKEN, GREGG. *Cardinal Choices: Presidential Science Advising from the Atomic Bomb to SDI,* rev. ed. Stanford, Calif.: Stanford University Press, 2000.

HOGAN, MICHAEL J., ed. *The End of the Cold War: Its Meaning and Implications.* Cambridge, U.K.: Cambridge University Press, 1992.

HOLLIS, MARK, and STEVE SMITH. *Explaining and Understanding International Relations.* Oxford: Clarendon Press, 1991.

HOLMES, KIM R., and BAKER SPRING, eds. *SDI at the Turning Point: Readying Strategic Defenses for the 1990s and Beyond.* Critical Issues Series. Washington, D.C.: Heritage Foundation, 1990.

HOSKING, GEOFFREY. *The First Socialist Society: A History of the Soviet Union from Within.* Cambridge, Mass.: Harvard University Press, 1993.

HOUGH, JERRY. *Russia and the West: Gorbachev and the Politics of Reform,* 2nd ed. New York: Touchstone, 1990.

HUGHES, ROBERT C. *SDI: A View from Europe.* Washington, D.C.: National Defense University Press, 1990.

HUNTER, KERRY L. *The Reign of Fantasy: The Political Roots of Reagan's Star Wars Pol-*

icy. American University Studies, Series X, Political Science, vol. 34. New York: Peter Lang, 1992.

JASANI, BHUPENDRA, ed. *Space Weapons and International Security*. New York: Oxford University Press, 1987.

JOHNSON, HAYNES. *Sleepwalking Through History: America in the Reagan Years*. New York: Anchor Books, 1992.

KAISER, ROBERT G. *Why Gorbachev Happened: His Triumphs and His Failure*. New York: Simon & Schuster, 1991.

KENNEDY-PIPE, CAROLINE. *Russia and the World, 1917–1991*. London: Arnold, 1998.

KISSINGER, HENRY. *Diplomacy*. New York: Touchstone, 1994.

KORT, MICHAEL. *The Columbia Guide to the Cold War*. New York: Columbia University Press, 1998.

LEEBAERT, DEREK. *The Fifty-Year Wound: How America's Cold War Victory Shapes Our World*. Boston: Back Bay Books, 2003.

LINENTHAL, EDWARD TABOR. *Symbolic Defense: The Cultural Significance of the Strategic Defense Initiative*. Urbana, Ill.: University of Illinois Press, 1989.

LONG, FRANKLIN, DONALD HAFNER, and JERRY BOUTWELL, eds. *Weapons in Space*. New York: W. W. Norton & Co., 1986.

LOUIS, WM. ROGER, and HEDLEY BULL, eds. *The "Special Relationship": Anglo-American Relations Since 1945*. Oxford: Clarendon Press, 1986.

LUONGO, KENNETH N., and W. THOMAS WANDER, eds. *The Search for Security in Space*. Ithaca, N.Y.: Cornell University Press, 1989.

MAYERS, DAVID. *The Ambassadors and America's Soviet Policy*. New York: Oxford University Press, 1995.

McCAULEY, MARTIN, ed. *Gorbachev and Perestroika*. London: Macmillan, 1990.

McCGWIRE, MICHAEL. *Military Objectives in Soviet Foreign Policy*. Washington, D.C.: Brookings Institution, 1987.

———. *Perestroika and Soviet National Security*. Washington, D.C.: Brookings Institution, 1991.

McCLELLAND, DOUG. *Hollywood on Ronald Reagan: Friends and Enemies Discuss our President, the Actor*. Winchester, Mass.: Faber and Faber, 1983.

McMAHON, K. SCOTT. *Pursuit of the Shield: The U.S. Quest for Limited Ballistic Missile Defense*. Lanham, Md.: University Press of America, 1997.

MIKHEYEV, DMITRY. *The Soviet Perspective on the Strategic Defense Initiative*. Foreign Policy Report, Institute for Foreign Policy Analysis. Washington, D.C.: Pergamon-Brassey's, 1987.

The Military Balance (multiple years). London: The International Institute for International Studies, multiple years.

MILLAY, EDNA ST. VINCENT. *Aria da Capo: A Play in One Act*. New York: Harper & Brothers, 1920.

MORRIS, EDMUND. *Dutch: A Memoir of Ronald Reagan*. London: HarperCollins, 1999.

NOGEE, JOSEPH L., and ROBERT H. DONALDSON. *Soviet Foreign Policy Since World War II*. New York: Pergamon Press, 1988.

NOONAN, PEGGY. *When Character Was King: A Story of Ronald Reagan*. New York: Viking, 2001.

OBERDORFER, DON. *From the Cold War to a New Era: The United States and the Soviet Union, 1983–1991*, 2nd ed. Baltimore: Johns Hopkins University Press, 1998.

ORMAN, STANLEY. *Faith in Gods (Global Orbiting Defence System): Stability in the Nuclear Age*. London: Brassey's (U.K.), 1991.

OSGOOD, ROBERT E. *The Nuclear Dilemma in American Strategic Thought*. Boulder, Colo.: Westview Press, 1988.

OYE, KENNETH A., ROBERT J. LIEBER, and DONALD ROTHCHILD, eds. *Eagle Defiant: United States Foreign Policy in the 1980s*. Boston: Little, Brown and Co., 1983.

PATERSON, THOMAS, and DENNIS MERRILL, eds. *Major Problems in American Foreign Relations*, vol. 2. Lexington, Mass.: D. C. Heath, 1995.

PAYNE, KEITH B. *Strategic Defense: "Star Wars" in Perspective*. Lanham, Md.: Hamilton Press, 1986.

PEARSON, RAYMOND. *The Rise and Fall of the Soviet Empire*. London: Macmillan, 1998.

PEMBERTON, WILLIAM E. *Exit with Honor: The Life and Presidency of Ronald Reagan*. Armonk, N.Y.: M. E. Sharpe, 1997.

PIPES, RICHARD. *Survival Is Not Enough: Soviet Realities and America's Future*. New York: Simon & Schuster, 1984.

PRADOS, JOHN. *Keepers of the Keys: A History of the National Security Council from Truman to Bush*. New York: William Morrow, 1991.

PRESSLER, LARRY. *Star Wars: The Strategic Defense Initiative Debates in Congress*. New York: Praeger, 1986.

QUAYLE, DAN, ROBERT E. HUNTER, and C. ELLIOTT FARMER, eds. *Strategic Defense and the Western Alliance*. Significant Issues Series, vol. 8, no. 6. Washington, D.C.: Center for Strategic and International Studies, 1986.

REISS, EDWARD. *The Strategic Defense Initiative*. Cambridge, U.K.: Cambridge University Press, 1992.

RENWICK, ROBIN. *Fighting with Allies: America and Britain in Peace and at War*. New York: Times Books, 1996.

SCHEER, ROBERT. *With Enough Shovels: Reagan, Bush and Nuclear War*. London: Secker & Warburg, 1983.

SCHMERTZ, ERIC J., NATALIE DATLOF, and ALEXEJ UGRINSKY, eds. *President Reagan and the World*. Westport, Conn.: Greenwood Press, 1997.

SCHULZINGER, ROBERT. *American Diplomacy in the Twentieth Century*. New York: Oxford University Press, 1994.

SCHWEIZER, PETER. *Victory: The Reagan Administration's Secret Strategy That Hastened the Collapse of the Soviet Union*. New York: Atlantic Monthly Press, 1994.

SERVICE, ROBERT. *A History of Twentieth Century Russia*. London: Penguin, 1997.

SHARP, PAUL. *Thatcher's Diplomacy: The Revival of British Foreign Policy*. London: Macmillan, 1997.

SHERRIFF, R.C. *Journey's End: A Play in Three Acts*. New York: Brentano's, 1929.

SIMON, JEFFREY, ed. *Security Implications of SDI: Will We Be More Secure in 2010?* Washington, D.C.: National Defense University Press, 1990.

SMITH, GEOFFREY. *Reagan and Thatcher*. London: Bodley Head, 1990.

SMITH, HEDRICK. *The Power Game: How Washington Works*. New York: Ballantine Books, 1988.

SNYDER, CRAIG, ed. *The Strategic Defense Debate: Can Star Wars Make Us Safe?* Philadelphia: The University of Pennsylvania Press, 1986.

SOOFER, ROBERT M. *Missile Defenses and Western European Security: NATO Strategy, Arms Control, and Deterrence*. New York: Greenwood Press, 1988.

Star Wars Quotes: Statements by Reagan Administration Officials, Outside Experts, Members of Congress, U.S. Allies, and Soviet Officials on the Strategic Defense Initiative. Washington, D.C.: The Arms Control Association, 1986.

TALBOTT, STROBE. *Deadly Gambits: The Reagan Administration and the Stalemate in Nuclear Arms Control*. London: Picador, 1984.

———. *The Master of the Game: Paul Nitze and the Nuclear Peace*. New York: Alfred A. Knopf, 1988.

———. *The Russians and Reagan*. New York: Vintage Books, 1984.

TELLER, EDWARD. *Better a Shield than a Sword: Perspectives on Defense and Technology*. New York: Free Press, 1987.

THOMAS, TONY. *The Films of Ronald Reagan*. Secaucus, N.J.: Citadel Press, 1980.

VAUGHN, STEPHEN. *Ronald Reagan in Hollywood: Movies and Politics*. Cambridge, U.K.: Cambridge University Press, 1994.

VOLKOGONOV, DMITRI. *Autopsy for an Empire: The Seven Leaders Who Built the Soviet Regime*. New York: Free Press, 1998.

WALDMAN, HARRY. *The Dictionary of SDI*. Wilmington, Del.: SR Books, 1988.

WALLER, DOUGLAS C., JAMES T. BRUCE, and DOUGLAS M. COOK. *The Strategic Defense Initiative: Progress and Challenges, A Guide to Issues and References*. Claremont, Calif.: Regina Books.

WESTAD, ODD ARNE, ed. *Reviewing the Cold War: Approaches, Interpretations, Theory*. London: Frank Cass, 2000.

WINIK, JAY. *On the Brink: The Dramatic, Behind-the-Scenes Saga of the Reagan Era and the Men and Women Who Won the Cold War*. New York: Simon & Schuster, 1996.

WOHLFORTH, WILLIAM C., ed. *Witnesses to the End of the Cold War*. Baltimore: Johns Hopkins University Press, 1996.

WOODS, NGAIRE, ed. *Explaining International Relations Since 1945*. Oxford: Oxford University Press, 1996.

Additional Source

"Reagan." *The American Experience with David McCullough*. PBS Home Video, 1998.

ACKNOWLEDGMENTS

I AM DEEPLY INDEBTED to Anne Deighton for her guidance, wisdom, and wit. And I am grateful to the late Richard Challener, whose teaching and advising were enriching and enjoyable.

Lawrence Freedman, John Lewis Gaddis, Kurt Gaubatz, Daniel Markey, and Hew Strachan read the manuscript with care and made helpful suggestions. Edmund Morris and Don Oberdorfer kindly provided research material and pointed me in the direction of still more.

At Writers' Representatives, Lynn Chu and Glen Hartley were always thoughtful and considerate and provided expert help at key times.

Any author would be fortunate to have Robert Loomis at Random House as his or her editor. His insights and well-honed skills are deservedly legendary. Thanks are also due to Casey Reivich and Daniel Barrett at Random House for their assistance and sound advice.

Special mention must be made of Michael Barone, who made time for consultation at a number of stages in the preparation of the manuscript. His counsel and encouragement have been invaluable.

William Thomas and David Hine exemplify graciousness and generosity.

I owe much to Catherine Lettow, the late Carl Lettow, and the late Mary Jane Stangland Todoroff.

Finally, for their continuing influence and inspiration, I thank Renée, Craig, Anna, and Elias, Carl and Alexandra, and John, Phoebe, and Ely.

INDEX

M

N

O

P

Weinberger, Caspar, 21–22, 23, 26, 44,
47–48, 55, 60, 61, 68, 69, 97, 98,
99, 101, 107, 108, 113, 115–16, 138,
143, 144, 146–47, 149, 156, 158, 160,
162, 167, 189, 193, 203, 204, 208, 215,
217–18, 245, 261n, 271n
dense-pack concept and, 84–85
early SDI deployment initiative and,
231–32
Geneva summit and, 178–79
missile defense debate and, 86–88
missile defense leaks and, 103–4
MX controversy and, 84–85
on NSDD 12, 56–57
resignation of, 235
on RR's SDI aims, 119
SDI management and, 139–40,
141
Welles, Orson, 11

White House Science Council, 105
World War II, 4, 10, 232

X

x-ray laser technology, 58, 81–82, 96

Y

Yugoslavia, 125

Z

zero ballistic missiles proposal, 208–12,
213, 216, 231
"zero-zero" proposal, 60, 211, 233

About the Author

Paul Lettow received an A.B. in history, summa cum laude, from Princeton University, and a D.Phil. in international relations from Oxford University. He has taught American history at Oxford University. He lives in Cambridge, Massachusetts, and the Washington, D.C., area.

About the Type

This book was set in Electra, a typeface designed for Linotype by W. A. Dwiggins, the renowned type designer (1880–1956). Electra is a fluid typeface, avoiding the contrasts of thick and thin strokes that are prevalent in most modern typefaces.